# The Berkeley UNIX Environment

## Second Edition

**R. Nigel Horspool**

*Department of Computer Science*
*University of Victoria*

Prentice-Hall Canada Inc., Scarborough, Ontario

Canadian Cataloguing in Publication Data
Horspool, R. Nigel, 1948-
The Berkeley UNIX Environment

2nd ed.
First ed. published under title: C programming in the
Berkeley UNIX Environment.
Includes index.
ISBN 0-13-089368-4

1. UNIX (Computer operating system). 2. C (Computer
program language). 3. Programming (Electronic
computers). I. Title. II. Title: C programming
in the Berkeley UNIX Environment.

QA76.73.C15H67 1991      005.4'3   C91-095640-5

Prentice Hall Inc., *Englewood Cliffs, New Jersey*
Prentice-Hall International, Inc., *London*
Prentice-Hall of Australia, Pty., Ltd., *Sydney*
Prentice-Hall of India Pvt., Ltd., *New Delhi*
Prentice-Hall of Japan, Inc., *Tokyo*
Prentice-Hall of Southeast Asia (Pte.) Ltd., *Singapore*
Editora Prentice-Hall do Brasil Ltda., *Rio de Janeiro*
Prentice-Hall Hispanoamericana, S.A., *Mexico*
Whitehall Books Limited, *Wellington, New Zealand*

ISBN 0-13-089368-4

Acquisitions Editor: Jacqueline Wood
Production Editorial: Marta Tomins
Production Coordinator: Anna Orodi
Cover Design: Monica Kompter
Page Layout: R. Nigel Horspool

Printed and bound by R.R. Donnelly and Sons in the United States of America

1   2   3   4   5   RRD   96   95   94   93   92

UNIX® is a registered trademark of UNIX System Laboratories, Inc. SunOS is a trademark of SUN Microsystems, Inc. The term Berkeley UNIX refers to the implementation of the UNIX Operating System that was developed at the University of California at Berkeley.

The author and publisher have used their best efforts in preparing this book. These efforts include the development, research and testing of the theories and programs to determine their effectiveness. The author and publisher make no warranty of any kind, expressed or implied, with regard to these programs or the documentation contained in this book. The author and publisher shall not be liable in any event for incidental or consequential damages in connection with, or arising out of, the furnishing, performance, or use of these programs.

# CONTENTS

# SECTION II   Systems Programming in C

# SECTION III   Managing and Maintaining Software

# LIST OF TABLES

# PREFACE

It seems to me that almost as soon as *C Programming in the Berkeley UNIX Environment* had appeared in print, the publishers were already nagging me to work on producing a second edition. I resisted the pressure for as long as possible, but the Berkeley UNIX system has now evolved to the point that I had to concede defeat.

As well as bringing the book up to date, I have taken the opportunity to change its orientation completely. I would estimate that only about half of the original book remains intact. It is arguable as to whether this book should be described as a new book or as a second edition. The change in title reflects the new orientation. Most of the material that provided an introduction to the C language has gone and has been replaced by new material, which I will describe in a moment. I apologize to anyone who would have liked a gentler C introduction to be part of the book. However, the size of the book would have grown significantly if I had attempted to compete with other C books and if I covered both the classic Kernighan & Ritchie and the new ANSI C dialects. This book contains only a single, albeit large, chapter that summarizes the ANSI C language. I propose that you, the reader, should obtain your introduction to C from a book that concentrates on just that one topic. Then, when you are ready to write interesting programs that require interaction with operating system facilities, you can forget the other book and switch to this one.

The new material is intended to make the book more suitable as an additional source of UNIX programming information for various senior undergraduate courses. The new chapters on lex and yacc should be helpful for courses in compiler construction that use C as their implementation language. Software engineering courses that require projects to be implemented in C may benefit from the chapter on the use of SCCS and RCS for project management. A new chapter on the command-level aspects of computer networking and electronic mail generally improves the coverage of the UNIX system. The choice of material that is presented in the book reflects my personal biases as to what is important.

Camera-ready copy for this book was produced using FrameMaker running on a Macintosh IIci. I offer my grateful thanks to everyone at Frame Technology Corporation for building a miraculous software product that creates such beautiful output. I also wish to thank Henry Spencer for a careful and critical reading of most of the chapters and for saving me the embarrassment of having many errors get into print. Also, several of my colleagues and my graduate students have helped by answering questions, by reading chapters, and for generally providing a pleasant working environment. Thank you everyone.

While I have tried to get every last detail right, I would be naïve if I thought that the book was totally free of errors. (In that respect, writing a book is remarkably like writing a gigantic program.) If you should find a mistake, no matter how trivial, please do send me a message by electronic mail so that I can make the appropriate corrections (and, perhaps, learn something new).

R. Nigel Horspool
`nigelh@csr.uvic.ca`

*Victoria, B.C., Canada*

# SECTION I

# *The User Environment*

# CHAPTER 1    *GETTING STARTED WITH UNIX*

UNIX has steadily grown in popularity since it was first released to the world in the early 1970s. Initially, UNIX was developed by Ken Thompson as an operating system for an otherwise unused PDP-7 computer at Bell Laboratories. The system was ported to the PDP-11 series of computer soon afterwards and it was this PDP-11 version that was subsequently released at a nominal charge to universities. Dennis Ritchie designed the C language for use with UNIX and wrote the compiler for it. He and Thompson rewrote as much of the UNIX source code in C as was reasonably possible, leaving only a small portion of the operating system kernel programmed in assembly language.

For a while, it appeared that UNIX would remain as merely a research tool in university computing laboratories. Although UNIX exemplified many interesting design ideas, it was a poor man's system in comparison to the operating systems provided by manufacturers for their mainframe computers. All that changed when the University of California at Berkeley added virtual memory support and ported the system to the DEC VAX series of computers. Instead of being able to support a few interactive users on a PDP-11, UNIX could now support a dozen or two users. Furthermore, the minuscule limits on the sizes of programs imposed by the PDP-11 architecture were removed. UNIX became a system with possibilities.

Bell Laboratories had produced some useful and important software for use with UNIX. For example, they provided text formatting software in the form of the nroff and troff programs, file searching programs like grep, desk calculator programs like dc, and so on. But in comparison to operating systems supplied by computer manufacturers, UNIX was lacking software for basic commercial applications. There was no COBOL compiler, no report generation facility, no programs for maintaining large databases, and so on. Consequently, UNIX continued to remain an academic system used mainly within universities and colleges.

Berkeley continued the Bell Laboratories policy of distributing the system at nominal charge to universities. This had the effect of introducing many tens of thousands of computer science students to UNIX. Many of these students helped develop new programs for use with UNIX. Many student projects at Berkeley and elsewhere were devoted to improving the operating system itself. The best improvements were incorporated into later releases of UNIX, resulting in some dramatic improvements to its power and to its efficiency. Some specific improvements, such as support for networking, were created through research projects at U.C. Berkeley funded by DARPA (the Advanced Research Projects Agency of the U.S. Department of Defense).

While U.C. Berkeley continued to develop and improve UNIX, Bell Laboratories were not neglecting UNIX either. This activity increased when Bell Laboratories was incorporated into the AT&T empire. Two increasingly different versions of UNIX competed, one distributed under the name Berkeley UNIX or bsd UNIX, and the other under the name System V UNIX. Meanwhile, perhaps because so many computer science graduates were demanding access to UNIX in their jobs, the computer manufacturers were porting UNIX to their own machines and making their own improvements to the system. Instead of two UNIX variants, there were many more – ULTRIX for DEC machines, HPUX for Hewlett Packard computers, AIX for IBM computers, UTX for Amdahl computers ... the list seems endless. One factor that lead to the proliferation of UNIX variants was that nearly all of UNIX is programmed in the C language. To port UNIX to a new computer, you mostly need to implement a C compiler for that computer and then re-compile the UNIX source code. The small portion of UNIX coded in assembly language and the small portions that are specific to a computer architecture are the only parts that need to be re-designed. Other, proprietary, operating systems are normally coded in assembly language and the thought of transferring such a system to a different computer architecture is a truly daunting one. So daunting, in fact, that it has never been attempted.

The role of workstation manufacturers must not be forgotten in this story of the growth of UNIX. In the late 1970s, Bill Joy left U.C. Berkeley to found SUN Microsystems. At that time, workstations were seen as moderate cost computers to be used by scientists and engineers for calculations. Particular attention was paid to graphics display ability on these computers. SUN produced a design for a workstation that was extremely successful and their operating system was, naturally, another variant of Berkeley UNIX. Although other workstation manufacturers competed for market share, notably Apollo and Hewlett Packard, SUN has won the dominant position. Their version of UNIX, called SunOS, is another strong competitor for the hearts and minds of the UNIX user community.

The proliferation of differing UNIX versions is, of course, counter-productive. Users expect their UNIX skills acquired on one machine to be transferable to other machines.

Software developers do not like having to create different versions of their programs for each UNIX variant. The trend is toward 'open systems' and standardization. At the time of writing, no single standard for UNIX exists. AT&T are cooperating with SUN to develop a UNIX standard, while other computer manufacturers and software developers are working on a different standard.

Most books on UNIX are based on *pure* AT&T System V UNIX. A few books attempt to cover both System V UNIX and Berkeley UNIX. There are very few books which are solely oriented towards Berkeley UNIX, even though this is the more popular system within the colleges and universities. This book will help to rectify the balance by concentrating exclusively on Berkeley UNIX. It may occasionally be biased toward the SunOS implementation of Berkeley UNIX, but that bias should not affect the reader.

## 1-1    *The Interactive Environment and the Shell*

Let us suppose that you, the reader, are sitting in front of a terminal or a workstation and that you have just started a session on a computer running UNIX. The computer is waiting for you to type a command.

You should be able to see a *prompt character* or *prompt string* on the screen, and a cursor symbol located just to the right of that prompt. The prompt may be indicated by a rectangle in reverse video, or perhaps by an underscore. The prompt may be blinking. It all depends on which kind of display device you have. The prompt character or string may be almost anything. Throughout this book, we will use the percent character as the prompt since it is a standard default choice for UNIX systems. However, it is easy to change the default and have the computer display something more useful than a percent character. Chapter 4 will tell you how.

Now, suppose that you enter the command ls (list), which is the command for listing the names of the files in a directory[1], and then complete the command line by hitting the return key. Using my computer and my UNIX account, we might see the following dialogue on the screen,

```
% ls
a.out         bin       core        dead.message
letter.roff   secrets   calc_pi.c   calc_pi.o
%
```

and the prompt from the computer indicates that it is again waiting for another command to be typed in.

---

1. This, and many other, cryptic command name abbreviations form probably the biggest stumbling block for new UNIX users. Here, and throughout this chapter, the source of each acronym is shown.

What really happened here? When we started the computer session, the UNIX system started running a UNIX program called the shell. The shell program output the prompt string to the screen and then attempted to read from the keyboard. Until we actually typed some characters on the keyboard, the shell program was *blocked* – its execution was temporarily suspended. As we hit the three keys 'l', 's' and the return key to end the line, the shell program read these characters into an internal array. The shell program analyzes the line in its array to extract the command name (ls) and its arguments (none). For some commands, such as cd to change the current directory, the shell executes the command directly. In the case of ls, the shell program searches several directories (these directories are named by the shell variable path) looking for an executable file named "ls". If all goes well, the file will be found and the shell will invoke a service of the operating system to execute the file as a program. (Chapter 10 will tell you how to write a program that executes other programs in this way.) The shell program suspends execution until the ls program has finished sending its output to the screen, at which point it is re-awakened by the operating system and it displays a new command prompt on the screen.

The shell program is not a special program. It does not do anything that you could not write a program to do, assuming that you had the proper expertise. Because it is possible (although difficult) for users to create their own shell programs, several do exist. The standard shell provided with System V UNIX is called the *Bourne shell* (after its implementer Steve Bourne). The standard shell for Berkeley UNIX systems and their derivatives is called the C shell (for which Bill Joy is largely responsible). As the shell program is just another UNIX program, it has a command name. The command name for the Bourne shell is sh, that for the C shell is csh. Other shell programs that you might encounter are ksh (the Korn shell), vsh (a visual, menu-driven, shell) and tcsh (an extended version of csh). Berkeley UNIX systems provide both sh and csh. Each user can select which shell program they want to be running at the beginning of a session.[2] This book assumes that you are using the C shell.

Perhaps you are wondering why a program that analyzes and executes your interactive commands is called a *shell*? The UNIX operating system itself provides a number of services including creation of files, writing files, and loading executable files into memory and executing them. The purpose of the shell program is to package the system services into a form that is more suitable for access by an interactive user. In a sense, the shell program is an outer layer of software that is wrapped around the system to provide the external interface.

---

2. The chsh command is provided for changing the shell selection.

## 1-2    Basic Shell and UNIX Concepts

When you use UNIX interactively, your perception of the system is greatly influenced by the shell program. However, in most cases, the shell is providing an interface for facilities that are built into the system. We will now review some of the concepts that you need to understand when using UNIX. Much fuller explanations are provided later in Chapter 4 when the C shell is described and in the chapters found in Section II of this book where facilities provided by the operating system are covered. We conclude by listing some of the basic UNIX commands.

### Files and Directories

The most important concept is probably that of the *file*. A file is a collection of data items written onto a disk. The fact that the data is held on a disk means that the information is not lost when you end your UNIX session. Many UNIX programs can create files, and the shell program can too.

As an ordinary user, you will normally own three different kinds of files. One kind of file is an ordinary *data file*. You will use a data file to hold things like the source code of a program, the output from a program, the input to a text formatter, and various other things. A second kind of file is an *executable file*. An executable file contains a program that the UNIX system can copy into the memory of the computer and execute. The third kind of file is a *directory file*. Directories can be viewed as folders which hold other files. Directory files can contain other directory files and this leads to a tree-structured directory hierarchy.

If you execute the command `ls -F`, you can see the names of the files that are in the current directory. The extra argument to `ls` asks it to indicate what kinds of files they are too. Executing the command on my UNIX account causes the following information to be displayed.

```
% ls -F
a.out*       bin/        core        dead.message
letter.roff secrets/    calc_pi.c   calc_pi.o
%
```

The asterisk after the name "a.out" indicates that "a.out" is an executable file. Similarly, the slash characters after the names "bin" and "secrets" indicate that they are directories. The fact that "a.out" is executable means that we should be able to type its name as a command.[3] Trying this with the executable program in my UNIX account has the following outcome.

```
% a.out
The value of pi isSegmentation fault (core dumped)
%
```

---

3. The word *should* is significant. If you try this and the shell replies "Command not found," you should read about the *path* variable and the `rehash` command in Chapter 6.

The partial line "The value of pi is" was output by my program, but before the line could be completed something went badly wrong in the program. It apparently generated a wild memory reference, perhaps due to an array index that is out of bounds. When the operating system detects such an error, it halts the program and copies the current state of the program into a file named "core". (Now we know why there was a file with this name in my directory.) The dbx program, covered in Chapter 15, can be used to analyze a core file and help in discover the nature of the programming error.

As well as an executable file, my UNIX account also contains a directory file named "secrets". One way we can find out what files are contained in that directory is by using the ls command again.

```
% ls -F secrets
chesstool*      gammontool*      highscores
savedgames/     suntetris*
%
```

As you see, the ls command can be given the name of a directory file as an argument and ls will report the contents of that directory.

Since the directory "secrets" contains yet another directory, we can ask ls to go one level further in the hierarchy as follows.

```
% ls -F secrets/savedgames
game1           game2           game3
%
```

## Pathnames and Navigating Through Directories

As you have just seen, directories can contain other directories and thus we can form a hierarchy of directories. All the files that are accessible on the UNIX system belong to a single hierarchy. The directory that you can see when you login into UNIX and execute ls is not the root of the hierarchy. It is merely a directory that happens to be your *home directory.* You can see where you are in the hierarchy by executing the pwd (print working directory) command. This is what I see when I run that command on my UNIX account.

```
% pwd
/csr/a/nigelh
%
```

The sequence "/csr/a/nigelh" is an example of an *absolute pathname.* The directory at the root of the hierarchy has the special name "/". In the directory named "/", there is another directory named "csr"; that directory contains another one named "a", which contains, in turn, my home directory named "nigelh" (corresponding to my login name).

An absolute pathname has the general form

```
/directory/directory/directory ... /filename
```

After the initial slash character (the name of the root directory), it consists of a sequence of file names separated by slash characters. All except the last file name must be directory names.

It would, of course, be inconvenient if we had to use absolute pathnames to refer to all of our files. For example, using the absolute pathname notation with the `ls` command to see what is in my "savedgames" directory, I would have to type the following.

```
% ls -F /csr/a/nigelh/secrets/savedgames
```

The UNIX system, therefore, remembers a current working directory for each running program, including for your shell program. When you start a UNIX system, the current working directory is your home directory. When I earlier typed an `ls` command as

```
% ls -F secrets/savedgames
```

I was using a *relative pathname*. The pathname is taken to be relative to the current working directory. That is, if the current working directory is "/csr/a/nigelh" and the relative pathname is "secrets/savedgames", the two parts are combined by the operating system software to obtain the full absolute pathname. The sole distinguishing characteristic of a relative pathname is that it does not begin with a slash character.

You may change the current working directory with the `cd` command. For example, after logging in to my UNIX account, I could execute the following commands.

```
% cd secrets
% ls -F
chesstool*      gammontool*     highscores
savedgames/     suntetris*
% cd savedgames
% ls -F
game1           game2           game3
%
```

Each of the `cd` commands, above, is being used to navigated one level further down the hierarchy.

In general, the argument to `cd` is the pathname of a directory. I could, for example, execute the command

```
% cd /csr/a
```

to navigate to a directory one level above my home directory. If all you want to do, however, is navigate to a higher level in the hierarchy, there is an easier way. Every directory contains an entry for the name '..' (two consecutive period characters). The name ".." refers to the directory one level higher. Therefore, I can use the command

```
% cd ..
```

to move up one level, and I can use a command similar to

```
% cd ../aturing
```

to move across to a sibling directory (i.e. another directory that shares the same ancestor as the current directory).

As a final note about the cd command, it is worth knowing that if the command is used without an argument, it resets the current working directory to your home directory.

## Creating and Deleting Files and Directories

Many commands create new files in the course of their execution. For example, if I have a C source code file named "calc_pi.c" in my directory, I can compile that file to obtain a relocatable binary file named "calc_pi.o" by executing the command

```
% cc -c calc_pi.c
```

and I can link that binary file with library functions to obtain an executable program named "a.out" by executing the following command.

```
% cc calc_pi.o
```

The C compiler and its usage is explained more fully in the next chapter.

Many commands create output that is simply displayed on the screen. The date command provides a simple example, it simply outputs the current date and time. If I type the command, I should see a result similar to the following.

```
% date
Mon Feb 25 18:18:48 PST 1991
%
```

But if I change the command to the following, a new file named "timenow" is created. The new file contains all the output created by the date command.

```
% date > timenow
%
```

The '>' operator is a feature of the shell program. You can read more about this operator and related operators in Chapter 4. You can use '>' in conjunction with the cat command (catenate) to type text directly into a file. For example,

```
% cat > testdata
First line of test file.
Second line of test file.
^D
%
```

When you have finished typing the text, you must type the end-of-file character, *Control-D*. (I.e., you hold down the *Control* key on the keyboard and type a *d*.) You would not, however, want to enter more than a few lines of text this way. An interactive text editor is much better because it will let you go back and make corrections to previously typed lines.

The rm command (remove) is used to delete any file except a directory. The cp (copy) command is used to make a duplicate of a file and the mv command (move) is used to rename a file. The following commands show some simple examples of their use.

```
% cp timenow copy_of_file
% mv copy_of_file new_name    # rename the copied file
% rm timenow                  # delete the original file
```

A new directory is created with the mkdir command (make directory) and an empty directory may be deleted with the rmdir command (remove directory). The command 'rm -r' may be used to remove a non-empty directory (automatically removing all files and subdirectories in that directory). Here is a short example of how we might create a new subdirectory in our home directory and start to use it.

```
% cd            # return to home directory
% mkdir notes   # create subdirectory
% cd notes      # change to new directory
```

## Interactive Editors

If you are a typical UNIX user, you will spend more time editing files with an interactive editing program than you do performing any other task. The most widely used editing program on Berkeley UNIX systems is vi (visual editor). Chapter 3 contains a detailed description of vi. Another popular editor, particularly among university and college users, is emacs. This is described in Appendix A.

If you use a workstation, you may prefer to use an editor that lets you use a mouse to select text for editing. The editor used with the SunView windowing system on SUN workstations is named textedit. You may also come across other editors on UNIX with the command names ed, ex and sed. The first two editors are intended for use with hardcopy terminals or with dumb terminals connected to the computer by slow-speed links (so slow that you do not want to wait while 20 lines or so of your file are displayed on the screen). The last named editor, sed, is useful when you wish to edit a file non-interactively (in batch mode).

## 1-3   Obtaining Help Information

The UNIX system has an on-line help facility. The command name to use is man (on-line manual). Its purpose is to provide you with descriptions of commands, operating system functions, library functions, formats of special files, and other topics related to your UNIX system.

The normal usage of man is to obtain information about how to use some command. If, for example, you wish to read a description of the rm command, you can execute the following.

```
% man rm
```

Naturally, help information about the man command itself is obtained as follows.

```
% man man
```

The major hurdle that UNIX beginners face is that commands tend to have cryptic abbreviations. If you cannot remember the name of the command that does what you want, how do you proceed? Another facility of the help command provides a partial solution. If, for example, that you want to know which commands will help you profile a program (to find out where it spends the most execution time), you may execute either

```
% man -k profile
```

or

```
% apropos profile
```

These two commands are identical in effect (indeed, they invoke the same program). They cause a small database that associates keywords with command names to be searched. The output is a list of all manual entries, along with one-line descriptions, that are associated with the keyword *profile*. The output from 'apropos profile' that my UNIX system gives me is reproduced in Figure 1-1. The parenthesized numbers indicate which section of

---

**Figure 1-1   Sample Output from the *apropos* Command**

```
% apropos profile
fusage (8)            - RFS disk access profiler
gprof (1)             - display call-graph profile data
kgmon (8)             - generate a dump of the operating
                        system's profile buffers
monitor, monstartup, moncontrol (3) - prepare execution
                        profile
prof (1)              - display profile data
prof (3)              - profile within a function
profil (2)            - execution time profile
pxp (1)               - Pascal execution profiler and
                        prettyprinter
tcov (1)              - construct test coverage analysis and
                        statement-by-statement profile
%
```

---

the on-line help manual contains the full description. There are normally eight sections, organized as follows.

- Section 1: User commands.

- Section 2: Operating system services (invoked as functions from C programs).

- Section 3: Library functions (that may be included in C programs).

- Section 4: Devices, networks and interfaces.

- Section 5: System file formats.

- Section 6: Games and demonstration programs.

- Section 7: Miscellaneous (text formatting macro packages, the ASCII character set, and so on).

- Section 8: System maintenance commands (these are not normally relevant to an ordinary UNIX user).

Some sections are further subdivided. For example, section 1 has a subsection named 1C. However, the subsections need not concern you when using the man or apropos commands. To return to the profile example, we see that we can restrict our attention to just the prof, gprof, pxp and tcov entries listed in Figure 1-1 and we can use the man command to obtain more information about each one.

There are a couple more points to observe with the man command. It sometimes happens that there are two entries with the same name in two different sections of the manual. This occurred with the profile example. The command

```
% man prof
```

will display the entry on prof from section 1 of the manual. It will tell you about a user command named prof. However, there is a different entry, describing a library function named prof, in section 3 of the manual. To read this entry, you must specify the section number in the man command, as follows.

```
% man 3 prof
```

The second useful point to know is that each section of the manual has an introduction that summarizes all the entries. To read the introduction to section 2, say, just execute this command.

```
% man 2 intro
```

## 1-4    Basic UNIX Commands

The following tables list some of the more useful commands. These are not complete lists. In particular, commands that are built into the shell are not mentioned (see Chapter 4 for these commands). Only simple forms of the commands are shown below. You should use the `man` command to learn more about each command.

### Table 1-1    Directory Handling Commands

| | |
|---|---|
| `cd` *dir* | change current working directory to *dir* |
| `cd` | change current working directory to the home directory |
| `ls` *dir* | list the contents of the named directory |
| `ls` | list the contents of the current directory |
| `pwd` | print the full path of the current working directory |
| `mkdir` *dir* | create a new directory named *dir* |
| `rmdir` *dir* | remove an empty directory named *dir* |
| `rm -r` *dir* | remove directory *dir* and everything contained in it. |
| `du` *dir* | report how much storage is used by all the files in directory *dir*. |
| `find` *expr dir* | search all the files in directory *dir* for files with the characteristics given by *expr*. |

### Table 1-2    Creating, Copying, Deleting Files

| | |
|---|---|
| `cp` *file newfile* | copy *file*, naming the copy *newfile*. |
| `mv` *file newname* | rename a file or directory to *newname*. |
| `rm` *file* | remove *file*. |
| `chmod` *how file* | set access permissions on *file* according to the *how* parameter. |

## Table 1-3 Commands to Perform Operations on Files

| | |
|---|---|
| diff *file1 file2* | compare two text files for differences. |
| fmt *file* | format a text file by right justifying lines. |
| indent *file* | format a C source code file. |
| grep *pat file* | display lines in *file* that match the pattern *pat*. |
| egrep *pat file* | display lines in *file* that match the pattern *pat*. |
| fgrep *pat file* | display lines in *file* that match the pattern *pat*. |
| sort *file* | sort lines of *file* into alphabetic order |
| tr *how file* | translate characters of *file* according to the *how* parameter. |
| compress *file* | squash *file* using data compression techniques (typically, text files squash to half the original size). |
| uncompress *file* | restore the compressed file to its original state. |
| zcat *file* | display a compressed file, without restoring it. |

## Table 1-4 Commands to Display, Inspect or Print a File

| | |
|---|---|
| more *file* | browse through *file*, one screenful at a time. |
| cat *file* | display the file without halting. |
| head *-n file* | display the first *n* lines in a file. |
| tail *-n file* | display the last *n* lines in a file. |
| file *file* | report the nature of the named file. |
| ls -l *file* | show the size, owner and access permissions for a file. |
| wc *file* | give the size of *file* (as numbers of characters, words and lines). |
| lpr *file* | send *file* to the standard printer. |
| pr *file* | display *file* with page numbers, suitable for printing. |

## Table 1-5   Miscellaneous Commands

| | |
|---|---|
| `man topic` | look up on-line manual information on the named topic. |
| `man n topic` | look up on-line information on the named topic in section *n* of the manual. |
| `man -k keyword` | list entries associated with the keyword in the on-line manual. |
| `apropos keyword` | same as `man -k keyword`. |
| `login username` | start a UNIX session. |
| `logout` | terminate the UNIX session. |
| `w` | see who is logged in, and their current commands. |
| `mail username` | send a mail message to the specified user. |

# CHAPTER 2    *C PROGRAMMING OVERVIEW*

The C language was designed and implemented by Dennis Ritchie in the early days of UNIX. It was used as the implementation language for UNIX and for most of the programs that come with UNIX. Knowledge of C is essential for systems programming on UNIX because all the systems services are called as C functions. The definition of the C language was effectively provided by the first edition of the book *The C Programming Language* by B. W. Kernighan and D. M. Ritchie (Prentice-Hall 1978). It, however, left several gaps in the language definition. In addition, a few extensions (such as enumeration types) were added to the language later.

C has become important as a language, independent of its use within UNIX, because of its availability on almost all kinds of computer and because of its versatility and efficiency. If one wishes to construct a program that will work, with little or no change, on any computer, C is a good language to choose.

Recently, C has been standardized by the American National Standards Institute (ANSI). The standardization committee deliberated for about three years, examining every language construct and defining the behavior of each construct as precisely as possible. While the committee did their best not to make changes to the language that would invalidate existing C code, there were some important additions made. The new language is called ANSI C and is defined by the standard numbered ANSI X3.159-1989. We will use the name *classic C* to refer to the original C language plus the commonly adopted extensions (such as enumeration types). You may also come across the name K&R C (for Kernighan and Ritchie C), sometimes further refined to K&R1 and K&R2 to indicate whether the extensions are included or not. ANSI C is consistently used for examples throughout this book.

This chapter contains only a condensed overview of the ANSI C language. It is neither a complete reference manual for C nor a gentle introduction to C. Instead it is a collected series of examples of nearly every construct and statement type, with a minimum of explanation. Most of the examples are applicable to both classic C and ANSI C. The exceptional features, specific to ANSI C, are tagged with a dagger symbol (†). A summary of the differences is given at the end of the chapter.

If you need an introduction to ANSI C, there a few books listed at the end of this chapter. For the reference manual, there is, at present, no real alternative to obtaining a copy of the ANSI standards document.

## 2-1  Compiling a C Program

At the time of writing, the Gnu C compiler, gcc, distributed by the Free Software Foundation, may be the only ANSI C compiler available on your system. However, computer companies and software companies should be distributing C compilers that conform to the ANSI standard in the near future (perhaps by the time this book is printed).

To compile a complete ANSI C program contained in the file named "prog.c", use the following command.

```
gcc -ansi prog.c -o prog
```

The −ansi flag causes gcc to require ANSI C constructions and the −o flag names the resulting executable program "prog". If the −o flag is omitted, the executable program will be named "a.out".

If you require maximum conformance to the ANSI C standard, you should use the command

```
gcc -ansi -pedantic -trigraph -undef prog.c -o prog
```

but it is very unlikely that you will notice any difference. The extra flags are explained in the gcc manual page entry.

To compile a multi-file program composed of files named "part1.c", "part2.c" and "part3.c", the following sequence of commands will suffice.

```
gcc -ansi -c part1.c
gcc -ansi -c part2.c
gcc -ansi -c part3.c
gcc -ansi part1.o part2.o part3.o -o prog
```

## 2-2   *Lexical Elements of the Language*

The lexical elements, or tokens, of C are identifiers, keywords, constants of various kinds, operator symbols, and punctuation symbols. The tokens of a program may be separated by white space characters and comments.

### Identifiers

```
A    last_index    cnt123a
```

Note that upper and lower case letters are distinct and that an underscore character is considered to be a letter.

### Integer Constants

```
123    99                          /* decimal integers */
0    037    01                     /* octal integers */
0xff   0x12AE0   0XFF0eeF          /* hexadecimal integers */
123L   077L                        /* long integers */
0xffffffffU                        /* unsigned integer† */
```

### Character Constants

```
'X'    '*'    '\n'    '\043'    '\x21'
```

A complete list of the special forms (using a backslash) appears in Table 2-1.

### String Constants

```
"String 1\n"   "she said \"%s\""
```

The same backslash forms of characters given in Table 2-1 may be used in strings. In ANSI C, adjacent string constants are automatically combined by the compiler into a single string – providing a convenient way to split long strings across several lines of the program.†

**Table 2-1**   **Special C Character Constants**

| | | | |
|---|---|---|---|
| `'\a'` | bell (alert) character† | `'\\'` | backslash |
| `'\b'` | backspace | `'\''` | single quote |
| `'\f'` | form-feed | `'\"'` | double quote |
| `'\n'` | linefeed | `'\?'` | question mark† |
| `'\r'` | carriage return | `'\ooo'` | octal notation |
| `'\t'` | tab | `'\xhhh'` | hexadecimal notation† |
| `'\v'` | vertical tab† | | |

### Floating-Point Constants

```
3.1416   1.0e-31   2e6   2E6    /* double type */
3.1416f  1.0e-31F                /* float type */
3.14159265358979323L            /* long double type† */
```

### Comments

```
/* any sequence of characters not containing an
   asterisk followed by a slash character ... */
```

Note that comments cannot be nested.

## Trigraph Sequences

It is unlikely that you will ever need to use the trigraph[†] feature. More likely, you will need to avoid accidentally triggering the trigraph mechanism. You therefore need to know of its existence so that you may avoid it.

A few important characters, such as square brackets, are not provided in the international character set defined by the ISO 646 standard. To guarantee that there is always a way to pass a C program from one computing device to another, the ANSI standard provides alternative methods of specifying these characters. Every one of these sequences consists of three characters (hence the name *trigraph*), where the first two characters are question marks. There are nine trigraphs in all, they and their single character equivalents are listed in Table 2-2. The compiler replaces any occurrence of a trigraph with its single character equivalent, even occurrences inside string constants. (Hence the need for the character escape code '\?' which provides you with a way of having two consecutive question marks inside a string constant.)

Note: the Gnu C compiler does not recognize any trigraph sequences unless the -trigraph flag is supplied on the command line.

## Table 2-2   ANSI C Trigraph Sequences

| ??! | \| | ??) | ] | ??< | { |
|-----|-----|-----|---|-----|---|
| ??' | ^ | ??) | ] | ??> | } |
| ??- | ~ | ??/ | \ | ??= | # |

## *2-3 Datatypes and Declarations*

### Elementary Datatypes

```
int cnt1, NumSteps = 0;
char ch;
float delta = 1.0e-10;
double e = 2.71828;
unsigned int flags;
signed char smallnum; /* † */
unsigned char c;
long double pi = 3.14159265358979323L; /* † */
short int temp1;
short temp2;    /* same type as temp1 */
long int timenow;
```

Note that int will be assumed if, as in the *temp2* example, you use just short, long, signed or unsigned as the complete type name.

### Boolean Type

There is no Boolean (or logical type) in C. Instead the integer value 0 serves as the logical value *false* and any non-zero integer serves as a representation of *true*.

### Enumeration Types

```
enum spectrum {violet, indigo, blue, green,
                yellow, orange, red} v1, v2, v3;
enum coin {cent=1, nickel=5, dime=10, quarter=25} tip;
```

The enumeration types are implemented in the same way as the int type, with enumeration constants being names for particular integer values. You may use the cast operator, see below, to convert between an enumeration value and an integer. Enumeration types were not part of the original Kernighan & Ritchie C language, but are supported by most C compilers.

### Arrays

```
int A[10];
float Potential[500][100];
```

Note that all subscripts are numbered from zero. The integer appearing between the square brackets is the number of elements in the array. Hence the subscript of *A* ranges over 0 to 9. Similarly, the first subscript of *Potential* ranges over 0 to 499 and the second subscript over 0 to 99.

The size of the first dimension of an array may be omitted if the declaration refers to an array that is fully defined elsewhere. The size may also be omitted if initialization values for the array are provided.

```
extern char CharacterMap[];
extern float CostMatrix[][100];
short DaysInMonth[] = { 31, 28, 31, 30, 31, 30,
                        31, 31, 30, 31, 30, 31 };
```

## Pointers

```
int *ptr1, *ptr2; char *cp;
void *gp;    /* generic pointer† */
```

A generic pointer can be cast to any pointer type using the cast operator (see below). Casting between other pointer types, say from int* to char*, may be possible with your C compiler but is not guaranteed to be possible with other C implementations.

The integer constant 0 is used as a *null* pointer. (A null pointer in C is used for the same purpose as the pointer **nil** in Pascal, say.) Thus, the assignment

```
ptr1 = 0;
```

is allowed by the compiler, regardless of what pointer type is declared for *ptr1*. The macro NULL, defined as 0 in standard include libraries, is normally used to write null pointers in C programs.

## Structures and Unions

```
struct cmplx { float x, y; } z1, z2;
struct listelement {
        char *strvalue;
        struct listelement *next;
    };
struct listelement *head, *tail;

union overlay {
        int x;
        char c[4];
    } trick;

void *uptr;   /* may point at objects of any type */
```

Note that the void* type is used as a generic pointer type.† For example, malloc can allocate storage for any kind of object and therefore the result type should be given as void*.

To allow data to be packed more efficiently and to permit convenient access to machine-dependent data structures, C provides bit-fields. A bit-field is a group of one or more consecutive bits that does not cross the boundary of a natural storage unit (a four byte longword on SUN-3 and SUN-4 computers). Bit-fields must be declared as fields in a structure. The type of a bit field is treated as an integer whose range is determined by the number of bits in the field. Its type may be `int`, `signed int`, or `unsigned int`.[†] Here is an example that corresponds to one of the formats for instructions on the IBM/370 architecture.

```
struct rx_format {
        unsigned int opcode: 8;
        unsigned int dest_register: 4;
        unsigned int index_register: 4;
        unsigned int base_register: 4;
        unsigned int offset: 12;
};
```

In this example, the field named *offset* may hold integer values in the range 0 to 4095 (since $2^{12}$ equals 4096). The fields with names ending in *_register* may hold values in the range 0 to 15, and the *opcode* field may hold values in the range 0 to 255. If we changed the `unsigned` qualifier of the *offset* field declaration to `signed`, then *offset* would be able to hold values in the range -2048 to 2047.

If you just declare a bit-field as having type `int`, an ANSI C compiler is free to choose whether it implements the field as being `signed` or `unsigned`.

If one or more bits must remain unused in a packed data structure, you do not have to give a name to the unused bit-field. Here is an example.

```
struct flags_word {
        unsigned int changed, must_save : 1;
        : 6;   /* unused - reserved for future use */
        int id_code : 8;
};
```

## Naming a Type with Typedef

```
typedef short int_16_bits;
typedef struct complex { float x, y; } COMPLEX;
typedef struct le { char *strval; struct le *next; }
        ListElement, *ListElementPtr;
```

The above definitions define new type names that may be used in subsequent declarations. If the keyword `typedef` were to be removed from such a definition, it would be an ordinary declaration of one or more objects. The addition of the `typedef` keyword causes the types that those objects would have had to be remembered by the compiler for later re-use. Some sample declarations that use the `typedef` names introduced above follow.

```
int_16_bits counter1, stack[100];
COMPLEX z1, z2;
ListElementPtr Head, Tail;
```

The `typedef` feature has several uses. It provides a way to parameterize the program for different environments. For example, the preprocessor (see below) may be used to select one `typedef` statement for one computer and a different `typedef` statement for another computer. Another use is as a primitive form of type encapsulation, as with the definition of COMPLEX, above. A third use is as a means of decomposing complex datatype declarations into a series of much simpler ones. For example, suppose that we wish to declare a variable *V* as being a pointer to a 10 element array of pointers to functions that take one argument of type `double` and return an `int` result. The direct way of making the declaration is as follows.

```
int (*(*V)[10])(double);
```

But, if (like me) you are unsure of getting all the parentheses and operators in the right places, you can use a series of `typedef` statements to build up the desired datatype.

```
typedef int FID(double); /* FID == function with
                                  int result, double arg. */
typedef FID *FIDP;       /* pointer to FID */
typedef FIDP AFIDP[10];  /* array of FIDP */
typedef AFIDP *PAFIDP;   /* pointer to AFIDP */
PAFIDP V;
```

The hardest part is inventing the names to represent the different datatypes.

## Storage Duration and Storage Class Specifiers

Variables declared in a C program either have their storage allocated before the program begins execution and that storage persists as long as the program executes, or else their storage is allocated each time an enclosing block is entered and de-allocated each time it is exited. The former possibility is called *static storage duration* and the latter is called *automatic storage duration*.

Every variable whose declaration is global, that is, whose declaration occurs outside a function, has static storage duration. A variable whose declaration occurs inside a function has automatic storage duration unless the declaration includes the type modifier `static` or `extern`. If the `static` modifier is used, the storage is static and the name is visible only within the block that contains the declaration. If the `extern` modifier is used, the declaration does not create a new variable but provides a reference to an existing variable with the same name that is declared outside the function (and therefore has static storage duration).

A variable that is declared inside a function without use of the `static` or `extern` modifiers has automatic storage duration. The `register` modifier may be used as a request to the compiler to implement the storage of that variable as a machine register. The request may be ignored by the compiler if the datatype of the variable is unsuitable for implementation in a register or if a register is not available for the purpose. The `auto` modifier is unnecessary, it simply requests automatic storage duration without using a register (and that is the default anyway).

```
int g;     /* static storage duration */
void f( register int b ) {
    static char buffer[10];       /* static storage */
    register char *cp = buffer;   /* auto storage   */
    float g = 1.5;                /* auto storage   */
    if (b == 0) {
        extern int g;       /* reference to global g */
        auto float h;                 /* auto storage */
        g = 1;              /* assignment to global g */
        ...
        ...     remainder of function omitted
```

## Const and Volatile Modifiers

The `const` modifier[†] indicates to the compiler that the object does not change its value. The compiler will disallow assignments that attempt to assign a value to the object directly. (Indirect assignments via pointers are harder to detect and may not be prevented by the compiler.) By placing the modifier at different positions in a declaration, it is possible to define variables such as a constant pointer to an array, where the contents of the array may change, or define a variable pointer to an array whose contents are constant.

```
const double pi = 3.14159265358979;
const char *ptr_to_constant_string;
char A[] = "abcdef";
char *const constant_ptr_to_string = A;
```

Thus, the following statements are legal or illegal as indicated.

```
ptr_to_constant_string    = "xyz";    /* OK */
ptr_to_constant_string[1] = 'X';      /* NOT OK */
constant_ptr_to_string[1] = 'X';      /* OK */
constant_ptr_to_string    = "xyz";    /* NOT OK */
```

The `volatile` modifier[†] indicates to the compiler that the object may change its value even without an assignment to the object inside the program. It is unlikely to be needed in normal programs. (A memory location that is updated by a hardware interrupt would be an example of a volatile variable.) The `volatile` modifier warns the compiler that it cannot assume that the object retains its value from one statement to the next and thus inhibits certain kinds of code optimization. The modifier is used in the same way as const, as follows.

```
volatile int *clock_address = (int *)0X000100;
```

## 2-4    *Accessing Values*

The following simple statements are consistent with the datatype declarations used in the preceding examples.

```
cnt1 = 10;      /* access a simple variable */
tip = nickel;   /* use an enumeration variable */

/* access array elements */
A[2] = 3;
Potential[cnt1][0] = 1.0;

ip = &cnt1;     /* ip holds address of cnt1 */
*ip = 0;        /* store zero, indirectly, in cnt1 */

/* access members of structures or unions */
z1.x = 3.0; z1.y = 2.0; z2 = z1;
trick.x = 37154890;
Head->strval = "Aardvark";
Tail->next = NULL; /* same as: (*Tail).next = NULL; */
```

## 2-5    *Expressions and Operators*

All the C operators are listed in Table 2-3. The operators are grouped according to their precedence levels, with thin lines separating groups of operators with the same precedences. The highest precedence operators are placed at the top of the table, and the lowest at the bottom.

The assignment operators are all right-associative. For example, the following two compound statements are equivalent.

```
{ i += j -= 2; }      { j = j - 2; i = i + j; }
```

All the unary operators are right-associative, so that, for example, the following two expressions have the same meaning.

```
*p++            *(p++)
```

The conditional expression operator is also right associative, so that these two expressions have the same meaning.

```
i>0?1:j>0?2:3      (i>0)?1:( (j>0)?2:3 )
```

All the other operators are left associative.

Examples and explanations for the various operators follow.

## Table 2-3  C Expression Operators

| | | |
|---|---|---|
| `expr[expr]` | | array indexing |
| `expr(expr, ... )` | | function invocation |
| `expr.fieldname` | | member selection |
| `expr->fieldname` | | pointer qualification |
| `expr++` | `expr--` | post-increment, post-decrement |
| `++expr` | `--expr` | pre-increment, pre-decrement |
| `&expr` | `*expr` | address of, pointer dereferencing |
| `+expr` | `-expr` | unary plus, unary minus |
| `~expr` | `!expr` | bitwise inversion, logical negation |
| `sizeof expr` | `sizeof(type)` | size of (in bytes) |
| `(type)expr` | | cast (convert to a datatype) |
| `expr*expr` | `expr/expr` | times, divide |
| `expr%expr` | | mod (or remainder) |
| `expr+expr` | `expr-expr` | add, subtract |
| `expr<<expr` | `expr>>expr` | shift left, shift right |
| `expr<expr` | `expr>expr` | less than, greater than |
| `expr<=expr` | `expr>=expr` | less-or-equal, greater-or-equal |
| `expr==expr` | `expr!=expr` | equal, not equal |
| `expr&expr` | | bitwise and |
| `expr^expr` | | bitwise exclusive or |
| `expr|expr` | | bitwise or |
| `expr&&expr` | | logical and |
| `expr||expr` | | logical or |
| `expr?expr:expr` | | conditional expression |
| `expr=expr` | | assignment |
| `expr+=expr` | `expr-=expr` | add-and-assign, subtract-and-assign |
| `expr*=expr` | `...` | times-and-assign, etc. |
| `expr , expr` | | comma expression |

## Arithmetic Operators

The infix arithmetic operators are '+', '−', '*', '/' and '%' meaning addition, subtraction, multiplication, division and remainder. The operands of the '%' operator must be integers. The other four operators work with either integer or floating point operands.

The ANSI C standard requires that the identity

```
a = (a/b)*b + a%b
```

should hold provided that a/b is representable (i.e., the calculation does not overflow). When either a or b is negative, the sign of a%b is left unspecified in the standard. Given that the divide instruction always leaves a positive remainder on some computer architectures but can leave a negative remainder on others, the lack of precision in the ANSI standard is a necessary concession to efficiency.

The infix addition and subtraction operators may also be used, subject to restrictions, with pointer operands. If p and q are variables with the same pointer type and if they point to elements in the same array, then all four of the following example expressions may be acceptable.

```
p+2     1+p     p-3     p-q
```

If p points at the array element, A[6], say, then p+1 is a pointer value that points at A[7], and p+2 points at A[8]. The expression 1+p is another way of writing p+1. Similarly, p−3 points at A[3]. If q points at A[10], then p−q has the value −4. If any of the forms *pointer±integer* goes off the end of the array, the result is undefined. Similarly, p and q must refer to elements in the same array for p−q to be defined. (To simplify array manipulation, the ANSI C standard allows a pointer value to reference a fictitious extra element at the high end of an array.)

The prefix '+' and '−' operators are available for integer and floating point operands.[†] Their effect should need no explanation.

The '++' and '−−' operators exist in both prefix and postfix forms and are applicable to integer or pointer operands. The prefix '++' operator causes its operand (which must represent a memory location) to be incremented by one and the new value of the operand is taken as the value of the expression. For example, the assignment

```
k = ++j * 2;
```

is equivalent to these two statements.

```
j = j + 1;   k = j * 2;
```

The postfix '++' operator causes the current value of the operand (again representing a memory location) to be taken as the value of the expression. Sometime later, but before the next statement in the program is executed, the operand of '++' is incremented. For example, the assignment

```
k = j++ * 2;
```

is equivalent to these two statements.

```
k = j * 2;   j = j + 1;
```

The '--' operator works similarly, except that it decrements its operand by one. If you use an incrementing or decrementing operator in a statement, the precise order in which actions take place is undefined. For example, the result of

```
i = 2;   j = i++ * i;
```

could result in j being assigned either 4 or 6, depending on whether the second operand of the multiplication is fetched before or after the incrementing takes place.

## Array Indexing

An array reference A[I] can be defined in terms of pointer arithmetic and dereferencing. The array name, by itself, is equivalent to a pointer to the first element of the array, which is A[0]. Therefore, given suitable declarations such as

```
float A[20]; int I;
```

the following two expressions are entirely equivalent.

```
A[I]            *(A + I)
```

Somewhat surprisingly (but not if you accept the equivalence to pointer arithmetic), A[I] is also equivalent to I[A].[1]

## Pointer and Structure Handling Operators

The prefix '&' and '*' operators are complementary. The former is the '*address of*' operator. It takes the address of an object, returning a pointer value. The latter is the '*dereferencing operator*'. It takes a pointer value and returns the object that it refers to. For example,

```
float X, Y, *pf;
pf = &X;        /* pf points at X */
*pf = 2.0;      /* sets X to 2.0 */
Y = *pf + 1.0;  /* sets Y to 3.0 */
```

The infix '.' and '->' operators are used for access to members of a structure or union type. Given the declarations

```
typedef struct node {
    int x, y; struct node *next;
} ELEMENT, *ELEMENT_PTR;
ELEMENT_PTR head;
```

---

1. Fortunately for people who have to read C code, such examples are found only in the annual obfuscated C code contest.

we may write accessing code such as the following.

```
head = (ELEMENT_PTR)malloc( sizeof(ELEMENT) );
if (head == NULL) abort();
head->next = 0;
head->x = 1; head->y = head->x * 2;
```

The expression (head->x) is equivalent to ((*head).x). That is, the '.' operator selects a field of a structure or union provided as the left operand. The '->' operator selects a field from a structure or union that is referenced by a pointer supplied as the left operand. The malloc function used in the above example is the general function for dynamically allocating new storage; its result is a pointer to the new storage. The cast to the ELEMENT_PTR type is redundant, as an ANSI C compiler will coerce the actual result type of malloc, void*, to the necessary pointer type. It is good practice to test the result returned by malloc. The result is NULL when there is insufficient remaining storage to satisfy the request. (A more user-friendly program would print an error message before calling abort.)

## Bitwise Operators

Several of the C operators correspond to bit manipulation instructions. The infix '&', '|' and '^' operators perform bitwise *and-ing*, *or-ing* and *exclusive or-ing* of their operands, which must be integers. For example, given the declarations and initializations

```
int X = 0x00005a1f;
int Y = 0x0000f187;
```

then X&Y has the value 0x00005007, X|Y has the value 0x0000fb9f, and X^Y has the value 0x0000ab98. To understand these results, it is necessary to look at the bit patterns of the operands and to apply the operation to pairs of bits taken from identical bit positions. The bit pattern calculation for X^Y would proceed as follows.

```
      0000 0000 0000 0000 0101 1010 0001 1111
^     0000 0000 0000 0000 1111 0001 1000 0111
     ─────────────────────────────────────────
=     0000 0000 0000 0000 1010 1011 1001 1000
```

The prefix '~' operator performs a bitwise inversion of all the bits in its operand, which must have an integer type. Thus, ~X would have the value 0xffffa5e0.

It is important to note that '&', '|' and '~' are *not* equivalent to the Boolean *and, or* and *not* operators. (Although they will very often yield the same answers.) For Boolean expressions, you should use the '&&', '||' and '!' operators, described below.

The '<<' and '>>' operators cause logical shifts left and right, respectively. The operands must be integers. The right operand, a non-negative integer, specifies the number of bit positions to shift the left operand. For example, X<<4, using the declaration for X given above, would produce the value 0x0005a1f0 and X>>4 would produce the value 0x000005a1. If the left operand of '>>' is an unsigned integer or a positive integer, the vacated bits at the left must be filled with zeros. If the left operand is a negative signed integer, the result is dependent on the implementation (thus allowing arithmetic shift instructions to be used in some implementations). Additionally, the result is undefined if you shift more positions than the number of bits in the operand or if the number of positions to shift is a negative number.

## Comparison Operators

The usual six comparison operations are '==' for equality comparison, '!=' for inequality, '<' for less than, '<=' for less-or-equals, '>' for greater than, and '>=' for greater-or-equals. The result of a comparison is the integer value 1 or the integer value 0, to represent true or false respectively.

You may compare two values of the same type for equality or inequality. If the types are compatible, so that one type can be converted to the other type, they again may be compared for equality or inequality.

The four operators '<', '<=', '>' and '>=' may be used if the operands are integers or floating point values. They may be used to compare values from the same enumeration type. (ANSI C does not prohibit comparisons between values from different enumeration types, but some compilers issue a warning message.[2]) Finally, they may be used to compare two pointer values, provided that the pointers reference elements in the same array.

## Boolean (Logical) Operators

The '&&', '||' and '!' operators perform the logical operations of *and*, *or* and *not*. The operands normally have integer type, where 0 is equivalent to *false* and any non-zero value is taken as equivalent to *true*. (The operands may also have pointer types, where NULL takes the role of false, or have floating point values where 0.0 is considered as false.) The result of the operation is either 1 or 0, corresponding to *true* or *false*, respectively.

The '&&' and '||' operators are known as conditional operators because they do not evaluate their right operands if the result can be determined from the left operands. This property is useful. For example, the following statement cannot cause an error due to the variable *i* having a value of zero.

```
if (i != 0 && k/i == 0) { ... }
```

---

2. The Gnu C compiler gcc permits such a comparison.

## Conditional Expressions

The statement

```
max = a>b? a : b ;
```

is equivalent to the statement

```
if ( a > b ) max = a; else max = b;
```

## Assignment Operators

The simple assignment operator is '='. It stores the value of the right operand in the location represented by the left operand. In addition, the entire expression containing the assignment operator has as its value the value of left operand after the assignment. Treating the assignment operator in this manner allows assignments to be embedded inside larger expressions (a practice that does not lead to readable code), and it allows multiple assignments. Here are a few examples.

```
i = j*k;
j = k = 3;          /* assigns 3 to both j and k */
i = j + (k = 2);   /* assigns 2 to k and 5 to i */
```

There are several other operators that combine assignment with an infix operator. These composite assignment operators are '+=', '-=', '*=', '/=', '%=', '<<=', '>>=', '&=', and '|='. Taking '%=' as an example, the following two statements are entirely equivalent.

```
x %= y;        x = x % y;
```

The other composite assignment operators are defined similarly.

## Cast Operator

The cast operator is used to convert a value from one datatype to another. Some sample conversions are the following.

```
int i; float f; char *cp;
enum {off, on} q;
...
i = (int)q;    /* i is assigned 0 for off, 1 for on */
i = (int)f;    /* f is rounded toward zero */
f = (float)27;      /* same as: f = 27.0; */
i = (int)cp;   /* an implementation-defined result */
cp = (char *)100;   /* ditto */
```

## The sizeof Operator

The `sizeof` operator may be applied to any expression or to a datatype name that is enclosed in parentheses. If the operand is an expression, that expression is not evaluated. Only the datatype of the expression is considered. The result of the operator is the size in bytes that a value with the operand datatype would occupy in memory. If applied to an array type, the result is the size of the entire array. If applied to a structure or union type, the size may include padding bytes that are allocated within the object or even at the end of the object in order to maintain alignment. Here are a couple of examples.

```
i = sizeof(int);    /* result is 4 on Sun computers */
i = sizeof p->b;
```

Note that the second example does not require *p* to have a valid pointer value, since the expression is not evaluated.

## The Comma Operator

The comma operator evaluates and discards its left operand, and then returns the value of its right operand as the result. The operator is not useful unless the left operand is an expression with side-effects. A simple, but silly, example is the following.

```
i = (j = 2), 3;
```

The example is silly because equivalent and more readable coding style would be the following.

```
j = 2;   i = 3;
```

The comma operator is most often needed in constructing expressions for controlling `for` loop constructs. For example, the following loop steps two index variables towards each other from opposite ends of a range.

```
for( i=0, j=99;  i < j;  i++, j-- ) {
... /* remainder of loop omitted */
```

## Implicit Arithmetic Type Conversions

The C compiler will automatically convert the datatype of a value to make it suitable for the context. For example, if you use the expression

```
5 / 2.0
```

the compiler will convert the `int` constant 5 to 5.0 with the `double` type, so that the divide operation may be performed as a floating point division. The example is, unfortunately, one of the simpler cases. Here is a summary of the ANSI C rules.

You may use a `char`, `short int`, `int` bit-field (including `signed` and `unsigned` versions of any of these) or an enumeration constant in an expression where an `int` value or an `unsigned int` value would be legal. If the `int` type can hold all the values of the original type, the conversion will be to int. Otherwise the conversion will be to unsigned int. These conversions are guaranteed to preserve the original value.

Conversions from a signed int to an unsigned int, or *vice versa*, are more difficult because it may not be possible to represent the value in the new type. First, if the value *can* be represented in the new type, the value is unchanged. If a negative integer value is converted to an unsigned int with greater size, the value is first converted to a signed int with the larger size and then (assuming a two's complement representation of the integers) the bit pattern of this result is assumed to be an unsigned int.

When an integer value is converted to an unsigned int with smaller size, the bit pattern of the value (assuming two's complement again) is simply truncated, discarding bits on the left. If an integer value is converted to a signed int with smaller size and if the value is outside the range of values that can be represented in the new type, the result is left to the implementer of the compiler.

When a floating-point value is converted to an integer value, the fractional part is discarded (i.e., the number is rounded towards zero). If the value is too large to be represented in an integer type, the result is undefined. When an integer value is converted to floating point, the conversion is performed as exactly as possible. A float value may be converted to double and a double value converted to long double, preserving the value. Conversions in the opposite direction are performed as exactly as possible. If the value cannot be represented in the new type, the result is undefined.

When an infix operator *op* is used in an expression, *expr1 op expr2*, the two operands must be converted to the same type and this must be the same type as the result. The ANSI C rules for the conversions are summarized in the table below. Given the types of the two operands, the rules should be tried in order until one of them matches. X represents any of the arithmetic types; the order in which the two types are listed is immaterial..

| | Operand Combination | | Conversion Action |
|---|---|---|---|
| 1 | long double | X | X $\Rightarrow$ long double |
| 2 | double | X | X $\Rightarrow$ double |
| 3 | float | X | X $\Rightarrow$ float |
| 4 | unsigned long int | X | X $\Rightarrow$ unsigned long int |
| 5 | unsigned int | long int | unsigned int $\Rightarrow$ long int, or both to unsigned long int |
| 6 | long int | X | X $\Rightarrow$ long int |
| 7 | unsigned int | X | X $\Rightarrow$ unsigned int |
| 8 | int | int | no conversion needed |

The action for rule 5 depends on the implementation. If the `long int` type can represent all the values in the `unsigned int` type (this is not the case for the `gcc` implementation on SUN computers), the `unsigned int` operand is converted to `long int`. Otherwise both operands are converted to `unsigned long int`.

## 2-6    Statement Types

### Expression Statements

Any expression may be used as a statement. The statement

```
27;
```

is valid C code but useless (and should generate a warning message from a good C compiler). But expressions that have side-effects when evaluated are useful. Therefore, the following are all syntactically expressions but are also plausible statements in a program.

```
cnt1 = 0;
cnt1++;
A[cnt1++] <<= 2;
fn(A, 37L, "call #1"); /* call a function */
```

### Selection Statements

```
if ( i < MAXSIZE) {   i++; A[i] = A[i-1];   }

if ( j > 0 )
   if (k > 0)
      printf("j, k are both positive");
   else
      printf("j > 0, k <= 0");
```

Note that an *else* part is associated with the closest unmatched *then* part (the same rule as in many programming languages) and that curly braces must be used to enclose groups of statements if used in a *then* part or an *else* part.

```
switch( cnt1+1 ) {
case 0: case -1: printf("A"); break;
case 3*2:        printf("B"); break;
default:         printf("-"); break;
}
```

The selecting expression in a `switch` statement must have an integer, character or enumeration type. Similarly, the constant expressions used in the case labels are restricted to the same types and must be compatible with the type of the selecting expression. Without the break statement, control would simply flow into the following case. This is because the case label and default label have the same status as the label used as a target of a goto statement.

## Iteration Statements

```
while( *cp != '*' ) {
    cp++;
    if (len++ > 10) break;
}

do {
    A[i] = B[i];
    i++;
} while( B[i] != 0 && i < 10 );

for( i=0; i<10; i++ ) {
    A[i] = 0;
    if (B[i] <= 0) continue;
    B[i]--;
}
```

The break statement may be used to exit from the nearest enclosing iteration statement (or switch statement). The continue statement may be used to skip over the remainder of the loop body and, if the test controlling the loop iteration is satisfied, repeat the loop.

The for loop header probably deserves a little explanation. The parentheses enclose three optional expressions, separated by semicolons. The first expression normally performs initialization prior to entry into the loop. The second expression performs a test that determines whether the loop body should be executed – the test is performed even for the first iteration of the loop. The third expression is executed after each loop iteration and is normally used to step loop control variables to their next values. A good way to understand the effect of a for loop is to think of it as a macro ...

```
for( expr1; expr2; expr3 ) loop-body
```

that expands to the following code pattern.

```
expr1;
while( expr2 ) {
    loop-body;
    expr3;
}
```

This expansion gives the correct semantics of the for loop with just one small exception – it does not properly explain the effect of a continue statement inside the loop body. (A continue statement inside a for loop causes *expr3* to be evaluated, followed by a test of *expr2*, and so on)

## Goto Statement

The `goto` statement may be used to transfer control to a label within the same function. (Labels defined in other functions are not visible in any case.)

```
        if ( (f = fopen(filename,"r")) == NULL )
            goto QUIT:
        ...

QUIT:
        return 1;
```

## Return Statement

The `return` statement may be used anywhere inside a function and causes an immediate return to the caller of the function. If the function has `void` type, no function value may be returned by the statement. Otherwise, the `return` statement must provide a value to be returned as the function result.

```
int max( int a, int b, int c ) {
    if (a >= b && a >= c) return a;
    if (b >= c && b >= a) return b;
    return c;
}

void zero_array( int *p, int n ) {
    for( ; ; ) {
        if (n-- <= 0) return;
        *p++ = 0;
    }
}
```

## 2-7   *Functions*

### Function Prototypes

A function prototype is used to specify the types of parameters accepted by a function[†] and the type of the returned result, if any. The prototype allows the compiler to check that the function is called correctly, and to coerce arguments to the correct types. The function may be defined in the same C module or in another module. Parameters may optionally be given names in function prototypes (see the *drawbox* example below), these names are for documentation purposes only and have no other significance.

The modifier `extern` is used to signify that the function is callable from a module other than the module in which the function is defined. The alternative is the modifier `static` which means that the function can only be called within the same module as where it is defined. If neither modifier is provided, the compiler assumes `extern`. If no result type is shown for the function, the compiler assumes `int`.

The `const` modifier[†] is useful in conjunction with a pointer argument as it can indicate that the object referenced by the pointer is not changed by the function. Here are several examples.

```
/* Function max takes exactly two arguments */
extern int max( int, int );


/* Function drawbox takes two arguments, the meanings
      of the arguments are indicated by their names */
void drawbox( int width, int height );


/* Function exchange does not return a result */
extern void exchange( int *, int * );


/* Function printf takes one or more arguments, the
second and following arguments may have any types.
      The first argument is not changed by printf. */
extern int printf( const char *, ... );


/* Function readstring takes no arguments */
extern char *readstring(void);


/* Function count accepts any number and any types of
      arguments. This form is provided for backwards
      compatibility with classic C code.3 */
extern int count();


/* Function localfn is defined in the same module.
      Its result type defaults to int. */
static localfn( double );
```

---

3. This is the only prototype out of all the examples given that is compatible with classic C.

## Function Definitions

A function definition begins with declarations for the arguments and for the result type of the function. There are two styles of argument declaration, one is identical to the classic C syntax (and is retained for backwards compatibility[4]) and the other corresponds to the ANSI C style for function prototypes.

```
int max( int a, int b ) {
    return a >= b? a : b ;
}

/* compatible with classic C syntax */
int min( a, b )
int a, b;
{
    return a < b? a : b ;
}

char *readstring( void ) {
    static buffer[100];
    return fgets( buffer, 100, stdin );
}

/* compatible with classic C syntax */
char *readstring2() {
    static buffer[100];
    return fgets( buffer, 100, stdin );
}
```

If you use the classic C syntax, you may omit declarations for arguments that have type int. Therefore, the declarations for *a* and *b* in the *min* function may be omitted. With either syntax, you may omit the function result type if it is int.

## Passing Parameters and Returning Results

The parameter passing mechanism is call-by-value. That is, a function receives copies of the argument values used in a call to the function. The arguments may have any datatype except void (but an argument with an array type is a special case, as explained below). The result type of the function may be any datatype except an array type. A result type of void is used to indicate that the function does not return a result (i.e., it is equivalent to a procedure in other languages).

---

4. The ANSI C standard describes the classic C syntax as *obsolescent*, implying that it is likely to be dropped from some future revision of the standard.

The compiler will automatically convert the types of the arguments to match the types declared for them,[5] provided that you have provided a suitable function declaration. One situation when conversion will occur is when the function definition precedes the function call in the compilation unit and the classic C format was not used (i.e., the argument types were included in the argument list). The other situation when the compiler can perform the conversion automatically is when a function prototype declaration has been provided and the argument list was not left empty (the form provided for compatibility with classic C). For example, if the declaration

```
extern double sin(const double);
```

has been provided, and the *sin* function is called by the code

```
int i;  double x;
...   /* omitted code */
x = sin( i );
```

the compiler will cause the `int` argument to be converted to `double` before it is passed to the function. But if you use the classic C declaration for *sin*, as follows

```
extern double sin();
```

you have to write the function call as

```
x = sin( (double)i );
```

or else you will simply get wrong answers from the program, without any warning from the compiler that a problem might exist.

If an array name is used as an argument in a call to a function, the compiler passes the address of the first element of the array to the function. It does *not* make a copy of the array to pass. This means that if the argument used in the call is an array of `int` values, the function parameter should be declared as having the type `int *`.

Here is an example function whose arguments and result have `struct` types.

```
/* type COMPLEX is defined by a typedef, as above */
COMPLEX cadd( COMPLEX a, COMPLEX b ) {
    COMPLEX result;
    result.x = a.x + b.x;   result.y = a.y + b.y;
    return result;
}
```

and a call to the `cadd` function would take the following form.

```
COMPLEX u, v, w;
...
w = cadd(u, v);
```

---

5. The classic C compiler never performs automatic conversion when passing function arguments. You have to specify the conversions yourself using a cast operator.

Here is an example that illustrates use of an array parameter.

```
/* count number of zero elements in the array */
int count( int *ap, int size ) {
    int cnt = 0;
    while( size-- > 0 ) {
        if (*ap == 0) cnt++;
        ap++;
    }
    return cnt;
}


...
int A[50]; int n;
...
n = count(A, 50);
```

If, in the above example, we had declared the function arguments as

```
int count( int ap[], int size ) { ... etc.
```

it would have made no difference. The parameter *ap* would still be considered as having the type int *. The explanation is that an array parameter is always passed by reference. If the compiler did not silently convert the type of ap to be a pointer, it would imply that a copy of an argument array's value is to be passed as the parameter – and copying an array in an assignment or when passing a parameter is not part of the C language design.[6]

It is possible to pass a pointer to a function as an argument to another function. Suppose that we wish to plot graphs of various functions, such as the *sin* function, the *tan* function, and so on. The function that performs the plotting can be constructed in the following manner. (In practice, we would probably want to add extra parameters to control the range of values to plot and to control the scaling of the plot.)

```
void plotgraph( double (*f)(double) ) {
    double x, y;
    for( x = 0.0; x <= 1.0; x += 0.1 ) {
        y = f(x);
        ... /* output a dot at coordinate (x,y) */
    }
}
```

---

6. In the original Kernighan & Ritchie C language, only simple values that would fit into a machine register could be passed as parameters and returned as results from functions. This had the virtues of efficiency and ease of implementation for the compiler writer. The later addition of struct parameters and results means that you can pass an entire array, provided that it is made a member of a struct value and the entire structure is passed.

The statement that invokes the parameter f as a function should, strictly, be written as

```
y = (*f)(x);
```

but the compiler automatically performs the dereferencing if needed to convert a pointer to a function into the function itself. Similarly, if the parameter f is declared as

```
double f(double)
```

the compiler will automatically and silently convert the declaration to the correct form as a pointer to a function.

Calls to the *plotgraph* function may be programmed as follows.

```
extern double sin(double), tan(double);
...
plotgraph( sin ); plotgraph( tan );
```

## The Function main

Every complete C program must contain a function whose name is *main*. The ANSI standard specifically states that two prototypes are possible for *main*. They are

```
int main(void);
```

and

```
int main( int argc, char **argv );
```

The first, parameterless form for *main* is used if the program does not need to access arguments on the UNIX command line that invokes the program. The second form is used otherwise. In this case, *argv* is a pointer to an array of character strings where each character string is the text of one command line argument. The array includes the text of the command name itself as the first element. An extra NULL pointer is provided as the last element of the array. The integer *argc* is the number of elements in the array, excluding the trailing NULL pointer.

The *main* function should return an integer as its result. The result is returned either by using the `return` statement or by calling the library function *exit*. A result of zero is supposed to indicate that the program terminated successfully. A non-zero value is supposed to represent an error code.

## 2-8   The C Preprocessor

Each C source file named as an argument on the command line of the UNIX command that invokes the C compiler is passed through the C preprocessor. The C preprocessor implements a simple macro processing language that has no direct relationship with the C language. The hash character '#' indicates a preprocessor action, such as a definition for a macro. The preprocessor checks each identifier found in its input to see if it has a macro definition. If it does, the macro is expanded using simple textual substitution.

The command line flag −E causes the C compiler to display the result of the preprocessing phase. The result is simply sent to the standard output stream, so you may feed it into a suitable browsing program such as *more*. The −E flag is useful if you get an inexplicable syntax error message – often the bad syntax is caused by macros that expand in unexpected ways. A sample command that uses the −E flag is the following.

```
gcc -ansi -E program.c | more
```

A preprocessor command is distinguished by having the hash character appear as the first non-blank character on a line (where only spaces and horizontal tabs are acceptable as white space characters preceding the hash character).

## File Inclusion Directive

```
#include <stdio.h>
#include "mydefs.h"
```

Both directives cause the contents of a file to be inserted into the program at this point, replacing the corresponding #include line. The inserted files are themselves passed through the C preprocessor (and may therefore contain nested #include directives). The first form, where the filename is enclosed in angle brackets, causes the preprocessor to look for the file in the directory "/usr/include". The second form, where double quote characters are used, causes the preprocessor to look in the current directory for the file. If it is not found there, the preprocessor would then look in "/usr/include". On UNIX systems, the file may be specified using normal pathnames, so that

```
#include "../phase2/mydefs.h"
```

would work. However, this is not portable to all non-UNIX systems.[7]

The general usage is that the angle bracket form is used for system header files, and the double quote form is used for files supplied by the user. Note that additional directories where the preprocessor will search for files can be specified with the −I option on the compile command.

---

7. Furthermore, the notion of *current directory* for a nested #include directive is now ambiguous and the effect is implementation-dependent.

## Conditional Compilation

```
#if VERSION == 1
    ...    /* text included if VERSION has a
            macro definition equivalent to 1 */
#endif

#ifdef DEBUG
    ...    /* text included if DEBUG has any
            macro definition whatsoever */
#else
    ...    /* text to be included otherwise */
#endif

#ifndef DEBUG
    ...    /* text included if DEBUG is not defined */
#endif

#if VERSION==1
    ...    /* text included if VERSION is 1 */
#elif VERSION==2
    ...    /* text included if VERSION is 2† */
#else
    ...    /* text included otherwise */
#endif
```

Each #if must be matched with a closing #endif. A #else component is optional. The #elif construct† has an effect similar to #else #if on consecutive lines (except that an extra #endif is not required). Conditional inclusion directives may be nested if desired.

After a #if directive, a constant expression must be supplied. The text on the following lines up to a #else, #elif or #endif directive is included if the expression has a non-zero value. Elements of this constant expression may be integer constants or character constants (after macro expansion) or one of the forms

```
defined M
```

or, using optional parentheses,

```
defined ( N )
```

where M and N represent arbitrary identifiers.[8] The 'defined M' construct† is replaced by the value 1 if M has a macro definition and by 0 otherwise. If you use an identifier that does not have a macro definition in a position other than as an operand of defined, it will

---

8. The defined test is not available with many classic C compilers.

be replaced by $0.$[9] Apart from the special def ined test on an identifier, the constant expression may be composed using constants and operators of the C language. A simple example is the following.

```
#if defined VERSION && VERSION == 0
   ...
#endif
```

## Macro Definitions

In its simplest form, a macro provides a sequence of one or more tokens that are to be substituted for all subsequent occurrences of the defined identifier in the current compilation unit.

```
#define MAXSIZE    10
#define CHECK_N    if (N < 0 || N > MAXSIZE) {      \
        printf( "N is out of range! (%d)\n", N ) \
    exit(1);   }
```

As seen in the two examples, above, macro definitions may use other macros and the definitions may be continued over several lines, if desired. If a macro definition contains a use of the macro being defined, that inner macro will be left un-expanded.[10] A common convention among C programmers is to capitalize macro names.

Macros may be parameterized. Here are three examples.

```
#define MAX(X,Y)    ((X)>(Y)? (X)  : (Y))
#define sin(X)      (callcnt++, sin(X))
#define INC()       (stepcnt++)
```

The apparently redundant parentheses in the above macro definitions are a wise precaution. The preprocessor performs textual substitution without regard to the syntax of the C code, either before or after the substitution. If we were to define MAX as

```
#define MAX(X,Y)    X>Y? X : Y
```

and use the macro in the call

```
i = MAX( j&0xff, k&0xff );
```

it would appear from the C source code that we were taking the maximum of two expressions, j&0xff and k&0xff. However, the expanded text would be

```
i = j&0xff>k&0xff? j&0xff : k&0xff;
```

---

9. The behavior of classic C compilers with respect to this point is not defined.

10. The behavior of classic C compilers on such recursive macro definitions is not defined.

and the relative precedences of the '&' and '>' operators in C cause the expanded text to be parsed as though it were written as

```
i = j&(0xff>k)&0xff? (j&0xff) : (k&0xff);
```

– a statement that is correct C but unlikely to give the desired result. Extra parentheses in the macro definition eliminate the possibility of such surprises.

The *sin* macro example illustrates the property that recursive uses of macros are not expanded. If we use the macro in a statement like

```
y = r * sin( theta );
```

the expanded text will be

```
y = r * (callcnt++, sin(theta));
```

and, given the meaning of the comma operator, this statement has the same effect as the pair of statements

```
callcnt++;  y = r * sin(theta);
```

Thus we have used the macro to implement a *wrapper function*, where some extra actions are attached to each call of a function.

As a final note, it is worth noting that a macro only be re-defined if the second macro definition is identical to the original definition. That is, the number and names of the parameters must be the same and the sequences of tokens provided as the macro body must be identical.[†] This eliminates a common annoyance with header files compiled by the classic C compiler where several header files might define the constant NULL as

```
#define NULL    0
```

If you ever do need to replace a macro definition with a different one, you have to un-define the macro first (see below).

## Stringification and Token Concatenation

To make macros more powerful, ANSI C introduced two preprocessor operators that are not provided in classic C. The first is the *stringify*[†] operator '#'. It may be used to construct a string constant from a macro argument. If, for example, the macro

```
#define CHECK(V,N)    if (V>N) {                \
    fprintf(stderr, "%s > %d\n", #V, N); \
    exit(1); }
```

is invoked in the source line

```
CHECK(Count, 99);
```

the preprocessor will expand the line to read as follows.

```
if (Count>99) {
    fprintf(stderr, "%s > %d\n", "Count", 99);
    exit(1); }
```

The second operator is '##' which may be used to combine two tokens to create a new one.[†] The newly created token is usually an identifier (and this identifier can be the name of a macro that is expanded further). As an example, if the `stmt` macro defined as

```
#define stmt(N)    { cnt##N++; fn##N(); }
```

is invoked in the source line

```
stmt(27);
```

the preprocessor will expand the line to the following.

```
{ cnt27++; fn27(); };
```

If *fn27* is the name of a macro, further expansion will take place.

## Un-defining a Macro

If a macro definition is not needed further in a file, it is a good idea to remove that definition so that it cannot, accidentally, interfere with compilation of the remainder of the file. The `#undef` directive removes a definition. For example,

```
#undef MaxSize
```

removes any definition that *MaxSize* may have. It is not an error if *MaxSize* does not have a macro definition, the directive is just ignored.[11]

## Line, Error and Pragma Directives

When the preprocessor or the C compiler issue an error or a warning message about something in the program, they report the line number and the name of the file where the problem was encountered. The `#line` directive can be used to reset the line number and the filename. This ability is only useful when a C program is generated by a translator (such as when the `yacc` program generates a C program from a grammar file), so that error messages can be made to correspond to the original file. Two examples follow.

```
#line 37
#line 16 "pascal-grammar.y"
```

If only a line number is provided, as in the first example, the filename used in error messages is not changed. It is unlikely that you will find a use for the `#line` directive, but you will certainly see it if you look at C code after it has passed through the preprocessor.

---

11. Some classic C compilers may consider this to be an error however.

The #error directive[†] causes the preprocessor to generate an error message. It can be combined with conditional inclusion directives to test that macros have been given appropriate value. For example, we might include the following preprocessor test in a C program.

```
#if MaxSize < 16
#undef MaxSize
#error MaxSize is too small!!
#endif
```

Note that if the #undef directive is omitted in the example, the error message that would be generated if *MaxSize* has the value 11, for example, would read "11 is too small!!".

The #pragma directive[†] has been specifically provided in ANSI C as a way for the user to control some aspects of the compilation process. It is implementation dependent.

## Predefined Macros

An ANSI C preprocessor must provide the following predefined macros[12] and it is not supposed to provide any others.[13]

| | |
|---|---|
| _ _LINE_ _ | The current line number in the source file. |
| _ _FILE_ _ | The name of the current source file. |
| _ _DATE_ _ | Today's date as a character string constant. |
| _ _TIME_ _ | The current time as a character string constant. |
| _ _STDC_ _ | The integer constant 1. |

The last macro, _ _STDC_ _, is provided so that preprocessor commands can test if the program is being compiled by an ANSI C compiler. A classic C compiler is not supposed to define this macro.[14]

Additional macros may be predefined in particular implementations. It is common for the macro unix to be predefined in C compilers on UNIX systems. Another common macro is one that describes the computer architecture. For example, the macro sparc may be defined on SUN-4 systems.

---

12. Of these macros, only _ _LINE_ _ and _ _FILE_ _ are likely to be defined in a classic C compiler.

13. However the Gnu C compiler gcc will normally provide some additional predefined macros, such as unix. The -undef command line flag must be supplied to remove the extra macros.

14. But, nevertheless, some compilers apparently do.

## Command Line Macro Definitions

Simple macro definitions may be given in the command that invokes the C compiler. This facility is used when the program must be customized (perhaps by building in the name of a special file) or when a special version of a program is to be created. For example, suppose that the program contains debugging print statements like the following.[15]

```
#ifdef DEBUG
    printf( "At line " #__LINE__ ", X = %d\n", X );
#endif
```

We can turn on the DEBUG flag by compiling the program with a command like

```
gcc -ansi -DDEBUG program.c
```

The −D flag is immediately followed by the name of the macro to define. When used in this manner, the macro is predefined with the value 1. A value other than 1 may be provided, if desired. Examples of this appear below. The −D flag may be used several times if more than one macro needs to be defined. Here is an example.

```
gcc -ansi -DVERSION=2 -DLOGFILE=\"/usr/local/log\"  \
        program.c
```

which works as though the preprocessor directives

```
#define VERSION    2
#define LOGFILE    "/usr/local/log"
```

were prepended to the program before being compiled. Note that the backslash characters are needed in the command line to prevent the double quote characters from being removed by the command shell and to continue the command over two lines.

## 2-9  Standard Header Files

If a program is to perform any useful action, it must interact with its external environment – normally by performing input and output. There are many library functions available for input-output, for dynamically allocating storage, for starting up new executing processes, and for performing many other useful tasks. The names and interfaces of a wide selection of useful functions have been specified in the ANSI C standard. These names and interfaces are defined as function prototypes in various standard header files. These and other standard header files also contain macro definitions for useful constants and typedef statements for useful datatypes.

---

15. This example uses two features of ANSI C, string concatenation and stringification, that are not provided in classic C.

In the following, the name of a header file is written as, for example, "<assert.h>". This indicates that a C program must contain the preprocessor directive

```
#include <assert.h>
```

in order to take advantage of the definitions contained in that header file. The header files are available for inspection. On Berkeley UNIX-based systems, you will normally find all the header files in the system directory named "/usr/include". Thus, for example, you may read the file "/usr/include/assert.h" to see how the macros in the "<assert.h>" header file are defined.

## Header File <assert.h>

Defines the `assert` macro, which causes the program to halt if a Boolean expression evaluates to *false*.

```
/* halt the program if n==0 or ptr is NULL */
assert(n > 0 && ptr != NULL);
```

This macro and program debugging in general are covered in section 15-1 of the book.

## Header File <ctype.h>

The file contains the prototypes for several functions[16] that test or convert characters. Each function returns a result of type `int`. Examples of use may be found in Chapter 9.

| | |
|---|---|
| `isalnum(int c)` | tests if `c` is an alphabetic character or a digit. |
| `isalpha(int c)` | tests if `c` is an alphabetic character. |
| `iscntrl(int c)` | tests if `c` is a control character. |
| `isdigit(int c)` | tests if `c` is a decimal digit. |
| `isgraph(int c)` | tests if `c` is a printing character (this excludes the space character). |
| `islower(int c)` | tests if `c` is a lower-case letter. |
| `isprint(int c)` | tests if `c` is a printing character (this includes the space). |
| `ispunct(int c)` | tests if `c` is a printing character other than a space or a character for which `isalnum(c)` is true. |
| `isspace(int c)` | tests if `c` is a white space character – one of space, `'\f'`, `'\n'`, `'\r'`, `'\t'`, and `'\v'`. |
| `isupper(int c)` | tests if `c` is an upper-case letter. |
| `isxdigit(int c)` | tests if `c` is a decimal digit or one of the letters *a* through *f* (either upper-case or lower-case). |
| `tolower(int c)` | if `c` is an upper-case letter, the result is the corresponding lower-case letter. Otherwise, the result is simply `c`. |
| `toupper(int c)` | if `c` is a lower-case letter, the result is the corresponding upper-case letter. Otherwise, the result is simply `c`. |

---

16. In classic C, the <ctype.h> file defines these functions as macros.

## Header File <errno.h>

The <errno.h>[†] file defines the external variable[17] errno which is set by many of the library functions to indicate an error number. The perror function (defined in <stdio.h>) or strerror function (defined in <string.h>) are normally used to construct a message based on the contents of errno. If you use either of these functions, you would not normally need to include <errno.h> in your program.

## Header File <float.h>

The <float.h>[†] file defines various macros that describe the properties of the floating-point numbers implemented by your C compiler. For example, FLT_DIG is the number of significant decimal digits that a value of type float has.

## Header File <limits.h>

The <limits.h>[†] file defines various macros that describe the numeric ranges of the integer types in the C implementation. For example, the macros INT_MIN and INT_MAX give the minimum and maximum integer values that may be assigned to a variable of type int. The full list of types and ranges described in <limits.h> is as follows.

```
signed char          SCHAR_MIN to SCHAR_MAX
unsigned char        0 to UCHAR_MAX
char                 CHAR_MIN to CHAR_MAX
short int            SHRT_MIN to SHRT_MAX
unsigned short int   0 to USHRT_MAX
int                  INT_MIN to INT_MAX
unsigned int         0 to UINT_MAX
long int             LONG_MIN to LONG_MAX
unsigned long int    0 to ULONG_MAX
```

In addition, <limits.h> defines CHAR_BIT as the number of bits in a byte (usually 8) and MB_LEN_MAX as the maximum number of bytes in a multibyte character (a subject that is ignored in this book).

## Header File <locale.h>

Different countries adopt different conventions for printing numbers and for printing currency amounts. For example, a sum of money in U.S. dollars is normally written in the style $1,995.95 whereas a sum in German marks would normally be written in the style DM 1.995,95. The <locale.h>[†] header file gives the prototype for a function localeconv which returns a structure that contains values for the national currency symbol, the separator characters, the sizes of the digit groups, and so on. The function is useful for

---

17. The ANSI C standard permits errno to be a macro that expands to a variable.

internationalizing business software; it is unlikely to be useful in ordinary systems programming. The header file contains definitions for a few macros and another function that control the operation of setlocale.

## Header File <math.h>

Prototypes for the following trigonometric and other mathematical functions are provided. All arguments and results in this first list have the type double.

| | |
|---|---|
| acos(x) | computes the arc cosine of x. |
| asin(x) | computes the arc sine of x. |
| atan(x) | computes the arc tangent of x. |
| atan2(y,x) | computes the arc tangent of y/x. |
| ceil(x) | computes the smallest integral value not less than x. |
| cos(x) | computes the cosine of x. |
| cosh(x) | computes the hyperbolic cosine of x. |
| exp(x) | computes $e^x$. |
| fabs(x) | computes the absolute value of x. |
| floor(x) | computes the largest integral value not greater than x. |
| fmod(x,y) | computes the floating-point remainder of x/y (i.e., the remainder after subtracting an integral multiple of y from x). |
| log(x) | computes the natural logarithm of x. |
| log10(x) | computes the logarithm to base 10 of x. |
| pow(x,y) | computes $x^y$. |
| sin(x) | computes the sine of x. |
| sinh(x) | computes the hyperbolic sine of x. |
| sqrt(x) | computes the square root of x. |
| tan(x) | computes the tangent of x. |
| tanh(x) | computes the hyperbolic tangent of x. |

There are a few more functions with an argument that does not have the type double. They are as follows.

frexp(double v, int *exp)

> computes two values. One is returned as the function result and the other is an integer stored in the int variable whose address is passed in exp. If the function result is $x$ and the integer result is $e$, then $x$ and $e$ are chosen such that $0.5 \le x < 1.0$ and v equals $x$ times two to the power $e$.

ldexp(double x, int e)

> computes x times two to the power e.

modf(double v, double *ip)

> breaks v into its integer and fractional parts, which both have the same sign as v. The integer part is stored in the double variable whose address is passed in ip. The fractional part is returned as the function result.

## Header File <setjmp.h>

The file contains definitions for the macro `setjmp`, the function `longjmp` and a `typedef` definition for the type `jmp_buf`. The `longjmp` function is used for jumping out of a function and returning through one or more function levels to a point in an ancestor function that was established with the `setjmp` macro. Examples of use may be found in Chapters 9 and 10.

## Header File <signal.h>

The file contains a definition for the `signal` function and related macros, a type and another function. This function is used to associate handler functions with various signals that may be sent to an executing program. When a signal is received, the associated handler is called. Examples of use may be found in Chapter 10.

## Header File <stdarg.h>[†]

The <stdarg.h>[†] file[18] defines a type and some macros needed for writing C functions that accept variable numbers and types of arguments. The `printf` I/O function is an example of a function with this property. Chapter 9 gives examples using the <stdarg.h> macros.

## Header File <stddef.h>

The <stddef.h>[†] file contains definitions of several types and macros that are useful in portable C code. The types are `ptrdiff_t` (the type of the integer value produced when one pointer value is subtracted from another), `size_t` (the type of the integer result produced by the `sizeof` operator), and `wchar_t` (an integer type whose values encompass all possible character codes). The macros are NULL (the null pointer) and `offsetof`. The `offsetof` macro is used to obtain the offset of a field in a structure relative to the beginning of that structure. An example use of the macro is

```
k = offsetof( struct complex, y );
```

which obtains the offset of the `y` field in the structure type provided as the first argument. Note that `size_t` and NULL are also defined in other header files, including <stdio.h>, and therefore there is usually no necessity to include <stddef.h> in your programs.

## Header File <stdio.h>

The file contains definitions for many macros, types and functions that are related to stream input-output operations. Chapter 8 contains a full description of stream input-output and provides programming examples. It is worth noting that <stdio.h> (like <stdlib.h> and <string.h>) contains a definition for the macro NULL that is conventionally used as the **nil** pointer in C programs.

---

18. The pre-ANSI C header file <varargs.h> defines similar facilities.

## Header File <stdlib.h>

The <stdlib.h>[†] file defines a miscellaneous collection of useful functions, types and macros. It is probably a good idea to include this header file in every non-trivial C source file that you compile.

Three string conversion functions that existed with classic C libraries are defined in <stdlib.h>. They are as follows.

```
double atof(char *s)
```
            scans the string s and converts a `double` value from its character string representation, returning it as the result.

`int atoi(char *s)`   scans the string s and converts an `int` value from its character string representation, returning it as the result.

```
long int atol(char *s)
```
            scans the string s and converts a `long int` value from its character string representation, returning it as the result.

In addition, the ANSI C standard has added extended versions of the three preceding functions. Their prototypes are also defined in <stdlib.h>.

```
double strtod(char *s, char **e)
```
            converts the initial portion of the string s to a `double` value. If e is not NULL, a pointer to the first character following the converted number is stored in the `char*` variable whose address is passed in e.

```
long strtol(char *s, char **e, int b)
```
            converts the initial portion of the string s to a `long int` value. The integer b is used as the base of the number system, where either $2 \leq b < 36$ or b=0 (in which case, normal C conventions are followed for converting the number). If e is not NULL, a pointer to the first character following the converted number is stored in the `char*` variable whose address is passed in e.

```
unsigned long strtoul(char *s, char **e, int b)
```
            is like `strtol` except that it converts the initial portion of the string s to an `unsigned long int` value.

Two functions for generating and seeding pseudo-random numbers are defined.

`int rand(void)`   returns the next random number in the range 0 to RAND_MAX (a macro defined in the header file that has a value of at least 32767).

```
void srand(unsigned int s)
```
            uses s as a seed to re-initialize the pseudo-random sequence.

The standard memory management functions for use with C programs are defined. Examples of these functions are given in Chapter 9. The `typedef` name `size_t` is used as an integer type that is sufficiently large for memory requests. In <stdlib.h> on SUN computers, `size_t` is defined as the `unsigned int` type. Recall that the `void*` type is used for generic pointers.

`void *calloc(size_t n, size_t s)`
      returns a pointer to a block of storage large enough to hold an array with n elements, each element having size s bytes. The result is NULL if the memory could not be allocated.

`void free(void *p)` de-allocates the block of storage referenced by the pointer p. This storage must have previously been obtained with one of the memory allocation functions.

`void *malloc(size_t s)`
      returns a pointer to a block of at least s bytes of storage. The result is NULL if the memory could not be allocated.

`void *realloc(void *p, size_t s)`
      changes the block of storage referenced by the pointer p to have the new size s. If the new size is larger, extra bytes of undefined value are appended. The result is a pointer to the re-sized block of storage and may or may not be equal to p. The result is NULL if the memory could not be allocated.

Functions for interacting with the environment are as follows.

`void abort(void)`
      raises the signal `SIGABRT` and this normally causes immediate termination of the program. (However, the signal may be intercepted by a signal handler.)

`int atexit(void (*f)(void))`
      registers a function referenced by f that is to be invoked just before the program terminates. At least 32 different termination functions may be registered. The result is zero if registration is successful and non-zero otherwise.

`void exit(int c)`
      causes successful termination of the program, passing the status code c back to the operating system. (The status code may be tested with an ensuing shell command or by a parent process, as explained in Chapter 10.) All the termination functions registered with `atexit` get called in reverse order of registration and all open files are closed.

`char *getenv(char *n)`
      searches the operating system environment for an environment variable whose name is n. The value associated with n is returned as the result. If no environment variable with the name exists, the result is NULL. (Environment variables are normally set by the `setenv` command in the shell; you may inspect their settings with the command `printenv`.)

`int system(char *s)`
      causes a new process to be created that executes a copy of the sh shell program, passing the string s to sh as a command

to be executed. The result is zero on Berkeley UNIX-based systems if creation of the shell was successful *and* if the command returned zero as its exit status.

The prototypes for a general sorting function and a general searching function are provided.

```
void *bsearch(void *k, void *b, size_t n, size_t s,
              int (*cf)(void *,void *)
```

searches a sorted array of n elements where b references the first element and each element has size s. The search is for the value that is contained in the object referenced by k. If the value is found, the function result references the element in the array that compared equal; otherwise, the result is NULL. The caller must provide a comparison function, referenced by cf, whose arguments are pointers to the two values to be compared. The result of this function must return a negative integer, zero or a positive integer to indicate whether the first argument is less than, equal to, or greater than the second argument, respectively.

```
void qsort(void *b, size_t n, size_t s,
     int (*cf)(void *, void *))
```

uses the quicksort algorithm to sort an array of n elements into order, where b references the first element and each element has size s. The argument cf references a comparison function with the same properties as the last argument to bsearch, above.

A few miscellaneous integer arithmetic functions are defined. They are as follows.

`int abs(int i)`  returns the absolute value of integer i.

`div_t div(int n, int d)`
computes the integer quotient and integer remainder when n is divided by d. The result is a structure containing the two fields quot and rem, holding the quotient and remainder respectively. Note that its rounding behavior is well-defined and may differ from that of the standard division operator.

`long int labs(long int i)`
is a version of abs that works with long int values.

`ldiv_t ldiv(long int n, long int d)`
is a version of div that works with long int values.

Finally, several functions for manipulating multibyte characters are defined. In the interests of brevity, they are not listed here.

## Header File <string.h>

This file[19] contains a definition for NULL. It also defines the type `size_t` and several functions related to string handling. They are described in Chapter 9.

## Header File <time.h>

The file defines macros, types and functions that are useful for manipulating time values. The possibilities for time include CPU time, and calendar dates and times (according to the Gregorian calendar). Descriptions and examples are given in Chapter 9.

# 2-10  Differences Between Classic C and ANSI C

The additions and changes to the classic C language are listed below. The list is grouped into three sections – changes to lexical structure, changes to syntactic structure, and changes to preprocessing rules.

## Lexical Changes

| | |
|---|---|
| trigraphs | available as alternate representations for some characters. |
| string concatenation | two adjacent strings separated only by white space are automatically concatenated. |
| extra escape characters | `'\a'`, `'\v'` and `'\?'` are new character escape codes. |
| hexadecimal codes | hexadecimal character constants have been added. |
| U, L, UL suffixes | may be appended to integer constants to indicate if the constant's type is `long` or `unsigned`. |
| F, L suffixes | may be appended to floating point constants to indicate if the constant's type is `float` or `long float`. |

## Syntactic and Semantic Changes

| | |
|---|---|
| unary + | added as a new operator. |
| new type qualifiers | `const`, `volatile` and `signed` have been added. |
| `signed char` | added as a new type combination. |
| `long float` | formerly a synonym for `double`, dropped from ANSI C. |
| `long double` | added as a new type. |
| function prototypes | types of arguments may be optionally specified. |
| `void *` | used as a generic pointer type. |

---

19. The pre-ANSI C header file <strings.h> defines some similar facilities.

| | |
|---|---|
| bit-fields | may have types `signed int` and `unsigned int`. |
| unary & operator | may be applied to an array value. |
| initialization | `auto` arrays and structures may be initialized to constant values; a union may also be initialized to constant values (the values are assigned to the first member of the union). |
| type conversions | are automatically performed on function arguments to match the types declared in the function prototype; also the conversion rules are subtly different. |
| enumeration constants | may be freely converted to the `int` type. |

## Preprocessor Changes

| | |
|---|---|
| `#elif` | added as a new preprocessor directive. |
| `##` | used as a concatenation operator during preprocessing. |
| `#` | used as a *stringification* operator during preprocessing. |
| `#error` | a new preprocessor command. |
| `#pragma` | a new preprocessor command. |
| `defined` | a new preprocessor operator. |
| recursive macros | macros used recursively are expanded once only. |
| predefined macros | `__DATE__`, `__TIME__` and `__STDC__` are new. |

## Standard Libraries

There are numerous changes. The header files <assert.h>, <errno.h>, <float.h>, <limits.h>, <locale.h>, <stddef.h> and <stdlib.h> did not exist with pre-ANSI C implementations. The <string.h> header file used to be named <strings.h>. The <stdarg.h> file used to be named <varargs.h>. There have been many small changes to the other header files, namely <ctype.h>, <math.h>, <stdio.h>, and <time.h>, and to the header files that have been renamed.

## 2-11  Further Reading

The ANSI C language is covered in *The C Programming Language* (Second Edition) by B. W. Kernighan and D .M. Ritchie (Prentice-Hall 1988). An authorative source covering many of the details is *C: A Reference Manual* (Second Edition) by S. P. Harbison & G. L. Steele Jr. (Prentice-Hall 1990). You might also consider *C: An Advanced Introduction* (ANSI C Edition) by N. Gehani (Computer Science Press 1988), *Programming in ANSI C* by S. G. Kochan (Hayden Books 1988), or *ANSI C Made Easy* by H. Schildt (Osborne/McGraw-Hill 1989). A book which covers both classic C and ANSI C is *C, A Software Engineering Approach* (Second Edition) by P. A. Darnell and P. E. Margolis (Springer-Verlag 1991).

# CHAPTER 3    *USING THE vi EDITOR*

---

## *3-1    Overview of vi*

The `vi` editor is the standard full-screen editor provided with the Berkeley UNIX system, but is available on most other UNIX systems too. It has a rather large repertoire of commands, which makes it forbidding to a first-time user. In this chapter, only a selection of the `vi` commands will be covered. This selection includes all the facilities that one should need when editing C source code files or English text.

`vi` (often pronounced by some people as *vee-eye* and by others like the English word *vie*) may be used to edit files containing ASCII characters. It cannot handle files containing non-ASCII characters or the ASCII NUL character (the character `'\0'` in C). Apart from this, the only restriction on an ASCII file is that a single line cannot contain more than 1023 characters.

The `vi` program may be invoked under three different names: as `vi`, as `ex` or as `view`. Using the name `vi` (short for *visual*) gives you access to a very powerful screen-oriented editor. The name `ex` is used when you wish to use a line-editor similar to `ed` but which is a little more powerful and more user-friendly. However, `ex` has a subcommand (`vi` – what else?) which changes its mode of operation to be the same as `vi`. The name `view` is used if you wish to obtain read-only access to a file. The facilities of *vi* are very convenient for browsing, but when you invoke `vi` as `view`, you are not allowed to store the file back (unless you explicitly override). This restriction is useful protection against accidentally destroying your file.

The concept of a full-screen editor is reasonably simple. The screen always shows a range of consecutive lines in the file. With standard terminals that have a display area of 24 lines, vi usually shows 23 lines of the file.[1] One line on the screen, at the bottom, is used for displaying information messages and for entering some types of command. vi has simple, one-letter, commands which move the cursor around on the screen. If your terminal keyboard has arrow keys, these keys should be usable as cursor movement commands too. Other commands may be used to change the information displayed on the screen at the current cursor position. These changes will be reflected in the edited file only when the file is subsequently saved. In addition to commands in the cursor movement and text replacement categories, there are many more commands for controlling vi.

## 3-2   Getting Started with vi

Before you try to use vi for the first time, you should make sure that vi will know what kind of terminal you are using and whether this terminal is suitable. CRT terminals have command sequences that perform actions such as clearing the screen, moving the cursor and for changing information displayed on the screen. Unfortunately, different kinds of terminals may use completely different control sequences. If vi assumes the wrong terminal type, you are likely to see some bizarre results when vi is in operation.

The vi program will normally try to determine your terminal type from the environment variable named TERM.   You can see the current value of this environment variable by executing the command

```
printenv
```

The value of TERM should be a short string that looks like an abbreviation for the name of your terminal. A typical setting might be "vt100" (for the DEC VT100 terminal) or "h1500" (for the Hazeltine 1500 terminal) and so on. If you run vi in a window on a workstation, you should see a setting like "sun" (a Sun workstation using the SunView windowing system), "sun-cmd" (a shelltool window on a Sun workstation running the OpenLook window manager), or "xterm" (a workstation using X-windows).

If the value looks like an abbreviation for some terminal type but does not match the kind of terminal you are using, it is not necessarily an error. Some terminals emulate other kinds of terminal and if your terminal is emulating the one listed for TERM, vi should work. If TERM is shown with a value like "dumb" or "su" you will definitely have to change its setting.

---

1.  This number can be reduced in some circumstances. For example, fewer lines may be displayed if you are using the terminal at a low baud rate.

Before you attempt to set the value of TERM, you can read through the standard list of terminal types by executing

```
setenv TERM dumb
more /etc/termcap
```

Note that TERM needs to be set to some safe value for more to operate properly! In the "/etc/termcap" file (the terminal capability database), lines beginning with a hash mark, #, are comments. Some of these comments make amusing reading. The file is very long, containing descriptions of scores of different kinds of terminal. These descriptions contain the command sequences needed to control the terminals. It is easy to recognize the beginning of a new terminal description in the file because a line that has a printing character in the first column is either a comment line or is the first line of a terminal description. Continuation lines for a terminal description are all indented by one tab character.

The first line of a description contains various names for the terminal, separated by vertical bars. The last name listed is intended to be the full name, readily recognizable by humans. You may set TERM to be the same as any of these names except for the last name. They are treated as synonyms by vi and other UNIX system software. However, it is not a good idea to use the first name, which is always a two-character abbreviation.

If you scan through "/etc/termcap" you should be able to find a suitable abbreviation for your terminal. If you cannot, it might be a good idea to ask for assistance. You can set the TERM environment variable to some string value, say "vt100", by executing one of the csh commands:

```
setenv TERM vt100
```

or

```
set term = vt100
```

The latter command is somewhat preferable for reasons that will be explained in the chapter on csh commands.

The easy way to test whether your setting of TERM is suitable is to invoke vi. Just type the following command.

```
vi
```

At this point, there are four different outcomes. If your screen is cleared, tilde (~) characters are written down the left column and the cursor is moved to the left of a line at the top of the screen, vi is working quite normally. However, you should insert a few lines and edit them a little to make sure. Sometimes a wrong terminal description is sufficiently similar to the correct one that vi will go wrong only in certain situations. If vi updates the screen incorrectly for some editing operations, then the terminal type is unsuitable. If starting up vi gives you the message "Visual needs addressable cursor or upline capability," your terminal must be an obsolete model that is too primitive to be used by full-screen programs. If you see the message "Using open mode" (accompanied by some other message) there is something wrong with the entry for your terminal in the terminal capability database and you should ask for assistance. Finally, if your terminal seems to go wild, scribbling strange characters over the screen in random positions, you must have an unsuitable terminal type.

Whatever the outcome of your test, you can exit from vi by typing the following four characters:

```
Escape : q !
```

The character *Escape* denotes the ASCII escape character. You should be able to find a key on your keyboard labelled *Esc* or *Escape* which transmits this character. If you cannot find such a key, you can transmit the escape character by pressing the *Control* key (perhaps labelled *Ctrl*) and the left square bracket key ( [ ) together. However, if your terminal keyboard really does not have an Escape key, it would be a good idea to find another terminal to use. The ASCII escape character is used in vi to terminate all text input or text replacement commands.

## 3-3 Invoking vi

If you have an existing file, say "prog.c" you can edit it with the command

```
vi prog.c
```

This command causes vi to make a temporary copy of the file, to display the first screenful of the file, to place information about the size of the file on the bottom line of the screen and finally to place the cursor at the beginning of the first line of the file.

If you wish to use vi to create a new file, say "newprog.c", the same form of command is used, namely

```
vi newprog.c
```

This command causes vi to clear the screen, place tilde characters down the left side of the screen, put an information line at the bottom of the screen that tells you that you are creating a new file, and to move the cursor to a blank line at the top of the screen. Each tilde character represents a non-existent line in the file. As you add lines to the file, the tildes will gradually be displaced from the screen. Vi does not leave completely blank lines on the screen, because you may be fooled into thinking that the file contains blank lines. In some circumstances, vi may also use the 'at' symbol (@) to represent a non-existent line in the file. It will usually be displayed after you have deleted lines from the file.

## 3-4 *Cursor Movement Commands*

The simplest cursor movement commands are those that move the cursor one position vertically or horizontally. If there are keys labelled with arrows on your keyboard, these *ought* to work as cursor movement commands. However, nothing is guaranteed. Depending on the terminal type, vi may not be able to use any or all of the arrow keys. Not all keyboards have arrow keys in any case. Consequently, there are other ways to move the cursor. First, the space and backspace characters will move the cursor horizontally in the way one would expect. The space character does not overwrite any characters displayed on the screen; only the cursor moves. If the keyboard has a linefeed key, it may be used to move the cursor down. In addition, the four lower-case letters, h, j, k and l, can be used as cursor movement commands. For example, when you type h, the cursor immediately moves left by one column. You do not have to hit the carriage-return key after the command. The h command does not have any effect if the cursor is at the first character on a line. Instead, you will probably hear your terminal beep.[2] The beep is simply a warning from vi – perhaps in case you are not looking at the screen.

Many useful cursor movement commands are listed in Table 3-2. This table and two others have, for convenience, been collected together in a Reference Guide at the end of this chapter. To gain experience with vi, it is probably a good idea to experiment with these commands on a sample file. Some of the cursor movement commands are relatively sophisticated. A simple step up in sophistication is the w command (short for *word*). This command advances the cursor to the beginning of the next word in the file. Two related commands are b (*back one word*) and e (*end of word*).

A command which is extremely useful to C programmers is %. If the cursor is currently located on a bracket character (one of { , } , ( or ) ), the cursor is moved onto the matching bracket in the program. This command makes it relatively easy to check whether your brackets are properly matched. If vi cannot find a matching bracket, it will not move the cursor and it should beep. Be aware, however, that vi can become confused if your C program has macros that generate unbalanced brackets or has comments or string constants that contain unbalanced brackets.

An important command is / which is used for searching. When you type /, the cursor jumps to the bottom line on the screen. Next you must type a pattern, terminated either by a carriage return or the *escape* character. This pattern has the same style as that used in the ed editor. If all you want to do is locate the next occurrence of some identifier, say *foo*, you would type

    /foo

---

2. For some terminal types, a *visible bell* may be used instead of a beeping sound. A visible bell shows up as a momentary flashing of the screen.

and this will cause vi to advance the cursor to the beginning of the next occurrence of *foo* in the file. If you then want to repeat the same search, you do not have to repeat the full command. The single letter command n (*next*) repeats the last search. The single letter command N is similar, except that it repeats the last search backwards through the file. If you want to search backwards initially, you should use ? instead of /. After performing a backwards search, n will repeat the search scanning backwards through the file. If you use N after a search begun with ?, the search will be repeated forward through the file. That is, n will continue a search in the same direction as was originally used for the pattern and N will search in the reverse direction.

The string following the / or ? command is a *pattern*. It is important that you know which characters have special meanings in a pattern. If you do not want to have to learn the details of pattern construction, you can simply avoid using the special characters, or you can remember to precede these characters with the escape symbol (\) or you can set the *nomagic* option (see below). The special pattern characters are

       ^ $ . * [ \

If, for example, you want to search for the character sequence $bill$, you have to type the vi command as

       /\$bill\$

We will not discuss patterns here. Their construction follows the same rules as the patterns used in lex, a UNIX program which is covered in Chapter 6.[3]

## 3-5  *Text Replacement Commands*

In a moment, we will look at some commands for inserting, deleting and replacing text in the file. These commands are summarized in Table 3-3, which appears at the end of the chapter. But before running through these commands, we should point out that the commands fall into two main categories. Commands from the first category operate on characters within a line and commands from the second category operate on entire lines. For example, the command i may be used to insert characters into the middle of a line, whereas the o command is used to insert entire lines into the file.

### Insertion

If you wish to insert characters into the current line, you would normally use either the i (*insert*) command or the a (*append*) command. The former, i, inserts characters at the current cursor position. The a command is similar except that it adds characters at the position immediately after the cursor position. Any number of characters may be inserted.

---

3. The same pattern constructions are used in other UNIX programs, notably ed, sed and awk.

Text insertion ceases only when the escape character is typed. You may even insert the carriage-return character, which causes the current line to be split into two lines. Variations on the character insertion commands are A, used to append characters to the end of the current line, and I, used to insert characters at the beginning of the current line.

To insert one or more lines into the file, either the o or the O command is used. These are known as the *open* commands because they cause the text on the screen to be opened up. When you type o, a blank line is created below the current line and the cursor is positioned at the beginning of this new line. Any text you type is now entered on the new line. Whenever you hit the carriage-return key, another blank line is inserted. Text insertion is halted only when you type the escape character. The O command is similar, the difference being that the new line is inserted immediately above the current line in the file.

## Deletion

The normal command used for deleting a character from the middle of a line is x. Presumably the command name is chosen because its effect is analogous to deleting words on an ordinary typewriter by typing letter *x*'s over the text. When x is typed, the character underneath the cursor is simply deleted.[4]

The character defined as your terminal delete character, often the key labelled *Del* on your keyboard, may also be used to delete a character. If you wish to delete several characters, you may precede the delete command with the character counts, as in 5x.

If you wish to delete an entire word from the line, you should position the cursor to the start of the word and then type dw (the *delete word* command). Finally, the D command will delete all characters from the current cursor position to the end of the line. Deleting an entire line is accomplished with the dd command. This deletes the current line. Several lines can be deleted by preceding this command with a number. For example, 13dd will delete thirteen lines.

## Replacement

With the exception of the r and R commands, replacement is equivalent to a deletion followed by an insertion. Therefore, we will look at these two commands first. The r command is used to replace a single character. The character underneath the cursor is replaced with whatever single character you type after the r. For example, if you type rq, the character at the current cursor position is changed to a letter *q*. There is no need to type an

---

4. Note that, unlike in editors on some other operating systems, you cannot directly delete a linefeed character ( \n ) from the file. Deleting this character is equivalent to joining two lines together and there is a special command, J, to perform this action.

escape character after using r. If you press the *return* key after typing r, you will replace the current character with a linefeed. This has the effect of splitting the current line into two lines, causing a re-arrangement of the displayed lines on your screen.

The R command is used to effect a one-for-one replacement of several characters. After you type R, the next character you type overwrites the character that is currently underneath the cursor. After this, the cursor is advanced by one column and you can replace a second character, and so on. Replacement stops only when an escape character is typed. Note that you can replace text only on the same line. You cannot, for example, jump down to the line below by typing a *return* or a *linefeed* character and carry on replacing text there. The effect of typing a *return* is actually to split the current line.

If you wish to replace one character with several characters, you would use the s (*substitute*) command. After typing s, all characters, up to an escape character, replace the one character that was underneath the cursor. If you wish to replace, say, three adjacent characters with several characters, you could use the command 3s. When you type the substitute command, the last character to be replaced is changed to a dollar character. This indicates the extent of the change that you are about to perform. The dollar symbol will disappear if you enter replacement text over the top of it, or when you terminate the replacement text.

If you wish to replace an entire word on the line, you would position the cursor at that word and type the command cw (*change word*). As before, the last character of the text to be replaced is temporarily changed to a dollar symbol and, as before, your replacement text continues until an escape character is typed. A group of consecutive words may be replaced if the command is preceded by a count, as in 3cw.

Replacing an entire line is performed with either the S or the cc command. After typing either command, you may enter any number of replacement lines, stopping when an escape character is typed. Several lines may be replaced by preceding the command with a count. For example, 5cc is used to replace five consecutive lines.

## Other Editing Actions

We will now look at some actions which change the file but which cannot be properly classified under the previous headings. The most important command of all, especially to a novice user, is the u (undo) command. If you have just executed a command that changed the file and you can see that your change is incorrect, you simply have to type u to undo the effect of the change. The file is instantaneously changed back to its state before your previous command. Unfortunately, you cannot repeat u to undo earlier changes, a second u simply undoes the previous *undo*. If you need to undo a deletion that you made a few commands earlier, Section 3-8 gives you a way of retrieving the deleted text.

A frequently required action is that of moving or copying a block of lines to another place in the file. These two actions are performed similarly in vi. The instructions for moving a block of lines are as follows. First position the cursor onto either the top line or the bottom line of the block to be moved (it does not matter which). Then type the command

mz

which *marks* the current line and gives the name z to this line. Second, move the cursor to the line at the other end of the block. Now type the command

d'z

which deletes all the lines from the current line to the line marked with the name z, inclusive. These lines are not irretrievably lost because vi retains a copy of them in a special buffer. Finally, position the cursor to a line immediately before the desired destination for the block of lines and type

p

which puts all the lines contained in the buffer back into the file. If you wanted to move the lines to the top of the file, you would have to move the cursor to the topmost line and use the command

P

This command puts back lines immediately before the current line. As a final note, any letter may be used instead of z to mark a line.

Copying a block of lines is almost exactly the same as moving them. The difference is that the y (*yank*) command should be used instead of the d (*delete*) command. That is, the second command should be

y'z

The y command causes lines to be copied into the same buffer that deleted lines are moved to.

If you only want to move or copy a few lines, the preceding instructions can be simplified a little. If, say, you wish to move three lines, you could move the cursor to the first of the three lines and type

3dd

to delete the lines. Then you can move the cursor to the desired insertion point and type p as before. To copy three lines, you would use the command

3yy

to copy the lines into the buffer, rather than deleting them.

## Command Structure

It should be obvious from the examples already given that commands can usually be preceded by a count. You can type a number before your command whenever it makes sense: 8k moves the cursor up eight lines; 8dw deletes eight consecutive words; 5rx replaces five consecutive characters with the letter *x*, and so on. Another convention is that commands whose name is a single lower-case letter normally apply to characters whereas commands whose name is an upper-case letter apply to entire lines.

What may have not been so obvious is the general structure of the *change*, *delete* and *yank* commands. When you type dw to delete a word, you are not using a *delete word* command as such. You are using a *delete* command, d, with an operand, w, that specifies how much is to be deleted. This operand may be recognized as the command to move the cursor to the next word. The general structure of the delete command is

```
d <motion command>
```

In other words, any command that causes cursor motion may be placed immediately after the *d*. For example, you may type d5l to delete five consecutive characters, dj to delete the current line and the following line, and dG to delete all lines up to the end of file. You may experiment for yourself to discover useful combinations. If the command letter is doubled, as with dd or yy, the command applies to lines rather than letters.

The yank command has a structure exactly like the delete command, and the change command is very similar. Its general structure is

```
c <motion command> <replacement text>
```

## 3-6    Miscellaneous Commands

When you type a colon character, the cursor jumps to the command line at the bottom of the screen. Then you may type a command, which will be displayed on that line. There is a large repertoire of commands, only a few of which are listed in Table 3-1, at the end of the chapter. The most important commands are those used to save the file and to terminate the edit session. Usually, you would use the command :wq at the end of the session. If, however, you have changed your mind about editing the file and wish to abandon your changes, you will have to use the command :q!.

If you wish to merge another file into the file being edited, you would first move the cursor onto the line that precedes the desired insertion point, and then use the :r command.

If you wish to exit temporarily from the vi editor to execute some shell commands, you have a choice of methods to use. Perhaps the easiest method is hitting the *Control-Z* key combination, an action that suspends the edit session and returns you to your command shell. You can later resume the edit session with the fg command of the csh command shell. Another method uses the shell escape mechanism of `vi`. All you have to do is type the command

```
:shell
```

which creates a subshell for you to use. If you wish to execute only one shell command (say the `ls` command), you may execute it with

```
:!ls
```

`Vi` has a large number of options that control its operation. These options may be displayed or changed with the `:set` command. To see all the option settings that are in effect, type the command

```
:set all
```

To set an option on, you give the name of that option after the `set` command. For example, to have line numbers displayed on the screen, you would type

```
:set number
```

And to disable an option, you should precede the name of the option with the word *no*. Thus, to turn off the display of line numbers, you can type

```
:set nonumber
```

Another option that you may wish to turn on and off is `magic`. If you execute

```
:set nomagic
```

you will disable the use of magic characters in search patterns. This can be much more convenient than having to escape each magic character by prefixing it with a backslash.


## 3-7    Using ex Commands

As mentioned earlier, `vi` and `ex` are two names for the same program. If you use the shell command

```
ex filename
```

to begin the edit session, you will invoke an editor that is much like the `ed` editor. All the `ed` commands are supported by `ex`.

When you invoke the editor with the name `vi`, you can still use all the `ex` commands. Some of these commands are easier to use than the equivalent full-screen commands. For example, if you wish to change all occurrences of the identifier *jack* to *jackie*, you can use the single command

```
:1,$s/jack/jackie/g
```

As before, the colon character causes the cursor to jump down to the command line at the bottom of the screen. The remainder of the command line is a use of the *substitute* command of the ed editor (and hence also of ex).

You can obtain more details about this command and other *ex* commands from the documentation for ed or ex.

## 3-8    Recovering from Problems

Soon after you first began to use a computer, you probably discovered that even the simplest program was likely to lead to unexpected problems. If you encounter some difficulty with vi, there is usually a way to recover from it. In this section, we will run through the recovery techniques – starting with the easy problems first.

First, what do you do if your screen becomes garbled? One common cause is a communications failure. If you are using a terminal connected to a computer via a modem and a telephone line, you will find that noise on the telephone line can cause many strange characters to be displayed. There is a simple command to redraw the screen correctly, but first you must make sure that any text you are about to type will not be inserted into the file. Therefore, you should type the *escape* character. (If you were not inserting text, vi will merely make the terminal beep.) Then typing *Control-L* will clear the screen and cause it to be completely redrawn. If *Control-L* does nothing, try *Control-R* instead. If your screen is consistently garbled in the same way, the reason is probably that the entry for your terminal in the terminal capability database, "/etc/termcap", is incorrect or that you have selected the wrong terminal type. It would be wise to ask for some assistance if this is the case.

Second, what do you do if you accidentally delete a large chunk of your file? If you realize what you have done immediately after executing the offending command, you can undo its effect with the u command. However, if you are a fast typist or do not look at the screen, you may already have typed commands after the one that deleted half your file. In this case, the undo command will not help you. But do not worry, vi keeps the last nine blocks of deleted text in named buffers. To re-insert the block of lines that were most recently deleted, type the command

```
"1p
```

To re-insert the last-but-one block of deleted text, use the command

```
"2p
```

and so on. You can even step through the buffers, inserting them into the file and deleting them again, until you hit the buffer that contains the text you want. You just have to continue the sequence

```
"1pu.u.u.
```

until you are successful. The u command undoes the insertion and the dot repeats the last command, p, but applies it to the next buffer.[5]

Third, what do you do if you lose your place in the file? This can happen if you are editing a very large file and you accidentally hit a key that sends you to a completely different region of the file (as happens with the G command). It may take some time to find your way back to the previous position in the file with scrolling commands. Fortunately, there is a command that allows you to return directly to the previous position in the file. This command is

    ' '

(two single quote characters).

Fourth, what do you do if you lose your connection to the computer or if the system crashes? Fortunately, vi always makes a temporary copy of your file to work with. Even if the system crashes or if you accidentally hang up your connection to the computer, this temporary file is preserved. Next time you log into the system, you can resume editing your file by initiating vi with the command

    vi -r filename

where *filename* is the name of the file that you were previously editing. (Vi will inform you of this possibility by sending UNIX mail to you.) When you restart the edit, you will probably find that the last couple of input lines or the last couple of minor changes in the file have been lost. It should only be a minor inconvenience to re-enter these last few changes.

## 3-9   *Further Reading*

For the full list of commands, you should obtain a copy of the document "Introduction to Display Editing with Vi" by William Joy. It is included in the documentation supplied with systems based on Berkeley UNIX. Your system administrator should be able to help you locate the documentation. There are also books available. One is *Learning the vi Editor*, third edition, by L. Lamb (O'Reilly 1988), a second is *The Ultimate Guide to the vi and ex Editors* published by Hewlett-Packard Press (available through Addison-Wesley), and a third is *vi: The UNIX Screen Editor*, fourth edition, by A. Hansen (Prentice-Hall 1985).

---

5. Note that the dot command can be used to repeat any command, not just the p command.

## *3-10 vi Reference Guide*

Although we have not stated it explicitly, `vi` is in one of three states at any moment. The normal state is called *Command* state. In this state, you can enter cursor movement commands, text deletion commands, etc. When you type a command like o (open) or i (insert), `vi` switches to *insert* state. In this state, all text that you type is inserted into the file. Only the *Escape* character or an interrupt (hitting the *Break* key for example) takes `vi` out of this state and back to command state. When you type one of the characters: :, /, ?, or !, the cursor jumps to the bottom line on the screen and all further text is echoed on that line. When the cursor is on the bottom line, `vi` is in the *last-line* state. Hitting the *Return* key or the *Escape* key at the end of the line causes the command to be executed and then `vi` returns to the normal command state. A partially typed command on the last line can be cancelled by backspacing back past the beginning of the line or by an interrupt (hitting the *Break* key).

All the `vi` commands described in this chapter are collected together here in three separate tables on the following pages. Remember that only about half of all the `vi` commands are listed. It is suggested that you become familiar with these commands before advancing to the full `vi` command language.

## Table 3-1  vi Control Commands

| | |
|---|---|
| `:w` | write the file back |
| `:w` *name* | write to the named file |
| `:q` | quit the editor |
| `:wq` | write the file and then quit |
| `:q!` | quit, discarding unsaved changes |
| `ZZ` | quit, saving the file only if any changes were made |
| `:r` *name* | read in the named file |
| `:shell` | temporarily escape to a subshell |
| `:!` *cmd* | execute the shell command *cmd* |
| `:set` *number* | display line numbers |
| `:set` *nomagic* | disable special characters in patterns |

## Table 3-2  vi Cursor Movement Commands

| | |
|---|---|
| h | move cursor left |
| *backspace* | move cursor left |
| j | move cursor down |
| *linefeed* | move cursor down |
| k | move cursor up |
| l | move cursor right |
| *space* | move cursor right |
| + | move cursor to first non-white character on next line |
| *return* | move cursor to first non-white character on next line |
| – | move cursor to first non-white character on previous line |
| ^ | move cursor to first non-white character on current line |
| $ | move cursor to end of line |
| w | move cursor to next word |
| e | move cursor to end of word |
| b | move cursor to previous word |
| % | move cursor to matching bracket (in C code) |
| 59| | move cursor to column 59 |
| G | move cursor to last line in file |
| 99G | move cursor to line number 99 |
| Ctrl-B | scroll up one screenful |
| Ctrl-D | scroll down several lines |
| Ctrl-F | scroll down one screenful |
| Ctrl-U | scroll up several lines |
| */pattern* | move to next occurrence of *pattern* |
| *?pattern* | move to previous occurrence of *pattern* |
| n | repeat previous / or ? search |
| N | repeat previous search but in opposite direction |

## Table 3-3  vi Text Editing Commands

| | |
|---|---|
| x | delete one character |
| D | delete characters up to end of line |
| dw | delete one word |
| dd | delete one line |
| i*text* | insert text at cursor position |
| a*text* | insert text after cursor position |
| I*text* | insert text at start of line |
| A*text* | append text at end of line |
| o*text* | insert lines after current line |
| O*text* | insert lines before current line |
| r*c* | replace current character with *c* |
| R*text* | replace several characters |
| s*text* | substitute text for current character |
| S*text* | substitute text for current line |
| cc*text* | substitute text for current line |
| cw*text* | change one word |
| J | join current line to next line |
| u | undo last change made |
| U | undo all changes made to current line |
| . | repeat the last edit command |
| yy | yank a copy of the current line into a buffer |
| m*c* | mark the current line with the name *c* |
| d'*c* | delete lines from here to line marked with *c* |
| y'*c* | yank lines from here to line marked with *c* |
| p | put contents of buffer at cursor position |
| P | put contents of buffer before cursor position |

# CHAPTER 4

# *THE C SHELL, csh*

---

## *4-1    Introduction*

---

### What Is The Shell?

Commands typed on the keyboard of your terminal are read by a command interpreter program. This program analyzes each command, determines what actions are to be performed and then performs the actions. For example, if you type the command

```
wc -l file1 > file2
```

the command interpreter performs all the actions in the following list, though not necessarily in the same order. First, it parses the command line and determines that the command to be executed is named wc, that it has two arguments (-l and file1), and that its output is to be directed to a file named "file2". It searches one or more directories determining that the wc program is located in the program library named "/bin". The command interpreter next makes a request to the operating system that a new *process* be created. This involves duplicating the current program (the command interpreter) and scheduling the copy (called a *child process*) for execution. The original copy of the program now waits for its child to finish. (If we had followed the command with an ampersand, it would not wait.) The child process opens *file2* for output (creating the file if necessary) and requests that the operating system re-direct its standard output to the open file. Then it asks the operating system to replace the currently executing code with the executable code found in "/bin/wc" and to pass it two strings (the command line arguments) as parameters. The wc program is now loaded into memory and scheduled for execution. When the operating system finishes executing wc, it sends a signal to the parent process (the original copy of the command interpreter). Sending the signal involves little more than restarting the program and providing a status value to indicate whether the child successfully completed execution. The re-awakened program now outputs a command prompt to the terminal and waits for a new command to be typed.

What you should observe from all of the above is that the command interpreter is, by no means, a magic program. You can write a C program that does everything the command interpreter can do. From within a C program, you can, for example, make requests to create child processes (look up the fork and vfork system calls). You can request that another program be loaded into memory and control be passed to it (look up execl and related system calls). The command interpreter has no special privileges in the UNIX system; it is just another C program. In fact, if you do not like the command interpreter, you are quite free to program your own. The purpose of the command interpreter is not to provide the user with special facilities – all its facilities are already available in the UNIX system as system calls. Its purpose is to make these facilities accessible. In other words, the command interpreter program is like an outer layer of software, or a *shell*, surrounding the system that provides an interactive interface for you to use. In standard parlance, a *shell* is a command interpreter.

Now that the command shell concept has been demystified to some extent, let us look at what is available. In the Berkeley UNIX system, you get a choice of at least two different shells. First, there is the standard shell available on all UNIX systems. It is sometimes called the *Bourne shell* (after its author, Steven Bourne) and its program name is "/bin/sh". The other shell was written at Berkeley and is called the C shell. Its program name is "/bin/csh". The two shells support command languages that, for simple command execution, are very similar. Our sample command with the wc program is the same for either shell. The two shells differ in what extra facilities they offer. The Bourne shell has better facilities for redirecting input-output and for intercepting interrupts. The C shell has, amongst other things, better job control facilities. It, for example, lets you switch jobs between foreground execution and background execution.

In this chapter, we describe the C shell command language. The Bourne shell language has been covered in many books, whereas the C shell has received relatively little coverage. If you are currently using the C shell, you can try out the Bourne shell by invoking it as a program. You just have to type the command

```
sh
```

And when you have tired of using this shell, you just have to type the end-of-file character, *Control-D*, to terminate sh and return to your previous shell. Conversely, if you are currently using the Bourne shell, you can invoke the C shell by typing

```
csh
```

To exit from `csh`, you can type the *Control-D* character unless you have set the shell variable `ignoreeof` (see below). In this case, you must use the `exit` command.

When you log into the UNIX system, a shell program is automatically started for you. If you care to inspect your entry in the "/etc/passwd" file, you will see your default shell specified at the end of the line that represents your entry. If your login name is *joanie*, say, you can see your entry in the password file with the command

```
grep joanie /etc/passwd
```

And if you should wish to change your choice of default shell from `sh` to `csh`, you should use the command

```
chsh joanie csh
```

The next time you logged in, you would be given `csh` as the start-up shell.

## Overview of Shell Facilities

As we explained above, the purpose of the shell is to provide a convenient interface to the UNIX operating system. The commands that you type at your terminal form a language with its own syntactic and semantic rules. This language is, in some respects, similar to a programming language. The main difference between the shell language and an ordinary programming language is that you are dealing with different kinds of objects. You are mostly concerned with requesting that programs be executed, with providing arguments to the programs, and with manipulating files. Thus, the facilities of the shell language are oriented towards providing easy access to programs and providing convenient notations for accessing files.

The `csh` shell includes the following facilities:

• Automatic command searching

When you type the name of a program to be executed, `csh` will search several directories to find an executable file with the given name. A hash table implementation is used to make these searches very fast.

• Input-output redirections

The standard input of a program may be redirected so that the program reads from a file. Similarly, the standard output and error output may be redirected into files.

• Pipelining commands

The standard output or error output from one program may be fed directly into the standard input of another program.

• Command aliasing

This feature allows you to provide aliases for commands (possibly including arguments).

• Job control

When you enter a command, you may indicate whether the command is to be run as a foreground or a background job. `Csh` permits you to suspend an executing job, to restart it, and to convert a job from foreground execution to background or vice versa.

• Command history

If you request it, csh keeps a list of the most recent commands you have executed. Csh provides convenient notations for repeating one of these commands (possibly with minor changes made to the command).

• Shell Control Flow

When csh commands are read from a file, it is desirable to be able to specify the conditions that must be satisfied before a program is to be executed. This is analogous to an *if* statement in an ordinary programming language. The csh shell language provides an if statement as well as other control flow constructs similar to those found in the C language (namely, the while loop, the switch statement, and the goto statement).

• Shell Script Files

Any collection of csh commands may be stored in a file and csh invoked to execute the commands in that file. Such a file is known as a *shell script*. Either a new instance of the shell can be created to execute the shell script or the commands in the file can be executed by the current invocation of the shell.

## 4-2    I-O Redirections and Pipelines

It is fairly standard practice for UNIX programs to read from their standard input (the C file pointer named stdin in <stdio.h> or the open file that has descriptor number 0) and to write results to their standard output (stdout or descriptor number 1). When such a program is invoked by csh, the default is for the standard input of the program to be connected to the same source as the standard input of the shell (usually the terminal keyboard). Similarly, the standard output of the program is, by default, connected to the same destination as the shell's standard output (usually the screen of your terminal). However, the csh language provides simple notations for redirecting input or output.

As a sample program, let us use fmt.  What fmt does is largely irrelevant, except inasmuch as it reads the standard input and writes to the standard output. In fact, fmt is a simple-minded text formatter which moves words from one line to another to try to make lines as long as possible without exceeding 72 columns. If you type the command

    fmt

the program is invoked and, by default, it reads standard input (your keyboard) and writes to standard output (the screen). To see any results, you must type some input to the program, terminated by *Control-D*. Unless you type a lot of input, the output will not appear on the screen until you hit *Control-D* because the program buffers its output.

Re-directing input to come from a file requires the use of the '<' operator. For example, to format text taken from a file, say the file "personal_letter" you would enter the command as

```
fmt < personal_letter
```

This causes a reformatted version of your file to be displayed on the screen.

Re-directing the standard output requires the use of the '>' operator. If you type the command

```
fmt > new_file
```

a reformatted version of the input you type at the keyboard will be stored into the file called "new_file". If this file did not already exist, csh will attempt to create it for you. If it did already exist, csh will attempt to let you overwrite the file.[1]

Of course, you can redirect both the input and the output in the same command. For example,

```
fmt < personal_letter > new_file
```

will reformat your file, storing the result in a new file. But be careful. You might think that a command like

```
### DO NOT EXECUTE THE FOLLOWING!
fmt < personal_letter > personal_letter
```

could be used to reformat the file in place. This does not work! Csh opens the file for output before fmt is ever invoked. Opening a file for output has the side effect of emptying the file. The fmt program will therefore read an empty file and produce no output. In other words, the command will destroy the file without producing any error messages.[2]

A variation on output redirection is the appending of output to the end of a file. The appropriate csh operator is '>>'. For example, the command

```
fmt >> personal_letter
```

will reformat any input you type at the terminal and append it to the file, "personal_letter". If the file did not previously exist, csh will attempt to create it before invoking fmt.

You may recall that typical UNIX programs use two output files. As well as the standard output, used for results, there is a standard error output file (corresponding to file descriptor number 2 or the name stderr). By default, the error output from any program you run is directed to the same destination as error output for your shell, which is usually

---

1. The word *attempt* is used because it is possible that access permissions on the current directory or on an existing file with the name "new_file" prohibit you from creating or modifying the file.

2. If this should worry you, there is a way to prevent files from being accidentally destroyed. See the noclobber variable on page 92.

the terminal screen. When you redirect the standard output, the error output file remains un-affected. Thus, if `fmt` should create any error message when it is invoked with

```
fmt < personal_letter > new_file
```

the message will still come to your terminal instead of being buried in the middle of your output file. This is probably the behavior you want for commands typed at the terminal. However, if the command is being run when you are not sitting at the terminal[3], there is a danger that the message will be lost. Therefore, it is desirable to be able to redirect error messages into a file. This re-direction is accomplished with the '`>&`' operator in the `csh` language. If you type the command

```
fmt < personal_letter >& new_file
```

then both the standard output and the error output are directed into the same file. No error messages generated by `fmt` are sent to the terminal. The operator '`>>&`' has a similar effect to '`>&`' except that both kinds of output are appended to the specified file.

The practice of chaining programs together so that the output of one program is passed to the input of the next is encouraged in the UNIX system. Let us take text format-ting with `troff`, for example.[4] If you have a `troff` input file that contains both tables and mathematical equations, it needs to be processed by three successive programs: `tbl`, then `eqn` and finally `troff` itself. A sequence of commands to run the programs, using temporary files for communication[5], would look like

```
tbl < text_input > #tmp1
eqn < #tmp1 > #tmp2
troff -me < #tmp2
```

But there is a tidier way to achieve the same effect, using *pipelines*. A pipeline can be thought of as a conduit through which data flows. The `csh` symbol that represents a pipeline is '`|`'. Using this operator, we can rewrite the earlier command sequence as

```
tbl < text_input | eqn | troff -me
```

As it happens, all of the programs `tbl`, `eqn` and `troff` have been programmed to take their inputs either from their standard input or from any files that are given as argu-ments. The rule is that if a file argument is provided, the program reads that. If no file is provided, the program reads its standard input. Thus, our last command is normally typed as

```
tbl text_input | eqn | troff -me
```

---

3. Look up the `at` command to see how to run a command after you have logged out.

4. Your particular UNIX system may require you to use a different command name instead of `troff`, perhaps `psroff` or `ditroff`.

5. It is recommended practice to give temporary files names that begin with a hash symbol. If you forget to delete these files, the system is supposed to remove them for you after a day or two.

Finally, we note that the operator ' | & ' has the expected effect. It causes both the standard output and the error output of the program on its left to be piped into the standard input of the program on its right. However its use is inappropriate in a normal pipeline. If we use

```
tbl text_input |& eqn . . .
```

and the tbl program generates an error message, the error message will be read by eqn. This situation is obviously undesirable. Yet there is a way to extract error messages from a command pipeline and redirect them elsewhere. Here is how it would be done for our text formatting example:

```
(tbl text_input | eqn | troff -me) >& msgs
```

Error messages generated by any of the three programs in this pipeline will be written to the file "msgs". This is our first use of parentheses in a command line. They cause the shell to fork and create a subshell which executes whatever commands are enclosed by the parentheses. The '>&' redirection after the parenthesized command redirects any output generated by the subshell. This output should consist only of error messages generated in the subshell.

A table of the file redirection and piping operators appears at the end of this chapter.

## 4-3   *Filename Expansions*

Shell commands usually perform operations on disk files. Therefore it is reasonable to expect that csh should provide some convenient notations for referring to files. Suppose, for example, you wish to compile all the C source files in your current directory and retain the object files for each of them. You could certainly list all the source files in the command, as in

```
cc -c file1.c file2.c file3.c
```

and so on. But you will not be glad of all the typing if you have twenty source files to list. The normal way to enter the command in the csh language is as

```
cc -c *.c
```

The asterisk character * is often called a *wild card* character  because the shell will take the asterisk as representing any sequence of characters at all.[6] Csh takes the string "*.c" as a pattern and attempts to match it against the names of all the files in your directory. If your directory contains the six files

```
file1.c   file2.c   file4.o
file3.c   abc.xyz.c  rubbish
```

---

6. There is an exception: csh will not expand either * or ? to match a period at the beginning of a filename.

then the pattern matches against "abc.xyz.c" "file1.c" "file2.c" and "file3.c". Therefore csh substitutes this list of filenames, in alphabetical order, for the pattern before executing the cc command.

You can use more than one wild card character in a pattern. For example,

```
cc *.*
```

will include the file "file4.o" as well as the four listed previously. (One command to watch out for is

```
rm *
```

which deletes *all* the files in your current directory.)

Other pattern features of filenames are as follows. First, ? is a wild card which matches any single character. Therefore,

```
cc file?.c
```

will compile three files in the example directory, and

```
rm file?.?
```

will delete four files. Second, if you want to match one character but you want to accept only certain characters (rather than any character as implied by "?"), you can enclose these characters in square brackets. Thus,

```
rm file[134].?
```

will remove "file1.c" "file3.c"and "file4.o" from the example directory and leave "file2.c" intact. You can also use a hyphen to denote a range of characters, as in

```
rm file[1-3].?
```

Another special character for filename expansions is the tilde (~). In, for example,

```
cd ~/bin
```

the tilde represents the full pathname for your home directory. This command will change the current directory to the subdirectory "bin" in your home directory. Similarly,

```
echo ~
```

will print the full pathname of your home directory.

The tilde character can also be used as a prefix for the user id of another user on the system, in which case, csh will expand the combination to the full pathname of that user's home directory. If there is a user named *cathy* on your system, you can execute

```
ls ~cathy
```

to see what files this user has in her home directory. (The command will work only if you have read permission on this user's home directory.)

A table of *magic* characters, including filename matching characters, appears at the end of this chapter.

## 4-4   *Command Aliases*

The csh alias command provides a simple means for you to give alternate names, or aliases, to commands. If, for example, you have trouble remembering that the command to delete a file is rm, you can provide an alias as in

```
alias delete rm
```

After the shell has executed this command, you can freely use the name *delete* as a synonym for rm.

A slightly more advanced use of aliasing is to force certain options to be provided on commands. For example,

```
alias ls ls -F
```

causes csh to expand all subsequent uses of the ls command to include the −F option. That is, if you subsequently typed the command

```
ls /bin
```

the shell expands the command to

```
ls -F /bin
```

before proceeding to interpret the command further. The −F option is a useful one that causes the types of files to be indicated in any directory listing. This feature lets you see at a glance which members of a directory are executable programs and which are subdirectories.

Another alias which many people find useful is

```
alias rm rm -i
```

It causes the rm program to double check with you before deleting any files. This provides useful protection against the accidental deletion of important files.

Of course, you should not have to retype all the aliases you use every time you log into the UNIX system. If you place your collection of alias commands in a special file named ".login" or ".cshrc" (see Section 4-11 below), the commands will be executed as soon as your shell is started up.

If you have created an alias for the rm command like that above, how can you ever execute rm without the −i flag? One way is to remove the alias with the command

```
unalias rm
```

The only other simple answer is to access the rm program under a name that csh will not recognize as aliased. For example, you can type the command as

```
/bin/rm *
```

to remove all your files non-interactively.

We will now look at a couple of trickier aspects of aliasing. First, aliases can expand to be several commands. For example,

```
alias status 'uptime; stty all'
```

causes status to expand to two commands which are executed one after the other. (The semicolon character is an alternative to the newline character as a command delimiter.) Second, there may be situations where you want to insert arguments into the middle of an alias expansion. For example, suppose that you frequently execute command pipelines like

```
tbl document | eqn | troff -me
```

It would be nice to provide an alias to reduce the amount of typing and to avoid having to remember whether tbl precedes eqn in the pipeline or vice versa. We cannot set up an alias like

```
alias format 'tbl | eqn | troff -me'
```

because when we use the command with arguments, as in

```
format doc1
```

the shell will expand the command to

```
tbl | eqn | troff -me doc1
```

To circumvent this problem, csh provides a notation for referring to command arguments. The correct way to create the alias is

```
alias format 'tbl \!* | eqn | troff -me'
```

Now our use of the format alias will expand with the argument in the correct place.

In fact, the notation !* represents *all* arguments. We can use a command like

```
format doc1 doc2 doc3
```

and this will be equivalent to executing

```
tbl doc1 doc2 doc3 | eqn | troff -me
```

Alternatively, you can use !:1 to refer to just the first argument, !:2 to refer to the second, and so on. Thus, you can create a command to exchange the names of two files as follows:

```
alias exch 'mv \!:1 #t; mv \!:2 \!:1; mv #t \!:2'
```

A backslash ( \ ) is required in front of the exclamation mark character to prevent csh from recognizing the exclamation mark as a special operator when the alias is defined. As in the C language, the backslash is used as an escape character. You might have noted that we enclosed some of our alias definitions within single quotation marks. Doing so was no accident. If the text is not enclosed within single quotation marks, csh attempts to perform filename expansion on the text. For example, if you try making the alias

```
alias print pr \!* | lpr
```

you will probably get the nasty message "No match." from csh. This means that csh tried to match \ ! * against the names of files in your directory but did not succeed. Thus, we have been using single quotation marks to prevent the asterisk character from being expanded and the backslash to delay interpretation of the exclamation mark.

Finally, it is useful to know that typing

```
alias
```

all by itself causes csh to print a complete list of current alias definitions. Typing

```
alias jack
```

will print out just the definition for *jack*, if there is one.


## 4-5   *Job Control*

Berkeley UNIX and csh provide convenient mechanisms for controlling several simultaneously executing jobs. A job is just a program whose execution has been initiated by you. At any moment, the job can be either

1)  *Running* – which means that the program is active and being executed at regular intervals (i.e. receiving time slices of the CPU), or
2)  *Stopped* – execution of the program has been suspended, perhaps because it is blocked waiting for an I/O device, but it can be restarted later.

In addition, a program may be running in the foreground or running in the background. A foreground job is a program which has control of your terminal. Anything you type at the keyboard is available for input by the program (although the program may not necessarily read it). While a foreground job is running, your keyboard input is not seen by the command shell. The command shell is simply in a wait state, waiting for the foreground job to terminate. Obviously there can be only one foreground job at any moment. On the other hand, there can be any number of background jobs or stopped jobs.

Csh gives you the ability to start and stop jobs and to switch them between foreground execution and background execution. A background job can be initiated by appending an ampersand (&) to the end of a command, as in

```
cc bigprog.c &
```

The shell will output a single information line about this job (specifying the UNIX process number or numbers for this job), and then it will give you a prompt for another command. Eventually the background job will complete and csh will output a one-line message to inform you of the job completion. This message will normally come to you at a convenient moment, just before the prompt for a new command.[7]

If we have started a background job, we can convert it into a foreground job with the fg command. For example, a session at the terminal which starts up two background jobs might look as shown in Figure 4-1. The notation [1] printed by csh shows that the C compilation is job number 1. Similarly, the troff job is assigned number 2. We can ask csh for the status of all current jobs with the jobs command, as in the figure. If we had used fg without an argument, we would have brought the most recently activated job (the troff job) into the foreground. (The most recently activated job is distinguished in the output of the jobs command by the plus symbol.) If we want to be explicit or to bring some other job into the foreground, we can supply an argument to fg. The argument can be written as %1 for job number 1, or it can be written as %cc to denote the most recent cc command.

To convert a job from foreground execution to background execution, we must first suspend execution. Suspending execution is normally accomplished with the *Control-Z* key combination which, by default, sends a *stop* signal to the program. Unless the program is deliberately intercepting and ignoring stop signals, the program is suspended and the shell

---

### Figure 4-1  Background Job Execution

```
% cc bigprog.c &
[1] 2974
% troff -me big_doc.roff &
[2] 2993
% jobs
[1] - Running cc bigprog.c
[2] + Running troff -me big_doc.roff
% fg %1
cc bigprog.c
^Z
Stopped
% jobs
[1] + Stopped cc bigprog.c
[2] - Running troff -me big_doc.roff
% bg %cc
[1] cc bigprog.c &
% jobs
[1] + Running cc bigprog.c
[2] - Running troff -me big_doc.roff
%
```

---

7. If you set the shell variable notify, csh will tell you as soon as a background job terminates.

will give you a prompt for a new command. The example shown in Figure 4-1 proceeds with the shell echoing the *Control-Z* character and outputting the message "Stopped". If we ask for a job status, we see that the C compile is shown as *stopped*. A stopped job can only be restarted or be killed. It can be restarted as a foreground job by using the fg command or as a background job with the bg command, as in the sample session at the terminal. When we restart a program, csh outputs a line to remind us what it is we are restarting. The use of the jobs command once more would verify that the program is indeed running again.

A stopped job or a background job can be terminated with the kill command. If we should change our minds about running the troff job, for example, we can kill the job with the command

```
kill -9 %2
```

or with a command similar to

```
kill -9 %tr
```

The notation %tr refers to the most recently created active job whose command name begins with the letters 'tr'. (The argument –9 should be included if you want to guarantee that the program is actually killed.)

Finally, we should note that the shell automatically stops a running background job that attempts to read from the terminal. Here is a sample session where this happens:

```
% mail fred &
[1] 34211
% Subject:
[1] + Stopped (tty input) mail fred
```

You can leave the program halted at the point where it is trying to read the subject of the mail message for as long as you like. Eventually, you will either have to kill the job or restart it by bringing it into the foreground. Once the program is brought into the foreground, you can enter the input that it was expecting and it will resume execution.

## 4-6   *The History Mechanism*

When you use the computer, you probably find yourself repeating commands. For example, when you are developing a new program, the sequence of commands you enter is likely to be something like edit a file, attempt to compile the file (but the compiler reports some errors), re-edit the file, attempt re-compilation, and so on. When you wish to repeat commands in this manner, you may avoid retyping each command in its entirety. Csh maintains a *history list*, a list of the most recent commands executed by you, and the command language provides a short notation for re-executing any command in this list. The number of commands in the list is controlled by a shell variable called history. By default, only the last command is remembered. To make use of the history mechanism, you must ensure that the variable is set to a suitably large number. (See the section on shell variables for more details.)

A reference to a command in the history list is introduced by the exclamation mark character. The exclamation mark may be followed by another exclamation mark to refer to the most recent command, by a number to refer to a specific command or by a few letters which identify the command. An example of a session at the terminal that uses the history mechanism is shown in Figure 4-2. In this sample command sequence, we simply had to type ! ! to repeat the vi edit command. Csh echoes the full version of this command before executing it. Later on, we used the notation !vi to repeat the most recently executed vi command and !c to repeat the C compile.

An alternative, but less usable, notation is to follow the exclamation mark with a command number. For example,

```
!23
```

---

**Figure 4-2   An Example of the History Mechanism**

```
% vi bigprog.c

   .
   . { perform some edits on the file }
   .
:wq { save the file back }
% !!
vi bigprog.c
   . { re-edit the file, we forgot to change something! }
   .
   .
:wq { save the file back }
% cc -c bigprog.c
bigprog.c: line 29: variable i not declared
% !vi
vi bigprog.c
   .
   . { edit the file again !! (sigh) }
   .
:wq
% !c
cc -c bigprog.c
%
```

---

will re-execute the 23rd command that you gave to the shell, provided that this command is still in the history list. Also, you can use the command form

```
!-2
```

to re-execute the last-but-one command, and so on. But for commands used much further back, you need to know the command numbers. One way to see them is to type

```
history
```

which gives a list of commands in the history list along with command numbers. Another means of knowing command numbers is to change the shell command prompt to always include the number of the next command. See below for the command which will change the prompt string to do this.

Finally, it is useful to know that there are ways to modify a command line before it is re-executed. If all you want to do is append some extra arguments, I/O redirections and the like to a command, you may do so easily. For example, if you have recently executed the command

```
cat somefile
```

you can repeat that command but with redirection and in the background as follows:

```
!ca > newfile &
```

If you have made a mistake in a command, there is a notation for changing the command before re-executing it. A short session might proceed as follows:

```
% cc -c -DDEBUG bigproh.c
0: No source file bigproh.c
% !!:s/oh/og/
cc -c -DDEBUG bigprog.c
%
```

The suffix `:s/oh/og/` indicates to `csh` that you wish to substitute the two characters "og" for "oh" in the command that you referenced. Actually, it is such a common occurrence to modify and re-execute the previous command that `csh` provides a shorter notation for it. The example command `!!:s/oh/og/` could have been typed as

```
^oh^og
```

## 4-7    *Shell Variables and Shell Expressions*

Just as a programming language like C has variables, the `csh` language also has variables. Some variables are used to control the operation of the shell. For example, a variable with the name `prompt` contains the string that is printed as your command prompt. Other variables can be created and used to control the operation of a shell script file (see below) or they can simply be used as a method of abbreviating commands.

## Setting Values

Shell variables have values which are lists containing zero or more elements. Elements of the lists are called *words* in the csh documentation, but words are really just character strings. Words may be used to represent either decimal or octal integer values. If the word consists of decimal digits, without a leading zero, it may be used as an operand for arithmetic operations listed below. If the word contains only octal digits and begins with a zero, it is treated as an octal integer (just as in C).

Shell variables are often used in a manner akin to Boolean variables. If the variable has a value, no matter what it is, the variable is used to represent *true* and if the variable is unset, with no value, then it implicitly represents *false*. The value that is commonly used to set such a variable is the empty list. A special test must be used to determine whether the variable has a value or not because it is an error to attempt to access the value of an unset variable.

The set command is used to change the value of a shell variable. The command has several forms, as illustrated in the following examples. The command

```
set V
```

will set variable *V* to have an empty list as its value. The command

```
set V = abc
```

will set *V* to have the string "abc" as its value. To be more precise, the value would be a list with one element and the value of this element is "abc". The command

```
set V = (123 def ghi)
```

sets the value of *V* as a list with three elements, these elements being the strings "123", "def" and "ghi". If *V* has been set to a list of words, as in the previous assignment, we can change one of the elements as follows:

```
set V[2] = xxxx
```

This command changes the second word in the list. Finally, if you type the command

```
set
```

csh will give you a listing of the values of all variables which are currently set.

## Referencing and Testing Shell Variables

The value of a shell variable is accessed by placing a dollar character before the name of the variable. Thus,

```
echo $term
```

will output the value of the variable term. This particular shell command should usually yield the same result as the command

```
printenv TERM
```

because csh maintains a one-way correspondence between the shell variables term, path, user and the environment variables TERM, PATH and USER. That is, if you change the shell variable term, you will find that the environment variable TERM has been changed to match. However, if you change TERM (with the setenv command), the term shell variable is unaffected. Csh does not maintain an equivalence for any shell or environment variables other than those listed above.

An alternative notation for accessing a shell variable is to enclose the variable name in curly brace characters and then to prefix the dollar symbol. Our previous example of the echo command could be typed as

```
echo ${term}
```

It has exactly the same effect. The need to use curly braces arises only when a string of alphabetic characters is to be catenated to the contents of the variable (see the section on expressions).

If a variable holds a list of words, a subscripting notation may be used to access one word or a range of consecutive words in the list. For example, if variable *V* holds a list of words, we may write shell commands like

```
echo $V[1]
```

to print the first word in the list, and commands like

```
echo $V[2-3]
```

to print the words in positions 2 through 3 inclusive. The command

```
echo $V[2-]
```

prints all words from the second position on. All these subscripting notations can be enclosed in curly braces, when necessary, as in the command

```
set W = ${V[3]}
```

Shell variables may be tested in a number of ways. The notations $#*name* or ${#*name*} may be used to find out how many words are in the list. For example, after executing the two commands

```
set V = (abc def ghi 123)
set N = $#V
```

the variable *N* will have the value 4.

The notations $?*name* or ${?*name*} can be used to test whether a variable has been set or not. The result of the test is 0 for *not set* and 1 for *set*.

## Shell Variables That Control The Shell

Some shell variables affect the way that the shell executes your commands. Some of the more useful control variables are briefly listed below.

- `filec`

  (short for *filename completion*) allows you to abbreviate filenames used in shell commands. When `filec` is set, you need type only the first few characters of a filename and then hit the *escape* key. The shell then checks the directory for files whose names begin with those characters and completes the filename as far as it is able. If the whole filename does not appear on the screen, you can type some more characters and hit the *escape* key again. If you want to see a list of all the filenames that match the prefix supplied so far, you can hit the *control-D* key.

- `prompt`

  contains the string which prints as your command prompt. The default value for this string ( `%` ) is rather uninteresting and many UNIX users change it. In environments where there are several computers, users frequently redefine `prompt` to remind them which computer they are using. For instance, if your computer is known to you as *Sun B*, say, you might set `prompt` with

  ```
  set prompt = 'B>> '
  ```
  If you want the prompt to show command numbers, use an assignment like
  ```
  set prompt = '\!> '
  ```
  The backslash is needed to protect the exclamation mark from being expanded at the time the `set` command is executed. And if you truly want your prompt to contain an exclamation mark, you will have to set the prompt in a manner similar to
  ```
  set prompt = 'HI THERE\\! '
  ```

- `ignoreeof`

  disables *Control-D* as a command input for terminating the shell. When the variable is set, the only commands to terminate the shell are `logout` (if this is the invocation of the shell that was initiated when you logged in) and `exit` (if this is not a login shell).

- `history`

  controls the number of previous commands retained in the history list. A reasonable number of commands is fifty and such a list can be set with

  ```
  set history = 50
  ```

- `mail`

  controls how often `csh` checks for new mail messages that have arrived for you and controls where it looks for the mail. If your login name is *joanie*, you would normally set `mail` with a command like

  ```
  set mail = (60 /usr/spool/mail/joanie)
  ```
  which specifies that `csh` should check the named file for new mail every sixty seconds. The directory containing incoming mail normally has the pathname shown in the example, but it would be wise to check whether a different path is needed for your particular UNIX system.

- `path`

    is a list of directories where `csh` will look for programs named in your commands. A fairly typical, but minimal, setting for `path` is

        set path=(/bin /usr/bin /usr/ucb .)

    The first three elements of the list are system directories where the standard commands are kept. The fourth element, a period, represents your current directory. If you are at all concerned about security, you should always put the period at the end of the path list.[8] If you have your own directory containing executable programs, say a subdirectory of your home directory called "bin" you would include it in the path list[9] as follows:

        set path=(~/bin /bin /usr/bin /usr/ucb .)

    A position at the front of the list is preferable because it gives you the freedom to create and use your own versions of system commands.

- `noclobber`

    is a flag which protects you from accidentally overwriting a file in a file redirection. If this flag is set and if the file "junk" already exists when you type a command like

        cat garbage > junk

    then `csh` will refuse to execute the command. If you really wish to perform this file redirection, you have to use a special override form of redirection:

        cat garbage >! junk

    (There is a similar override form for appending, namely '`>>!`'.) To set the flag, you need only execute

        set noclobber

- `noglob`

    turns off the filename expansion process of `csh`. This operation is useful if you are about to enter commands whose arguments contain wild-card characters and you do not want to be bothered with enclosing the arguments in quotation marks or using backslash escape characters.

---

8. This helps guard against the *Trojan Horse* subterfuge, in which some nasty person creates a program named `ls` and leaves it lying around in a directory that you might visit. This fake `ls` program could perform very malicious actions such as deleting all your files or it could be more subtle and create, unknown to you, a permanent loophole in the security of your files.

9. If you do include one of your own directories in the path list, make sure that you know about the `rehash` command, which is described later.

## Expressions

Shell variables have values which are lists of words. To the shell, a word is nothing more than a string of ASCII characters. These lists can be combined to create longer lists as in the following short extract from a session at the terminal:

```
% set single = xxx
% set List1 = (abc def)
% set List2 = (ghi jkl mn)
% set M = ($single $List1 $List2)
% echo 'value of M = ' $M
value of M = xxx abc def ghi jkl mn
%
```

The use of the `echo` command in this example illustrates that strings can be combined (or catenated) by juxtaposing them. More usually, strings are catenated to create filenames. Given the assignment to *single*, above, the command

```
set PROG = /tmp/${single}zz.c
```

would cause *PROG* to be assigned the filename "/tmp/xxxzz.c". This example also illustrates the need for the alternate (curly brace) notation for accessing a shell variable. Without the braces, the shell would look for a variable with the name *singlezz*.

Csh expressions use a syntax that is similar to that of the C language. Expressions may only be used in commands that begin with the keywords `if`, `while`, `exit` or the symbol `@`. All the `if` and `while` commands are explained in the following section of this appendix. The `@` command form will be discussed presently.

The most important expressions for controlling conditional execution of commands are those that yield results representing true or false. As in C, false is represented by the integer 0 and true by any non-zero integer. Comparison operations yield either 0 or 1 as their results. The operators `==` and `!=` may be used to compare either string values or number values. The other comparison operators that occur in C, namely `<`, `<=`, `>` and `>=`, may only be used to compare numeric values. There are two more comparison operators: `=~` and `!~`. The former operator, `=~`, is used to compare strings and is similar to `==`. It is a more powerful comparison operation, though, because the right-hand operand can include wild card characters such as `*` and `?`. For example, the expression

```
abcdefgh =~ a*d*
```

will evaluate to 1 (true). The other operator, `!~`, just yields the opposite result to `=~`.

Boolean values may be combined with the `&&` and `||` operators, which operate in exactly the same way as they do in C. And a Boolean value may be inverted with the `!` operator. Note that it is necessary to have a space following the exclamation mark to avoid confusion with the history mechanism notation.

Integer forms of all the arithmetic operators of C, including assignment, are available too. Although arithmetic expressions can be used as operands for the `if` and `while` commands, they are most often used in a special kind of shell command that is marked by having an "at" symbol (@) in the first column. The symbol indicates an arithmetic assignment statement. Here are some examples:

```
@ i = 10
@ j = $i * 2 + 5
@ i++
@ j *= ( $i - 5 ) / 2
```

The first of these assignments is equivalent to

```
set i = 10
```

None of the other assignment statements, however, can be reexpressed as a `set` command.

### Testing File Characteristics

Another form of shell expression is a test on a file. For example, the following expression

```
-w ~joanie/junk
```

is a test to see if the file "junk" in the home directory of *joanie* is writable. If the file can be written to, the result is 1, otherwise it is 0. The complete list of tests is given at the end of the appendix.

## 4-8  csh Control Structures

The `csh` command language includes facilities for conditionally executing a command and for repeatedly executing a group of commands. These facilities are most useful if you, yourself, are not sitting at the terminal to type these commands yourself or if you have to type the same group of commands repeatedly. That is, these shell facilities are needed for when the commands have been collected into a shell script file.

The `csh` control structures are modelled after those found in the C programming language. (Presumably this is how the *C shell* obtained its name.) The command language has two forms of the `if` statement, the `while` loop, a variation on the `for` loop, the `switch` statement, and the `goto` statement.

### The Shell *if* Command

There is a one-line form of the `if` command, which has the structure

```
if ( expression ) simple-command
```

The expression is evaluated and if it is a non-zero integer, the following command is executed. If the expression is zero, no command is executed. If the expression does not evaluate to an integer, the shell reports an error. An example of the command is

```
if (-w $file2) mv $file1 $file2
```

The one-line form of if command is not general because the following command must be simple and must not use pipes or I/O redirection. Furthermore, this form of if command is occasionally inappropriate because the shell expands uses of the history mechanism and of shell variables in the entire command line before determining whether the command after the test should be executed. Sometimes the occurrence of such an expansion in a command that will not be executed is unwanted and may result in an error message from csh. For example,

```
if ($?FILE) rm $FILE
```

will yield an error message if the variable *FILE* is not set.

To avoid problems, the multi-line form of if is recommended. The general structure for an if command without an else clause is

```
if ( expression ) then
     zero or more lines
     containing shell commands
endif
```

The first line in this layout must be typed as a single line. The line cannot be split into multiple lines (unless the end-of-line is escaped with a backslash) and no commands should appear after the keyword then on the same line. Similarly, the endif keyword must appear on a line by itself.

Just as in most programming languages, an else clause may be provided. The structure is then

```
if ( expression ) then
     zero or more lines
     containing shell commands
else
     zero or more lines
     containing shell commands
endif
```

Again, the else keyword must appear on a line by itself.

If statements may be nested. But if the else clause contains just a single if statement, there is a shorthand form. The lines beginning with the keywords else and if that appear consecutively may be joined and one of the `endif` lines eliminated. This leads to a structure like

```
if ( expression ) then
    shell commands
else if ( expression ) then
    shell commands
else
    shell commands
endif
```

## The Shell *while* Command

The `while` command may be used to repeat a group of commands. The general structure is

```
while ( expression )
    shell commands
end
```

The first line and last line must be typed as single lines, as shown. Within the loop body, the shell command `break` may be used to exit the loop (just as in C) and the command `continue` may be used to cause a transfer to the test at the top of the loop (again, just as in C).

## The Shell *foreach* Command

The shell provides a second form of looping construct. This loop has an index variable which takes on successive values from a list of words. The general structure is

```
foreach variable ( list of words )
    shell commands
end
```

Just as with the `while` loop, the commands within the loop body may include `break` and `continue`.

A simple example of the `foreach` command appears in Figure 4-3. This loop runs through all the C source code files in the current directory and prints only those that are not excessively large. The first command uses a `csh` feature that has not yet been mentioned. It is possible to access the output of a program in a shell command. If the command to invoke the program is written within a pair of backquote characters ( ` ), the program will be executed and its output treated as a list of words. The command invokes the `wc` program to count the number of lines in a file. The result is a single number which we assign to a shell variable.

---

### Figure 4-3  An Example Use of foreach

```
foreach F (*.c)
    set SIZE = `wc -l $F`
    if ($SIZE > 1000) then
        echo "$F too big to print"
        continue
    endif
    echo "Printing $F"
    pr $F | lpr
end
```

## The Shell *switch* Command

The `switch` command selects from among several possible groups of commands accord-ing to a selecting expression. The general structure is

```
switch ( string )
case string:
    shell commands
    breaksw
case string:
    shell commands
    breaksw

    .
    .
default:
    shell commands
endsw
```

The `default` clause is optional. If it is provided, it should appear after all other case labels. The `breaksw` causes an exit to the bottom of the `switch` construct, just like the `break` statement in C. If a `breaksw` command is omitted, execution will drop through to the next clause of the `switch` construct.

Although this structure is obviously modelled after C, the `csh` version of the `switch` statement is more powerful in two important ways. The first reason is that the val-ues appearing as `case` labels need not be constants. Since lines read by the shell are subject to expansion (of shell variables, of references to history events, etc.), the labels can be formed by catenating various substrings together. The shell interprets the `switch` com-mand by first expanding the selector string in the first line. Then the shell scans forward finding lines beginning with the keyword `case`, expanding these lines and comparing the selector string against the string appearing after the keyword. If the strings match, the fol-lowing command lines are executed. Since the search proceeds sequentially, it is not an error for two `case` strings to be the same, the shell simply stops at the first one that matches. The second reason this `switch` statement is more powerful than the one in C is that strict equality matching between the selecting expression and case labels is not performed. Instead, pattern matching between the selecting expression and the case label expression is performed (exactly as with the `=~` operator). In other words, case label expressions may contain wild card characters.

### The Shell *goto* Command

A label may be placed anywhere within a file containing shell commands. It is typed as an identifier followed by a colon and placed on a line by itself. A `goto` command may occur anywhere else in the file, either before or after the line where the label is defined. The general format is

```
label :
    .
    .
    .
goto label
```

## 4-9    *The Interpretation Process*

When `csh` reads a command line, it performs various manipulations on the text of this line before any commands get executed. It is necessary to know something about how this processing of the text proceeds if you want to become an adept shell programmer.

There are several stages to the processing of a command line. In the first stage, the command line is read and split into words.[10] Words are normally separated by one or more white space characters (blanks and tabs). However, some shell operator symbols will be recognized as separate words regardless of whether they are surrounded by white space. These symbols are

```
& && | || ; < << > >> ( )
```

In addition, text enclosed within pairs of single quote characters, pairs of double quote characters or pairs of backquote characters is not split into words.

The second stage is for `csh` to deduce the basic command syntax. That is, the line is decomposed into commands separated by semicolons. Components of pipelines are recognized, I/O redirections are recognized, and so on.

The third stage is for `csh` to perform alias substitution. The first word in a command line is checked to see if it has an alias definition. If it has, the substitution is performed.

---

10. The command line may consist of several input lines if all but the last of these lines end with the backslash character.

The fourth stage is for `csh` to perform history substitutions. The words in the line that have not been recognized as shell operators are scanned to search for exclamation mark characters. Any exclamation mark followed by another exclamation mark, by an integer or by alphanumeric text causes a search of the history list for the matching command. If the reference to a history event is followed by a colon (as in `"!!:s/fred/jack/"`), editing on the matching command is performed. The possibly edited command is then substituted into the command line.

The fifth stage is for `csh` to search words for references to shell variables. This search is keyed by the dollar character. The values of variables or the results of tests on variables are substituted as appropriate.

The sixth stage is for commands supplied as strings between pairs of backquote characters to be executed. The standard output of a command given between backquotes is substituted for the entire string (including the quotes). Unless the backquoted command itself appears inside a pair of double quotes, the command output is split into words at white space or at newline characters. If the command appears inside double quotes, only newline characters cause a split into separate words.

The seventh stage is filename expansion. The words in the command are scanned for the magic characters

```
    *   ?   {   [
```

and appropriate expansions are performed. In addition, if the word begins with the tilde character (~), the name of the specified home directory is substituted.

Finally, the command is executed. `Csh` checks the first word on the line to see which command has been given. Many commands, such as `echo` and all the control flow commands, are handled directly by the shell. Three of these commands, namely the `if`, `while` and `@` commands, require `csh` to perform expression evaluation before execution of the command is completed. A command that is not built into the shell causes `csh` to search the directories in the `$path` list for a program with that name. If the program is found, the shell forks and the child process executes the program.

It is frequently necessary to prevent the shell from performing some or all of the expansions listed above. How, for example, could we use the `echo` command to print a line containing an asterisk? The command

```
    echo *** WAKEUP!! ***
```

is quite incorrect because `csh` will perform both history and filename substitution. One mechanism to prevent a character from being treated as magic or special in some way is to precede it with a backslash character. Our example `echo` command could be written as

```
    echo \*\*\* WAKEUP\!\! \*\*\*
```

and it will work. It, perhaps, does not work perfectly because csh does not preserve the original spacing of our message. Remember that the line is split into words at white space. If we use three spaces to separate two words, that fact is forgotten. The proper way to write the command is as

```
echo '*** WAKEUP\!\! ***'
```

The single quote characters protect the enclosed text from being split into words and from all forms of expansion except history expansion. (Hence the need to retain backslash characters before the exclamation marks.)

If double quote characters are used, they protect the enclosed string only from being split into words at blanks and tabs. The string is still subject to all forms of expansion. Thus, we could personalize our sample echo command to include the name of the person at the terminal with

```
echo "\*\*\* WAKEUP $user\!\! \*\*\*"
```

Finally, we should mention that the order in which the parsing and various expansions are performed may not suit our needs. If this is the case, it may be necessary to force csh to reprocess the line. Reprocessing is requested with the eval command. An example of its use appears in the next section.

## 4-10 Shell Script Files

Although all the commands described above can be entered at the terminal, many of them are sensibly used only within shell command files. A file that contains shell commands is called a *shell script* file. If you have such a file named "SCRIPT" say, you can execute the script with the command

```
csh SCRIPT
```

If you are developing a new script and you have trouble getting it to work properly, you can enable trace output. Using either command form

```
csh -x SCRIPT
```

or

```
csh -v SCRIPT
```

will cause each command line in the script to be printed after some expansions have been performed and before the shell actually tries to execute the command. The −x flag causes the line to be printed at the latest possible moment, whereas −v causes the line to be printed immediately after history substitution.

We will now introduce shell script programming with the help of some examples.

---

### Figure 4-4   Csh Script for ZAP

```
1    # csh shell script for zapping processes
2
3    set ps_out = "`ps g`"
4    @ i = 1
5
6    while ( $i < $#ps_out )
7    @    i ++
8         set line = ($ps_out[$i])
9         set proc_no = $line[1]
10        if ($proc_no == $$) continue
11
12   RETRY:
13        echo -n "Kill this process? $line "
14        set ans = $<
15        if ($ans =~ n* || $ans =~ N*) continue
16        if ($ans =~ q* || $ans =~ Q*) break
17        if ($ans =~ y* || $ans =~ Y*) then
18             kill -9 $proc_no
19        else
20             echo 'Respond: y (yes), n (no) or q (quit)'
21             goto RETRY
22        endif
23   end
```

---

### Example of a Parameterless Script

A shell script for a program named ZAP is listed in Figure 4-4. If this script is held in a file named "ZAP" then, as mentioned earlier, we can execute the commands in the file by typing

```
csh ZAP
```

But if you prefer (and most people do), you can make the file executable by first executing the command

```
chmod +x ZAP
```

and then you should be able to execute the commands in the file with the simpler command

```
ZAP
```

When the UNIX system tries to execute this file, it will discover that the file does not contain executable binary and report this back to your current shell. (UNIX checks for a *magic number* in the first two bytes.) The csh shell then looks to see what the first line of the file contains. If a csh comment is recognized, a new instance of csh is created and given the file to read.[11] What does the ZAP shell script do? It finds out what active processes you have and then runs through these processes and asks you if you want to kill each one in turn. (You may occasionally find that you have a need for a script like this one.) We will now run through this shell script and explain all the mysteries in it.

For reasons just explained, the first line is a csh comment. The first executable command occurs in line 3 and invokes the ps program to obtain a list of all your processes. The output of ps when invoked from inside our shell script might look something like

```
PID TT STAT TIME COMMAND
 8609 h9 S 0:23 -csh (csh)
11258 h9 R 4:11 wild_program
11341 h9 I 0:00 csh ZAP
13342 h9 R 0:00 ps g
```

where the first process listed is your login shell, the second process is the one that you want to kill, the third process is a second instance of the shell that was created to run our script and the fourth process is the ps program itself. All this output replaces the string written with the backquote characters in the command line. Now this string is itself contained within double quote characters. The use of the double quotes is important to the shell script. If we had used the line

```
set ps_out = `ps g`
```

the output of ps would be broken up into words wherever there was white space (blanks, tabs or newline characters). With our sample output from ps, there would be twenty-eight words. However, when text is enclosed within double quotes, the shell splits the text into words only at newline characters. Thus, the command in the shell script will actually assign a list of five words to *ps_out* for our sample ps output. Of course, each of these words contains blanks and tabs.

The remainder of the shell script is a loop to run through the second and subsequent words in the list held in *ps_out*. We use an index variable *i*, initialized in line 4, and a while loop, occupying lines 6 to 23, to sequence through these words. Instead of this particular method of controlling the loop, we might equally well have used the foreach construct. Lines 4 through 7 could be replaced with the one line

```
foreach i ( $ps_out[2-] )
```

We will now trace through the first iteration of the loop, assuming that *ps_out* was assigned the five words above.

---

11. If you forget to begin your script with a csh comment, the shell will pass your file to an instance of the sh shell instead. This is likely to produce many strange error messages.

Line 6: This line is expanded by csh (as a result of variable substitution) to become

```
while ( 1 < 5 )
```

and, because the test evaluates to 1 (true), the loop body is executed.

Line 7: This one simply increments *i*, to give it the value 2.

Line 8: On the first loop iteration, this line expands to the command

```
set line = ( 8609 h9 S 0:23 -csh (csh) )
```

and so becomes a command which assigns a list of six words to *line*.

Line 9: The first of the six words in *line* is picked out and assigned to *proc_no*. Thus, *proc_no* is given the value 8609, which is the process number of the login shell.

Line 10: Here, we have a one-line if command which is expanded to

```
if ( 8609 == 11341 ) continue
```

($$ expands to the process number of the shell executing this script.) This test is provided so that our ZAP script does not permit the user to kill the instance of the shell that is executing ZAP. The test fails, so control continues past a goto label to the echo command.

Line 13: The echo command outputs the line

```
Kill this process? 8609 h9 S 0:23 -csh (csh)
```

and leaves the cursor at the end of this line on the screen. (The -n flag suppresses the newline character that is normally output at the end of the echoed line.)

Line 14: This line contains a construct, $<, which is a request for csh to read a line from its standard input. The user must type a line which csh will substitute for $<. This response is assigned to *ans*.

Lines 15-22:

There are three lines of tests on the current value of *ans*. Pattern matching forms of comparisons are used so that our ZAP script will recognize *n*, *no* and even *no thank you* as being equivalent ways of saying "no". A *no* response causes the continue command to be executed and this would cause csh to return to the top of the while construct. A *quit* response would cause the while loop to be immediately exited. A *yes* response would cause the kill program to be invoked. Any other response causes a line listing the valid responses to be printed and then control goes back to the *RETRY* label to prompt for a new response.

## Example of a Script with Parameters

There are many applications for which we can use a shell script file instead of writing a special program in C. We could, for example, write a C program that is equivalent to the ZAP script. The only discernible difference to the user would be that a C code version of ZAP would execute much faster. But for applications that are infrequently used or for applications that are subject to change, a shell script may be the sensible way to attack the problem.

To make shell scripts as usable as C programs, there needs to be a facility for accessing command line arguments. This facility is provided by the shell variable argv, which is a list containing the arguments. The first argument can be accessed by writing $argv[1] or ${argv[1]} and similarly for the other arguments. Alternatively, there is a shorter notation. $1 is equivalent to $argv[1], and so on. The notation $* is equivalent to $argv[*], a list containing all the arguments. An example shell script with arguments is reproduced in Figure 4-5. Our FORMAT script is designed for people who can never remember the correct order to run the various text preprocessors used on troff input. If your computer installation has pic (a preprocessor that lets you create pictures in your documents), you have a choice of at least three preprocessors to use. Of course, you could set up an alias that always runs all three preprocessors

```
alias FORMAT 'pic \!* | tbl | eqn | troff'
```

but this alias will not let you pass any options to troff. They would be given to pic instead. And there is a certain amount of inefficiency in invoking a preprocessor unnecessarily.

If the FORMAT script has been made executable with the command

```
chmod +x FORMAT
```

it can be invoked with commands like the following one:

```
FORMAT -T -o5- doc1 doc2
```

On this example, our shell script would set up and execute the following pipeline:

```
tbl doc1 doc2 | troff -o5-
```

We have used the flags, -P, -T and -E, to indicate that pic, tbl and eqn, respectively, are to be applied to all source files provided as arguments. Any other flags are assumed to be meant for troff.

How does it work? We begin with a foreach loop which looks at every command line argument in turn. A switch statement tests for our preprocessor flags and remembers if any of them are seen. Any other flags are appended to a list built up in the *tropts* variable. Any arguments which do not look like flags are assumed to be filenames and appended to a list built up in the *files* variables. After the loop, we run through each preprocessor in the order in which they should be applied and build up a command pipeline to process the file arguments. The pipeline is built as a list in the *cmd* variable. Finally, we append troff and any flags for troff to the end of *cmd* and execute the command that is now contained in the variable. The shell command eval is needed to make csh look at the line twice. Unless the shell is forced to process the line twice, it will not recognize the vertical bars as representing pipelines. It would, instead, pass the vertical bars as command line arguments to the first program listed in our pipeline. (This program would look for a file whose name consists of just the vertical bar character and report an error.)

## Figure 4-5 The FORMAT Shell Script

```
# csh script to control 'troff'
set tropts = () # options for ntroff
set files = () # list of troff source files
foreach arg ($*)
    switch ($arg)
    case -P: # run PIC processor
        set pic; continue
    case -T: # run TBL processor
    set tbl; continue
    case -E: # run EQN processor
        set eqn; continue
    case -?*: # troff options
        set tropts = ($tropts $arg)
        continue
    default:
        set files = ($files $arg)
        continue
    endsw
end
set cmd = ()
if ($?pic) then
    set cmd = (pic $files |); set files = ()
endif
if ($?tbl) then
    set cmd = ($cmd tbl $files |); set files = ()
endif
if ($?eqn) then
    set cmd = ($cmd eqn $files |); set files = ()
endif
eval "$cmd troff $tropts $files"
```

## 4-11 The .login and .cshrc Files

After you have become familiar with csh, you will undoubtedly find that there are several variables that you would like to set and several aliases that you would like to use. It would, of course, be inconvenient to have to type all the set and alias commands every time you log in. The obvious solution is to keep these commands in a file. So, if you have such a file named "my_aliases" say, how should you execute the commands in this file? If your answer to this question is to type the command

```
csh my_aliases
```

you are wrong. This command creates a new instance of csh to read and execute the commands. After csh has read the last line in the file, this instance of csh terminates and all the useful aliases are forgotten. Executing a new instance of csh simply has no effect on your login shell. And it does not help to make "my_aliases" executable because a new instance of csh will still be created to execute the commands.

The correct answer is to use the source command. If you enter the command

```
source my_aliases
```

the current shell will read the lines in the file as though you had typed them at the terminal.

But it is still a little inconvenient to have to type a command like

```
source my_aliases
```

every time you log in or create another instance of the csh program. Therefore, there is another mechanism. If you have a file named ".cshrc" in your home directory then every time csh is invoked, it will begin by reading and executing the contents of this file. In addition, if this invocation of csh is your login shell, it will look for and read a file named ".login" in your home directory immediately after reading the ".cshrc" file (if there was one). A fairly typical pair of ".cshrc" and ".login" files are reproduced in Figure 4-6 and Figure 4-7.

It is a good idea to keep the ".cshrc" file as short as possible. New shell instances are created fairly often, and a long ".cshrc" file can slow down your work at the terminal quite noticeably. All work that needs to be done once only should be performed in the ".login" file. It should be noted that those shell variables which have corresponding environment variables (term, path and user) are automatically inherited by subshells. Therefore they do not have to be reset in ".cshrc". Similarly, environment variables are inherited too. They do not need to be reset either.

Our ".login" file may need a little explanation. The first part of the file is concerned with initializing tty modes and setting the term shell variable (and therefore setting the TERM environment variable too). The most important part of this process is invoking the tset program in order to make a guess at the kind of terminal in use. In our example, the

---

### Figure 4-6   A Typical .cshrc File

```
# set up our favourite aliases
alias ls ls -F
alias rm rm -i
# initialize various shell variables
set history=50 time=5
set ignoreeof notify filec
```

---

### Figure 4-7   A Typical .login File

```
# initialize for our terminal type
set noglob
set term = `tset - -e -m '>9600:?sun' '?vt100'`
unset noglob
stty new crt
# initialize various shell variables
set path=(~/bin /usr/ucb /bin /usr/bin .)
set savehist=50
set prompt='\!> '
set mail=(60 /usr/spool/mail/$user)
# set environment variables used by misc. programs
setenv EDITOR /usr/ucb/vi
setenv MORE -c
# define an alias needed in the login shell
alias off logout
# check for system messages
msgs -fp
# show current system load
uptime
```

---

arguments of tset have been set up so that if you log in at a baud rate greater than 9600, it will guess the terminal type to be a SunView window on a Sun workstation. Otherwise, it will guess a vt100. (The question mark symbols cause tset to output its guess and wait for you to confirm the guess by hitting the return key or to override it by typing a different terminal type.) The result of the tset command is a terminal name which is used to set the shell variable term (and thus the environment variable TERM).  Note that the shell variable noglob is set before invoking the tset program. When this variable is set, csh does not expand any wild card characters in command lines. Although it actually does not need to be set in our particular example, it is a wise precaution because arguments to tset frequently contain characters that are special to the shell. Finally we invoke the stty program to initialize the tty modes so that they will be suitable for a CRT terminal.

## *4-12  Further Reading*

The definitive, most complete documentation for the C shell is "An Introduction to the C Shell" by William Joy and is supplied with the documentation for systems based on Berkeley UNIX.

The on-line manual entry for the `csh` command also provides a great amount of detail. You should be able to print your own copy of this voluminous manual entry with a command similar to

```
troff -man /usr/man/man1/csh.1
```

(assuming that the unformatted manual pages are provided on your UNIX system).

## *4-13  csh Reference Guide*

The remainder of this appendix contains several tables of commands, operators and variables that briefly summarize the `csh` command language. Some entries in these tables are not discussed elsewhere in this appendix. Further information can be obtained from the on-line manual entry for `csh`.

First, we begin with a table of all the special characters that you should use with care in `csh` commands. The special meaning of most of these characters can be removed by using a backslash before the character. Note that characters that only have meanings within expressions (such as + and −) are not included.

### Table 4-1   Special Characters in csh

| | |
|---|---|
| # | Start of a comment which continues up to the end of the line. A comment cannot be continued onto a second line. The first line of a `csh` script file should be a comment with the # character in the first column, otherwise you will have to explicitly invoke `csh` as a command to run the shell script. |
| @ | Perform expression evaluation. The @ character must appear in the first character position of the command line. |
| $ | Access to the value of a shell variable or a test on a shell variable. |
| ! | Access to an event in the history list or to an argument of an aliased command. |
| * | Wild card character in pattern matching or a range of list indexes. |
| ? | Wild card character in pattern matching. |

## Table 4-1   Special Characters in csh (Continued)

[     Introduces a list of characters to match. A matching right square bracket character must be provided.

~     When used at the beginning of a word, a tilde causes expansion to the pathname of a home directory.

{     There are two uses. It may be used with a matching right brace to form a *string product* when generating a list of filenames. E.g., abc{x,y,z}def is expanded to the list of three words, abcxdef abcydef abczdef. Its other use, again with a matching right brace, is to test the termination status of an enclosed command. For example,

```
{cmp -s file1 file2}
```
may be used in expressions as a subexpression with value 0, 1 or 2.

\     The escape symbol to disable the meaning of a special character. It may also be used as the last character on a line to permit an overly long command to continue onto the next line.

&     Background command execution.

|     Pipeline symbol.

<     I/O redirection symbol.

>     I/O redirection symbol.

;     Command terminator symbol. It terminates any command line except a comment.

(     The left parenthesis must be matched with a right parenthesis. There are two uses. The parentheses are used to enclose commands that must be run in a subshell and they are also used for grouping operations within expressions.

'     A pair of single quote characters protects enclosed text from variable substitution and from being split into words.

"     A pair of double quote characters protects enclosed text from being split into words (except at embedded newline characters).

`     A pair of backquote characters is used to enclose a command. When command substitution occurs, the output of the command replaces the quoted string.

## Table 4-2  I/O Redirection and Pipeline Operators

| | |
|---|---|
| `< file` | Take standard input from *file*. |
| `> file` | Send standard output to *file*. |
| `>> file` | Append standard output to *file*. |
| `>& file` | Send both standard output and error output to the named *file*. |
| `>>& file` | Like `>&`, but append to *file*. |
| `>! file` | Like `>`, but report an error if *file* exists and `noclobber` is set. |
| `>&! file` | Like `>!`, but redirect both standard output and error output. |
| `>>! file` | Like `>>`, but report an error if *file* does *not* exist and `noclobber` is set. |
| `>>&! file` | Like `>>!`, but redirect both standard output and error output. |
| `<< word` | Redirect standard input of the program on the left to come from the command input of the shell, up to an input line which is identical to *word*. It is normal to have quotes around *word*, which stops `csh` from expanding the input lines. |
| `\|` | Pipe standard output from program on left to standard input of program on right. |
| `\|&` | Pipe both standard output and error output from program on left to program on right. |

Shell expressions may appear in the `if`, `while` and `@` commands. Expressions may contain the string comparison operators in the next table. Parentheses may be used to group the operations within an expression.

## Table 4-3  Expression Operators

| | | | | | |
|---|---|---|---|---|---|
| `==` | `!=` | `=~` | `!~` | | string comparison operators |
| `!` | `&&` | `\|\|` | | | Boolean operators |
| `+` | `−` | `*` | `/` | `%` | arithmetic operators |
| `~` | `&` | `\|` | `^` | | bitwise integer operators |

Expressions may include the following tests on file accessibility. To avoid confusion with the subtraction operator, it may be necessary to parenthesize these tests. The result of a test is 1 to indicate success or 0 to indicate failure.

## Table 4-4   Tests on File Accessibility

| | |
|---|---|
| -r *file* | Test if *file* can be read. |
| -w *file* | Test if *file* can be written to. |
| -x *file* | Test if *file* can be executed. |
| -d *file* | Test if *file* is a directory. |
| -e *file* | Test if *file* exists. |
| -o *file* | Test if you are the owner of *file*. |
| -z *file* | Test if *file* is empty. |
| -f *file* | Test if *file* is an ordinary file, that is, not a directory, not a character special and not a block special file. |

It is possible to execute a command and use the status code set by that command within an expression. An example of a command which sets the status code in a useful way is cmp. You can use the construction

```
{ cmp -s file1 file2 }
```

as a component of an expression. The value of this subexpression will be 0 if the two files are identical and 1 otherwise. However, it is probably a better idea to run a program in a separate command line and to test the status code set by this program by using the status shell variable.

## Table 4-5   Special Shell Variables

| | |
|---|---|
| $$ | Contains the process number of the shell. |
| $< | An input line read from the standard input of the shell and supplied as the value of this variable. |
| $argv | A list of command line arguments to the shell. |
| $cdpath | A list of directories to search for subdirectories if the cd command cannot find the subdirectory in the current working directory. |

## Table 4-5   Special Shell Variables (Continued)

| | |
|---|---|
| $cwd | The pathname of the current working directory. |
| $echo | Causes command lines to be echoed after all expansions have occurred but before execution. |
| $filec | Enables filename completion. |
| $history | The number of commands remembered by the history mechanism. |
| $home | The pathname of the home directory. |
| $ignoreeof | Disables end-of-file (^D) from terminals as a means of terminating the shell. |
| $mail | Controls the frequency of checks for new mail and gives the names of files to check for mail. |
| $noclobber | Prevents > redirections from destroying existing files and >> from using non-existent files. |
| $noglob | Disables filename expansions. |
| $nonomatch | Disables error reporting when filename expansion fails to match any file. |
| $notify | Causes csh to report completion of a background job as soon as the event occurs. |
| $path | Provides a list of directories that csh searches for executable programs. |
| $prompt | Contains the command prompt string. |
| $savehist | Specifies the number of commands to be remembered as history from one login session to the next. |
| $shell | The file containing the shell program. |
| $status | The completion status of the last command. Normally, zero means that the last command was successful and non-zero implies that it was unsuccessful. |
| $time | Causes a summary of resource utilization to be printed for any job that uses more than $time CPU seconds. |
| $verbose | Causes command lines to be echoed after history substitution has occurred. |

## Table 4-6  Control Flow Commands

| | |
|---|---|
| ```if (expr) then```<br>    ```commands```<br>```else if (expr) then```<br>    ```commands```<br>```else```<br>    ```commands```<br>```endif``` | Conditional execution of groups of commands. |
| ```if (expr) command``` | Conditional execution of *command*, which must be a simple command. |
| ```while (expr)```<br>    ```commands```<br>```end``` | Conditional repetition of commands. |
| ```foreach vrbl (list)```<br>    ```commands```<br>```end``` | Definite repetition of commands with an index variable, *vrbl*, that takes on successive values from *list*.. |
| ```break``` | Exit from an enclosing ```while``` or ```foreach``` loop. |
| ```continue``` | Return to the top of an enclosing ```while``` or ```foreach``` loop. |
| ```switch(string)```<br>```case pattern:```<br>    ```commands```<br>    ```breaksw```<br>```case pattern:```<br>    .<br>    .<br>```default:```<br>    ```commands```<br>```endsw``` | Selection among groups of commands according to the results of successively matching *string* against *case* label patterns. |
| ```repeat count command``` | Repeatedly execute *command count* times. The command must be simple. |
| ```goto label``` | Unconditional transfer to *label*. |
| ```onintr label``` | Transfer to *label* if an interrupt occurs. If *label* is omitted from this command, all interrupts will be ignored. If a minus sign character is used instead of *label*, default handling of interrupts is restored. |
| ```label:``` | Define a *label* used as a target of *goto* and *onintr* commands. The label definition must appear on a line by itself. |

The current working directory provides the starting point for relative pathnames used in references to files. Csh keeps track of your working directory in the variable $cwd and provides commands (cd or chdir) to change the working directory. Csh actually maintains a stack of working directories. The top element of this stack (with position number 0) is the current working directory. There are two commands to manipulate the directory stack.

In addition, csh maintains two lists of directories. One list, $path, contains the names of all the directories that should be searched to find an executable program. Because searches for programs are very frequent, csh compiles a hash table which lists all the programs in the search path. This hash table is compiled when the shell is started. For the most part, you need not be aware that command searches are being implemented as hash table look-ups. The exception arises if new programs are added to any directories in your search path. If this happens, csh will be unaware of the existence of these programs and will fail to find them. Therefore, the rehash command is provided to force csh to recompile its hash table. A second list of directories can be held in the variable $cdpath. If the cd (or chdir) command cannot find the specified subdirectory in the current directory, it will search all the directories named in $cdpath for it.

## Table 4-7 Shell Commands for Directory Management

| | |
|---|---|
| cd | Change working directory to $home. (chdir is an alternate command name for cd.) |
| cd *name* | Change working directory to *name*. (chdir is an alternate command name for cd.) |
| dirs | Print the directory stack. |
| popd | Pop the directory stack. |
| popd +*n* | Delete the *n*-th entry in the directory stack. |
| pushd | Exchange the top 2 elements in the directory stack. |
| pushd *name* | Push *name* onto the directory stack. |
| pushd +*n* | Exchange the *n*-th entry with the top entry of the directory stack. |
| rehash | Recompile the hash table of programs in the $path list of directories. Use this command after you have added new programs to any of the directories in $path. (Otherwise the shell will say that these programs cannot be found when you try to use them.) |
| hashstat | Print hash table statistics. |
| unhash | Stop using hash table searching for commands. This means that csh takes longer to invoke a command, but you no longer need to execute rehash every time you add a new program to a library on your search path. |

## Table 4-8 Commands for Job Control

| | |
|---|---|
| `bg` | Put current job into background. |
| `bg %job` | Resume the specified job in the background. The same effect can be achieved by just typing `%job &` |
| `fg` | Bring current job into foreground. |
| `fg %job` | Bring specified job into foreground. The same effect can be achieved by just typing `%job`. |
| `history` | Print the history list. |
| `jobs` | List all active jobs. |
| `kill %job` | Send the TERM (terminate) signal to the specified job. |
| `kill -9 %job` | Definitely kill the specified job. |
| `notify` | Report when the current job terminates. |
| `notify %job` | Report when the specified job terminates. |
| `stop` | Stop the current job. |

## Table 4-9 Other Shell Commands

| | |
|---|---|
| `alias` | List all aliases in effect. |
| `alias name` | List any alias for *name*. |
| `alias name wordlist` | Set an alias for *name*. |
| `unalias pattern` | Remove all aliases with names matching *pattern*. |
| `echo wordlist` | Print the arguments on the standard output. |
| `echo -n wordlist` | Print the arguments without a terminating newline. |
| `eval wordlist` | Reparse and execute *wordlist* as a command. |
| `exit` | Exit from the shell with termination status 0. |
| `exit(expr)` | Exit from the shell with status *expr*. |
| `login` | Terminate the current (login) shell and login again. |

## Table 4-9 Other Shell Commands (Continued)

| | |
|---|---|
| `logout` | Terminate a login shell. |
| `set` | Print the values of all shell variables. Just typing @ symbol as a command by itself has the same effect. |
| `set name` | Set the value of *name* to be an empty list. |
| `set name=word` | Set the value of *name* to be *word*. The same effect is achieved with the command form<br>`@name=expr` |
| `set name=(wordlist)` | Set the value of *name* to be a list. |
| `set name[index]=word` | Change the value of one list element. (*name* must have a list value and *index* must be a valid index.)<br>The same effect is achieved with the command form<br>`@name = index[expr]` |
| `unset pattern` | Unset all variables whose names match *pattern*. |
| `setenv name value` | Set the specified environment variable. |
| `unsetenv pattern` | Unset all environment variables whose names match pattern. |
| `shift` | Delete the first element of the `argv` list (in effect, shifting the list left). |
| `shift variable` | Delete the first element of the *variable* list. |
| `source file` | Read and execute shell commands contained in *file*. |
| `suspend` | Suspend the current shell (which cannot be a login shell). |
| `time` | Summarize CPU time usage of this shell and all its child processes. |
| `time command` | Report CPU time usage of *command*. |
| `umask` | Print the value of the current file creation mask. |
| `umask value` | Set the file creation mask to *value*. When `csh` creates a file as a result of an I/O redirection, it uses the umask value to set the access permissions on the new file. |

# CHAPTER 5

# *NETWORKING PROGRAMS*

Unless you use a microcomputer at home, it is very likely that your computer is just one of several that are linked by a local area network (or LAN). The most common method of connecting the computers in a LAN is by means of ethernet cable. Another possibility uses fibre optic cable (FDDI). But it should not really matter to you as a UNIX user how the network is implemented, all you need to know it that data transfers from one computer to another in the network are very fast.

In the future, we may all be using distributed operating systems. This kind of system would give each user the illusion that he or she was using a single computer, while making the resources of the entire network available. The system would automatically execute your programs on whichever computer has idle capacity, perhaps moving the programs around as the situation changes. For now, however, we have to live with UNIX as it currently exists, and UNIX is *not* a distributed system.

While the operating system itself may not be distributed, the file system may be. Software known as Network File System (NFS) allows a user to have direct access to files that reside on a disk attached to another computer in the network. The access is said to be transparent, meaning that the user does not treat a file accessed through NFS any differently to any other file. There are few differences between a file on your own computer and a file accessed through NFS on another computer.

If your computers are located at a school or commercial organization of any size, they are probably connected to many thousands of other computers around the world using one or more networks. These *wide area networks* have names like Arpanet, CSNet, and BIT-NET. They permit you to exchange electronic mail (or e-mail for short) with correspondents at other computer sites on the network. You may also have the capability to obtain files from other sites, or even to login to another computer that is situated thousands of kilometers away. Some of the possibilities are discussed below.

# 5-1    Connecting to Other Berkeley UNIX Computers

Let us imagine that your organization has three computers named *A*, *B* and *C* linked via a LAN and all three computers run a UNIX that was derived from Berkeley UNIX. If you have accounts on all three computers, you can normally choose which one to login to. When you have logged on to one computer, say A, what do you do if you later find that you need to access a file on B or run a program on C? The NFS software may or may not eliminate the need to explicitly access that file on B, depending on how your system is organized. Similarly, the C computer may have a different architecture to the A computer so even if you can access the executable file from A, you may not be able to execute it directly. There are several ways to solve these problems, and they are explained below.

The commands described below do not depend on the computers being connected by a LAN. The commands will work just as well, perhaps with slower response times, if the computers are geographically far apart and connected by the Internet. All that is required is that the network communications operate using a protocol named TCP/IP and that the computers at both ends are running a Berkeley UNIX derivative.

## Remote Commands: rlogin, rsh and rcp

Assume that you are currently logged in to computer A and that you wish to perform some work on computer C. If you type the command

```
A% rlogin C
```

and if the network is operating correctly, you will receive a prompt for a password from computer C. If your login attempt is successful, all your command prompts will come from the shell executing on C and all your commands will be executed on C. The fact that all inputs and responses must go via computer A should be totally invisible to you.

If you need to remotely login to other machines frequently, you can speed up the process by creating a file named ".rhosts" in your home directory on computer C. Assuming that your login name on computers A and B is *jane*, the file could contain these lines.

```
A jane
B jane
```

These two lines tell the `rlogin` program not to prompt for a password when a user with login name *alfred* on machines A and B attempts to login.

If you have unfortunately been assigned a different login name on computer C or if you need to login into someone else's account, you have to add an extra argument to the `rlogin` command. If you need to login to an account named *tarzan* on C, you would enter this command.

```
A% rlogin -l tarzan C
```

(That flag is a lower-case letter 'L', not the digit '1'.) If the home directory for the *tarzan* account has a ".rhosts" file that lists *jane* on A, no password would be requested.

When you logout from computer C, you will simply find yourself back at computer A. However, if you need to alternate between executing some commands on computer A and some commands on computer C, there is no need to logout. You can suspend the `rlogin` program by typing the two consecutive characters "~" and "*Control-Z*". Without a preceding tilde character, the *Control-Z* character would simply be passed to the program or shell running on the remote computer. The tilde character is used as a special prefix to tell the `rlogin` program that the *Control-Z* is meant for it.

If you are currently logged into computer A and you need to execute just one command on computer C, you may be able to avoid using `rlogin`. The `rlogin` approach requires full execution of the ".login" and ".cshrc" files on the remote computer and so may be relatively time consuming. The alternative is the `rsh` command (`rsh` is short for *remote shell*). However, you must have a ".rhosts" file on the remote computer, as described for the `rlogin` command. A sample use of `rsh` is as follows.

```
A% rsh C ls /usr/bin | more
```

This executes the command "`ls /usr/bin`" on computer C. The output from the command is fed into the `more` program on the current computer, A. As you can see, the shell operators like '`|`', '`>`', etc., are assumed to belong to the shell running on computer A. If you need to include such operators or other magic characters in the command that gets executed on the remote computer, you must disguise them. One possibility is to enclose them in quote characters, as in the following example.

```
A% rsh C ls -l '/usr/bin/g*' '|' grep gcc
```

The `rsh` command cannot be used properly if the command to be executed on the remote computer is interactive, such as `vi`. Partially interactive commands like `more` can be used after a fashion, but you will find that your inputs do not properly synchronize with the actions performed by the command, as though it lags one character behind in its input.

As with `rlogin`, the `rsh` command accepts a '`-l`' flag followed by a login name if the account name on the remote computer does not match the one on the originating computer.

If you need to copy a file named "mydata" located in your home directory on computer B to your current computer, A, one possibility that would work for a textfile is to execute the command

```
A% rsh B cat mydata > data-from-B
```

and this will create a duplicate file named "data-from-B" on computer A. However, a more convenient approach is available. To obtain the same effect, you need only execute the following command.

```
A% rcp B:mydata data-from-B
```

The command is used in a similar manner to `cp`, except that the filenames are generalized. Either or both of the source and destination filenames may be prefixed by a label that specifies the computer that has the file. Thus you may copy to or copy from a remote computer. An interesting possibility is that you can copy between two different remote computers. For example,

```
A% rcp B:mydata C:mydata
```

copies the file named "mydata" on B to machine C. The command works as long as appropriate entries exist in the ".rhosts" files on both computers B and C.

A powerful feature of the `rcp` command is its ability to copy directories and all the files in the directories. The '`-r`' flag enables this recursive copying mode.

## Network Security

This section of the chapter would not be complete without a warning. The ".rhosts" file is dangerous because it increases the chance that someone may break into your account and read or destroy your files. If an unscrupulous person can become a superuser on another machine, that person can access your files on that machine. A ".rhosts" entry for that other machine makes the situation worse by allowing him or her to violate other accounts of yours.

Therefore, you must balance security against your personal convenience. A reasonable compromise is to name only other computers within your own organization in your ".rhosts" file.

## Interactive Communication with Other Users

If you would like to communicate with another user, you could send a mail message (see below). But this is the electronic equivalent of writing a letter and it is not always the most convenient way to get a fast response to a question or to engage in a dialogue.

Perhaps the first thing you would like to do is determine whether your friend, with login name *tarzan*, is currently at his terminal or workstation. The most convenient command for discovering this information is finger. If the name of the computer that *tarzan* uses is *jungle*, you can type the command

```
A% finger tarzan@jungle
```

and this will tell you if *tarzan* is currently logged in, what time he logged in, and how long it is since he last typed a command at the keyboard (this is the idle time). You do not need an account on the *jungle* computer to be able to use this command. Depending on whether your friend maintains files named ".plan" and ".project" and whether extra information has been placed in his entry in the "/etc/passwd" file, finger may tell you other things – such as his office number, his telephone number and so on.

Note that finger works equally well across the network. You can use it to obtain information about users who are thousands of kilometers away. You can also use it to find out who is currently logged in. For example,

```
A% finger @downunder.oz.au
```

will give you a list of current users on a (hypothetical) machine named *downunder* located in Australia. (The '.au' suffix indicates that the address belongs to the national network of Australia.)

If your friend *tarzan* is currently logged in, you can exchange messages with him by first typing this command.

```
A% talk tarzan@jungle
```

Provided that he has not disabled interruptions (using the "mesg n" command), *tarzan* will see a message similar to

```
Message from Talk_Daemon@jungle at 11:34 ...
talk: connection requested by jane@A.
talk: respond with: talk jane@A
```

displayed on his screen or in a window on his workstation. If he responds with the indicated command, you will both be provided with a screen (or window) that is divided into two halves by a horizontal line. Anything you type is shown in the top half of your screen and, simultaneously, in the bottom half of your correspondent's screen. Similarly, anything he types appears in the bottom half of your screen. Thus, you have simultaneous two-way communication where you can see every character as it is typed (including all the backspacing to type over mistakes).

Again, physical distance is not, in itself, an obstacle to communication. The finger command will work just as well, albeit with delays, if the two computers are located far apart.

## 5-2    *Connecting to Other Systems*

Can you still use networking commands to reach other computers that do not use an operating system derived from Berkeley UNIX? The answer is often *yes*, but you may have to try the connection to be sure. Rlogin, rsh, rcp, finger and talk are all Berkeley UNIX programs and would normally be unavailable on other computer systems.

A more generic remote login program is called telnet. It is supported on other variants of the UNIX system as well as some non-UNIX operating systems, such as VMS. It works like a simplified version of rlogin. If you have an account on another computer whose network name is, say, "downunder.oz.au", you can execute the telnet command and, assuming that the connection succeeds, see a dialogue like the following.

```
A% telnet downunder.oz.au
Trying 123.456.78.9 ...
Connected to downunder.oz.au.
Escape character is '^]'.

SunOS UNIX (downunder)

login:
```

When you get the *login* prompt, you are connected to the remote machine and you can login to that machine in the normal way. The telnet program does not simulate any particular type of terminal. Therefore, either the ".login" file on the remote computer should set the terminal type to be the same as on your local computer or you should make the setting explicitly. (See Chapter 4 for an example of a suitable ".login" file.) The telnet program has a lot of special subcommands that are available if you type the character "*Control-]*". You may obtain the details from the on-line manual entry for telnet.

If you wish to obtain files from a remote computer, the ftp program (*file transfer protocol*) is the normal mechanism to use. Many organizations maintain large collections of public domain software and make the software available for public access. For normal, unrestricted, use of ftp, you need an account on the remote computer. However, the usual arrangement for public distribution of software provides a special guest account whose login name is *anonymous*. Figure 5-1 shows an example session using so-called *anonymous ftp*. To make this example easier to follow, characters typed by the user are shown in bold. (The text typed as the password is not echoed by ftp, and this is shown in a shadow font.) The example illustrates just a few subcommands of ftp. A selection of the more useful subcommands is listed in Table 5-1. The patterns used in the mget and mput subcommands are similar to filename patterns used with the shell.

The sample ftp session in Figure 5-1 retrieves a file named "gcc-1.39.tar.Z". (The wording and order of some of the messages shown in the figure may differ according to which version of ftp you have access to on your system.) The retrieved file is in a form known as a *compressed archive file*. A few words of explanation on what to do with this file are probably appropriate. The '.Z' suffix on the filename indicates that the file has been compressed with the `compress` program. This implies that the file is not in ASCII format and is the reason why the file transfer mode had to be set to *binary* in the `ftp` example. If you execute `uncompress` to re-create the original file, the new suffix would be '.tar'. This suffix indicates that the file is in an archive form created by the `tar` program. An archive is a collection of smaller files that have been joined together. Having a single file makes it easier to transmit one file over the network or write one file to a magnetic tape. The archive can be disassembled into its constituents by running it through the `tar` program again. The commands that you could execute to process the archive file retrieved in

---

### Figure 5-1   An Example ftp Session

```
A% ftp aeneas.mit.edu
Connected to aeneas.mit.edu.
220 aeneas ftp server (Version 4.136 Mon Oct 31
                23:18:38 EST 1988) ready.
Name (aeneas.mit.edu:jane): anonymous
331 Guest login ok, send ident as password.
Password: jane
230 Guest login OK, access restrictions apply.
ftp> ls
200 PORT Command successful.
150 Opening data connection for /bin/ls
                (128.189.66.45,1390) (0 bytes).
Index
archive
... several lines have been deleted
pub
226 Transfer complete.
81 bytes received in 0.06 seconds (1.3 Kbytes/s)
ftp> cd pub/gnu
250 CWD command successful.
ftp> binary
200 Type set to I.
ftp> get gcc-1.39.tar.Z
200 PORT command successful.
150 Opening data connection for gcc-1.39.tar.Z
                (128.189.66.45,1394) (2907533 bytes).
2907533 bytes received in 880.9 seconds (3.3 Kbytes/s)
ftp> quit
221 Goodbye.
A%
```

---

Figure 5-1 are shown below. They first move the compressed archive to a new, empty, directory where the extracted files can reside. Then the files are extracted using `zcat` and `tar` in series. Finally, assuming that `zcat` and `tar` work successfully, the archive file may be deleted.

```
A% mkdir workdir
A% mv gcc-1.39.tar.Z workdir
A% cd workdir
A% zcat gcc-1.39.tar.Z | tar xvf -
A% rm gcc-1.39.tar.Z
```

The `x` flag to `tar` tells it to extract files; the `v` flag tells `tar` to be verbose (reporting its progress); the `f` flag tells `tar` that the archive should be read from the source named in the next command line argument. The next argument is just '`-`' and this is interpreted by `tar` to mean that the archive must be read from its standard input. The `zcat` program performs the de-compression, sending the result to its standard output. Finally, the shell pipe operator '`|`' connects the standard output of `zcat` to the standard input of `tar`. When the `x` flag is used with `tar`, you may specify individual files to be extracted. However, in this case, no files are specified and `tar` automatically extracts every file in the archive.

## Table 5-1   Selected Subcommands of ftp

| | |
|---|---|
| `user `*`loginname`* | use this command to give your login name if you were not prompted for it. |
| `cd `*`dirname`* | change to a subdirectory on the remote computer. |
| `cdup` | change to parent directory on the remote computer (this command is not available in older versions of `ftp`). |
| `binary` | prepare to transmit binary (non-ASCII) files. |
| `ls` | list names of files in current directory on remote computer. |
| `get `*`filename`* | get a file from the remote computer. |
| `mget `*`pattern`* | get files whose names match the pattern. |
| `put `*`filename`* | send a file to the remote computer. |
| `mput `*`pattern`* | send files whose names match the pattern. |
| `help` | obtain a list of all the subcommands accepted by `ftp` |
| `help `*`command`* | get a synopsis of the named subcommand |
| `quit` | exit from `ftp` |

If you just wish to see the names of the files contained in the compressed archive file, the following command would suffice.

```
A% zcat gcc-1.39.tar.Z | tar tf -
```

To complete the digression on how to use compressed archive files, we may as well see the commands needed to create such a file. You will find these commands useful if you ever need to transmit a file using `ftp`. Suppose that you wish to combine all the files in your current directory to form an archive. The necessary commands would then be as follows.

```
A% tar cvf - ./* > /tmp/archive.tar
A% compress /tmp/archive.tar
```

The compressed archive file would end up with the name "archive.tar.Z" and be located in the temporary file directory named "/tmp". (We do not create the archive in the current directory or else the list of files that ". /*" matches would include "./archive.tar".)

## 5-3    Electronic Mail – The mail Program

The standard program for sending electronic mail (or just *e-mail*) is called `mail`. If you use a SUN workstation with the SunView or OpenView environment, you may use an interactive mail program called `mailtool`. If you operate in a X-windows environment, you may be using the `xmail` program. We will focus on the `mail` program here.

### Sending a Message

If you wish to send a message, you need an e-mail address for the intended recipient. Assuming that address is "tarzan@jungle", you might type a quick message as follows.

```
A% mail tarzan@jungle
Subject: food supplies
Do we have enough bananas for supper tonight?
- Jane
.
A%
```

Everything typed by you is shown in bold. The line that contains just a period terminates the input to the `mail` program.

### Receiving a Message

Sometime later, the message sent above arrives at the destination computer. The recipient, *tarzan*, will receive a notification

```
You have new mail.
```

the next time he logs in, or he may see it sooner if he is already logged in when the message arrives. (The csh command shell checks for new mail at intervals determined by the *mail* variable – see Chapter 4.) If he types the command mail, with no arguments, he can read the message and any others that may be waiting to be read.

The mail program can be more than a little confusing to use. Part of the reason is that the program can be in two different modes. If you type the command

        mail

to read messages that have been sent to you, the program will start off in command mode. The program will display a numbered list of messages that are available for you to read. Each message is identified by its sender and a subject line (provided that the sender provided one). You may use the subcommands listed in Table 5-2 to select which messages to read, to print, to save, to delete and so on.

## Table 5-2   Selected Subcommands of the mail Program

| | |
|---|---|
| q | quit from the mail program, unsaved and undeleted messages are appended to the user's "mbox" file. |
| x | quit without updating the system mailbox. |
| p *n* | display message number *n*; (the command t *n* is a synonym). |
| \| *n* 'lpr -P*qms*' | print message *n* on the printer named *qms*. |
| r *n* | reply to sender of message number *n*. |
| R *n* | reply to sender and all recipients of message *n*. |
| s *n filename* | append message *n* to the named file. |
| w *n filename* | append message *n*, without *From* line, to the named file. |
| m *addressee* | compose a new message to the named recipient. |
| d *n* | delete message *n*. |
| u *n* | undelete message *n*. |
| h *n* | list message headers to be read, starting at message *n*. |
| set *variable*=*val* | set a parameter of the mail program to the given value. |
| alias *name value* | set *name* as an abbreviation for the address value. |

## Mail Subcommands

If you use one of the m, r or R subcommands to send a new message or if you start the mail program with a command like

```
mail tarzan@jungle
```

you will first be prompted for a subject line to go in the header of the message. Next, you may be prompted for a list of *carbon copy*[1] recipients of the message (depending on whether the askcc parameter is set). Finally, you will be in input mode, typing text to be included in the message body. A different set of commands, called *tilde escapes*, are available for use while in input mode. Some of the more important tilde escape sequences are listed in Table 5-3. To use one of the tilde escape commands, you must type the tilde as the first character on a new line. For example, the dialogue that our recipient with the login name *tarzan* has when he receives and replies to the message might go as shown in Figure 5-2. As before, the characters typed by *tarzan* are shown emboldened, everything else is generated by the computer. When he types ~m1 the text of Jane's message is copied into the message he is sending. If he had wanted to use an editor on the message, he would have typed ~v, and so on.

### Table 5-3   Selected Tilde Escapes of the mail Program

| | |
|---|---|
| ~p | list the message body |
| ~h | display the message header for editing |
| ~c *user* | add a new recipient to the CC list on the message |
| ~b *user* | add a new recipient to the BCC list on the message |
| ~v | invoke a visual editor on the message body |
| ~e | invoke a line-oriented editor on the message body |
| ~f *n* | insert message *n* into the message being composed |
| ~m *n* | insert message *n*, shifted right by one tab |
| ~r *filename* | insert contents of file into the message |
| ~q | abandon composing the message, saving it first in "dead.letter" |
| ~x | abandon composing the message, without saving it |

---

1. The term carbon copy is rather obsolete, especially when applied to electronic mail. However its abbreviation *CC* is built into the mail program.

---

**Figure 5-2   Replying to a Message**

```
jungle% mail
Mail version SMI 4.0 ... Type ? for help
"/usr/spool/mail/tarzan": 1 message 1 new
>N 1 jane        Thu Mar 28 13:08 15/472    food supplies
& p1
Message 1:
From jane@A Thu Mar 28 13:12:56 1889
Return-Path: <jane@A>
... a few lines of the message header are omitted
Subject: food supplies
Status: R

Do we have enough bananas for supper tonight?
- Jane

& r
To: jane@A
Subject: Re: food supplies
~m1
Interpolating: 1
(continue)
Yes. Lots!
Tarzan
.
& q
Saved 1 message in /usr/a/tarzan/mbox
jungle%
```

## Mailboxes

Messages that are waiting to be read are held in a system mailbox. Starting the mail program without any command line arguments causes mail to list all the messages for you in
this system mailbox. Those messages that you have read, saved to a file or explicitly
deleted are removed from the system mailbox when you use the q subcommand to quit the
mail program. The messages that you have read but have not saved or deleted are not lost.
They are automatically appended to a file owned by you. The name of this file is normally
"mbox" and resides in your home directory. (However, there is a mechanism to cause
mail to use a different filename.)

The messages that have accumulated in your "mbox" file from previous invocations of mail can be read and processed too. If you start up the mail program using the command

```
mail -f
```

it processes the messages in your "mbox" instead of in the system mailbox file. It is, of course, possible to have mail process messages in files other than "mbox". This will be explained when we get to the subject of mail folders.

## The .mailrc File

Some subcommands allow the `mail` program to be customized for your use. For example, the `alias` subcommand allows you make an abbreviation for the name and address of an e-mail recipient. If you collect these subcommands together in a file named ".mailrc" in your home directory, the `mail` program will automatically read the sequence of subcommands when it starts execution. An example ".mailrc" file showing some of the more useful subcommands is shown in Figure 5-3. The file typically contains a series of `set` subcommands that control parameters of the `mail` program, followed by a long list of aliases for all the people you frequently send e-mail to. The particular parameters referred to in the ".mailrc" file of Figure 5-3 have the following effects.

Setting `askcc` on (i.e., defining its value as *Yes*) causes `mail` to prompt you for a list of carbon copy recipients whenever you compose a new message. Setting `crt` to the value 24 causes `mail` to use a pager program to display any message that contains more than 24 lines. The default pager program is `more`, but the default can be overridden by setting the `PAGER` parameter. The `VISUAL` parameter provides the name of a full-screen editor to invoke when you edit a message body by using the `~v` tilde escape, for example. The setting of `VISUAL` in the example ".mailrc" file is actually redundant because the default editor is `vi`.

## Mail Folders

If you wish to keep messages, you can hold them in your "mbox" file. The `mail` program will automatically transfer any messages you have read, but not saved or deleted, to your

---

### Figure 5-3   A Sample .mailrc File

```
set askcc=Yes
set VISUAL=/usr/ucb/vi
set crt=24
alias tz tarzan@jungle
alias bb brigitte@st.tropez.fr
# The author of this book
alias nh nigelh@csr.uvic.ca
```

*Electronic Mail – The mail Program*   **131**

"mbox". However, as the number of messages held there grows, you will find that it becomes less and less convenient to find messages from particular correspondents or messages on particular subjects. If your messages were on sheets of paper, you would probably choose to arrange them in file folders stored in a filing cabinet.

The mail program provides analogous facilities. A directory acts the part of the filing cabinet and computer files within that directory act as file folders. To use these facilities, you should place the line

```
set folder=mailfolders
```

in your ".mailrc" file, where *mailfolders* is the name of the directory to use, given relative to your home directory. You may, of course, use any convenient name for the directory.

To file a message in a folder, you may use a save subcommand as in the following extract of a mail program dialogue.

```
& s1 +jane
"/usr/a/tarzan/mailfolders/jane" [Appended] 1301/6497
&
```

That is, the folder name is *jane*, and message 1 has been appended to the file named "jane" in the "mailfolders" directory. If the folder did not previously exist, mail would create it for you.

To find out what folders you currently have in your folder directory, you can use the mail subcommand folders.

Each folder file has the same format as your "mbox" file. If you want to read through the messages in a particular folder, you can start up the mail program using a command like the following,

```
jungle% mail -f +jane
```

which will display all the messages saved in folder *jane* and allow you to process them in the same way as other mail messages. If you are already running mail, you may use a subcommand like the following to switch to a folder.

```
& folder +jane
```

You may return to processing messages in the system mailbox with the subcommand

```
& folder %
```

or to processing messages in your "mbox" file with the following.

```
& folder &
```

## 5-4    Network Addresses

When you want to communicate with a particular computer, you need a network address for it. For example, Figure 5-1 shows a `ftp` session that communicates with the computer at address "aeneas.mit.edu". Let us examine this address in more detail. The address is hierarchically composed from a series of domain names. The top level domain is called EDU (short for *Education*) and is intended to include colleges and universities within the United States (it also includes one or two from Canada). The second level domain is MIT, obviously representing *Massachusetts Institute of Technology*. MIT is a large university and owns several hundred computers. The third level name, *aeneas*, is the name assigned to a particular computer (or a *host* as it would be called in networking jargon). This computer has users with their accounts on that machine and we can reach one of these users if we send mail to an address like "joe@aeneas.mit.edu". There may also be workstations which rely on that computer for their communications. If a particular workstation has been assigned the name *ws29*, we can send a message to a person who uses that workstation by using an address like "judy@ws29.aeneas.mit.edu".

The EDU domain in the example address identifies that address as belonging to a particular computer network known as the Internet. The Internet domain hierarchy has the structure shown in Figure 5-4, below. Of course, only a minuscule part of the entire network is represented here. It should be stressed that the diagram shows the administrative struc-

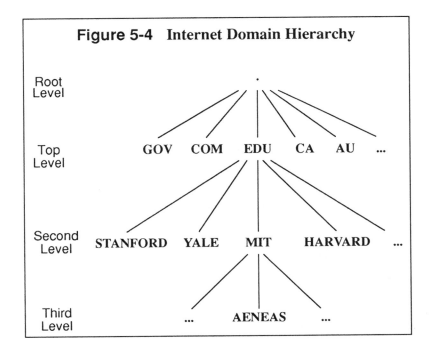

**Figure 5-4    Internet Domain Hierarchy**

ture of the network — it has almost no relation to the network topology (the connection graph showing which computers are connected by communication links).

There are other networks, for example BITNET and CSNET, which have their own hierarchical domain structure for addresses. You can recognize an address in the BITNET network, for example, because the address will end with the domain name '.BITNET'. The various networks can exchange messages with each other using gateway computers – these are computers that simultaneously belong to two different networks. Therefore, you should be able to send e-mail to a destination on any computer on any of the networks. However, you should only expect to be able to use the `rlogin`, `rcp`, `rsh`, `finger`, `talk`, `telnet` and `ftp` programs for communication between two computers within the Internet. These programs all rely on a particular set of communication protocols used by the Internet called TCP/IP (Transmission Control Protocol / Internet Protocol). Other networks do not necessarily use the same protocols.

The communication software actually uses addresses in the form of 32-bit numbers. Some of the networking commands, such as `ftp` and `telnet`, allow you to use either the symbolic address or the numeric address. For example, the `ftp` session of Figure 5-1 could have been commenced with the following command form.

```
ftp 18.71.0.38
```

The standard form for expressing the address is as byte values (i.e., numbers in the range 0 to 255 and known as *octets* in networking literature) separated by periods. The four-byte number is commonly known as an IP number (for *Internet Protocol*).

When you use a domain-style symbolic address, the software has to convert it to the numeric form. Your local site probably (but not necessarily) maintains a table containing equivalences between names and IP numbers. If you want to use short names such as *A*, *B*, *C* or *jungle* for your local machines, they will be in this table. The table is normally held in the file "/etc/hosts" on the machine that handles your communications. In addition to the table, your local site probably (but, again, not necessarily) maintains a cache containing the IP numbers for names that have had to be looked up in the recent past. If you use an address that is not in the table and not in the cache, your local site will send a message to another computer on the network that provides a *nameserver* service. That other computer should be maintaining a complete table of equivalences for its domain. If the name lies outside the domain, the request for the IP number is passed to the nameserver for the next higher domain. The nameserver for the root of the domain hierarchy is supposed to have a table containing all internet addresses and acts as the ultimate authority. The nameserver at the root of the internet hierarchy is maintained by an organization called NIC (Network Information Center). Before a site can be added to the internet, its administrators must contact NIC to obtain a unique IP number and to register its name.

Occasionally the nameserver service may fail to find an IP number for a computer on the network. This might happen if the administrators have failed to register the name or if the nameserver and the alternate nameserver provided for backup are temporarily unreachable. To guard against this, it is useful to know the IP number of a site as well as its name. Sites which provide anonymous ftp service often publicize their IP number for exactly this reason.

If you wish to find out the IP number of some site, you may use the nameserver service interactively. There is a program `nslookup` which allows you to choose a nameserver site and to ask that nameserver to look up a name for you. If the program is available on your computer, a description of its usage may be found in the on-line manual. An alternative to `nslookup` is a public-domain program named `host`. It provides similar functionality but is much easier to use for a single name look-up.

## Address Syntax

If you use the `mail` program to send a message to a person with an internet address, you will normally use an address with the format

*username@hostname*

where *username* represents the login name of the recipient and *hostname* represents the domain-style specification of the recipient's home computer.

If you wish to send a message whose home computer belongs to a different network to the one you use, you may have to use a more complicated form of address. As mentioned earlier, e-mail can be exchanged between two networks via gateway computers that belong to both networks. Therefore, you may have to send your message to the gateway computer for forwarding onto the other network. In this case, the e-mail address is written as

*username%hostname@gateway*

where *username* and *hostname* are as before and *gateway* is the name of the gateway computer. An example address in this format would be `joe%xxx.csnet@relay.cs.net`. However, most computers on the internet would accept `joe%xxx.csnet` as a valid address and forward the message to the appropriate gateway computer automatically.

The '`%`' and '`@`' symbols may be considered to be operators with the same meaning, but '`%`' has higher precedence than '`@`'. When an address of the form *xxx@yyy* is used, the message is sent to the computer named *yyy* and then that destination computer inspects the recipient name *xxx*. If *xxx* contains the '`%`' operator, the address is decomposed further and the message is forwarded. You will find the '`%`' operator useful in situations where you wish to reach a recipient whose computer is not registered with NIC, but you know that the computer can be reached from somewhere else on the network.

Finally, there is a style of address that is nearly obsolete but that you may still come across. This is the UUCP style of address. UUCP is an abbreviation for *Unix to Unix Copy* (recall that the copy command is abbreviated to `cp` on Unix), which was originally a protocol for Unix computers to exchange messages via telephone connections. It was later extended to allow message exchange by ethernet. A UUCP address has the following appearance.

```
aaa!bbb!ccc!ddd!joe
```

It defines a path through the network to reach the computer where the intended recipient *joe* has his account. Your computer must make regular UUCP connections to the first computer named in the path, *aaa*. In turn, *aaa* must make connections to *bbb*, which connects to *ccc* and so on.

The disadvantages of UUCP-style addresses are obvious. One problem is that you cannot conveniently publicize your e-mail address because the address depends on the location of the message's sender. The best that you can do is to give your address relative to some major computer site and assume that everyone knows how to send e-mail there. Following this idea, it used to be common to give one's e-mail address in the following manner:

```
{ubc-vision,uw-beaver}!uvunix!csr!nigelh
```

The computers named inside the pair of braces are well-known computers that know how to reach the next computer in the path, *uvunix*. Therefore, the sender of a message needs to construct a path that gets the message to one of the computers named within the braces and then complete the path as indicated.

Aside from the problem of specifying one's own address, UUCP-style addresses become very unwieldy because of the lengths of the paths that may be needed. Finally, it is simply not a good idea to specify a precise path for the message to follow. If one of the communication links is temporarily broken, your message may get held up for days or weeks even though an alternate routing may be available. In contrast, the internet will automatically choose the least congested route for your message and will definitely by-pass links that are broken.

You may come across UUCP-style addresses used in conjunction with domain-style addresses. Such mixed-format addresses can cause trouble. Here is an example.

```
sherwood!little!john@castle.nottingham.uk
```

If you are lucky, a message sent to this address will first be sent to the computer named "castle.nottingham.uk".[2] This computer will then forward the message to the computer named *sherwood*, which will, in turn, forward the message to *little*, where the recipient, *john*, has his account. The difficulty with the address is that it is ambiguous and not all software will decompose the address in the intended manner. (It works if the ' ! ' symbol is treated as an

---

2. Within the United Kingdom, this computer's address would be written as "uk.nottingham.castle". The UK national network, JANET, uses a scheme where the domain names are listed in the reverse order to the internet standard. The addresses are automatically converted when messages are exchanged between JANET and other networks.

operator with higher precedence than '%' and '@' when decoding addresses.) If the mixed-format address does not work, you can try replacing the '@' by '!' as follows,

```
castle.nottingham.uk!sherwood!little!john
```

but no guarantees of success are offered!

If your computer is not a member of the internet, but it has a UUCP connection to a computer that does (i.e., to a gateway computer), you will likely need to use the '!' operator. A plausible address that corresponds to this situation is

```
ggg!st.tropez.fr!brigitte
```

where *ggg* is the gateway computer on the internet and the intended recipient has the internet address `brigitte@st.tropez.fr`. The gateway computer *ggg* is supposed to transform the address it is given, `st.tropez.fr!brigitte` into the internet equivalent. (Be aware, however, that such address transformation is a complicated process and many computer systems do not perform it perfectly.)

Finally, it is worth noting that capitalization within e-mail addresses is not supposed to be significant. The addresses `joe@xxx.csnet` and `joe@XXX.CSNet` should be equivalent. However, changing the capitalization of the recipient's login name may have an effect. It depends on the operating system in use at the recipient's computer.

## 5-5    *Further Reading*

A survey of the many different computer networks, as of 1986, appears in the article "Notable Computer Networks" by J. S. Quarterman and J. C. Hoskins in *Communications of the ACM*, October 1986 (pages 932-971). It describes characteristics and capabilities of each network and gives examples of e-mail addresses used for communication within each network and for exchanging messages between networks. A more up-to-date and authoritative treatment by the first author is available as a book: *The Matrix* by John S. Quarterman (Digital Press, 1990). You may also find the following two books useful. The first is *!%@:: A Directory of Electronic Mail Addressing and Networks*, second edition, by D. Frey and R. Adams (O'Reilly and Associates, 1991) and the other is *Using UUCP & Usenet*, fourth edition, by G. Todino and D. Dougherty (O'Reilly and Associates, 1989).

The paperback book *The Cuckoo's Egg* by Cliff Stoll (Pocket Books, 1990) tells the story of how a hacker who broke into dozens of computers across the United States was tracked down. It gives numerous, if unorthodox, examples of use of the `telnet` command. It should be required reading as a lesson in why you need to be very careful with your passwords and your ".rhosts" files.

The domain name service is described in the SUN document *Administering Domain Name Service*. If you have a SUN computer at your site, your system administrator should possess a copy.

# CHAPTER 6     *COMPILER TOOLS –*
# *LEX*

## *6-1   What is lex Useful For?*

Most programs need to read textual input. In the majority of cases, `fscanf`, the routine for formatted input in the C library, provides all the necessary capabilities. However, `fscanf` may provide too low a level of interface for other programs. In such cases, the lexical analyzer generator `lex` may assist. It allows the programmer to specify a number of patterns (defined using regular expression notation) which are to be matched against the input text. Lex creates a C function that reads input and matches the patterns against the input. Each time a pattern matches, C code supplied by the `lex` user is executed. This C code may perform any desired action. An example of a `lex` pattern is the following which should match almost all English words:

```
[A-Za-z][a-z]*
```

The pattern matches a sequences of characters whose first character is a letter, either an upper-case letter in the range A to Z or a lower-case letter in the range a to z. Following the initial letter, the pattern matches zero or more occurrences of a lower-case letter (the asterisk denotes "zero or more repetitions" in the regular expression notation). The `lex` program processes a file containing a series of such patterns paired with actions defined in C. It generates a C function that will match those patterns against the input. Each time a pattern matches, the associated C statements are executed.

As the saying goes, "use the right tools for the right job." Lex is not appropriate for every input processing task. If efficiency is of paramount importance, you will find that you can hand-code lexical analyzers that are much smaller and much faster than the ones generated by the usual implementation of lex. Even when you are not so concerned about efficiency, and you simply want to create a working program quickly, there are alternatives. If the actions to be performed when a pattern matches are not too complicated you may find the awk tool to be more appropriate. The UNIX on-line manual pages contain a brief, but reasonably complete, description of awk. Another alternative to lex is the regexp package of functions for performing regular expression matching. This freely distributed package enables you to write the entire program in C and make calls to regexp for matching strings read from the input.

## 6-2   Writing lex Specifications

### The lex Input File Structure

A lex input file has three sections. The first section holds definitions; the second section contains rules – patterns paired with C statements to be executed each time the pattern matches; the third section holds arbitrary C code to be appended to the file created by lex.

A complete lex input file is shown in Figure 6-1. The first section of the file provides a definition for the name *Letter*, followed by C declarations for some variables needed in the generated program. The second section contains three patterns, which are given on the left-hand sides of the lines, and three associated actions, given as C statements on the right-hand sides of the lines. The third section provides a C declaration for the main program. The three sections are separated by %% delimiters. From the first and second sections of the file, lex creates a function named yylex. This function reads input (from the standard input stream) checking for occurrences of the three patterns. The first pattern matches an English word and, each time a match occurs, the C statement that increments the variable wordcnt is executed. The second pattern matches any character except the newline character – it matches characters that do not form part of a word. Each time such a character is read, a null action is performed. (If one or more characters in the input are not matched, the default lex action is to print them and then carry on.) The third rule counts the number of newline characters. The third section of the file defines a main program in C that calls the generated yylex function. The file generated by lex from the specification given above will be named "lex.yy.c" and will contain a complete C program. If the C program is compiled and executed, it will behave much like the wc program on UNIX for counting the numbers of word and lines in a file.

## Figure 6-1   A Sample Lex File

```
Letter                  [A-Za-z]
%{
int wordcnt = 0, linecnt = 0;
%}
%%
{Letter}+               { wordcnt++; }
.                       { /* do nothing */ }
\n                      { linecnt++; }
%%
main() {
    (void)yylex();
    printf("Words=%d; lines=%d\n", wordcnt, linecnt);
    exit(0);
}
```

## Regular Expression Notation in lex

### Simple Regular Expressions

Any character, except for the special characters listed below, is a simple pattern that matches this same character. Thus,

```
a
```

is a regular expression (normally abbreviated to R.E.) that matches the letter a.

Two R.E.s may be concatenated by writing them adjacently (with no intervening space). Thus

```
ab
```

is a R.E. that matches the sequence of two characters ab.

A choice between two R.E.s is indicated by an 'or' bar. Thus

```
yes|no
```

matches either the three character sequence yes or the two character sequence no. Note that concatenation has higher precedence than the 'or' operator.

Parentheses may be used in R.E.s to group the subpatterns in any desired manner. Thus, if one really wishes to match either of the strings yeso or yeno, the pattern may be written as follows.

```
ye(s|n)o
```

## Sets of Characters

There are special notations for matching any one character chosen from a set of characters. First, the period character may be written to denote *any* character except a newline character. Thus,

```
d.d
```

is a R.E. that matches a sequence of three characters: the first and last characters are the letter d and the middle character is anything (even a space character or a punctuation character, but not a newline).

Second, explicit sets of characters may be written using square brackets to enclose the characters in the set. Thus

```
[abc]
```

matches one occurrence of any of the characters a, b or c, and is exactly equivalent to the following R.E.

```
a|b|c
```

As a convenience, ranges of characters may be used inside the set notation. The first character in the range is simply followed by a hyphen and then the final character in the range. So

```
[a-zA-Z]
```

is a R.E. that matches any letter of the alphabet, either lower-case or upper-case.[1] If it is desired to have a hyphen character be a member of the set, it is necessary to place the character so that it does not separate two other characters (i.e., it must appear first or last). Thus, the set of all letters plus a hyphen could be written as follows.

```
[-a-zA-Z]
```

A variation on the notation is used to obtain the complement of a set. If the first character after the opening bracket is ^, the R.E. will match any single character that is not listed. Thus,

```
[^a-zA-Z]
```

will match any character *except* a letter. If you wish to write a set that contains a caret character, you should obviously not write it in the first position. For example,

```
[;,^]
```

matches one of the three characters: semicolon, comma or caret.

---

1. Note that a range like a-z may not match all the letters of the alphabet in a language that has accented characters.

## Repetitions

An asterisk is used to denote zero or more repetitions of the R.E. that immediately precedes it. For example,

```
re*d
```

is a R.E. that matches any of the sequences `rd`, `red`, `reed`, `reeed`, and so on.

A plus symbol denotes one or more repetitions of the R.E. that precedes it. Thus,

```
re+d
```

matches all the same sequences as in the preceding example with the exception of `rd`.

A question mark denotes zero or one repetitions of the preceding R.E. (i.e., it denotes an optional part of the pattern). For example,

```
hoo?t
```

matches `hot` or `hoot`.

There is a notation for full control over the degree of repetition. If, for example, we wish to limit identifiers to a maximum length of 31 characters, we can write the R.E. as follows.

```
[a-z][a-z0-9]{0,30}
```

The two numbers inside the curly braces specify the number of allowed repetitions of the preceding R.E.

## Macro Definitions

To simplify writing R.E.s, `lex` allows strings to be predefined and named in the first part (the definitions part) of the input file. For example,

```
Digit        [0-9]
```

defines `Digit` as being a name for the string `[0-9]`. In the second section of the file, we may write `{Digit}` and `lex` will textually substitute the appropriate string. For example, we may write a pattern for floating-point numbers, without an exponent part, as

```
{Digit}+\.{Digit}+
```

Note that this substitution facility is merely textual substitution (similar to that provided in the C compiler's preprocessor). It is possible to get confusing results if the substitution strings are not simple or are not fully parenthesized. Consider the following example.

```
AB           a|b
CD           c|d
%%
{AB}{CD}     return 1;
...
```

The rule will match any of the three strings

```
a  bc  d
```

because the pattern is the same as writing the R.E. (a|bc|d) whereas the user would probably expect the pattern to be equivalent to (a|b)(c|d).


## Metacharacters

It is obvious that certain characters, like asterisks and parentheses, are metacharacters of the R.E. notation. If it is necessary to write one of these characters to be matched as part of a R.E., the character can be escaped by preceding it with a backslash character. For example,

```
\([^)(]*\)
```

is a R.E. that matches a left parenthesis, then zero or more occurrences of any character other than a parenthesis, and then a right parenthesis. Note that the parentheses do not need escaping inside the set (fewer characters are special inside a set). An alternative way of escaping characters is to enclose them within double quote characters. Thus,

```
"(*)"
```

is a R.E. that matches three consecutive characters: left parenthesis, asterisk, right parenthesis. The complete list of all characters that might need escaping consists of the white space characters (space and tab) plus the following:

```
( )  [  ]  {  }  %  |  .  ,  *  ?  +  -  <  >  \  /  ^  $  "
```

Some additional escapes are defined for specifying non-printing characters. These are the usual C language escape sequences of \n for a linefeed character, \t for a tab, and \b for a backspace.


## Beginning and End of Line Context

A frequent requirement is to match a pattern only if it occurs at the beginning of a line or at the end of a line. For this purpose, lex provides two metacharacters. The caret character matches a fictitious symbol at the start of a line and the dollar character matches a fictitious character at the end of the line. For example,

```
^#include
```

is a R.E. that matches the 8 characters "#include", but only if they start at the beginning of the line. Similarly,

```
\.$
```

matches a period appearing at the end of a line.

## Other Context Restrictions

Lex provides more powerful context restrictions than the beginning and end-of-line contexts. The notations for specifying left and right contexts are not described here. They are not usually required for defining the lexical structure of modern programming languages (they are required for Fortran IV, for example).

## Associating Patterns with Actions

The second section of the lex input file is written as a sequence of rules. Each rule is a pairing of a R.E. with an action given as a C statement. Whenever the pattern matches the input, the associated action is executed. The R.E. must be written at the beginning of a line (i.e., it cannot be preceded by spaces or tabs). An action must always be provided, even if it is a null C statement. One or more spaces or tabs must separate the R.E. from the associated action.

Figure 6-1 contained a complete example of a lex specification file and showed how actions are paired with patterns. It also illustrated two more points. First, global declarations of variables may be added to the generated file by putting them in the definitions section, enclosed by the special brackets %{ and %}. Second, the example shows that rules may overlap. The second rule has the potential for matching a letter of the alphabet and thus conflicts with the first rule. Lex resolves the ambiguity by using the rules in the order that they are given. When there is a choice of rules to apply, lex uses the rule that is given first.

Another form of ambiguity arises when patterns contain instances of other patterns (or even of the original pattern). For example, the rule

```
[a-z]+        {cnt++;}
```

applied to the input ab could match once or it could match twice. The R.E. can match the two characters ab, or it can match the single character a. After matching the single character, the rule can be applied again to the input to match the character b. The ambiguity is resolved by the *longest match* principle. That is, lex will try to match as many characters as possible with the R.E.

If some part of the input fails to match any pattern, lex applies a default rule of printing the non-matching characters. Except when debugging the lex patterns, this is likely to be undesirable behavior.

The characters matched by a pattern are held in an array named yytext. The characters are followed by an ASCII null character and you may therefore use yytext as a normal C character string. The length of the string is available in the integer variable yyleng. It is common for actions in rules to access the yytext array.

## 6-3 *Efficient Use Of lex*

It is tempting to list the keywords of a language as regular expressions. For example, an extract from a `lex` file for Pascal might read as follows:

```
    . . .
%%
program         { return 1; }
procedure       { return 2; }
begin           { return 3; }
end             { return 4; }

    . . .
{Letter}({Letter}|{Digit})*
                        { return 27; /* identifier */ }

    . . .
```

Do *not* do this if there are more than a few keywords! The finite state automaton that `lex` generates to recognize these regular expressions is likely to have thousands of states and you will end up with an extremely large C program. Much better is to catch all keywords and identifiers with a single pattern and then look the word up in a table of keywords. That is, the `lex` specification should be written in the way shown in Figure 6-2. (Of course, a hash table look-up function would be preferable to the linear search programmed in the

### Figure 6-2  Matching Keywords in Lex

```
%{
int kwd_lookup();
%}
%%
{Letter}({Letter}|{Digit})*  { return kwd_lookup(); }
    . . .
%%
struct { char *name; int code; } keyword[NUMKWDS] = {
        {"program", 1}, {"procedure", 2}, ... };
int kwd_lookup() {
    register int i;
    for( i = 0; i < NUMKWDS; i++ ) {
        if (strcmp(yytext,keyword[i].name) == 0)
            return keyword[i].code;
    }
    return 27;
}
```

example.) As a matter of style, it is also preferable to use preprocessor identifiers instead of integers for the return values of the scanner. For example, it is better practice to write

```
return IDENTIFIER;
```

than the `return 27;` statement shown in the figure. Definitions for the preprocessor identifiers can be placed in a separate ".h" file, which is included in the generated scanner by a `lex` directive like the following.

```
%{
#include "filename.h"
%}
```

When a `lex`-generated scanner is used with a `yacc`-generated parser, `yacc` can optionally generate a suitable ".h" file.

Another practical issue is concerned with the processing of comments. In most programming languages, comments may have unlimited length. It is a very bad idea to write a R.E. in a `lex` specification to match an entire comment. The `yytext` array has a fixed size and therefore a long comment will overflow the array and overwrite other variables in the program. That is, a rule like this one for Pascal comments

```
\{[^}]*}          { /* ignore comment */ }
```

is dangerous. The simple solution is to provide a rule whose R.E. matches the beginning of a comment and whose action reads and discards input until the close of the comment is seen. The `lex` rule for matching a Pascal comment should be coded in the manner shown in Figure 6-3. The function `input()` is a macro supplied by `lex` that obtains the next input character. At the end of input, this macro returns the value 0 (*not* the special code EOF used by input functions in the library "<stdio.h>"). It is important to check for the end of input condition in user-supplied code for scanning text (otherwise an error like an unclosed comment can cause the scanner to get caught in an infinite loop). Note: if string constants are to be recognized by the scanner and if they can also have unlimited length, they should be processed using similar code.

---

### Figure 6-3  Matching Pascal Comments with Lex

```
"{"     {   register int ch;
            do {   /* skip to right brace or EOF */
                ch = input();
            } while( ch != '}' && ch != 0 );
            if (ch == 0) {  /* we hit EOF */
                (void)fprintf(stderr,
                    "error: unclosed comment\n");
                return 0;
            }
        }
```

---

## 6-4   Interfacing lex Scanners

The `lex` program creates a file named "lex.yy.c". This file contains a function named `yylex`, which takes no arguments. If this function is called, it will process input taken from the standard input stream until either a `return` statement is executed in one of the rules, or until the end-of-file is reached. In the latter case, the integer 0 is returned as the function result. The `yylex` function may be called repeatedly as long as input remains to be processed.

By default, the generated scanner reads from the standard input stream. If you want to read from a different source, it is easily accomplished. Just include code like the following in a function defined in the third section of the `lex` input file and call the function before `yylex` is invoked.

```
yyin = fopen("somefile", "r");
if (yyin == NULL) {
    perror( "somefile" ); exit(1);
}
```

This code opens a file named "somefile" and uses the result to override the source of input used by `lex`.

Sometimes it is desirable to read the input from more than one file. When the end of one file is reached, the file needs to be closed and a new file opened as the source of input. To provide such a capability, the lex-generated scanner will call an external function named `yywrap` whenever it reaches the end of file. You must provide this function (or else allow a default `yywrap` function to be loaded from the lex library, as explained below). Your `yywrap` function must return 1 (i.e., *true*) if there is no more input to be read from another file. If you do wish to handle multifile input, `yywrap` should close the `yyin` input stream, possibly output some data concerning the file that has just been processed, open a new file using `yyin` as the file descriptor again, and return zero (i.e., *false*) to the caller.

The number of the current input line is maintained in the integer variable `yylineno`. This variable is useful for generating error messages. The text string that matched the pattern is held in the character array `yytext`. (Note: the array size is given by the preprocessor constant `BUFSIZ` which is normally defined as 1024 in the <stdio.h> header file on Berkeley UNIX-based systems.)

## 6-5   Running lex

The specification file must have a name which ends with the suffix ".l". If, for example, the file is named "lang.l", you may simply execute the command

```
lex lang.l
```

If no errors are detected, the result will be a new file named "lex.yy.c".

If the `lex` specification file contained a function called `main` and does not need to be linked with any other C files, "lex.yy.c" should be a complete program. It could then be compiled with the command

```
cc lex.yy.c -ll
```

to create an executable program named "a.out". The '`-ll`' option on the command indicates that `lex` library functions are to be included, as required. If you omit this option, you will likely get a loader error message complaining that the function `_yywrap` is missing.

If your "lex.yy.c" file does need linking with other C files, you should compile it with the command:

```
cc -c lex.yy.c
```

When you subsequently link the object file "lex.yy.o" with the other files, do not forget to provide the '`-ll`' option on the command.

Note that a Gnu version of `lex` exists. It is distributed by the Free Software Foundation and is called `flex`. The usage of `flex` is identical to `lex`. (However, the scanner generated by `flex` is usually smaller and faster.)


## 6-6   Further Reading

Almost any compiler text contains a discussion of regular expressions and lexical analysis. In particular, *Compilers: Principles, Techniques and Tools* by A.V. Aho, R. Sethi and J.D. Ullman (Addison-Wesley 1986) contains several pages of material on `lex`. A complete chapter on `lex` may be found in *Introduction to Compiler Construction with UNIX* by A.T. Schreiner and H.G. Friedman Jr. (Prentice-Hall 1985). It features prominently in *Introduction to Compiling Techniques: A First Course using ANSI C, LEX and YACC* by J.P. Bennett (McGraw-Hill 1990). Another book is titled *Lex & Yacc*, by W.A. Mason and D. Brown (O'Reilly & Associates 1990). It contains complete examples showing `lex` interfaced with `yacc` as well as a good introduction to `lex` usage. Finally, the original description of `lex`, presented in a tutorial manner, may be found in a document supplied with the UNIX Programmer's Reference Manual. It is called *Lex - A Lexical Analyzer Generator* by M.E. Lesk and E. Schmidt.

# CHAPTER 7 — *COMPILER TOOLS — YACC*

---

## 7-1  *Introduction to Syntactic Analysis*

---

Many programs, particularly compilers and programs for processing natural languages, need to check and analyze the structure of their input. Let us take, for example, one line of an input file to be read by a Pascal compiler:

```
{find max} if a >= b then max := a else max := b;
```

Character-level analysis (or lexical analysis) is used to extract the language elements that appear on that line. These language elements (or lexical elements or tokens) are: the keyword `if`, the identifier `a`, the comparison operator `>=`, and so on. Note that the comment and the spaces in the line are not considered to be lexical elements. A lexical analyzer can be automatically generated by `lex` or equivalent tools from specifications of the lexical elements.

A higher-level form of analysis needs to be performed on the sequences of tokens. Syntactic analysis performs pattern matching on the sequence to discover that it corresponds to an if-statement, where an if-statement is described by the pattern:

```
<if-statement> ::= if <expression> then <statement>
                   else <statement>
```

In turn, the sub-sequence  a>=b is matched by the pattern:

```
<expression> ::= <expression> <comparison>
<expression>
```

and the two statements are matched by the patterns:

```
<statement> ::= <assignment>
<assignment> ::= <variable> := <expression>
```

Additional patterns, like the following, are needed to complete the analysis.

```
<expression> ::= <variable>
<variable> ::= <identifier>
<comparison> ::= >=
```

The complete set of patterns is known as a *grammar* and defines the syntactic structure of the language. Each pattern is called a *production rule*, or *rule* for short. The rules have been written using angle brackets to enclose the names of non-elementary concepts. Each such concept, <expression>, for example, must be defined by one or more rules. The symbol ::= can be read as the word "becomes". Other symbols that appear in the rules, such as >=, represent lexical elements. (An exception is made for <identifier>. If we write it without the angle brackets, it would suggest that there is a keyword in the language called **identifier**.)

As a shorthand notation, a group of rules with a common left-hand side may be compressed. For example the four rules

```
<comparison> ::= >=
<comparison> ::= >
<comparison> ::= <=
<comparison> ::= <
```

may also be written more succinctly as follows.

```
<comparison> ::= >= | > | <= | <
```

The vertical bar can be read as the word "or" and its role is to separate alternative right-hand sides.

To introduce more terminology, each name used on the left-hand side of the ::= separator in a rule is called a *non-terminal symbol* of the grammar. A name or symbol in the grammar that does not appear on the left-hand side of any rule is called a *terminal symbol*. A terminal symbol is a lexical element of the language.

One particular non-terminal symbol is the top-level concept that is being defined, and is known as the *start symbol*. In a complete Pascal grammar, the start symbol would likely be called <program> and have a definition like

```
<program> ::= program <ident> <options> ; <block> .
```

A grammar specifies which sequences of tokens have a desired structure. In other words, a grammar defines a *language*. (The language being formally defined as the set of all sequences of lexical elements that satisfy the grammar rules.) Our example grammar rules are written in a notation known as BNF (Backus-Naur Form). BNF or equivalent notations are commonly used to define the syntactic structure of programming languages.

It is usually either difficult or extremely tedious to construct a program that matches a sequence of lexical elements against the grammar rules. Fortunately there are programs to automate the task. One such is yacc. The yacc program reads a file containing syntactic rules (in a notation similar to BNF) and creates a C file containing a function for performing matches against the syntactic rules. Each time the function uses one of the rules, it executes some C statements (supplied in the specification file).

## 7-2    The yacc Input File Structure

### The Overall Format

A yacc input file has three parts (just as for lex): a definitions part, a rules part, and a C code part for appending arbitrary C code to the generated parser. An example yacc file that gives a grammar for a tiny subset of English is shown in Figure 7-1.

---

**Figure 7-1   An Example YACC File**

```
%start Sentence
%token chase chases hit hits
%token a an the cat dog ball house
%token I me he she him her
%%
Sentence: Subject Verb Object '.' ;
Subject: Article Noun
       | SubjPronoun ;
Verb: chase | chases | hit | hits ;
Object: Article Noun
      | ObjPronoun ;
Article: a | an | the ;
Noun: cat | dog | ball | house ;
SubjPronoun: I | he | she ;
ObjPronoun: me | him | her ;
%%
```

---

Note that angle brackets are not used to distinguish terminal symbols from non-terminal symbols. Instead, non-terminal symbols, such as `noun`, are written as identifiers. Terminal symbols may also be written as identifiers, in which case there must be a declaration for the identifier in the definitions section of the file. Alternatively, terminal symbols may be written as quoted strings, the period at the end of the first rule is an example. A colon character is used instead of the `::=` symbol of BNF and the end of a group of rules is marked by a semicolon.

If the name of the example file is "english.y" and is processed by `yacc` with the command

```
yacc -d english.y
```

two files are created. One, called "y.tab.c", contains the C code source for a function named `yyparse`. This C function will process a sequence of lexical elements (terminal symbols or tokens) and match it against the supplied grammar rules. The function assumes that each lexical element is represented by an integer code. The other file is called "y.tab.h" and contains preprocessor definitions for those terminal symbols that are denoted by identifiers in the grammar rules. For example, the ".h" file will contain a line like

```
#define chases 258
```

indicating that the integer code assumed by `yyparse` for the token `chases` is 258. The ".h" file can be included by a lexical analyzer, perhaps one created by `lex`, to ensure that the parser and the lexical analyzer conform to the same numbering scheme.

## Defining yacc Grammar Rules

A single grammar rule is written in the style:

```
lefthandside : righthandside ;
```

where *lefthandside* is an identifier used for a non-terminal symbol, and *righthandside* is a sequence of zero or more symbols separated by white space (spaces, tabs or newlines). Each symbol in a *righthandside* may be a non-terminal or a terminal symbol. When there are two or more rules with the same left-hand side, the rules may be combined in the following manner:

```
lefthandside : righthandside1
       |          righthandside2
       |          righthandside3
       ...
       |          righthandsideN ;
```

A terminal symbol may be written as an identifier, in which case, there must be a declaration for the identifier appearing in the first section of the `yacc` input file (see below). Terminal symbols may also be written as character strings. For example, `'+'` and `'=='` could be used as terminal symbols in the grammar. For reasons to be explained later, it is not a good idea to use the quoted string form for a symbol containing more than one character; i.e., the '+' example, above, is acceptable and normal but the '==' example will lead to some awkward interfacing problems.

The matching of input tokens against grammar rules proceeds according to a parsing algorithm called LALR(1). A description of the method may be found in most books on compiler construction. Not every grammar is suitable for use with the LALR(1) parsing method. Some grammars will cause error messages to be generated by yacc, and others may cause a warning message to appear. Even if the message is just a warning, it would be wise to attempt to understand the reason. Yacc's method of correcting the problem may result in the parser not recognizing the same language you thought you had specified.

The LALR(1) method used in the parser is a form of *bottom-up* parsing. Some understanding of the bottom-up approach is essential if you wish to use yacc for developing a compiler. Here is an example, using the grammar for a simple English sentence, as given above. We use the sentence "a dog chases me." as the example input. The parser maintains a stack of symbols and this stack is initially empty. The parser performs a series of actions, but there are only two basic actions. One action, called *shift*, is to obtain a token from the input and push it onto the stack. The other action, called *reduce*, is used when the parser has the right-hand side of some rule on top of the stack. The action is to pop all the symbols of that right-hand side off the stack and push the left-hand side symbol on instead. For our example input, the complete series of actions and subsequent stack contents is shown in Table 7-1.

## Table 7-1   A Trace of Parsing Actions

| | **Parse Action** | **Stack Contents** |
|---|---|---|
| 1. | *Shift* a | a |
| 2. | *Reduce*: Article ::= a | Article |
| 3. | *Shift* dog | Article dog |
| 4. | *Reduce*: Noun ::= dog | Article Noun |
| 5. | *Reduce*: Subject ::= Article | Noun Subject |
| 6. | *Shift* chases | Subject chases |
| 7. | *Reduce*: Verb ::= chases | Subject Verb |
| 8. | *Shift* me | Subject Verb me |
| 9. | *Reduce*: ObjPronoun ::= me | Subject Verb ObjPronoun |

## Table 7-1   A Trace of Parsing Actions (Continued)

| | | |
|---|---|---|
| 10. | *Reduce*: Object ::= ObjPronoun | Subject Verb Object |
| 11. | *Shift* . | Subject Verb Object . |
| 12. | *Reduce*: Sentence ::= Subject Verb Object . | Sentence |
| 13. | *Halt, and report success* | Sentence |

The main point to notice is that the parser applies the production rules in reverse – building up a right-hand side on top of the stack and then replacing it by a left-hand side. At the conclusion of a successful parse, all the input tokens have been read and the stack contains only the start symbol of the grammar.

## Defining Operator Precedences & Associativities

With normal mathematical notation, we are accustomed to particular ways of associating the operators. For example, we normally compute the value of

```
2 + 3 * 5
```

as if the expression had been written as follows.

```
2 + ( 3 * 5 )
```

The normal explanation given for this is that the multiplication operator has *higher precedence* than the addition operator, and so we should perform the multiplication before the addition.

Another example where mathematical conventions dictate a certain order of evaluation is the following.

```
7 - 2 - 1
```

Here it is evaluated as if it had been written

```
( 7 - 2 ) - 1
```

and not as this

```
7 - (2 - 1)
```

The normal explanation for choosing the first interpretation over the second is that the subtraction operator is *left-associative*. Right-associative operators are relatively unusual in programming languages, but a few examples exist such as the exponentiation operator in FORTRAN and the assignment operators in C.

In constructing a grammar, the precedences and associativities of the operators can be incorporated into the production rules. Thus, the following grammar for arithmetic expressions gives the operators their usual associativities and precedences.

```
Expression : Expression '+' Term
           | Expression '-' Term
           | Term ;
Term : Term '*' Factor
     | Term '/' Factor
     | Factor ;
Factor : Primary '^' Factor
       | Primary ;
Primary : '(' Expression ')'
        | identifier ;
```

To be precise, there are five operators. Exponentiation (represented by the '^' symbol) is given the highest precedence and is made right associative. Multiplication and division are given equal but lower precedence and are made left associative. Addition and subtraction have the lowest precedence and are also left associative.

You do not really need to understand how the preceding grammar rules caused some operators to be left-associative and another right-associative or determined their precedences.[1] This is because yacc provides a simpler mechanism to achieve the same effect. First, all the operators are treated equally when defining the grammar rules. Thus, the yacc version of the preceding example is the following.

```
Expression : Expression '+' Expression
           | Expression '-' Expression
           | Expression '*' Expression
           | Expression '/' Expression
           | Expression '^' Expression
           | '(' Expression ')'
           | identifier ;
```

Now this grammar is ambiguous – there are sequences of tokens that can be parsed in two different ways. For example,

```
id1 + id2 * id3
```

may be parsed as though (id1+id2) is one operand for a multiplication and id3 is the other. The alternative parse corresponds to the conventional interpretation; namely, id1 is one operand for an addition and (id2*id3) is the other operand. Yacc can disambiguate

---

1. The general approach is easy to imitate however. Left-associative operators are introduced in left-recursive production rules, similarly for right-associative operators. The expression grammar is organized as a series of as many levels as needed (Expression, Term, Factor and Primary in this example). The lowest priority operators are introduced in the rules for the first level, and so on.

the two parses, choosing the parse with the desired meaning, if it is given declarations for operator precedences and associativities. The following definitions should be included in the first part of the `yacc` input file to give the operators their conventional properties.

```
%left '+' '-'
%left '*' '/'
%right '^'
```

Each of these declarations specifies the associativities of the named operators. The order in which the operators are listed defines their precedence ordering. Operators that are listed on the same line all have the same precedence. An operator that appears on a later line has higher precedence than operators listed in earlier lines.

The possible declarations for operators are: `%left`, `%right`, and `%nonassoc`. The first two are self-explanatory. The third declaration, `%nonassoc`, means that the listed operators do not associate either to the left or to the right. Examples of such operators occur in FORTRAN where comparison operators cannot be applied to the result of a comparison. Consequently, the simple comparison

```
A .GE. B
```

is valid (meaning A>=B) but the compound comparison

```
A .GE. B .GE. C
```

is syntactically invalid. The `yacc` declaration

```
%nonassoc '.EQ.' '.NE.' '.GT.' '.GE.' '.LT.' '.LE.'
```

has the desired effect.

Sometimes the same symbol is used in more than way. For example, the minus sign is used to denote both the infix subtraction operator and a prefix negation operator in most languages. Similarly for the plus symbol which is used as both the infix addition operator and as a prefix plus operator in many languages. The two different uses cause a difficulty with the yacc mechanism for declaring precedences. If the grammar for arithmetic expressions includes the following rules

```
Expr :   Expr '+' Expr    |   Expr '-' Expr
     |   Expr '*' Expr    |   Expr '/' Expr
     |   '+' Expr         |   '-' Expr
     |   id               |   '(' Expr ')' ;
```

we would like to declare the infix version of '−' with a lower precedence than the prefix version. However, the `yacc` precedence declaration format does not permit us to specify which version of '−' is being given which precedence. The recommended solution is a subterfuge. We first invent fictitious terminal symbols to correspond to the extra meanings attached to operators. Let us invent the symbols UNARY_PLUS and UNARY_MINUS for the prefix versions of plus and minus. Then we can declare the precedences as follows.

```
%left '+' '-'
%left '*' '/'
%right UNARY_PLUS UNARY_MINUS
```

Next, we have to tell `yacc` that the prefix uses of plus and minus have the same precedences as these invented symbols. There is a special `yacc` construction for this. We simply replace the two rules that introduce the prefix plus and minus as shown here.

```
Expr :  Expr '+' Expr    |    Expr '-' Expr
     |  Expr '*' Expr    |    Expr '/' Expr
     |  '+' Expr   %prec UNARY_PLUS
     |  '-' Expr   %prec UNARY_MINUS
     |  id               |    '(' Expr ')' ;
```

When constructing the parser program, `yacc` normally uses the precedence and associativity that is declared for the last terminal symbol in the right-hand side of a rule. The `%prec` construction explicitly specifies a different terminal symbol to take this information from. It does not matter if the specified terminal symbol is not used in the grammar.

## Adding yacc Semantic Actions

Just knowing that the sequence of tokens matches the grammar rules is usually not sufficient. We normally wish to perform some processing on the input. `Yacc` provides a mechanism for attaching C code to the rules so that each time the rule is used, the C code is executed. For example, if the grammar contains only the following rules:

```
Input : List ;
List  : identifier
      | List ',' identifier ;
```

it would match a sequence of one or more identifiers separated by commas. We can attach C code actions to count the number of identifiers in the list as follows.

```
Input : List { printf( "%d\n", cnt ); } ;
List  : identifier { cnt = 1; }
      | List ',' identifier { cnt = cnt + 1; } ;
```

When an input like

```
a , b , c
```

is read and matched, the rule

```
List ::= identifier
```

is used to match the first identifier in the list, a. The attached action will set the variable `cnt` to 1. The next rule to be used is

```
List ::= List ',' identifier
```

---

### Figure 7-2    Conversion to Reverse Polish

```
%start Input
%left '+' '-'
%left '*' '/'
%token identifier integer
%{ extern char yytext[]; %}
%%
Input : Exp { printf("\n"); } ;
Exp :    Exp '+' Exp { printf( " +" ); }
    |    Exp '-' Exp { printf( " -" ); }
    |    Exp '*' Exp { printf( " *" ); }
    |    Exp '/' Exp { printf( " /" ); }
    |    '(' Exp ')'
    |    identifier { printf(" %s", yytext); }
    |    integer { printf(" %s",yytext); } ;
%%
```

---

which will match the list already seen followed by a comma and the identifier b. The attached action increments `cnt`. The rule is used a second time to match the second comma and the identifier c, so `cnt` is incremented again. Finally, the rule

```
Input ::= List
```

is used and the attached semantic action prints the value of `cnt`. Note: to complete the example, it is necessary to declare the variable `cnt` and this is accomplished by including the line

```
%{ int cnt; %}
```

in the first section of the `yacc` input file.

If the `yacc`-generated parser is combined with a `lex`-generated scanner, the actions associated with the rules have access to the text of each token (such as the name of the identifier) in the array `yytext`. (Other scanner-generators provide similar facilities.)

Figure 7-2 shows a complete example of a `yacc` file for reading an arithmetic expression and outputting that expression in reverse Polish notation (RPN). RPN is a notation where an operator follows its operands. Provided that we do not have two different operators with the same name (such as the infix minus and prefix minus operators), RPN removes the need for parenthesization. Given an input like

```
a * ( b - c )
```

the `yacc`-generated program will output the characters

```
a b - c *
```

---

### Figure 7-3 A Desk-Calculator Program

```
%start Input
%token int
%left '+' '-'
%left '*' '/'
%{
extern char yytext();
%}
%%
Input :    Exp { printf( " = %d\n", $1 ); } ;
Exp :      Exp '+' Exp { $$ = $1 + $3; }
    |      Exp '-' Exp { $$ = $1 - $3; }
    |      Exp '*' Exp { $$ = $1 * $3; }
    |      Exp '/' Exp { $$ = $1 / $3; }
    |      '(' Exp ')' { $$ = $2; }
    |      num { $$ = atoi(yytext); } ;
%%
```

---

## 7-3  The yacc Semantic Stack

### Introduction to Semantic Attributes

The example of converting arithmetic expressions to reverse Polish form did not require any information to be accumulated – it was simply printed. Consider now the problem of building a desk calculator. For example, when it is given the input

```
(7 * 4 + 2) / 3
```

our program should output the following line.

```
= 10
```

As the input is parsed, we will recognize subexpressions, e.g., $7*4$ is the first subexpression to be seen. They must be computed and their results saved. The natural way to look at the problem is to consider the non-terminal symbol that represents a subexpression in the grammar as having an associated value (the integer value of the subexpression). Yacc supports exactly this concept (and by default the associated values have int type). The desk calculator grammar may be specified in yacc as shown in Figure 7-3.

The notation $$ represents the value associated with the non-terminal on the left-hand side of the rule; $1 represents the value for the first symbol on the right-hand side, $2 for the second symbol, and so on.

It is instructive to trace part of the execution of the desk calculator example on an input, say

```
(7 * 4 + 2) / 3
```

The sequence of parsing actions and semantic action executions proceeds as shown in Table 7-2. In this table, the integer value associated with the *Exp* non-terminal is shown as a subscript.

## Table 7-2   A Trace of Semantic Actions

|  | Parse Action | Semantics | Parse Stack Contents |
|---|---|---|---|
| 1. | *Shift* '(' | — | ( |
| 2. | *Shift* num | — | ( num |
| 3. | *Reduce*: Exp ::= num | $\$\$=7;$ | ( $Exp_7$ |
| 4. | *Shift* '*' | — | ( $Exp_7$ * |
| 5. | *Shift* num | — | ( $Exp_7$ * num |
| 6. | *Reduce*: Exp ::= num | $\$\$=4;$ | ( $Exp_7$ * $Exp_4$ |
| 7. | *Reduce*: Exp ::= Exp '*' Exp | $\$\$=\$1*\$3;$ | ( $Exp_{28}$ |
| 8. | *Shift* '+' | — | ( $Exp_{28}$ + |

...

Semantic actions in a grammar used with `yacc` almost always take the form

```
$$ = some function of $1, $2, ...
```

This corresponds to a *synthesized attribute* evaluation, as it is called in books on compiler construction. Switching to the standard terminology, each grammar symbol may have zero or more *attribute values* associated with it.

Note that the integer attribute that `yacc` associates with each grammar symbol is held in a stack that grows and contracts in the same way as the parse stack. We can imagine the two stacks to be located side-by-side. For example, if the rule

```
Exp ::= '(' Exp ')'  { $$ = $2; }  ;
```

is being used, the notation $1 refers to the integer attribute of ' ( ' (if there is one), $2 to the integer attribute of the `Exp` used in the RHS, and similarly for $3. A semantic action such as the one shown is necessary to ensure that the attributes associated with the expression enclosed in parentheses are propagated to the entire expression, corresponding the use of *Exp* on the left-hand side of the rule.

In a rule of the following form,

```
Exp1 ::= Exp2 { $$ = $1; };
```

the semantic action code is unnecessary. Just writing

```
Exp1 ::= Exp2 ;
```

has the same effect. The explanation is that the locations used for $$ and $1 on the semantic stack are the same location. Conceptually, the $1 value is popped and then the $$ value must be pushed back on. But since the stack entry does not get overwritten, an explicit assignment to $$ is unnecessary. Even if the right-hand side of the rule contains several symbols, the semantic action

```
{ $$ = $1; }
```

may still be omitted.

Yacc does not prohibit you from using the notation $0 to refer to the integer attribute of whatever symbol happens to be located immediately below the ' (' symbol on the parse stack, $-1 to access the symbol below that, and so on. However, it is unwise to take advantage of this feature because its correct operation requires you to have an excellent understanding of how the parsing process operates.

You are allowed to embed a semantic action anywhere in the right-hand side of a rule. Here is a highly contrived example of a rule with an embedded action:

```
A : a B { $$ = $2 * 2; } b C { $$ = $3 + $5; } ;
```

For the purposes of parsing and executing the semantic actions, yacc considers this rule to be equivalent to the following two rules:

```
A :      a B Temp1 b C { $$ = $3 + $5; } ;
Temp1 : { $$ = $0 * 2; } ;
```

The use of $0 is *not* a misprint. The explanation is as follows. A semantic action does not cause any parsing actions to occur, so therefore we can replace its occurrence by an invented non-terminal defined by a rule with an empty right-hand side (as shown). Next, we can consider that invented non-terminal symbol (Temp1) to have an associated attribute and it is that attribute that is referenced by the $$ notation in the embedded semantic action. The notation $2 used in the embedded action refers to the attribute of B. In the transformed version of the grammar, B will be the top entry on the parse stack whenever the rule

```
Temp1 ::= ε
```

is used. It will be located one position below the (fictitious) first symbol on the right-hand side of this rule and hence it can be accessed as $0. The action at the end of the first rule,

```
$$ = $3 + $5;
```

takes the value for the embedded action (corresponding to `Temp1`) and adds it to the value for `C`, the symbol in the fifth position. To summarize, when you use `$$` in an embedded action, it refers to an attribute for the action *itself* (not for the LHS of the rule). However, when you use `$1`, etc., in an embedded action, it simply refers to an attribute of a symbol in the RHS of the enclosing rule.

The final rule of the desk calculator grammar read as follows.

```
Exp : num { $$ = atoi(yytext); } ;
```

To avoid problems synchronizing actions performed in the parser with actions performed in the lexical analyzer, it is desirable to simplify this rule to the following.

```
Exp : num ;
```

This can be arranged by having the lexical analyzer provide an integer-valued attribute for the token num. The global variable `yylval` (short for "lexical value") may be assigned the desired attribute value in the lexical analyzer just before it returns the num token to the parser. For our example, the lexical analyzer could contain the following lines.

```
extern int yylval;
...
yylval = atoi(yytext); /* set the attribute of num */
return num; /* return code for num token */
```

The synchronization problem that was alluded to, above, can be exemplified with the following scenario. Suppose we were to add the following production rule to the grammar.

```
Exp : num { $1 = atoi(yytext); } '!'
          { $$ = factorial($1); };
```

The intention is that our desk calculator should be able to accept an input such as

```
3! + 4
```

and get a result of 10 (using the *factorial* function). However, the extra rule forces the parser to read the token that follows a *num* token to determine whether to reduce by the rule Exp→num or to reduce by the rule Exp→num!. Thus the `yytext` array that contains the text of the num token gets overwritten (by the text of the following token) before the semantic actions that use the `yytext` array are executed. Associating the integer value with the token in the lexical analyzer avoids this catastrophe.

## Specifying Semantic Attribute Types

For almost all compiler applications, a single integer attribute is insufficient. More likely, you would like to have an attribute that is a pointer to a structure that contains several pieces of information. Another possibility is that some grammar symbols have one kind of attribute (such as a pointer to a structure) while some other grammar symbols have a different kind (such as a character string).

The parser generated by `yacc` defines grammar symbol attributes as having the type `YYSTYPE`. By default, `yacc` supplies a preprocessor macro definition for `YYSTYPE` that expands to the type `int`. However, if you provide your own preprocessor definition for `YYSTYPE`, this will override the default definition. Therefore, if you wish to make every attribute have a C structure as its type, you can include a declaration like the following.

```
%{
typedef struct { int a; char * b; } attrtype;
#define YYSTYPE attrtype
%}
```

in the first section of the grammar file. (Warning: you have to be careful because the generated parser accesses the name `YYSTYPE` in a declaration similar to the following.

```
YYSTYPE a, b;
```

Therefore, a definition similar to

```
#define YYSTYPE char *
```

leads to a type mismatch when you try to compile the generated parser.)

## Using the %union Declaration

The ability to define the attribute type for every symbol as a C structure or as a C union type is adequate for any application. However, as a convenience to the user, an alternative mechanism for defining attribute types is provided. It is frequently the case that you want some grammar symbols to have one type, say `char *`, and other grammar symbols to have a different type, say `float`. Since an entry in the semantic value stack represents only one symbol at a time, we could define the semantic attribute type as being a union type, e.g.,

```
union { char *name; float val; }
```

Then, if `FExp` is a non-terminal symbol with a `float` attribute, a rule such as the following would be possible.

```
FExp : '-' FExp { $$.val = - $2.val; };
```

However, `yacc` can supply all the necessary ".name" and ".val" suffixes automatically. To take advantage of this feature, the first section of the grammar file must contain a `%union` declaration that names all the different attribute types. Then `%type` declarations are required for every non-terminal symbol that has an attribute value. If any terminal symbols have attribute values that are returned by the lexical analyzer (in the global variable `yylval`), the types can be added to the `%token`, `%left`, `%right`, or `%nonassoc` declarations for these symbols. Figure 7-4 shows a small example using a `%union` declaration.

---

### Figure 7-4  An Example Using %union

```
%start S
%union {  char *name;
          float val; }
%type <val> FExp
%token <name> ident
%token <val> number
%left '+' '-'
%%
S :        FExp { printf("result = %f\n", $1); };
FExp :     FExp '+' FExp { $$ = $1 + $3; }
     |     FExp '-' FExp { $$ = $1 - $3; }
     |     ident { $$ = lookupvalue($1); }
     |     number ;
... etc.
```

In this example, we assume that there is a function lookupvalue which when invoked in a call like lookupvalue("pi") will return the value 3.14159. We also assume that the lexical analyzer stores attribute values for the ident and number tokens in the yylval variable using code like that shown in Figure 7-5.

In the lexical analyzer, the appropriate members of the union type must be explicitly accessed. However, in the generated parser, the correct member qualifications are automatically appended to all accesses to semantic attribute values.

There is one special case that should be mentioned. If an embedded semantic action has an attribute value, yacc will not be able to deduce a type for that value. In this situation, the user must supply a type. Here is a very contrived example.

```
FExp : READ { scanf("%f", &($<val>$) ); }
       ';' { $$ = $<val>2; } ;
```

The type name, enclosed in angle brackets, is simply placed after the initial $ character of the attribute reference.

---

## Figure 7-5   Returning Attributes from the Lexical Analyzer

```
#include "y.tab.h" /* this include file contains
                      a definition for YYSTYPE */
extern YYSTYPE yylval;
extern char *strdup(const char *);
extern float *atof(const char *);
    ...
int yylex() {
    ...
    /* code to return an ident token */
    yylval.name = strdup(yytext);
    return ident;
    ...
    /* code to return a number token */
    yylval.val = atof(yytext);
    return number;
    ...
}
```

---

## 7-4   *Grammar Debugging*

Successful operation of the parser depends on making the correct choice for each action. At each step, the parser must select one of the four possible actions listed below.

- A shift action, which causes a state number to be pushed onto an internal stack and a new token to be obtained from the `yylex` function.
- A reduce action, which causes state numbers on its internal stack to be coalesced.
- An accept action, which causes `yyparse` to return with a success indication.
- An error action, which causes the `yyerror` function to be invoked followed by an attempt to recover from the syntactic error. If the recovery fails, `yyparse` returns with an error indication.

If it selects a reduce action, it must also select which production rule to use. The LALR(1) parsing method uses a table that specifies the correct next action given the current stack contents and given knowledge of the next input token. There is at most one action stored in a table entry – thus execution of the parser is completely determined for every possible input. (A missing entry represents an error action.) That is, the parser is always *deterministic*.

When the LALR(1) parser construction method is applied to a grammar, it may find more than one valid parsing action for a given parse stack state and input combination. In this situation, yacc will apply some rules to disambiguate the actions. Consider the following example grammar.

```
Exp : Exp '/' Exp
    | id ;
```

For the case when the input is

```
id / id / id
```

there is a choice of parsing actions after the third token has been read. The parser could either reduce the input read so far to an Exp or it could read the next symbol (performing a shift action). The first choice corresponds to treating the input as though it were parenthesized as (id/id)/id and the second choice corresponds to id/(id/id). If the user has provided a declaration such as

```
%left '/'
```

then it is used to disambiguate the two choices, since the first choice corresponds to making / left-associative and the second to making it right-associative. If, in this example, the user has provided no precedence declaration, yacc applies a simple rule. It always chooses a shift action in preference to a reduce action. (This default rule makes / right-associative in our example.) Yacc will, however, issue a warning message that it found a *shift-reduce conflict* in the grammar.

There is another situation where the parser has a choice of actions. It is called a *reduce-reduce* conflict and it occurs when there are two or more rules that can be used in a reduction. Here is an example where such a conflict arises.

```
Stmt : { printf("type 1\n"); } RETURN
     | { printf("type 2\n"); } RETURN Result ;
Result : ident | number ;
```

If the semantic actions are removed, the reduce-reduce conflict goes away – this illustrates that inserting semantic actions can cause problems with a LALR(1) grammar. (Adding an action to the end of a rule, however, will never introduce a new problem into a grammar.) As explained previously, the grammar with the semantic actions is automatically transformed by yacc into the following.

```
Stmt : Temp1 RETURN
     | Temp2 RETURN Result ;
Result : ident | number ;
Temp1 : ;
Temp2 : ;
```

and where semantic actions are executed whenever reductions by the null rules Temp1 ::= ε and Temp2 ::= ε are performed. If the parser sees the keyword RETURN as an input symbol, it must choose one of the two null rules to reduce by. But it cannot know which rule is applicable without looking at the input that follows the keyword RETURN. In a LALR(1) parser, this is not permitted (though it would be in some other kinds of parser). Thus, `yacc` discovers a reduce-reduce conflict between the two null rules. The disambiguating strategy adopted by `yacc` is to choose whichever rule appears first in the grammar. In this case, it is the null rule for `Temp1`. As a consequence of choosing the `Temp1` null rule, further matching is forced to use the first rule given for `Stmt`. The second rule for `Stmt` can never be used (a clear indication that the parser is not going to accept the same language as was intended). Warning messages, reporting both the reduce-reduce conflict and the unused rule, are printed by `yacc`.

If you get a warning message from `yacc` that conflicts were detected in your grammar, you should verify that they were disambiguated in a suitable way. For shift-reduce conflicts, the strategy of preferring the shift usually gives a satisfactory result. But the strategy for resolving reduce-reduce conflicts is hit-and-miss. You should re-run `yacc` to obtain diagnostic output (you must provide the '–v' flag on the command). The output is stored in a file named "y.output". If you browse through the file, you will find a group of lines describing each state in the generated parser. For example, you might find the following lines in the file.

```
state 2
    S : E_  (1)
    E : E_ + E
    E : E_ - E

    +  shift 5
    -  shift 6
    .  reduce 1
```

These lines say that when the parser is in state 2, and the input symbol is a plus symbol, a shift action will performed in order to match one more symbol on the right-hand side of the rule "E ::= E + E". As a consequence of the shift, the parser will enter state 5. Similarly, a plus symbol will cause a shift to state 6. If the input symbol is anything else (denoted by the dot), a reduction by the rule tagged "(1)" will be performed. The underscore character is used in the listing of a rule to indicate how much of the right-hand side has been matched already. Another convention used in the "y.output" file is to use a created name like $$1 to denote a non-terminal symbol that has been invented to correspond to a semantic action.

If the grammar has conflicts, the "y.output" file contains lines giving the numbers of the states where the conflicts occur. You should scrutinize the listings of these states very carefully to try to understand why the conflicts have occurred.

## 7-5    *Interfacing with a yacc Parser*

The parser generated by `yacc` will call a function named `yylex` to obtain each token. Its function prototype is

```
int yylex(void)
```

The function result returned by a call to `yylex` is the integer code of a terminal symbol (or of an end-of-file indication). The parser assumes a particular numbering scheme for the terminals, and it is up to you to make sure that the lexical analyzer uses the same numbering. The scheme is detailed in the next few paragraphs.

Zero or a negative integer may be used to indicate the end-of-file. Thus, if the parser calls `yylex` and the lexical analyzer reaches the end of file without finding another lexical element, you would normally return zero or EOF (which is defined as −1 in the <stdio.h> include file). A `lex`-generated scanner automatically returns 0 at the end-of-file.

Every single character token is assigned a number equal to the ASCII code of that character. Thus, the token `'+'` is numbered 43 because that is the ASCII code for the plus symbol. A token identifier composed of a single letter is treated in the same way as if the character had been enclosed in quotes. For example, the token declared by

```
%left z
```

will be assigned the number 122 because that is the ASCII code of the letter *z*.

Any token not covered by the above rules will be assigned a number in the range 257 and above. Although you can deduce the number assigned to each token by looking through the grammar file to determine the order of first appearance of the tokens, this is not convenient. It is also subject to change if the grammar is edited. Fortunately, there is a way to obtain the numbering scheme for token identifiers. If `yacc` is invoked with the '−d' option ('d' stands for *defines*), a file named "y.tab.h" will be created. This file is a C header file containing the definition of YYSTYPE (if a `%union` declaration was used) and a preprocessor `#define` statement for every token that is in identifier form. Thus, if the grammar file included a declaration like

```
%token identifier
```

then the "y.tab.h" file will contain a corresponding line

```
#define identifier 258
```

(with whatever number is assigned). The header file may be included by the lexical analyzer file, and it therefore becomes possible to use statements such as

```
return identifier;
```

inside the `yylex` function.

There are two pitfalls to watch out for. First, be careful not to use token names that coincide with C keywords or with identifiers used by the generated parser. If, for example, your grammar file contains the line

```
%token int
```

you will be in for a surprise when you try to compile the parser or a lexical analyzer that includes the "y.tab.h" file. The reason is that there will be a preprocessor definition

```
#define int 259
```

that will cause every occurrence of the keyword `int` to be replaced by the number 259. To avoid identifiers used in the parser itself, do not give any token a name that begins with the letters 'yy'. If you intend to include the "y.tab.h" in a `lex`-generated scanner, you also have to avoid several more names that are used by `lex`. The complete list is: BEGIN, ECHO, FILE, U, NLSTATE, INITIAL, REJECT, input, output, unput, stdin, and stdout.

The second pitfall is that it is permissible to use multicharacter token names that are not identifiers. For example, the rule

```
Exp : '++' Exp ;
```

uses a token named `'++'`. No line giving the number of this token will be placed in the "y.tab.h" file. Therefore, you should always give a name to such a token. For example, we could replace the example rule by

```
Exp : PLUSPLUS Exp ;
```

and add the line

```
%token PLUSPLUS
```

to the first section of the file.

As mentioned previously, the lexical analyzer may pass additional information back to the parser. The external variable `yylval` with type `YYSTYPE` may be assigned the attribute value for the token that is about to be returned. This attribute value can be accessed by using the $k$ notation in a subsequent semantic action. The definition of `YYSTYPE` is obtainable from the header file "y.tab.h" if it has been constructed from a `%union` declaration.

The parser function itself is called `yyparse` and has this function prototype:

```
int yyparse(void);
```

It returns to the caller only on completion of parsing (or when forced to return earlier by syntax errors or by an explicit semantic action). The integer returned as the function result indicates success or failure of the parser. Zero indicates that there were no syntax errors detected and one indicates that one or more errors were encountered.

The parser requires a function named `yyerror` to be provided. The function prototype is as follows.

```
int yyerror( char *message );
```

The function is called when a syntax error is discovered. No result is returned (the parser is not coded in ANSI C). The argument is a message (usually saying nothing more specific than the string *syntax error*). You should provide this function. Sample coding for it is as follows.

```
int yyerror( char *message ) {
    extern int yylineno;
    (void)fprintf(stderr, "line %d: %s\n",
        yylineno, message);
    return 0;
}
```

The integer variable `yylineno` is defined in `lex`-generated scanners and holds the current input line number. If you wish to improve the quality of the error message further, you should note that the number of the current input token is available in the external integer variable `yychar`.

If the order in which the parser applies production rules is mysterious, you can ask the `yyparse` function to trace its actions. Provided that you used the '`-t`' option on the `yacc` command when the parser was created, you need only set the external integer variable `yydebug` to a non-zero value. From then on, every parsing action will generate a line on the standard output file.

## 7-6    Syntax Error Handling

On detection of a syntax error, the normal action is for the parser to call `yyerror` and then to abandon parsing, returning a result code of one back to the caller of `yyparse`. However, a mechanism is provided for continuing after an error. The mechanism is simple, but some experimentation may be required before it gives acceptable results.

The word `error` indicates a recovery point for a syntactic error. It may be used in the right-hand side of one or more special recovery rules. After control returns from `yyerror`, the parser proceeds as follows.

1. The parser pops its stack until it enters a state where the token "error" is legal.
2. The parser makes a shift transition on the token "error".
3. If the "error" token is followed in the recovery rule by a terminal symbol, then input symbols are discarded until that symbol is seen and another shift transition performed.
4. Parsing now continues almost as normal. Until three tokens from the input have been successfully matched, however, the parser is in an error state. While in the error state,

an unexpected input symbol will simply be ignored and no error message is generated. (This behavior is intended to prevent a cascade of error messages caused by an unsuccessful recovery from a single error.)

A common strategy when a syntax error is found in a C or Pascal program is to throw away everything associated with the current statement, skip through the input until a semicolon is found, and then resume parsing a new statement at the following symbol. This method (often called *panic mode*) is represented by the following `yacc` recovery rule.

```
Statement : error ';' { .... } ;
```

The semantic action code will be executed when recovery using this rule occurs. It should *undo* any effects that actions associated with the partially recognized erroneous statement may have had. (This is easier said than done.)

There are some special macros available for use by semantic action code associated with a recovery rule. One is invoked by the statement

```
yyerrok ;
```

to reset the parser mode from the error state back to its normal state. It is useful if you are sure that your recovery rule has corrected the problem and you therefore do not want syntax errors involving the next two symbols to be ignored. The statement

```
yyclearin ;
```

performs another special action. It causes the current input token to be discarded. This is useful if the recovery rule does not specify a token that must follow the "error" token (so no skipping of input occurred) but you provided a semantic action that did perform some skipping or that modified the input stream in some way. In such a situation, you may need a means of clearing the erroneous symbol that is the parser's current lookahead token.

If the semantic code attached to a recovery rule needs to abandon the recovery attempt, it can execute the statement

```
YYABORT ;
```

and this causes `yyparse` to return with an error indication. In fact, any semantic action code, not just that in a recovery action, may contain this statement. A statement with the opposite effect also exists. It is:

```
YYACCEPT ;
```

but its usefulness seems limited.

## 7-7   Running yacc

The grammar file must have a name that ends with the suffix ".y". If "gram.y" is such a file, then the command

```
yacc gram.y
```

will result in the creation of a file named "y.tab.c" containing the C code for the parser.

Command line options for `yacc` are:

-d    to create a header file named "y.tab.h" that contains definitions of the terminal tokens;

-v    to create a file named "y.output" that contains a listing of the parser states.

-t    to include code for tracing parsing actions in the parser; the trace output is produced when the variable `yydebug` is non-zero).

When the parser is compiled and an executable program is created, you may supply the '-ly' loader option. This will cause the `yacc` library to made available. If your program does not have a function called `main`, a main function that simply calls `yyparse` will be loaded from the library. Similarly, if you do not have a `yyerror` function, a very simple one will be loaded from the library. Usually, however, you would supply your own main function and error routines, so the loader option is not often required.

## 7-8   Further Reading

The definitive description of `yacc` is provided as a document in the UNIX Programmer's Reference Manual. It is called *YACC: Yet Another Compiler-Compiler* by S.C. Johnson. Another useful source, full of practical information about `yacc`, is *Introduction to Compiler Construction with UNIX* by A. T. Schreiner and H. G. Friedman Jr. (Prentice-Hall 1985). An alternative book is *Lex & Yacc*, by W. A. Mason and D. Brown (O'Reilly & Associates 1990). Its coverage is more complete, including complete examples of `lex` interfaced with `yacc` as well as a general introduction to compilers and interpreters. A compiler text that uses `lex` and `yacc` is *Introduction to Compiling Techniques: A First Course using ANSI C, LEX and YACC* by J. P. Bennett (McGraw-Hill 1990).

For information about the LALR(1) parsing method and for help in constructing a grammar, almost any recent text on compiler construction may be consulted.

# SECTION II

# *Systems Programming in C*

# CHAPTER 8   *LIBRARY FUNCTIONS FOR INPUT-OUTPUT*

---

## *8-1    Standard Libraries*

---

### What is a Library?

Up to this point, there has been an assumption that C programs can simply include calls to various standard functions. Now is the time to take a closer look at the standard functions, what services they provide to the user, the rules for accessing them and where they reside in the UNIX system.

Consider, for example, this C statement:

```
fprintf(stderr,"error in line %d\n", lineno);
```

The `fprintf` function used in this statement is not part of the C language. In this matter, C does not follow the same path as PASCAL. In PASCAL, the equivalent operation, *writeln*, is defined as a standard procedure and has a special status in the language. The call on the `fprintf` function in C has no special status is treated like a call on any other function. In the interests of maintaining a consistent programming environment, however, the interface and operation of `fprintf` is precisely defined in the ANSI C standard.

In principle, the source code of the `fprintf` function could be made available for inclusion in your program with a `#include` directive. However, this approach would be grossly inefficient because even the smallest C programs could easily require that several thousand lines of function definitions be included. In addition, much of the work would be repetitious because the same functions would be compiled over and over by different users.

The normal solution to the problem, adopted in all major computer systems, is to precompile a large collection of useful functions. The compiled versions of these functions are in a form called *relocatable binary code*; in other words, as ".o" files. This is the form of file created when a C source file is compiled with the −c flag in effect. Since it is a little inconvenient to have hundreds of tiny ".o" files, collections of these compiled functions are combined into larger files called *libraries* or *archive libraries*. These libraries are identified by having the special suffix ".a". To speed up searches for functions within an archive, a special section, similar to a table of contents, can optionally be inserted at the front of the file.

If you have a directory containing a large number of ".o" files, you can create your own archive library by executing commands similar to the following:

```
ar crv mylib.a *.o
ranlib mylib.a
```

The ar program may be used to create an archive library, to extract particular files from a library or to replace members of an archive. The c and r options used in the above invocation of ar request creation of a new archive, and the v option specifies that the program should be verbose (reporting every action it performs). The ranlib command inserts a table of contents at the front of an archive library (or replaces the table of contents if one was already present).

It is unlikely that you will need your own private archive libraries. They are likely to be useful only in the largest software projects. For normal programming, it is only necessary to know of the existence of the standard archive libraries provided with the UNIX system. The most important library is the C library which is automatically searched for functions whenever you use the cc or gcc command to create an executable program. This library is usually the file "/lib/libc.a", which contains almost all the standard functions mentioned in this book. If you are interested, you can obtain a list of all the ".o" files that were merged to create this library by executing this command:

```
ar t /lib/libc.a
```

(This list is very long.) You can also see all the names (mostly of functions) listed in the table of contents section by executing this command:

```
ar p /lib/libc.a __.SYMDEF | strings | more
```

The table of contents section, added by ranlib, has the name "__.SYMDEF". This is extracted by the ar command. The strings command scans the table looking for all ASCII strings and outputs them.

## Loading Functions from a Library

If you wish to use one of the many standard functions and if you do not require a result from that function or if its result has type `int`, no declaration for the function need appear in your program. For example, you can simply code

```
length = strlen(somestring);
```

in the middle of your program. As the final stage of compilation, the system loader program `ld` simply looks for the precompiled code of the `strlen` function in the "/lib/libc.a" library and adds it to your program. There is no checking by the loader program that the function is being used correctly. This particular example does work because the C compiler assumes that undeclared functions have the attributes `extern` and `int`, and because the argument passed to `strlen` does not require any conversion. However, it would be better to include the preprocessor directive

```
#include <string.h>
```

because the header file contains a prototype for `strlen` (and several other string handling functions). This allows the compiler to check that `strlen` is used correctly and to perform datatype conversion on argument values and the result value, when required.

When the function you want to use returns a result with a type other than `int`, a declaration of the function prototype is normally required in the program. To use the `getenv`[1] function, for example, the prototype declaration

```
char *getenv(const char *);
```

should be provided. Then, when you call this function in a statement such as

```
term_type = getenv("TERM");
```

the C compiler will be able to check that the function is used correctly. Without the prototype declaration, the C compiler assumes that `getenv` returns an `int` result and will issue an error message that the `int` value is incompatible with the required `char*` type.

The prototype of the `getenv` function is part of the <stdlib.h> header file. You will find a great number of prototypes for the more commonly used library functions in that header file. It would therefore be good practice to include the directive

```
#include <stdlib.h>
```

at the beginning of all your C source files.

Many standard functions operate on structures with particular formats. For such functions, there is usually a special *include* file which contains the necessary type and structure definitions. For example, the identifier `FILE` (an important feature of input-output processing) is defined by a `typedef` statement in the include file <stdio.h>. This header file also

---

1. Use of the `getenv` function is covered in Chapter 9.

includes type declarations for the various input-output functions. The input-output functions and the <stdio.h> header file are discussed more fully later in this chapter.

The standard functions are documented in section 3 of the UNIX on-line manual. You may see succinct one-line descriptions of all these functions by executing

```
man 3 intro
```

If you have a lot of spare time, you can browse through all these manual entries and see what is available by executing

```
cd /usr/man/cat3; more *
```

The directory named in the `cd` command normally holds preformatted copies of all the on-line manual entries. If this directory does not exist or is empty, you will have to read through the unformatted versions instead.[2] To see the unformatted entries, execute

```
cd /usr/man/man.3; more *
```

Each manual entry gives a brief synopsis of how to call the function and tells you if there is any associated include file.

In addition to the on-line manual files, the manual entries are also available in hard-copy form. Your system administrator should be able to help you obtain a copy. This person may also be able to direct you to supplementary documentation that is available for many system programs.

It should be noted that there are several archive libraries. When you use the C compiler, only the standard C library (in the file "/lib/libc.a") is actually searched for the functions that you use. If you use mathematical functions, such as *sin* or *sqrt*, you must ask for the mathematical library to be searched. This library is normally held in the file "/usr/lib/libm.a". You can request that the mathematical library be searched by supplying the −lm flag to the `cc` or `gcc` command when it is used to create the final executable program. For example, the command

```
gcc *.o -lm -o math_problem
```

will suffice if you have already compiled several C source files to produce object files.

Similarly, there is a library of functions for terminal handling, which is searched if you provide the flag −ltermcap and there is a library of functions for full-screen I/O (the *curses* screen package), searched by including the flag −lcurses. If you browse in the "/usr/lib" directory, you will find many archive libraries. They are, of course, easily identifiable by the ".a" suffix.

---

2. On some systems, the unformatted manual pages may not be provided – only the preformatted versions may have been distributed with the system.

*Chapter 8: Library Functions for Input-Output*

## 8-2 Files and Directories

This section of the chapter provides a brief introduction to the implementation of files and directories in the Berkeley UNIX system. This material can be skipped if you just need to know how to perform simple input-output. The Ritchie and Thompson paper, cited at the end of the chapter, provides additional reading on the file system structure.

### Implementation of Files and Directories

The data in a file is organized as a collection of blocks, which are not necessarily contiguous on the disk surface. Each file has a special disk block, called an *inode* (for *index node*), which gives the disk addresses of the data blocks and which contains other information needed by the system. In theory, all you need know to access a file is the *inode* number for that file. But, of course, users would be unhappy if files had to be referenced by numbers. Directories are therefore used to maintain a correspondence between names (which are just character strings provided by users) and inode numbers. A directory is nothing more than a list of names and matching inode numbers. The fact that a directory is itself a disk file should not confuse you. An implication is that one directory file can contain the inode number of another directory file, and so the familiar tree-structured hierarchy of files can be built up.

When a directory is created, it is automatically provided with two entries. One entry has the name " . " (a single period) and gives the inode number of this directory. The other entry has the name " . . " (two periods) and gives the inode number of the parent directory in the hierarchy. These two entries cannot be changed or deleted.

If a directory *D1* contains the name and inode number for a file *F*, *D* is said to contain a link to *F*. There is no inherent restriction in the UNIX system which prevents a second directory *D2*, say, from containing a link to *F*. The *D2* directory might even associate a different name with the inode number for *F*. Thus, we can have one file which has two, quite different, pathnames. (The shell command `ln` can be used create extra links to files.) Figure 8-1 illustrates a directory structure which permits a file to be accessed with two different pathnames. If the current working directory is the directory file at the left of the figure, the data file at the right of the figure then has the two names "D1/F1" and "D2/F2".

The directory links that we have just described are sometimes known as *hard links*. The term *hard link* is used whenever it is necessary to distinguish this kind of link from another kind of link, the *symbolic link*, that is available in the Berkeley UNIX system. Symbolic links are covered later in this chapter.

A disk is normally divided into separate regions called *file systems*. (You can see a list of all the file systems on your computer by executing the `df` command.) Each file system has its own set of inodes, numbered from one upwards. An inode number, therefore, does not completely specify a file unless you also state which file system it refers to. Names in directories are associated only with inode numbers, and so these inode numbers are assumed to belong to the same file system as the directory itself. This assumption implies that a directory cannot contain links to arbitrary files, only links to files in the same file system are allowed. Another restriction is that links to directory files cannot be created by the `ln` command. This restriction is imposed to eliminate the possibility of cycles in the file system structure. If directory *A* could contain a link to directory *B* and *B* contain a link to *A*, many system programs would fail.

## Symbolic Links

Although all the files owned by a single user are likely to be contained in the same file system, the user may wish to make links to files owned by other users. Such links would simplify project management in cases where individual project members let others access their files. Often, however, the files may be resident on different file systems. To get around this problem and around the restriction that `ln` must not create links to directories, Berkeley UNIX has another kind of directory link, called a *symbolic link*. When a symbolic link is stored in a directory, a correspondence is still made between a name and an inode. However, the file corresponding to this inode contains the pathname of the file that we are symbolically linking to, and the mode bits contained in the inode indicate that this file is a

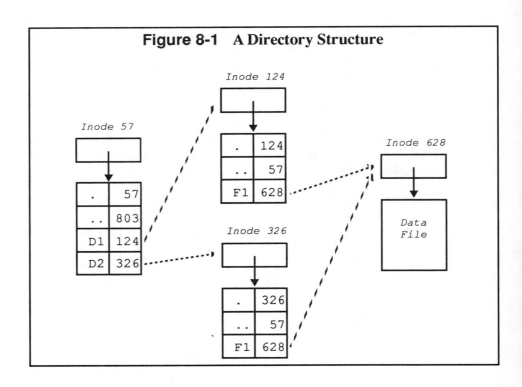

**Figure 8-1   A Directory Structure**

symbolic link. An example should make symbolic links a little clearer. If you execute the command

```
ln -s /usr/include/stdio.h io_header
```

an entry in your current directory is created. This entry contains the name `io_header` and the inode number of a new file. The new file contains only the string "/usr/include/stdio.h" and nothing else. The mode bits of the new file, held in a field of the inode block on disk, specify that the new file is a symbolic link. If you now execute a command, such as

```
pr io_header
```

the `pr` program will request that the file "io_header" be opened for input. When the UNIX system processes this request, it finds that the file mode indicates a symbolic link. It therefore reads the value of the symbolic link, the string "/usr/include/stdio.h" and repeats the file open process using this name instead. Hence, the user obtains access to the file without being aware that there is anything special about the route taken to locate the file. It is quite possible for the pathname found as the value of a symbolic link to lead to another symbolic link, and so on. This implies that there must be a limit on how many symbolic links that the system will follow when trying to access a file. It should also be clear that it is inherently less efficient for the system to follow a symbolic link than a hard link.

Each file has, stored in its inode block on disk, information about the file owner, the file size, when the file was last changed, when it was last accessed, and who has permission to access this file and in what manner. The *mode* bits for the file control access to the file and say a little about what kind of file it is (e.g., a directory or a symbolic link). The mode bits are set when a file is created and can be changed with the `chmod` command or the function of the same name.

## Current Working Directory

The UNIX system remembers a current working directory for each executing process. This directory provides a starting point for following file pathnames if the path does not begin with the slash (/) character. The full pathname of the current working directory can be determined by calling the `getwd` function. The current working directory can be changed with the `chdir` function.

## Miscellaneous File Handling Functions

We will briefly list, but not fully explain, some of the operations and corresponding system functions which are applicable to files. Details about the usage of these functions may be obtained from the on-line manual entries.

- The access modes on a file may be set with the `chmod` function.
- Creation of a hard link in a directory is performed with the `link` function. This function does not create a new file, it simply makes an extra link to an existing file.
- Creation of a symbolic link with the `symlink` function.

- A file may be renamed with the rename function.
- New files are created with the creat function. However, a file may also be created as a side effect of the open or fopen function. These two functions are described later in this chapter.
- A link to a file may be deleted with the remove function.[3] (When the last hard link to a file has been deleted, the file is physically deleted from the disk.)
- Directory files may be created with the mkdir function and removed with the rmdir function.
- The entries in a directory file (i.e., the names of the files that belong to a particular directory) may be read using the readdir function. reading a directory is modelled after reading a file (see below), so that the directory must first be opened for reading with a call to the opendir function, and there should be a final call to closedir.

## 8-3    *Stream-Oriented Input-Output Functions*

The UNIX system provides two families of functions for handling input-output and for managing files. One family is relatively low-level and is best suited for handling large blocks of data, say 1024 characters at a time. These functions are used mostly by systems programmers who are striving to achieve extraordinary efficiency. The other family of functions deals with input-output on a character-by-character or line-by-line level, known as *stream* input-output. The stream input-output functions are actually implemented in terms of the low-level routines.

The stream I/O functions should be used in normal applications. As well as having a more usable interface, they also provide automatic blocking of data, so that file input-output is performed efficiently. Another reason to use the stream I/O functions is that this makes your program more portable. Most implementations of C on non-UNIX computer systems provide the standard library of stream I/O functions, but most do not provide a compatible library of low-level I/O functions.

The ANSI C standard distinguishes between text streams and binary streams. When you open an I/O stream, you are supposed to specify which kind you wish to use. However, on most UNIX systems you will not notice any difference between text and binary streams. Before the ANSI C standard, the notion of a binary stream did not exist on UNIX. Text streams are line-oriented, where the lines are terminated by new-line characters and contain only printing characters or horizontal tab characters. In theory, the routines that implement text streams are permitted to insert or remove blanks at the ends of lines and to remove or translate characters non-printing characters (other than horizontal tabs). Therefore the sequence of characters read from a text file may not be identical to the sequence of characters

---

3. This is the ANSI C name for the function. In pre-ANSI C systems, the function is called unlink.

written to the file. Binary streams, on the other hand, may contain sequences of arbitrary byte values. The sequence of bytes read from a binary file should exactly match the sequence that was written. Even though your UNIX system typically will implement text streams and binary streams in the same way, it would be good practice to distinguish between them as this will improve the portability of your programs.

We will now go through most of the stream I/O functions in some detail. Additional information about these functions may be found in the on-line manual entries.

## Preliminaries

Any program that intends to perform stream input-output should contain the directive

```
#include <stdio.h>
```

somewhere near its beginning. The included file defines several macros, several constants and a special data type called FILE, which is needed for processing files.

Every program started from the shell automatically has access to a standard input stream and two standard output streams. One output stream is intended for use in normal program output; the other is intended to be used for error messages and other exceptional output. Suppose that we have compiled a C program and saved the resulting executable code in the file called "cprog". If we simply type

```
cprog
```

at the terminal, this program will read characters from the terminal keyboard (up to a *control-D* character) and it will print all its output at the terminal. If we type

```
cprog < datafile > results
```

the program will read its input from "datafile" and write its normal output into the file "results". Any error messages are still printed at the terminal. Finally, if we are using the csh command shell (see Chapter 4) and if we should want error messages to be saved in a file along with the normal output, we could type the command

```
cprog < datafile >& results
```

This last form is most suitable for running cprog as a background process, while the terminal is being used for other things.

Since the UNIX shell command processor, csh, provides the I/O redirections described above (and the *pipe* facility), there is no great need for the simpler C programs to make explicit accesses to disk files. That is, they can usually get by with just the standard input and output streams that are provided automatically.

The three standard I/O streams are defined to have the names stdin, stdout and stderr in the <stdio.h> include file. These names correspond to "standard input", "standard output" and "standard error output", respectively. These three identifiers are declared to be pointers to a type with the name FILE. FILE is a typedef name for a complicated structure, whose inner details are irrelevant to normal programmers.

The stream input-output functions automatically provide buffering. Buffering of I/O is performed in order to improve efficiency. If a program is reading a continuous stream of characters from a disk file, it would be extremely inefficient to access the disk each time the program needs the next character. The usual approach is to begin by copying a large chunk of the file, 1024 bytes on the Berkeley UNIX system, into an area of main memory called a *buffer*. Then when the program asks to read individual characters with the getc function, the characters are taken from the buffer instead of from the disk. In this manner, slow and expensive accesses to the disk occur only once per 1024 characters read by the program. Similarly, if a program is outputting characters to a disk file, the characters are normally accumulated in a buffer until the buffer is full. When the buffer is full, the entire contents of the buffer are written to the disk in a single operation.

If the program is reading from a keyboard and writing to a terminal instead of using disk files, it still makes sense to buffer the input and output. Again, the reason for buffering is efficiency. If input is unbuffered, the program must be suspended from execution each time it requests an input character and the program must be made to wait until the user types a character. The system overhead involved in suspending and restarting the program for each character is fairly high, although there are some programs, such as the vi editor, where unbuffered input is necessary. Similarly, the software overhead is reduced if output characters destined for the terminal screen are accumulated in a buffer and transmitted in small chunks.

By default, standard output to a terminal is line-buffered. Output characters generated by the program are accumulated in the output buffer until either the buffer is full or until a *linefeed* character is output or until the program attempts to read from the terminal. (This last reason for transferring the buffer contents to the output terminal is to simplify interactive prompting for input.) Standard error output is, by default, either line-buffered or unbuffered. One consequence is that error output is performed inefficiently. It is unsuitable for large volumes of data. A second consequence is that if a program crashes, we can be fairly confident that we have not lost any messages that were in the buffer when the program failed. Input is also, by default, buffered. However, input from a terminal is actually buffered by a program (the tty driver) that is not part of the stream I/O functions. Control over terminal input buffering is performed with a function, ioctl, which will not be described until Chapter 11.

If buffering defaults are unsuitable for your application, they are fairly easy to change. The occasions when they need to be changed, however, are relatively rare.

## Character-by-Character I/O

The simplest functions perform input and output of a single character. The function call

fgetc(fp)     returns the next character read from the file referenced by the pointer *fp*, and the call

fputc(c, fp)  outputs the character *c* to the file referenced by the pointer *fp*.[4]

Because input-output of characters is so frequent and, in particular, input from the standard input and output to the standard output are so common, special versions of `fgetc` and `fputc` implemented as macros are also provided:

`getc(fp)`      has the same effect as `fgetc(fp)`.

`putc(c,fp)`      has the same effect as `fputc(c,fp)`.

`getchar()`      returns the next character read from the standard input. It is defined to be the same as `getc(stdin)`, and

`putchar(c)`      outputs the character *c* to the standard output. It is defined to be the same as `putc(c,stdout)`.

Given these functions and given the fact that `fgetc` (and `getc` and `getchar`) return the special code EOF[5] at the end of input we can code a simple program to strip comments from C source code. It is reproduced in Figure 8-2. (Use of this program on your source files is *not* recommended!)

## Line-by-Line I/O

Another group of functions, `gets`, `fgets`, `puts`, and `fputs`, handle input/output of entire lines. To read a line, you must supply a character array to receive the line. If, say, your program declares the array as

```
#define MAX_LENGTH 256
char input_line[MAX_LENGTH], *result;
```

you can read a line from `stdin` with the call

```
result = gets(input_line);
```

If the line has been read successfully, `result` will be assigned the address of the array `input_line` and the array will contain the input line. The line is supplied as a string terminated by a null byte (the character `'\0'`). The string does not contain the *newline* character. If the read operation fails because we are at the end of input, NULL is assigned to `result`.

When using the `gets` function, you must be sure to supply an array that is guaranteed to be larger than the longest input line. It is preferable and safer to use the `fgets` function instead. We can read into the same array as before with the call

```
result = fgets(input_line, MAX_LENGTH, stdin);
```

This statement reads input characters up to the next *newline* character (but at most `MAX_LENGTH-1` characters are read) into the `input_line` array. If the *newline* character is read, it is stored in the array too. (This behavior is incompatible with `gets`.) As with `gets`, the function result is either the address of the array or NULL (to indicate end-of-file).

---

4. Actually, `putc` and `getc` are defined as macros in the <stdio.h> include file.

5. EOF is defined as a constant with the value -1 in <stdio.h>.

---

**Figure 8-2    A Comment Stripper Program**

```c
#include <stdio.h>
#include <stdlib.h>

int main(void) {
    register int ch;

    for( ; ; ) { /* loop forever */
        ch = getchar();
        /* copy non-comment text to the output */
        while(ch != '/' && ch != EOF) {
            putchar(ch);
            ch = getchar();
        }
        if (ch == EOF) break;
        ch = getchar();
        if (ch == '*') {
            /* output a blank instead of the comment */
            putchar(' ');
            /* search for the end of the comment */
            do {
                do {
                    ch = getchar();
                } while(ch != '*' && ch != EOF);
                if (ch == EOF) break;
                do {
                    ch = getchar();
                } while(ch == '*');
            } while(ch != '/' && ch != EOF);
        } else
            putchar('/');
        if (ch == EOF) break;
    }
    return 0;
}
```

There are two corresponding routines for output of lines. One, `puts`, outputs its argument string on `stdout` and then outputs an extra *newline* character. The other, `fputs`, outputs its first argument, a string, on the stream indicated by the second argument. No extra *newline* character is output. For example

```
puts("TABLE OF RESULTS");
```

sends a complete line, terminated by a *newline* to the standard output. This is the same effect as is obtained with

```
fputs("TABLE OF RESULTS\n", stdout);
```

Notice that we had to supply our own *newline* character here.

## Formatted Output Functions

A further group of functions handles formatted input-output. The formatted output functions convert data values into character strings for output according to format specifications. The formatted input functions perform the opposite conversions. These functions are unusual in that they do not have a fixed number of arguments, and the arguments do not have to have predefined data types. Let us begin with one of the output functions, `fprintf`. Its first argument is a file pointer (like `stdout` or `stderr`); its second argument is a format specification; all subsequent arguments are values which are to be converted to character strings and printed according to the format specification. Here is an example call of `fprintf`:

```
fprintf(stderr,
    "error at line %d, input value is %d\n",
    lineno, invalue);
```

All the characters appearing in the format specification are printed as written, except where there is a percent symbol followed by a special code (the letter *d* here). The `%d` combination indicates that an integer is to be printed in decimal notation. The first use of `%d` corresponds to the print-out of the variable `lineno`; the second use corresponds to `invalue`. Thus if `lineno` has value 10 and `invalue` has value -99, the function call will output

```
error at line 10, input value is -99
```

with a skip to a new line at the end. The message will be transmitted to the standard error stream.

The valid output format codes are listed in Table 8-1. When upper-case alternatives are given (e.g., `%x` and `%X`), the lower-case version generates output including lower-case letters (i.e., *a* through *f* for hexadecimal digits) and the upper-case version generates upper-case letters.[6] A couple of special format codes (`%p` and `%n`) that have been added as part of the ANSI C standard are omitted from the table.

---

6. However, some older C implementations interpret the upper-case codes differently. It may be advisable to avoid them unless you are using an ANSI C compiler.

## Table 8-1   Printf Format Codes

| | |
|---|---|
| `%d` or `%i` | Decimal output of an integer. |
| `%o` | Unsigned octal output of an integer. |
| `%x` or `%X` | Unsigned hexadecimal output of an integer. |
| `%u` | Unsigned decimal output of an integer. |
| `%c` | Output of a single `char` value. |
| `%s` | Output of a string; the argument must be a pointer to a null-terminated string. |
| `%e` or `%E` | Output of a `float` or `double` value in exponent notation. |
| `%f` | Like `%e` except that fixed point notation is used. |
| `%g` or `%G` | Output of a `float` or `double` value, using whichever of `%d`, `%e` or `%f` produces the shorter output without dropping significant digits. |
| `%%` | Output a single percent symbol. |

Between the percent symbol and the format code, optional further information may be included. The format code may be immediately preceded by the letter *l* (*ell*) which acts as a modifier to indicate that the data item has the `long` attribute. For example, a possible format specification is

```
fprintf(stderr, "Big number = %ld\n", bignum);
```

Since the `int` and `long int` types are identical in the Berkeley UNIX system, this modifier is redundant. It is, however, important to use the modifier if you wish to make your programs portable to other computers and to other versions of UNIX. Alternatively, the *h* modifier may be supplied to indicate that an integer value has the `short` attribute. In addition to the *l* and *h* modifiers, field width and precision information may be specified. This optional information has the following structure:

1. A minus sign may be given to specify left adjustment within the output field.
2. A decimal number which specifies the minimum field width. By default, output items will be padded with blanks to achieve this minimum width. Padding with the digit zero will be performed if the field width is written as an integer with a leading zero.
3. A period to separate the preceding number from the following one (if it is provided).
4. A decimal number (the precision) which specifies the maximum number of characters to be printed from a string or the number of digits to be printed after the decimal point (for output of `float` or `double` numbers).

Either or both of the decimal numbers (items 2 and 4) may be written as an asterisk character. In this case, the corresponding field width or precision is taken from an extra argument passed to the `printf` function. The extra argument(s) must have `int` type.

The `printf` routine is like `fprintf` except that the standard output file `stdout` is used. Its argument structure is

```
printf( format-specification, arg1, arg2, ... )
```

A third function, `sprintf`, is very used very similarly to `fprintf`, but does not actually perform any output. (It is mentioned here only because this seems to be the most appropriate place.) It generates a formatted string and stores it in a character array that is supplied as the first argument. For example,

```
char buffer[128];
int cpu_secs, total_secs;
     .
     .
sprintf(buffer, "CPU usage = %.2f%%\n",
    cpu_secs*100.0/total_secs);
```

Be careful when using `sprintf` because it does not check whether the data it is writing will fit into the destination array.

We close this description of the formatted output functions with a warning. A very common mistake in C programming is to match data arguments with the format codes used in the format string argument incorrectly. A failure to match the arguments properly will, at best, cause garbage to be printed. More likely, however, it will cause the program to abort with a bus error or segmentation fault.

## Formatted Input Functions

Formatted input of data is performed by the `fscanf` and `scanf` functions. A sample use of `fscanf` is

```
nd = fscanf(stdin, "%d%c", &n, &ch);
```

where n has type `int` and ch has type `char`. The `fscanf` function reads the specified file (standard input) looking for a decimal integer (as required by the `%d` format code). It will skip white space (blanks, tabs and *newline* characters), but no other characters when seeking this number. The number is read and assigned to variable n. The very next character (matched by the `%c` format item) is assigned to variable ch.

The `fscanf` function requires that it be passed pointers to variables in the third and following argument positions. (The word *pointers* must be stressed, because this represents a major difference in usage between the formatted input and output functions.) The function result returned by `fscanf` is the count of how many input items have been successfully read and assigned. Thus, if nd does not have the value 2 after executing the statement above, we know that there has been an error in the input. (Perhaps a character that is not a decimal digit has been found when reading the number to be assigned to n.) The result assigned to nd would be EOF if the end-of-input is reached.

The valid input format items are listed in Table 8-2. A modifier may optionally precede the format code. A modifier which may precede the d, o and x format codes is the letter *l* (*ell*) to indicate that the corresponding variable has the long int type. The *l* modifier may also precede the e or f codes to indicate that the corresponding argument has the double type. A second possible modifier is the letter *h* which may precede the d, o and x codes to indicate that the corresponding argument has the short int type. Between the percent symbol and the format code, a maximum field width can be specified. This defines a limit on the number of characters which will be read, converted and assigned to the corresponding argument. An example is

```
char linebuf[50];  int nd;
    ...
nd = fscanf(stdin, "%49s", linebuf);
```

where a limit of 49 characters is imposed on the string to be read. (This leaves one element in the array to hold the null terminator.) Note that no ampersand prefixes the array name. This is because an unsubscripted array name is treated as being a pointer, a pointer to the first array element.

## Table 8-2   Scanf Format Codes

| | |
|---|---|
| %d | Input a decimal integer and assign it to an int variable. |
| %o | Input an octal integer and assign it to an int variable |
| %x or %X | Input a hexadecimal integer and assign it to an int variable. |
| %u | Input a decimal integer and assign it to an unsigned int variable. |
| %c | Input a single character. Unlike the other format codes, no white space is skipped before the character is read and assigned to the corresponding char variable. Thus, a blank can be read with the %c format. |
| %s | Input of a string of non-white space characters. The corresponding argument must be a character pointer pointing to a character array large enough to hold the string and a terminating null character. The null byte is supplied by fscanf. |
| %e or %f or %g | Input a floating-point number and assign it to a float variable. The two format codes may be used interchangeably for input. |
| %[ ... ] | (See the explanation in the text.) |

Format strings may include characters other than format codes. If these characters are not white space characters (blanks, tabs or *newline* characters), they must match characters found in the input. White space in the format matches optional white space in the input, but the kind of white space characters and how many are present is irrelevant. To match a percent symbol in the input, the format string may contain the code %%.

The %s format code is often inappropriate for reading a sequence of characters into an array with char elements because the number of characters to be read must be known in advance. For example, you might wish to read the characters that comprise an English word – that is, you wish to read letters up to but not including the first character that is not a letter. The special format code % [...] provides for this possibility. The format code works similarly to the %s code except that only characters in a specified set of characters are read. The set of characters is specified in the same way as the [...] regular expression notation used in the lex program (see Chapter 6). Thus, if you wish to read one English word from the input, you might use a C statement similar to the following.

```
char word[128];
. . .
nd = fscanf(infile, " %127[A-Za-z]", word);
```

As with lex, the caret character ('^') may appear immediately after the left square bracket to obtain the complement of the set.

The scanf function is the same as fscanf except that the standard input file is assumed. Here is an example:

```
nd = scanf("%2d%2d", &n1, &n2);
```

Finally, sscanf works similarly to fscanf except that the input characters are read from an array instead of from an input stream. For example, if the array buffer contains the string "45677873 jones" when the statement

```
nd = sscanf(buffer,"%3d%d %s", &i, &j, s);
```

is executed, variable i will be assigned 456, j will be assigned 77873, the string "jones" will be copied into the array s, and nd will be set to 3.

If the input data is line-oriented, a good programming approach is to read each line of data into an array (the fgets function is convenient for this purpose) and use sscanf to dissect the data in the array. This makes it easier to keep track of line numbers and to report an error if a data item is missing or malformed.

Just as we closed the preceding section of this chapter with a warning, we should give a warning about scanf and its two companion functions too. It is a common error to forget that variables which are to receive values are not passed directly. Pointers to the variables are passed instead. If you forget to prefix an argument with the & operator, your program will probably fail with a bus error or segmentation fault.

## File Handling

Input from or output to a disk file requires a file pointer variable and a call to the function fopen to allocate a buffer and prepare the file. This function takes two string arguments: the first argument is the name of the file, the second argument is a string specifying the access mode. The primary access mode strings are "r" for read access, "w" for write access, and "a" for writing to the end of a file (i.e., *append* mode). The fopen function returns a file pointer result, referring to a newly created stream, if it was able to access the file (or if it was able to create a new file to receive output). If fopen is unsuccessful, perhaps because the file is unreadable, it returns a null pointer as its result. (NULL is defined as the null pointer value 0 in the <stdio.h> header file.)

Thus, the following code will read the first line from the on-line manual file "/usr/man/cat1/ls.1"

```
#define MAXLEN 256
FILE *fp;
char line[MAXLEN];
char *filename = "/usr/man/cat1/ls.1";
        .
        .
fp = fopen(filename, "r");
if (fp == NULL) {
    /* error -- could not open the file */
    perror(filename);  exit(1);
}
if (fgets(line, MAXLEN, fp) == NULL) {
    /* error -- could not read from the file */
    perror(filename);  exit(1);
}
```

The perror function, used twice in the above code, is useful for printing a message on the standard error stream. When an input-output function fails, an integer code identifying the nature of the error is stored in an external variable named errno. The perror function prints a one-line description of the error code, prefixed by the string passed as the function argument. When reporting a problem with a file, the obvious argument to pass is the name of the file.

If the first character in the filename argument is not a slash (/) character, fopen will try to locate the file from within the current working directory, that is, the directory that was current when this C program began execution or that was made current by a call to the chdir function. Note that shell command language metacharacters, such as *, ? and ~, are not recognized as metacharacters if used in filenames that are passed to fopen.

It is possible to open a file for both input and output. But, because of buffering by the stream input-output functions, you will not get correct results if you freely intermingle input requests and output requests on a file. The rules are that you can only switch from reading to writing (or vice versa) if you have read up to the end-of-file indicator (EOF) or if you call fseek or rewind. The simultaneous input-output modes are "r+" where the file is initially positioned for reading/writing at its beginning, "w+" where the file is created or emptied if the file already exists, and "a+" where the file is initially positioned for reading/writing at its end.

When you have finished working with a particular file, you may close the file with the fclose function. Its sole argument is a file pointer for an open stream. It is not *essential* to close files in your program as open files are automatically closed when the program terminates. There are, however, some reasons why you should close a file when you have finished using it. One is that the last bytes that the program writes to a file may not actually be stored in a disk file until the file is closed (i.e., the data is buffered). A second and very important reason is that fclose returns a code to indicate that all the writes to the file were successful. It is good practice to test this result code in the program so that a suitable warning can be issued. A third reason is that there is a limit (of at least 20) on the number of files that are simultaneously open. If you should get close to the limit, it may be necessary to close one file before opening another.

## Binary I/O Functions

File are not restricted to being text files or to containing only ASCII characters. Indeed, relocatable binary (".o") files contain mostly non-ASCII data. Such files can be read one character at a time with the *getc* and *getchar* functions. Use of other input functions such as gets would be inappropriate. Non-ASCII data can be written with any of the output functions discussed so far.

The ANSI C standard provides the special mode character b for use when opening a binary file. The letter b is used in addition to the mode characters listed earlier. Thus, the possible mode strings used with the fopen function for opening a binary file are "rb", "wb", "ab", "r+b", "w+b" and "a+b".

You need to be careful when reading non-ASCII data or data in extended ASCII (extended by the addition of 8-bit codes). If you read the characters one at a time into a variable whose size is one byte (as is the case for a char variable), the special character code, EOF, does not work as an unambiguous indication of the end of file. The value returned by getc has the unsigned char type, and all values in the range 0 to 255 are possible. If getc returns the end-of-file indicator, EOF, which is defined as -1, the value stored into the variable will be truncated and will give the same result as if 255 had been read. There are two ways around the problem. One is to read the character into a signed integer variable – thus guaranteeing that -1 and 255 are distinct. The other way is to use a special function, feof, which tests for the end-of-file condition. The call feof(fp) returns non-zero if the stream referenced by the file pointer fp is at the end of file.

If you wish to read non-ASCII data in larger chunks than one byte at a time, you have a choice of two functions. The *get word* function, getw, returns an integer composed of the next *w* bytes from an input stream, where *w* is the word size of the computer. The fread function can be used to read an arbitrary amount of data into an array. Similarly, putw is used to output one word at a time, and fwrite is used to output an arbitrary amount of data from an array.

## Other Stream I/O Functions

If you wish to reread a file, referenced by the file pointer fp, that is currently open, the call

```
rewind(fp);
```

will suffice. The next call to getc on this file would read the first character in the file again. A call to the rewind function performs just a particular kind of file positioning. General positioning capabilities are provided by the fseek function, which permits an arbitrary file position to be specified. A file position is defined by an integer, which represents an offset in bytes. This offset can be made relative to the start of the file, to the current position in the file or to the end of the file. A typical call is

```
status = fseek(fp, offset, kind);
```

where kind is 0, 1 or 2 to indicate that the offset is given relative to the file start, current position, or end of the file, respectively. The result returned by fseek is zero if the seek is successful and −1 if not.

When writing to a file, you can freely seek to a position way beyond the current end of the file. For example,

```
fseek(fp, 1000000, 2);
putc('*', fp);
```

seeks to a position one million bytes past the current end of file and writes a single character there. This does not cause the UNIX system to waste one million bytes of disk space. Holes in files, created by seeks similar to the above, consume very little storage. If you later attempt to read from a region in a file within a hole, the system will supply null bytes as the characters read, but these null bytes are not physically present on the disk. You should note, however, that the ability to create holes in files is peculiar to the UNIX system. If you transport your C program to a non-UNIX system, you should not expect files to have quite the same properties.

If you ever need to know the current position within a file, the ftell function should be used. The result of a call like ftell(fp) returns an offset relative to the start of the file.

Another useful function is ungetc. It can be used in conjunction with character-oriented input to "unread" one character. Frequently, program functions have to read one character too many. For example, a function to input a decimal number cannot determine that it has read the entire number unless it reads one extra character appearing after the number.

This extra character may, perhaps, be a significant (non-blank) character that should be read in another part of your program. Rather than introducing extra flags and tortuous logic into the program to handle the situation, C lets us simply "unread" the extra character. This is accomplished with

```
ungetc(c, fp)
```

where c is the character and fp is the appropriate file pointer (such as stdin). The very next character to be read, by getc or gets etc., will be c. Note that c need not be the same as the excess character that was originally read. There are naturally some restrictions on the use of ungetc. There cannot be two successive calls to ungetc without a read operation in between. Also, ungetc will not permit you to unread the end-of-file marker (EOF).

## 8-4    *Low-level File Handling Functions*

### Introduction to Low-Level I/O

As explained in the previous section, all the stream I/O functions are implemented in terms of lower level functions. A few of these functions, such as chdir and chmod, are useful in programs that use the stream I/O interface. Many others are not. However, it is probably still a good idea to know what the low level functions do and what their interface is.

The low level functions maintain a table called the *object reference table* or, sometimes, the *descriptor table*. This table contains, amongst other things, information about all open files in use by the current process. Each open file is identified by its index in the table. The files corresponding to standard input, standard output and standard error output initially have indexes 0, 1 and 2. These indexes are known as *file descriptors*. File descriptors are small integers, in the range 0 to 19 or so,[7] and should never be confused with streams or file pointers, which are pointers to structures maintained by the stream I/O functions. We will now examine some of the functions for manipulating files at the level of file descriptors.

### Opening and Closing Files

A file may be opened (and created if necessary) through the use of the open function. Its first argument is the pathname of the file, just as it is for the first argument of the fopen function. The second argument is an integer containing flags that control the mode that the

---

7. Berkeley UNIX guarantees only that each process has at least 20 slots in the object reference table. The table may be a little larger at your installation. The getdtablesize function may be used to find out what the actual size is.

file should be opened in. The third flag defines the file access modes that should be given to the file if the file is created by this call to open. An example of a call follows:

```
#include <sys/file.h>
char *filename = "/tmp/junk";
int fd;
    ...
fd = open(filename, O_WRONLY|O_CREAT, 0644);
if (fd < 0) {
    perror(filename);
    exit(1);
}
```

The names O_WRONLY and O_CREAT are flag values defined as macros in the include file. They indicate that we wish to open the file for output and to create the file if it does not already exist.[8] If the file is created, it will be assigned the access modes 0644 (an octal constant).[9]

These particular modes permit reading by anyone but writing only by the current user. The result returned by open is a file descriptor. If the file could not be opened, an error code is set in the external variable errno and the function returns a negative integer as its result. (And, as before, the perror function may be used to output a message corresponding to the error code set in errno.)

When we have finished using the file, it should be closed with the close function.

## Reading and Writing

Only functions for reading and writing blocks of data are provided. To read a large number of bytes of data from the file with descriptor fd, a code sequence like:

```
char inbuffer[1024];
int fd, nread;
    ...
nread = read(fd, inbuffer, 1024);
if (nread < 0) {
    perror(filename);
    exit(1);
}
```

may be used. The result returned by read is the count of characters actually read. This count may be smaller than the size of the input buffer (specified in the third argument) if

---

8. The full list of flags can be found in the manual entry for open.

9. The full list of file mode values can be found in the section 2 manual entry for chmod. Execute the command: man 2 chmod to see this entry.

we reach the end of file or if the input is being read from a terminal. An error is indicated by a negative result. The buffer size used in our example is a size that leads to fairly efficient I/O. The actual size specified in the call can be any number from one upwards. But specifying a buffer size of one makes file processing quite inefficient, because the system overhead involved in reading one character is about the same as for reading 1024 characters. If you really wish to read characters one at a time, you should probably use the stream input-output package.

Output via a file descriptor proceeds similarly. The code sequence looks like

```
char outbuffer[1024];
int fd, nwritten;
    ...
nwritten = write(fd, outbuffer, 1024);
if (nwritten < 0) {
    perror(filename);
    exit(1);
}
```

The result of the function call is the count of bytes that were actually written. This number will equal to the buffer size specified in the third argument unless there has been an I/O error. If there is an error, the result is -1.

## Other Functions

We should mention here that the lseek function is available for changing the current position within a file. It is used in a way that is very similar to the fseek function in the family of stream I/O functions. Another useful function is fdopen which can be used to convert a low-level file descriptor to the higher-level stream interface. If fd is a descriptor for a file open for input, we can execute

```
int fd;
FILE *fp;
    ...
fp = fdopen(fd, "r");
```

to obtain a stream file pointer. The read-write mode used in the fdopen call should match the mode of the file descriptor. The opposite conversion, finding the file descriptor corresponding to a stream file pointer, is performed by the fileno macro.

## 8-5    *Further Reading*

An older, but still relevant, article is "The UNIX Time-Sharing System," *Communications of the ACM* by D. M. Ritchie and K. Thompson, vol. 17, Issue 7 (July 1974), pp. 365-375. It provides a brief overview of the UNIX system and of its implementation. The description of the file system is particularly relevant to the material in this chapter. Chapters 4 and 5 of the book *The Design of the UNIX Operating System* by M. J. Bach (Prentice-Hall 1986) contain a very detailed description of how the input-output system is implemented. Even further information, more specific to Berkeley UNIX implementations, may be found in Chapter 7 of the book *The Design and Implementation of the 4.3BSD UNIX Operating System* by S. J. Leffler, M. K. McKusick, M. J. Karels and J. S. Quarterman (Addison-Wesley 1988).

# CHAPTER 9    *ADDITIONAL LIBRARY FUNCTIONS*

---

## *9-1   String and Character Handling*

### String Handling

The ANSI C standard describes a large family of string handling functions that should be provided with an ANSI C compiler. The functions whose names begin with the three letters 'str' require that input strings be terminated by a null byte (as per normal C conventions). A few additional functions whose names begin with the characters 'mem' are appropriate for handling arrays of byte values (i.e., blocks of memory). Summaries of nearly all the functions for handling strings and blocks of memory are given in Table 9-1 . The include file <string.h> contains prototype definitions for all the functions listed in the table. Therefore, you should include preprocessor directive

```
#include <string.h>
```

in any program that uses these functions. An example program that uses a few of the string handling functions appears in Figure 9-3 at the end of the chapter. The SUN implementation of UNIX has a few additional string functions that are not part of the ANSI standard. These are listed in Table 9-2.

The <string.h> include file also (indirectly) defines the datatype size_t that is used by some of the function interfaces. The size_t type is defined by a typedef statement as unsigned int in the <string.h> include file on computers with 32 bit integers. (It may be defined as unsigned long int on 16-bit computers.)

## Table 9-1  String Functions

```
char *strcpy(char *dest, char *src)
```
copies the string src into the array dest. The result is the value of dest (i.e., a pointer to the string copy).

```
char *strncpy(char *dest, char *src, size_t n)
```
copies no more than n characters from string src into the array dest. If the src string has m characters where m<n, n−m null bytes are appended to the string in dest. The result is dest.

```
char *strcat(char *dest, char *src)
```
appends the string src to the string in the array dest. The result is dest.

```
char *strncat(char *dest, char *src, size_t n)
```
appends at most n characters from the string src to the string in array dest. A terminating null byte is always written. The result is dest.

```
int strcmp(char *s1, char *s2)
```
compares the string s1 with the string s2. The result is a negative, zero or positive integer depending on whether s1<s2, s1=s2 or s1>s2, respectively.

```
int strncmp(char *s1, char *s2, size_t n)
```
compares at most n characters of the strings s1 and s2. The result is a negative, zero or positive integer depending on whether these portions of the strings compare less than, equal to or greater than (as with strcmp).

```
size_t strlen(char *s)
```
returns the length of the string s.

```
size_t strspn(char *s, char *set)
```
returns the length of the initial portion of string s that consists of only characters contained in the string set.

```
size_t strcspn(char *s, char *set)
```
returns the length of the initial portion of string s that consists of characters that do *not* appear in the string set.

*... continued on next page*

## Table 9-1  String Functions (Continued)

`char *strchr(char *s, int c)`
    searches string s for the first occurrence of character c, returning a pointer to that character if it is found. Otherwise the result is NULL.

`char *strpbrk(char *s, char *set)`
    searches string s for the first occurrence of any character that appears in the string set, returning a pointer to that character if it is found. Otherwise the result is NULL.

`char *strrchr(char *s, int c)`
    searches string s for the last occurrence of character c, returning a pointer to that character if it is found. Otherwise the result is NULL.

`char *strstr(char *s, char *pat)`
    searches string s for the first occurrence of the substring pat, returning a pointer to the located string if it is found. Otherwise the result is NULL.

`char *strtok(char *s, char *delim)`
    searches string s for the first substring that does not contain any characters contained in the string delim. The character following the substring (a token) is overwritten by a null byte and a pointer to the token is returned as the result. If the function is called again with the NULL pointer as the first argument, the search for a token resumes in the previous string at the character following the null byte that was written. The result is NULL if no token was found.

`void *memcpy(void *dest, void *src, size_t n)`
    copies n bytes from the object referenced by pointer src into the object referenced by the pointer dest. The result is dest. If the src and dest objects overlap in memory, the effect is undefined.

`void *memmove(void *dest, void *src, size_t n)`
    is like memcpy except that the effect of overlapping src and dest objects is fully defined. The effect should be equivalent to copying src to a temporary buffer and then copying the buffer to dest.

`int memcmp(void *s1, void *s2, size_t n)`
    compares the first n bytes of the object referenced by s1 with the first n bytes of the object referenced by s2. The result is a negative, zero or positive integer corresponding to the s1 and s2 objects comparing less than, equal or greater than.

`void *memchr(void *s, int c, size_t n)`
    searches up to n bytes of the object referenced by s for the first occurrence of the character c. The result is a pointer to that character, or NULL if it is not found.

## Character Handling

There is a large family of functions for testing and converting single characters. To use these functions, the C program must include the directive

```
#include <ctype.h>
```

These functions implement tests for a character being alphabetic (isalpha), being a decimal digit (isdigit), being a white space character (isspace), etc. In addition, there are functions for converting a letter from lower case to upper case (toupper), and from upper case to lower case (tolower). The full list of functions appeared in Chapter 2.

There are two major differences between ANSI C and classic C concerning the character handling functions. The first difference is that in classic C, the tests are implemented as macros. (This may have unforeseen consequences if you use an argument that has side-effects when evaluated.) Secondly, in classic C, the behavior of the character testing macros isalpha, isdigit, etc., is undefined if the argument is outside the range for ASCII characters. The isascii macro is provided in classic C to test whether the argument is in the ASCII range.

These functions are particularly useful if you intend to transport your program to another computer. For example, the test for a character being a letter of the alphabet must be coded differently on machines that use the ASCII and EBCDIC character sets. If you use the isalpha macro to perform the test, you do not have to worry about how the test should be coded.

## Table 9-2  Additional (Non-ANSI) String Functions

char *strdup(char *s)
> allocates new storage (using malloc) in to which the string s, including its trailing null byte, is copied. The result is a pointer to the string copy. If storage cannot be allocated, the result is NULL.

int strcasecmp(char *s1, char *s2)
> compares two strings like strcmp except that the comparison ignores the difference between upper and lower case letters. The ASCII character set is assumed when mapping between cases.

int strncasecmp(char *s1, *char *s2, int n)
> compares two strings like strncmp except that the comparison ignores the difference between upper and lower case. Again, ASCII coding is assumed.

## 9-2  *Storage Allocation Functions*

Storage can be dynamically allocated by the `malloc` function. Its argument is the number of bytes to allocate, its result is a pointer to the newly allocated storage. If `malloc` cannot obtain sufficient storage, it returns a null pointer result. A typical code sequence for using `malloc` is

```
#include <stdio.h>
#include <stdlib.h>
struct xx *sp;
...
sp = (struct xx *)malloc(sizeof(struct xx));
if (sp == NULL) {
    fprintf(stderr,"out of storage\n");
    exit(1);
}
```

The standard include file <stdlib.h> contains prototype definitions for `malloc` and the related storage allocation functions described in this section. Brief summaries of the functions are given in Table 9-3.

### Table 9-3  Storage Allocation/De-Allocation Functions

`void *malloc(size_t s)`

dynamically allocates a block of storage of size `s` bytes and returns a pointer to it. If the storage cannot be allocated, the result is `NULL`.

`void *calloc(size_t n, size_t s)`

dynamically allocates a block of storage for an array of `n` elements where each array has size `s` bytes. The storage is initialized to zero. The result is a pointer to the first element of the array.

`void free(void *p)`

deallocates the storage referenced by `p`. The storage must have been previously allocated by one of the allocation functions (`calloc`, `malloc` or `realloc`).

`void *realloc(void *p, size_t s)`

changes the size of the previously allocated block of storage referenced by `p` to have a size of `s` bytes. If the size is being reduced, the result will normally be the same as `p`. If the size is being increased, the object may be copied to a new location and the function result will be a pointer to that new copy (while the original is deallocated). The result may be `NULL` if insufficient memory is available.

Dynamically allocated storage can be de-allocated through the `free` function. Its argument is a pointer to an area of storage that was previously obtained from one of the allocation functions. For example, to release the storage obtained in the code sequence above, we can execute

```
free(sp);
```

Of course, once you have released the storage, you should not subsequently attempt to access it in your program.

A useful alternative to `malloc` is the `calloc` function. This function is intended for allocating storage to arrays. The storage it returns holds binary zero patterns, the same as static storage that has no explicit initialization in C programs. The `calloc` function requires two arguments. The first is the number of elements in the array, the second is the size of each element in bytes. We might, for example, use `calloc` in a program as follows:

```
#include <stdlib.h>
#define ARRAYSIZE 256
int *array1;
    ...
array1 = (int *)calloc(ARRAYSIZE, sizeof(int));
if (array1 == NULL) {
    fprintf(stderr,"out of storage\n");
    exit(1);
}
/* initialize the array */
for( i=0;  i<ARRAYSIZE;  i++ )
    array1[i] = -1;
```

Storage obtained via `calloc` can be returned to the system with the `free` function, just as for `malloc`.

There is one more storage allocation function, `realloc`. It is used to re-size a dynamically allocated array. If you browse through the on-line manual entries, you will find two more functions called `brk` and `sbrk`. These are the low-level routines which obtain storage directly from the operating system; `malloc` and the other functions listed above are implemented as calls to `brk` and `sbrk`. Normal programs should not call them directly.

## 9-3    Date and Time Functions

A group of functions provide access to the system clock and provide conversions to calendar time, etc. Prototypes for these functions and some related types and macros may be included in your program with the directive

```
#include <time.h>
```

Some of the functions treat time as being an integer that counts the number of ticks of a clock. The number of clock ticks per second is specified by a macro whose name is CLOCKS_PER_SEC. The type clock_t is an arithmetic type that can hold the number of clock ticks that occur during execution of the program. The type time_t is an arithmetic type that can hold the number of clock ticks since the time instant 0:00 on January 1, 1900. If the clock rate is reasonably high, this value will not fit into a single 32-bit integer. Therefore, you should use of the difftime function for manipulating time_t values, as this will improve the portability of your code.

Other functions manipulate a structure that describes a calendar time. This form of time measure is called a *broken down* time in the ANSI standard. The structure contains at least the nine fields shown below. Additional implementation-dependent fields may also be present.

```
struct tm {
    int tm_sec;     /* seconds, 0 - 61 */
    int tm_min;     /* minutes, 0 - 59 */
    int tm_hour;    /* hours,   0 - 23 */
    int tm_mday;    /* day of month, 1 - 31 */
    int tm_mon;     /* months since January, 0 - 11 */
    int tm_year;    /* years since 1900 */
    int tm_wday;    /* days since Sunday, 0 - 6 */
    int tm_yday;    /* days since Jan. 1, 0 - 365 */
    int tm_isdst;   /* Daylight Saving Time flag */
};
```

The comments describe the contents of each field and the range of possible values. (The peculiar range for tm_sec allows for leap seconds when clocks are corrected at the end of a year.) The tm_isdst flag is positive if DST is in effect and zero if it is not. (The ANSI C standard says that the value may be negative to indicate that information about DST is unavailable.)

The basic functions for handling dates and times are summarized in Table 9-4. Note that the arguments to the ctime, gmtime and localtime functions are pointers to time_t values (and not the time_t values themselves). This non-intuitive interface exists for historical reasons. In addition, there is one more function strftime introduced by the ANSI standard that may be used as a general-purpose function for formatting dates. It is appropriate for use if the 25-character string created by the asctime or gmtime function does not meet your needs.

## Table 9-4  Date and Time Functions

`clock_t clock(void)`
> returns the total CPU time of the program as a multiple of the number of clock ticks.

`double difftime(time_t time1, time_t time0)`
> computes the difference `time1-time0`.

`time_t mktime(struct tm *tp)`
> converts the broken down time referenced by `tp` into a calendar time (expressed as the number of clock ticks since Jan. 1, 1900). The `tm_wday` and `tm_yday` fields are ignored. On return, all fields of the argument structure will have been forced into their appropriate ranges and the `tm_wday` and `tm_yday` fields will have been set (overwriting any previous contents).

`time_t time(time_t *timer)`
> returns the number of clock ticks since Jan. 1, 1900. If the argument is not NULL, the result will also be stored in the referenced object.

`char *asctime(struct tm *tp)`
> converts the broken down time supplied by the argument into a character string (containing 25 characters plus a terminating null byte) and returns a pointer to that string. An example result from the function might be `"Mon Apr 22 16:45:47 1991\n"`.

`char *ctime(time_t *timer)`
> produces a similar result to `asctime` except that the argument supplied to the function is a calendar time expressed in clock ticks.

`struct tm *gmtime(time_t *timer)`
> converts a calendar time expressed in clock ticks to a broken down structure representing the corresponding Coordinated Universal Time (UTC). This used to be known as Greenwich Mean Time (hence the name for the function).

`struct tm *localtime(time_t *timer)`
> converts a calendar time expressed in clock ticks to a broken down structure representing the local time (in the local time zone).

## 9-4   *Macros for Handling Variable Arguments*

The printf function is an example of a C function where the number and types of arguments can differ according to what the user wishes to print. In some, but not all, implementations of classic C it is possible for the user to construct a function similar to printf. When this ability is available, the language facilities needed to write the function may depend on the compiler being used. The ANSI C standard now provides a uniform mechanism for writing functions like printf (and this mechanism is available with the Gnu C compiler).

The standard include file <stdarg.h> provides definitions for a special type named va_list and three macros needed to implement variable arguments.

The best way of explaining the use of the macros is through an example, and what better example is there than the printf function? To keep the example to a reasonable size, we will show a simplified version called myprintf that supports just the %c, %s, %b format codes. You may be unfamiliar with the %b code (because the real printf does not provide it) – this code prints a logical value (implemented by zero for *false* and non-zero for *true*) as the letter 'F' or the letter 'T'. The function coding is given in Figure 9-1.

Consider the following sample invocation of the myprintf function in the figure.

```
myprintf("condition=%b, text=%s", i>j, buffer);
```

The variable ap in the myprintf function is used to point at successive arguments in the argument list. Its type must be declared as va_list. The macro va_start is used to initialize ap. The second argument to va_start must be the name of the last argument that appears before the '...' part of the function prototype. In our example that is the argument named format. Thus, after this initialization, ap will refer to an integer object holding the value of the comparison  i>j.

When the myprintf function advances through its format string argument and reaches the %b code, it invokes the va_arg macro. This macro returns the current argument referenced by ap and advances ap to the next argument. The second argument is the expected type of the argument being accessed, in this case it is type int. (If it does not match the actual type of the next argument, it is possible that none of the following arguments will be accessed correctly and undefined results will be obtained). Subsequently, the %s format code will be encountered and va_arg is invoked again, but this time requesting a string value (char *) to be returned. Note that, in a function call, arguments of type char or short are automatically promoted to have the int type, similarly a float argument is promoted to the double type. The va_arg macro should specify the type which is actually received by the function. The %c format code is an example of this, where int and *not* char is specified as the argument type.

Finally, before the function returns control, the va_end macro should be invoked to terminate the variable argument processing.

---

### Figure 9-1   Variable Argument Processing Example

```
#include <stdarg.h>
#include <stdio.h>
#include <stdlib.h>

void myprintf( char *format, ... ) {
    va_list ap;
    int i; char c, *cp;

    va_start(ap,format);   /* initialize ap */
    for( ;  *format != '\0';  format++ ) {
        if (*format != '%') {
            putchar(*format);
            continue;
        }
        switch( *++format ) {
        case 'b':
            i = va_arg(ap,int);
            putchar( (i == 0)? 'F' : 'T' );
            break;
        case 'c':
            c = va_arg(ap,int); /* Note that the type is
                                    is not given as char */
            putchar(c);
            break;
        case 's':
            cp = va_arg(ap,char *);
            while( *cp != '\0' )
                putchar( *cp++ );
            break;
        default:
            fprintf(stderr,"bad format code: %c\n",*cp);
            goto EXIT;
        }
    }
EXIT:
    va_end(ap);   /* finish variable argument handling */
}
```

## 9-5 *Functions for Non-Local Jumps*

The C language requires that the destination label of a `goto` statement must be located within the same function. Some languages, such as Pascal, allow a jump to a label in an enclosing function as an alternative way of exiting from a procedure or function. It provides a useful way of escaping from a long series of function calls without returning one level at a time back through the call chain. The ability to exit many functions in this manner is made available by means of two functions (or macros, depending on the C implementation) called `setjmp` and `longjmp`. They are, perhaps, most useful when used in conjunction with signal handling – a topic covered in the next chapter. However, signals are difficult enough to master without adding the complexities of `setjmp` and `longjmp` that we will cover a simple example based on syntax analysis.

Suppose that we wish to read textual input consisting of a single list, but where the elements of that list may themselves be lists. For example, given the input

```
( (a b)  (c d)  ((e)  f g)  )
```

we might like our program to construct a data structure whose diagram is the following.

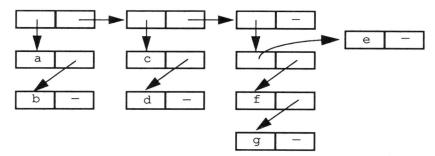

We might choose to use the `lex` and `yacc` tools to help build this program. But if the list structures are the only syntactic construct to worry about, the programming task is easily accomplished by means of a couple of recursive functions. These functions should, however, take account of syntax and exit all levels of recursion if a required right parenthesis is missing or if an unexpected character is encountered. The `setjmp` and `longjmp` functions provide the mechanism for implementing the multiple exit. Figure 9-2 shows our code for the function that builds the data structure.

The jump that implements the multiple exit is implemented by the `longjmp` function. The argument of this function is a value that indicates the destination for the jump and it has the datatype `jmp_buf`. This datatype and prototypes for the `setjmp` and `longjmp` functions are provided in the standard include file <setjmp.h>. A value of type `jmp_buf` is established by the `setjmp` function. When the following code is executed,

```
jmp_buf exitloc;
setjmp(exitloc);
```

---

### Figure 9-2  A Setjmp/Longjmp Example

```c
#include <stdio.h>
#include <stdlib.h>
#include <setjmp.h>
#define readchar()  do ch=getchar(); while(ch == ' ')
static jmp_buf exitloc;
typedef struct elem { short kind;
    union { struct cell *subl; char c; } val; } ELEM;
typedef struct cell { ELEM e; struct cell *link; } *PTR;
static char ch;  /* current input character */
static PTR read_tail(void);

ELEM read_element(void) { ELEM result;
    if (ch == '(') { readchar();
        result.kind = 1;  result.val.subl = read_tail();
        if (ch != ')') longjmp(exitloc,1);
    } else {
        if (!isalnum(ch)) longjmp(exitloc,2);
        result.kind = 0;  result.val.c = ch;
    }
    readchar();  return result;
}

PTR read_tail(void) { PTR rp;
    if (ch == ')') return NULL;
    rp = (PTR)malloc(sizeof(*rp));
    rp->e = read_element(); rp->link = read_tail();
    return rp;
}

ELEM build_list_structure(void) {
    ELEM bad_result = { 1, NULL };
    readchar();
    switch( setjmp(exitloc) ) {
    case 0: return read_element();
    case 1: fprintf(stderr, "missing rt parenthesis\n");
            break;
    case 2: fprintf(stderr, "invalid char: 0x%2x\n", ch);
    }
    return bad_result;
}
```

---

the return address of the call to setjmp is stored in the argument, exitloc. Then control is returned from setjmp as normal. If a call to longjmp is subsequently executed, passing it the argument exitloc, control is transferred to the address held in exitloc. Of course, this causes a minor programming problem because the caller of setjmp can receive control back in two different ways – initially via the normal return from setjmp and subsequently via calls to longjmp. To alleviate the programming problem, the setjmp function returns an integer result of zero for a normal return and a different integer, supplied as a second argument to longjmp, for other returns. Therefore, the caller of setjmp can test the returned result to know which case applies.

In the example program of Figure 9-2, the build_list_structure function initializes the exitloc variable with a call to setjmp. Control comes back with the result zero and this causes the read_element function to be invoked. If all goes well, read_element builds the desired data structure and returns it as its result. If an error at some level of recursion is encountered, longjmp is invoked and control is immediately transferred back to the build_list_structure function. The return code is either 1 or 2, indicating the reason for the forced return and is used to select an appropriate error message.

It should be noted that the destination for a longjmp call must be inside an active invocation of a function. When setjmp is called, the function that makes the call to setjmp provides an environment in which local variables exist and have storage allocated to them. That function must not have exited when longjmp is called, otherwise the proper environment to continue execution will no longer exist.

The final comment on longjmp is a warning. When control returns to a function via longjmp, you should not expect the local variables of that function to have the values that were previously assigned unless the variables were declared with the volatile modifier. Here is some sample code to illustrate the problem.

```
{
    int i;

    i = j*k;
    if ( setjmp(exitloc) == 0 ) {
        /* i equals j*k on this path */
        ...
    } else {
        /* we got here by a call to longjmp;
            the variable i is not necessarily equal
            to j*k on this execution path */
        ...
    }
    ...
```

Some compilers, especially optimizing compilers, may evaluate $j*k$, but defer storing the result into the memory location for i. Very often, such a deferred store is found to be unnecessary (perhaps because another value is assigned to i) and the compiler has avoided some unnecessary work when the program is run. If, however, control re-enters the function in a manner that the compiler does not expect, the strategy of deferring stores to memory may not work correctly. The ANSI C solution is as follows. If variable i is declared as

```
volatile int i;
```

the compiler will not defer any assignments to i, and thus leave the compiler free to optimize the use of other variables not declared with the volatile attribute.

## 9-6    Environment Interfacing Functions

There are several functions that permit interaction between a C program and the environment provided by the command shell. The getenv function allows a program to interrogate the settings of environment variables. For example, the csh command

```
setenv PAGER more
```

sets a shell variable named PAGER to have the string value indicated. Several programs interrogate the value of this variable to see which program should be invoked to scroll through display output that does not fit within the window. A program obtains the value by executing C code like the following

```
#include <stdlib.h>
char *value;
...
value = getenv("PAGER");
```

The result is NULL if the environment variable is not currently set. (In case you are wondering, the operation of setting or changing an environment variable by a function call inside the program is not possible.) Figure 9-3 shows a program that uses the getenv function, though you should probably read about the popen and pclose functions, described below, before studying the program in detail.

Another way that a program can interact with the command shell environment is by returning a status code when the program terminates. The function call

```
exit(0);
```

causes the program to terminate execution and return zero as the completion code to the shell. A code of zero is the conventional indication of successful completion, whereas any non-zero code is taken to be an indication of some sort of failure. A common convention in UNIX programming is to use a code of two to indicate that the arguments to the command were incorrect and a code of one to indicate other kinds of error. A few programs (e.g., the cmp program that compares two files) use the completion code to indicate the main result.

An alternative to `exit`, to be used for serious failures, is the following function call.

```
abort();
```

It causes the program to be terminated immediately and, unless the default action is over-ridden, a core dump file is generated. There is no purpose in using `abort` instead of `exit` unless you think that you will need the core file to track down a programming error. The `dbx` or `dbxtool` programs (covered in Chapter 15) may be used to analyze a core file.

Any `sh` shell command may be executed from within a C program. The argument to the `system` function is a string containing the command. If this command creates output, it writes directly to the standard output and, possibly, the standard error output. If the command expects input, it will read from the standard input. For example, if we would like a program to include a directory listing in its output, we might write the following code:

```
fflush(stdout);
system("ls -alx");
```

The call to `fflush` is usually required so that any previous output generated by the program actually appears before the output of the command executed by `system`.

If we are not content to have the output of the system command sent to the terminal, that is, if we need the output returned to our program for further processing, a *pipe* must be created. If, for example, you would like your program to execute the `ls` command and read its output as though a file were being read, code similar to the following could be used:

```
FILE *lspipe;
...
lspipe = popen("ls -alx", "r");
if (lspipe == NULL) {
    fprintf(stderr, "ls command failed!\n");   exit(1);
}
...
/*      Now the program can read the output of "ls"
        using the file pointer "lspipe".  At the end of
        input, the EOF code will be read, as usual. */
...
pclose(lspipe);
```

The first argument to `popen` is the command to be executed. It is passed to the `sh` shell for interpretation and execution. The second argument indicates the I/O direction. If we specify `"r"`, as above, then we will be reading the standard output generated by that command. If we specify `"w"`, we would be writing to the pipe and thus providing standard input for the command. The result of the call to `popen` is a stream which may be used like any other stream (except that a few operations, such as `fseek` cannot be performed). When we have finished reading from or writing to a pipe, `pclose` is used to terminate it.

A complete example of a program that uses a pipe is given in Figure 9-3. This program, *print_cmds*, will print the names of all the executable files that may be typed as sim-

## Figure 9-3    Printcmds: A Program to List Executable Files

```
/* printcmds program */
#include <stdlib.h>
#include <stdio.h>
#include <string.h>
#define MAXLEN    1024

void print_members( char *dirname ) {
    FILE *lspipe;
    char command[MAXLEN], line[MAXLEN];

    strcpy(command, "/bin/ls -F ");
    strncat(command, dirname, MAXLEN-strlen(command));
    lspipe = popen(command, "r");
    if (lspipe == NULL) {
        fprintf(stderr, "can't run %s\n", command);
        return;
    }
    printf("%s:\n", dirname);
    while(fgets(line, MAXLEN, lspipe) != NULL) {
        int astpos = strlen(line) - 2;
        if (astpos > 0 && line[astpos] == '*')
            printf("\t%.*s\n", astpos, line);
    }
    pclose(lspipe);
}

int main(void) {
    char *pathlist, *dir;
    pathlist = getenv("PATH");
    if ( pathlist == NULL ) {
        fprintf(stderr, "No PATH variable\n"); exit(1);
    }
    for( ; dir=strtok(pathlist,":"); pathlist=NULL )
        print_members(dir);
    return 0;
}
```

ple command names. That is, excluding some commands that are built into the shell (such as t ime), you will obtain a list of all the commands that may be entered on the keyboard. Print_cmds uses the getenv function to obtain the value of the PATH environment variable. This variable holds a list of all the directories where the shell will look for an executable program. The string consists of directory names separated by colon characters. The strtok function is used to extract one directory name at a time and pass it to the print_members subroutine. The string copying commands strcpy and strncat are used to construct a shell command such as "/bin/ls -F /bin" which is supplied as the first argument to the popen function. Assuming that the popen call succeeds, the program will be able to read file names one at a time from the pipe stream using the fgets function. The '-F' option to ls causes executable files to be flagged with a trailing asterisk character. For example, one of the lines that fgets might read is the string "ls*\n". By checking the last but one character in the string to see if it is an asterisk, we can determine if the file is executable (and can thus be used as a command name). If the test succeeds, the format pattern "%.*s" is used to print the file name up to but not including the trailing asterisk and linefeed characters.

If the print_cmds program were intended to be widely used, some effort might be spent on making it more efficient. In particular, the multiple use of popen to execute the ls command could be replaced by function calls that directly obtain the names of directory members. At the other extreme, if the print_cmds program were only needed for very occasional use by just a few people, we should probably implement it as a shell script.[1]

Pipes involve the creation of parallel processes. The command passed as an argument to popen is executed by a separate process. We will be looking at the creation and management of parallel processes in more detail in Chapter 10.

# 9-7    *Further Reading*

Further information and examples of use of the library functions and macros covered in this chapter may be found in any of the numerous books on C programming. However, it would be preferable to consult a book that focuses on ANSI C, such as *C: A Software Engineering Approach* by P. A. Darnell and P. E. Margolis (Springer-Verlag 1990).

---

1. The overhead of starting up a shell instance and interpreting the commands is not so great when compared to the overhead inherent in performing input-output. It can be argued, on maintenance grounds, that a shell script implementation is preferable.

# CHAPTER 10

*PROCESSES AND*
*SIGNALS*

---

## 10-1  *Parallel Processing*

Most computers, probably including the one you use, can only execute one machine instruction at a time. Yet, if your computer is under the control of the Berkeley UNIX operating system, several people could be using the computer at the same time. It appears to each user that the computer is executing instructions solely on his or her behalf. The ability of a single computer with a single processing unit (CPU) to execute several programs simultaneously is known as *multiprogramming*. The computer system executes, perhaps, several thousand instructions of one user's program, then suspends execution of that program and switches to another user's program. By regularly switching from one user to another (a scheme called *time-slicing*), each user has the illusion that his or her program is continuously executing. As more users sign on to the system, programs receive time slices less often and the illusion of continuous execution may begin to break down.

So far we have considered situations in which each user has only one program executing at a time, but the UNIX system allows each user to have several simultaneously executing programs. All one need do to have two programs running is to start up the first program as a background job. We could, for example, type the commands

```
gcc -ansi giantprog.c -o giantprog &
vi anotherprog.c
```

which initiate a long-running C compilation and then, while that compilation is running, edit a file using the vi editor. Having two or more programs running simultaneously does not represent any great problem to the UNIX system. The operating system just has to share the CPU among a few more programs using the time-slicing mechanism.

We do not need the shell command language to create two simultaneously executing programs. The same effect may be achieved by including the appropriate function calls inside a C program. But, before we can examine these functions, we have to become more precise in our use of terminology. In particular, we have to introduce the concept of a *process*. A process is a program, consisting of instructions and data and machine register contents, with an environment and an instruction pointer that indicates the next instruction that is to be executed in the program. The process environment is information maintained by the system about the process. It includes the file descriptor table, accounting information, a unique identification number for the process, and a few other details.

At first sight, it might seem that our definition for a process also seems to describe a program. That is correct: a process is just a special case of a program. In general, however, a program may split itself into two or more separate pieces, each of which execute independently. These pieces are called *processes*. Initially, a program begins execution as a single process. This process executes by receiving regular time slices from the operating system. In the course of its execution, the process may call a function that causes the operating system to create a new process. Both the original process and the new process receive time slices from the operating system and, therefore, appear to execute simultaneously. After the new process has been created, we would say that the program consists of two processes. Possibly the two processes execute the same sequence of machine instructions, but this is not necessarily the case. Possibly the two processes share the same data area in memory, but this too is not necessarily the case. The only thing that we can say with certainty is that the program has two threads of control. In other words, there are two separate instruction pointers indicating two, independent, next instructions to be executed.

Any C program can fork into two instances of itself by making a call to the `fork` system function. A simple program that does exactly that is shown in Figure 10-1. The new process that is created by the call to `fork` is an exact duplicate of the process that makes the call. The duplicate process is provided with a copy of the data area of the original process, but in a different region of main memory, and it is provided with a copy of the original process' environment. Since the new process has the same data and environment as the original process, it has access to exactly the same open files. The only easily discernible differences in the environment are that the accounting information shows that the new process has consumed no CPU time, the new process has a different identification number and the identity of its parent process is different. Every active process in the system has a unique identification number, which is called the *process id*. A process can find out its process id by calling the `getpid` function.

The program of Figure 10-1 clones itself into two separate processes and then each process repeatedly outputs its process id. If you care to execute this program, you will see output similar to the following

```
Hello, my name is 7050!
Hello, my name is 7050!
Hello, my name is 7050!
Hello, my name is 7051!
Hello, my name is 7051!
Hello, my name is 7050!
    etc.
```

You see several output lines with one process id, then several with another process id, then several more with the first process id, and so on. The number of consecutive lines with the same process id corresponds to how many lines can be output in a single time slice. The faster the computer you use, the greater the number of identical adjacent lines that you will see. You will not see individual output lines broken up, interrupted by a line from the other process, because the standard output functions normally use line buffering.

It is important to be clear that each process has its own data area. If one of the processes writes to a global variable, that assignment can have no effect on any other processes. This behavior is exemplified to some extent by the program in Figure 10-1 because there is apparently only one variable named `pid` in the program, yet two different process ids are printed. Figure 10-2 should help to make the situation even clearer.

In this next example, we can see that the `fork` function returns a result, or in fact, two results – one result for the original process that invoked `fork` and a different result for the new process. The result returned to the original process, called the *parent* process, is the

---

### Figure 10-1   An Experiment in Forking (#1)

```c
#include <stdio.h>
#include <stdlib.h>

int main(void) {
    int pid;
    fork();
    pid = getpid();
    for( ; ; ) {
        printf("Hello, my name is %d!\n", pid);
    }
    return 0;
}
```

process id of the new process. The result returned to the other process, the *child* process, is zero. If you care to run the second program, you will see forty numbered lines from the child process interwoven with forty numbered lines from the parent process. The fact that you see forty correctly numbered lines from each should prove to you that there are two copies of variable *i* after the forking operation.

A new function, wait, is used in the example. This function causes the process that calls it to be suspended until a child process has completed execution.[1] The parameter to wait is a pointer to a word in memory. When control returns from the call to wait, this word holds flags that indicate the completion status of the child process. The wait function also returns the process number of the child process that completed as its result. Our program needs to check the process number only if it is possible that there is more than one child process running (or perhaps no child process running).

If necessary, our program could test the flags to see whether the child process terminated abnormally. A suitable definition for the layout of flags in the status word can be found in the header file <sys/wait.h>. Since completion status is unimportant to us in the sample program, we will not go into the details until later.

---

### Figure 10-2   An Experiment in Forking (#2)

```
#include <stdio.h>
#include <stdlib.h>
#define NLINES 40
int i, pid, status;

int main(void) {
    pid = fork();
    if (pid == 0) {          /* this is the child process */
        for( i=1; i<=NLINES; i++ )
            printf("%d. I am the child!\n", i);
    } else {                 /* this is the parent process */
        for( i=NLINES; i>0; i-- )
            printf("%d. I am the parent!\n", i);
        wait(&status);
    }
    return 0;
}
```

---

1. Or until the calling process receives some signal. Signals are discussed later in this chapter.

There is no requirement that the parent process wait for its child processes to finish before exiting itself. If the parent process terminates first, all its child processes become so-called orphaned processes, but carry on executing normally. It is almost always poor programming practice to create orphaned processes, because there may be no indication to the user that there are still processes running. If one of the orphaned processes gets into an infinite loop, the user may be completely unaware of this, and the orphaned process may continue execution even after the user has logged out. By having the parent process wait for its children, the user will have a more explicit indication that there is a running program. (If the program is run as a foreground job, no command prompt will appear until the parent process completes.)

What use is the fork function in a program? To a certain extent, the creation of a new process may let you get more computational work done because you would have two processes receiving time slices from the system rather than one. However, exploiting this fact could make you unpopular with other users, who might notice a degradation in their service. There are two real reasons why a new process might be needed. The first reason is that we may want the new process to watch for some external event that is logically unrelated to the task being performed by the parent process. Possible external events include timer interrupts or inputs received from a communications line. The second reason is that we may want the new process to execute some other program in the system. Possibly the parent process and the new process will communicate via standard input-output in the same manner as pipes. Whatever the reason for creating the new process, there would usually need to be some means for the processes to communicate with each other. But to simplify matters, let us begin with an example where there is no need to communicate.

Our example will emulate the system function, which was mentioned in the previous chapter. If you insert the statement

```
system("date >> logfile");
```

into a C program, the string argument will be passed to a new instance of the sh shell command processor for execution. Our program example will be code that imitates the effect of the system function, but where we will invoke the csh shell instead. The few lines of C code needed to achieve this effect are given in Figure 10-3.

To be more generally useful, we should, of course, package our code as a function that is used in the same way as system. In the example, we clone a child process as in the earlier examples. A second copy of the original program is of no use to us, so we have the child process immediately transfer control to the csh program. The transfer is achieved with the execl function. This function makes a request to the UNIX system to replace the current process (the one calling execl) with a new process. The new process is an executable program whose pathname is given by the first argument. The second and subsequent arguments are the parameters that will be supplied to the program and may be accessed by that program via its argv argument. The end of this list of parameters is indicated by a zero. In our example, we are asking the UNIX system to execute the program "/bin/csh" and for this program to see the argument values:

```
argv[0] = "csh"
argv[1] = "-c"
argv[2] = the csh command
```

The −c flag indicates that a shell command is provided as the next argument (instead of having the shell read a command from the standard input). Control does not normally return from the call to execl. If it does, it means that the UNIX system was unable to execute the program named in the first argument.

Before continuing with the explanation of the sample program, we should note that execl is but one function in a family of seven similar functions for overlaying the current process with a new program. The most general of these functions is execve, which is used if the number of arguments to be passed to the program is not known in advance and if the program is to be supplied with a new set of environment variables. Further details can be obtained from the on-line manual entries for execve and execl.

---

### Figure 10-3   Execution of a csh Command

```c
#include <stdio.h>
#include <stdlib.j>
#include <signal.h>
int pid, status, wait_result;
char *command; /* the csh command */
void (*old_INT_handler)(), (*old_QUIT_handler)();
    ...
    command = "date >> logfile" ;
    ...
    pid = fork();
    if (pid == 0) { /* child process */
        execl("/bin/csh", "csh", "-c", command, 0);
        fprintf(stderr, "unable to invoke csh!\n");
        exit(127);
    }
    old_INT_handler = signal(SIGINT, SIG_IGN);
    old_QUIT_handler = signal(SIGQUIT, SIG_IGN);
    do {
        wait_result = wait( &status );
    } while(wait_result != pid && wait_result != -1);
    signal(SIGINT, old_INT_handler);
    signal(SIGQUIT, old_QUIT_handler);
    ...
```

---

While the child process in our sample program is using the `csh` shell to execute the command, the parent process waits for the child to complete. The calls to the `signal` function should be ignored for the moment; they will be explained later in this chapter. The parent process in this program uses a more general, and more reliable, method of waiting for a child to complete than in the program of Figure 10-2. The code checks that it is really the child process that has completed when control returns from the call to `wait`. If control returns because some other child has completed (or for some other reason), we repeat the wait request. One more detail is taken care of too. If there are no children processes when the call to `wait` is made, the result returned by `wait` is −1. In our sample program, it would be possible to obtain this −1 result only if the earlier call to `fork` fails. Although such a failure is unlikely,[2] it is desirable to code the wait loop in such a way that it is guaranteed to terminate.

To conclude the discussion of `fork`, we should note that systems based on Berkeley UNIX provide a function named *vfork*. In our example of Figure 10-3, the system creates a duplicate copy of the program and then immediately discards this program copy, replacing it with the `csh` program. It is clearly inefficient to create a new process whose first action is to call `execl`, especially if this process was occupying a large region of memory. (Recall that the data space of the process is completely duplicated by the call to `fork`.) If you have code similar to that shown in the figure, you may substitute `vfork` for `fork` and `_exit` for `exit` (in the child process only) and thereby avoid the inefficiency. The child process should not make any assignments to global variables before calling `execl` or else there may be some surprising results. This is because `vfork` suppresses the duplication of the parent process' data space. The manual entry warns that `vfork` represents only an interim solution to the efficiency problem and is likely to be dropped in some future UNIX release.[3] (A more permanent solution would presumably use a *copy-on-write* scheme where the pages in data space are tagged as read-only; if either process writes to a data location, a hardware interrupt occurs and the operating system makes a duplicate of just the page of memory that holds the data location.)

## 10-2  *Signals*

When a program forks into two or more processes, rarely do these processes execute independently of each other. The processes usually require some form of synchronization or some method of passing data between them. Data has to be passed using input-output functions and we will be looking at the *pipe* and *socket* approaches to doing this in the next chapter. The UNIX method of synchronizing processes is based on the `signal` mechanism. To keep explanations simple, we will start by considering signals in situations where there is only a single process running.

---

2. The `fork` function will fail to create a new process if you already have the maximum allowed number of processes.

3. On SUN-4 systems, a program that uses `vfork` should include the header file <vfork.h>.

## Introduction to UNIX Signals

A signal is very similar in concept to a machine interrupt. When a computer detects an unusual event, it stops executing the current program and transfers control to an interrupt routine that is located somewhere in the code of the operating system. When a C program receives a signal, control is immediately passed to a function called a signal handler. The signal handler function can execute some C statements and exit. It can exit in three different ways: it can return control to the place in the program which was executing when the signal occurred; it can return control to some other point in the program; or, finally, the signal handler can terminate the program by calling the `exit` or `_exit` functions.

There are many kinds of signal supported in UNIX systems derived from Berkeley UNIX. The different signal types have numbers which range from one upwards. However, for readability and portability reasons, programs should not use these numbers directly. Preprocessor names for the signal types are defined in the header file <signal.h>. A list of the more standard signal types appears in Table 10-1. The list is probably not complete for your implementation of the Berkeley UNIX system. In particular, the SUN implementation has additional signals used for managing windows. Only the first few signals, marked by a dagger symbol, are likely to be portable from one system to another.

Several signals, such as the `SIGFPE` signal (floating point exception), correspond to machine interrupts. If your C program attempts to divide by 0.0, say, a machine interrupt is generated. An interrupt routine in the operating system will trap the interrupt and pass control to the signal handler function in your program that is currently responsible for the `SIGFPE` signal. Other signals are directly generated by your program or by other programs within the UNIX system or by typing certain characters on the keyboard. The characters that generate interrupts are normally chosen to be control characters (two key combinations that include the *Control* key). The default choices for these characters can be changed with the `stty` command. But, assuming that you have not changed the defaults, the keyboard-generated signals used most often are as follows: typing the *Control-Z* key combination while a program is running generates a `SIGTSTP` signal and this would normally cause the program to be temporarily suspended; hitting the *break* key or *Control-C* combination generates a `SIGINT` signal and this normally causes the program to be terminated; hitting the *Control-\* key combination generates a `SIGQUIT` signal and this normally causes the program to be terminated and a core dump file to be generated.

Initially, a default action is provided for each kind of signal. The default action for several signals is to terminate the program. For another group of signals, including `SIGFPE`, the action is to terminate the program and generate a file named "core". This file contains a memory image of the program for use by the `adb`, `sdb` or `dbx` debuggers. For another group of signals, including `SIGTSTP`, the default action is to suspend execution of the program. Finally, there are a few signals where the default action is to do nothing. That is, the signal is ignored.

## Table 10-1   List of Signal Types

| Name | Description | Default Action |
|---|---|---|
| SIGABRT | abnormal termination[†] | TC |
| SIGFPE | floating point exception[†] | TC |
| SIGILL | illegal instruction[†] | TC |
| SIGINT | interrupt[†] | T |
| SIGSEGV | segmentation fault[†] | TC |
| SIGTERM | termination signal[†] | T |
| SIGHUP | hangup | T |
| SIGQUIT | quit signal | TC |
| SIGTRAP | trace trap | TC |
| SIGIOT | IOT instruction | TC |
| SIGEMT | EMT instruction | TC |
| SIGKILL | kill signal | T |
| SIGBUS | bus error | TC |
| SIGSYS | bad argument to system call | TC |
| SIGPIPE | write to a closed pipe | T |
| SIGALRM | timer alarm | T |
| SIGURG | urgent socket message | I |
| SIGSTOP | unignorable stop signal | S |
| SIGTSTP | keyboard stop signal | S |
| SIGCONT | continue after stop | I |
| SIGCHLD | change in child status | I |
| SIGTTIN | background terminal input | S |
| SIGTTOU | background terminal output | S |
| SIGIO | I/O has become possible | I |
| SIGXCPU | CPU time limit exceeded | T |
| SIGXFSZ | file size limit exceeded | T |
| SIGVTALRM | virtual time alarm | T |
| SIGPROF | profiling time alarm | T |

*where* **T** = terminate; **TC** = terminate with core dump; **I** = ignore; **S** = stop.
Note that signals tagged by a dagger (†) are part of the ANSI C standard.

For nearly all signal types, the default action can be changed. The two signal types where the default action cannot be overridden are named SIGKILL and SIGSTOP. The inescapable action for a SIGKILL signal is to terminate the process. The existence of SIGKILL means that there is always a guaranteed method of terminating a process (short of the drastic step of shutting the computer system down). The action for SIGSTOP is to stop the process and this provides a guaranteed method of temporarily halting a process. Changing the action to be performed when a signal is received is accomplished through the signal or sigvec functions. The former function has a simpler interface and is part of the ANSI C standard so we will consider it exclusively.

A simple example involving signals appears in Figure 10-4. What happens if we enter this program, compile it and run it? The computational part of this program is uninteresting, to say the least. Every several seconds, the program outputs a dot on the screen. When you get tired of this behavior, you can interrupt the program. Hitting the break key on your terminal should generate the SIGINT signal and cause the signal handler function to be exe-

---

### Figure 10-4 An Experiment with Signals (#1)

```c
#include <stdio.h>
#include <stdlib.h>
#include <signal.h>
int i = 0;

void quit( int code ) {
    fprintf(stderr,
        "\nInterrupt (code = %d, i = %d)\n", code, i);
    exit(1); /* abnormal termination */
}

int main(void) {
    /* intercept various termination signals */
    signal(SIGINT, quit);
    signal(SIGTERM, quit);
    signal(SIGQUIT, quit);
    /* show the passage of time */
    do {
        i++;
        if (i % 100000 == 0) putc('.', stderr);
    } while( i != 0 );
    /* terminate successfully (after a few hours) */
    return 0;
}
```

cuted. You can send the program some different signals by typing various control character combinations. You can see which control characters have special purposes by executing the command

```
stty all
```

The character appearing under the heading *intr* is an alternative to *break* for generating the SIGINT signal, while the character under the *quit* heading generates the SIGQUIT signal. (If, for example, the notation ^\ appears under *quit* this means that the *control-\* key combination generates the signal.)

If you run the program as a background job, you can try sending an even greater variety of signals to the program. Assuming that you are using the csh command shell and that you have just started this program, you can send it the SIGTERM signal by executing the command

```
kill %+
```

You can send it any signal you like by including another argument in the command. For example,

```
kill -9 %+
```

will send it the SIGKILL signal, and this will terminate the program immediately. Either signal names (without the *SIG* prefix) or signal numbers may be used in the kill command; so

```
kill -KILL %+
```

is an alternative method of giving the same command. In addition to the kill command, a C process can send a signal to itself or to any other process by calling the library function named kill. The kill function is discussed later in the chapter.

## Proper Use of the `signal` Function

Before proceeding to more difficult examples, we should be clear about what the signal function is doing and how it works. For each process, the UNIX system maintains a table of the action that should be performed for each kind of signal. When the process calls the signal function, the table entry for the signal type named as the first argument is changed to the value provided as the second argument. There are three possibilities for the second argument. It may be: SIG_IGN (ignore the signal), SIG_DFL (perform the default action), or a pointer to a signal handler function. (SIG_IGN and SIG_DFL are names defined in the <signal.h> header file.) The signal function returns the old table entry as its result. If you eventually wish to restore the original signal handling action, you should save this result. The data type of the result is *pointer to function with **int** argument returning **void***. The variable used to hold the result should therefore be declared in the following manner.

```
void (*signal_result)(int);
```

The result returned by `signal` explains the signal handling code that was included in Figure 10-3 earlier. In that code, the parent process disabled the `SIGINT` and `SIGQUIT` signals while it was waiting for the child process to finish. Later, when the child has terminated, the original signal handling actions are restored. Why should the parent process not respond to these signals? It should not in case the child process installs handlers for either kind of signal. If it does, the parent process may be killed by the signal while the child continues – and this orphaned process can become a nuisance. (It may, for example, try to read from the keyboard and so interfere with your shell commands.)

This is, perhaps, an appropriate point to consider another problem with signal handling. It is often the case that a parent process wishes to ignore a certain kind of signal and so executes a call like

```
oldhandler = signal(SIGHUP, SIG_IGN);
```

in which we use `SIGHUP` as a plausible example of a signal that might be ignored. But if the parent process spawns a child that performs an `execl` call to execute a self-contained program, it is quite possible that this program will contain a call similar to the following.

```
oldh = signal(SIGHUP, myhandler);
```

This call has the effect of causing the child process to accept signals that are being ignored by the parent. There are undoubtedly some situations where this behavior is desirable. But it is more likely to be the case that the child process should not start intercepting signals whose default action has previously been changed (by the parent) to `SIG_IGN`. Therefore, the *normal* method of installing a new signal handler is to use a code sequence like the following:

```
oldhandler = signal(SIGHUP, SIG_IGN);
if (oldhandler != SIG_IGN)
    signal(SIGHUP, newhandler);
```

That is, before installing our new signal handler, we should check to see that the current action for this signal is not `SIG_IGN`.

Now that we have been through all the details of installing a signal handler, let us consider the actions that take place when a signal handler is called. If a signal occurs and control is transferred to a signal handler function, further occurrences of this kind of signal are temporarily inhibited. This signal type is said to be *blocked*. If and when control is returned from the signal handler, this signal type will automatically be unblocked. But only this one kind of signal is blocked while the signal handler is executing. It is quite possible for a different kind of signal to interrupt the signal handler.

When a signal handler function is invoked, it is passed three arguments. The first argument is the number of the signal. The second argument is an integer code that, for some signal types, refines the reason for the signal occurring. For example, the `SIGFPE` signal is generated for almost any kind of arithmetic error that includes integer divide by zero, floating point divide by zero, and floating point overflow. The third argument provides information on where the program was interrupted.

## Returning Control from Signal Handlers

The previous example simply terminated the program when the signal was received. But what if we want to resume the interrupted code? Or, what if we would like to continue execution at a different place in the program? Figure 10-5 illustrates both possibilities.

---

### Figure 10-5    An Experiment with Signals (#2)

```c
#include <stdio.h>
#include <stdlib.h>
#include <signal.h>
#include <setjmp.h>
jmp_buf return_pt;
int i;

void trap_int(void) {           /* SIGINT signal handler */
    char answer[80];
    fputs("\nDo you wish to restart? ", stdout);
    gets( answer );
    if (*answer != 'y' && *answer != 'Y')
        exit(1);
    longjmp(return_pt, 1);
}

void trap_quit(void) {        /* SIGQUIT signal handler */
    printf("\ni = %d\n", i);
}

int main(void) {
    signal(SIGQUIT, trap_quit);
    if (setjmp(return_pt) == 0)
        signal( SIGINT, trap_int );
    for( i=1; i!=0; i++ ) {
        if ( i%100000 == 0 ) {
            putchar('.');  /* show the passage of time */
            fflush(stdout);
        }
    }
    puts("\nFinished!");
    return 0;
}
```

---

In this short program, the signal handler for the SIGQUIT signal prints the current value of the variable *i* and then returns control to the point in the main program that was interrupted. If you run this program, you can generate the signals (normally with the *Control-\* key combination) and see that variable *i* is continually increasing in value. If, however, you generate the SIGINT signal (with the *break* key or your interrupt control character), you will be prompted for input from the keyboard. Typing a letter "y" (or "Y") causes the computation loop in the main program to be restarted. Typing anything else causes the program to be terminated.

Restarting the main loop requires a control transfer to a point in the program different from the point of interruption. The setjmp and longjmp functions, covered in the previous chapter, are useful in this case. We will briefly review their operation. When a call to setjmp is executed, the return point of this function is remembered in the buffer supplied as the function argument. The function returns zero as its result. Subsequently, if we execute a call to longjmp and supply this buffer as the first argument, control will be transferred to the position remembered in the buffer. This point in the code is at the return from setjmp. Thus it might seem to the user of setjmp that control returns from the call more than once. It may be important to your program to distinguish the original return from setjmp from apparent returns generated by longjmp. Therefore, you must supply a value to longjmp (as its second argument) that will be used as the return value of setjmp. Any non-zero value is sufficient to distinguish the two kinds of return.

Notice that our program is careful not to set the SIGINT signal handler until after initializing the return_pt buffer with setjmp. (Otherwise the occurrence of a SIGINT signal between setting the signal handler and initializing the buffer could cause a wild jump of control.) We need only set the signal handler if the result from setjmp is zero.

There is one important point to note with the use of setjmp and longjmp. When longjmp is executed, the function that contained the call to setjmp which set the buffer must still be active. If this function has returned or even if it has returned and been re-entered, execution of the longjmp can cause chaos. The local variables of the function to which longjmp returns may contain garbage and when this function attempts to return to its caller, a wild jump may occur. This happens because the local variables and return address for active procedures are held on a data stack. When longjmp is executed, the stack is popped so that it has the same height that it had had when the setjmp was executed. If this fails to restore the stack to its earlier configuration, there will almost certainly be chaos.

## Signalling Between Processes

One process may send a signal to another process, provided that this other process also belongs to you.[4] The signal mechanism may be used for various purposes. It may be used to kill errant processes, to temporarily suspend execution of processes, to make processes aware of the passage of time, or to synchronize the actions of processes.

---

4. To be precise, the two processes must have the same effective user id.

To send a signal to a process, you will usually need to know the number of that process (its *process id*). The only exception occurs when you need to send the same signal to all processes in a *process group*. (If your program has been forking and has created several processes, all these processes should belong to the same group.) A parent process can always know the numbers for its child processes, because the `fork` function returns the number of the new child process to the parent. A child process can always determine the number of its parent because there is a system function `getppid` that returns this number. And, a process can always determine its own number with the `getpid` function. The function call that sends a signal is `kill`. Its name is, perhaps, misleading because it does not necessarily kill the process that receives the signal. A possible call is

```
kill(getppid(), SIGINT);
```

which sends the `SIGINT` signal to the parent of the current process.

The necessity of knowing process numbers and the requirement that the processes have the same effective user id will, in practice, restrict the signal mechanism to processes that have a common parent. If you use it only for processes that belong to the same program, you should not encounter any difficulties.

## Use of Timer Signals

There are many situations in which a program needs to be aware of the passage of time. Perhaps we would like to terminate a process that is taking too long, perhaps there is some action that must be performed periodically, such as writing checkpoint information to a file.

UNIX systems derived from Berkeley UNIX maintain three interval timers for each process. These timers are counters which are being continuously decremented. When a timer reaches zero, a signal is sent to the process. One timer is used for measuring real time. Real time is time as it is measured by a clock on the wall; the rate of passage of real time is completely independent of what the computer is doing. For example, if you set the real interval timer to hold 10 seconds, then 10 seconds later, a `SIGALRM` signal is delivered to the process. A second timer measures virtual time. This timer is like a stopwatch that runs during time slices received by the process and is stopped at other times. In other words, the virtual timer measures the amount of CPU time that the process is consuming. When the virtual interval timer expires, a `SIGVTALRM` signal is delivered. The third timer measures virtual time plus system time. That is, the timer is being decremented while the process is executing and while the UNIX system is executing a request on behalf of the process. When this timer trips, a `SIGPROF` signal is delivered. As the signal name suggests, this timer is intended to be useful to program profilers (such as those described in Chapter 15).

An interval timer is set with the `setitimer` function. This function both sets the timer to hold a new value and returns the old value of the timer. To simply inspect the value held in an interval timer, the `getitimer` function can be used. As a short example of the use of the virtual timer, Figure 10-6 shows the use of a function that prints regular progress reports on how much CPU time has been consumed.

## Figure 10-6   A CPU Time Meter Function

```c
#include <stdio.h>
#include <stdlib.h>
#include <signal.h>
#include <sys/time.h>
int interval=10;                /* report every 10 seconds */

void vt_tick(void) {
    static int total_time = 0;

    fprintf(stderr,"\nCPU Usage = %d secs.\n",
            (total_time += interval));
}

void start_cpu_meter(void) {
    struct itimerval vt_val;

    if (interval <= 0) return;
    signal(SIGVTALRM, vt_tick);
    vt_val.it_value.tv_sec = interval;
    vt_val.it_value.tv_usec = 0;
    vt_val.it_interval.tv_sec = interval;
    vt_val.it_interval.tv_usec = 0;
    setitimer(ITIMER_VIRTUAL, &vt_val, NULL);
}

int main(void) {
    int i = 0;

    start_cpu_meter();
    for( ; ; ) /* consume some CPU time */
        i++;
    /* this line is never reached */
    return 0;
}
```

As the code illustrates, timer values are split into two separate words. One word (the field named `tv_sec`) holds seconds. The other word (`tv_usec`) holds microseconds. The fact that intervals can be expressed to microsecond accuracy should not be understood to imply that operating system can time processes to that degree of accuracy. Some room for improvement in timing accuracy has been left to accommodate faster computers.

Which of the three interval timers to use is specified in the first parameter of `setitimer`. A pointer to a structure containing the new timer value is passed as the second parameter. A pointer to a structure that would receive a copy of the old timer value could be passed as the third parameter. The old value is not returned if `NULL` is passed.

The structure passed to `setitimer` actually contains two timer values. One value, the `it_value` field, specifies the time until the next signal is generated. The other value, the `it_interval` field, can be used to obtain repeated signals at regular intervals. For example, if we set `it_value` to 5 seconds and `it_interval` to 3 seconds, we would receive signals after 5 seconds, 8 seconds, 11 seconds, and so on.

A simpler version of `setitimer` is available. It is called `alarm` and is available on all versions of the UNIX system, whereas `setitimer` is available only on Berkeley-based UNIX systems. The call `alarm(n)` generates a single SIGALRM signal after a delay of $n$ seconds. Other functions useful for timing purposes include `sleep` and `pause`. The `sleep` function causes the calling process to be suspended for the period of time specified by its argument. The `pause` function suspends the calling process until after the next timer signal has arrived and the signal handler function returns from handling that signal.

## Handling the SIGTSTP Signal

A program executing as the foreground job can normally be suspended by hitting the *Control-Z* key combination. This control character causes a `SIGTSTP` signal to be sent to every process in the job[5] and the default action for the `SIGTSTP` signal is to suspend the process. A suspended process can later be restarted by sending it the `SIGCONT` signal. The `csh` commands that restart a stopped job send this signal to every stopped process in the job (process group).

Some programs must intercept the `SIGTSTP` signal to perform some special actions. The `vi` editor, for example, normally operates with the terminal in the *raw* and *noecho* modes.[6] (Raw mode implies that none of the special characters such as *Control-U* to erase a line, etc., will work.) If `vi` is simply stopped in its tracks, the terminal will be left in a strange state in which no characters echo on the screen, backspacing will not erase mis-

---

5. To be more accurate, the signal is sent to every process in the *process group*. All processes in a Berkeley-based UNIX system belong to some group, each group being identified by a process group number. The `csh` command shell creates a separate process group for execution of each job.

6. We will be looking at terminal modes and how to change them in the next chapter.

takes, and so on. Consequently, `vi` and programs like it must intercept `SIGTSTP` to restore the terminal to its usual mode. Later, when `vi` is restarted, it must set the terminal modes again and redraw the screen. The signal handler for `SIGTSTP` in a program like `vi` should have the structure shown in Figure 10-7.

Assuming that the main program installs this signal handler by executing

```
signal(SIGTSTP, suspend);
```

a *Control-Z* character will cause control to enter our `suspend` function. This function should begin by restoring the terminal modes, and flushing output that is pending for the terminal and for any open files. In general, the function should ensure that the program environment is returned to the state that the user expects. The user of the program is likely to be unhappy if, for example, subsequent commands typed on the keyboard do not echo on the screen. Next, the function unblocks `SIGTSTP` signals with a call to the `sigsetmask` function (recall that further deliveries of a signal are automatically blocked while control is in the handler for that signal). It then restores the default processing action for the `SIGTSTP` signal. Now that we are ready for the process to be stopped, we send the `SIGTSTP` signal to ourself with the `kill` function, and our process is stopped because that is the default action for the signal.

---

### Figure 10-7   A SIGTSTP Signal Handler

```c
#include <signal.h>

void suspend(void) {
    .
    . /*     restore terminal to normal operating mode,
    .           and move the cursor to last line */
    .

    fflush(stdout);    /* flush pending output */
    sigsetmask(0);
    signal(SIGTSTP, SIG_DFL);
    kill(0, SIGTSTP);
    /*  control returns here after
        the process is restarted */
    signal(SIGTSTP, suspend);
    .
    . /*     set the terminal modes
    .           and redraw the screen */
    .
}
```

Later, when the program is restarted, control resumes at the statement following the call to `kill`. We immediately reinstall the signal handler and then we can go about setting terminal modes to whatever the program requires, redrawing the screen, and doing anything necessary to put the program back in a suitable state for resuming execution. Finally, control can return from the signal handler to where we were when the *Control-Z* character took effect.

# 10-3  *Further Reading*

For background information on the process concept and on using interrupts to control software, almost any text on operating systems may be consulted. One possibility is *Operating System Concepts* by A. Silberschatz and J. L. Peterson (Addison-Wesley 1988). Detailed technical information on processes and signals as implemented in Berkeley UNIX systems is contained in Chapter 4 of *The Design and Implementation of the Berkeley 4.3BSD UNIX Operating System* by S. J. Leffler, M. K. McKusick, M. J. Karels and J. S. Quarterman (Addison-Wesley 1989).

# CHAPTER 11 *TERMINAL AND WINDOW HANDLING*

## *11-1  The Terminal Driver*

The characters that you type on the keyboard of your terminal or workstation do not go directly to the program you are running. They are first processed by an interface program known as the terminal driver or the TTY driver.[1] Similarly, output characters to the terminal or workstation screen are also subject to some processing.

When operating in its normal mode, the terminal driver reads characters from the keyboard, echoes these characters to the screen and also saves them in a line buffer. When the line is completed with a linefeed or carriage return character, the line is made available to whatever program you are currently executing. Certain characters you type are treated specially by the terminal driver. One special character is the backspace character. If the terminal driver is operating in a mode suitable for CRT terminals, typing a backspace causes three characters to be echoed to the screen and a character to be deleted from the line buffer. When you type a backspace, the driver echoes a backspace, then a space to blank out the position on the screen that you are about to overwrite and then another backspace to put the cursor back on the space. Another special character is your *kill* character, usually '@' or *Control-U*, which causes the line buffer to be cleared. Other special characters, such as

---

1.  *TTY* is an abbreviation for teletypewriter, once the only kind of terminal supported by the UNIX system. Even though teletypewriters are rarely seen now, the abbreviation occurs throughout the system documentation.

*Control-\*, cause signals to be sent to whatever program is currently executing (and therefore has control of the terminal). The character sent by the *return* key of your keyboard is also subject to processing: the terminal driver echoes both a carriage return and a linefeed to the screen and sends a linefeed character to the program. This is why programs that read several lines of data might check for the linefeed character, '\n', in the input but not for the carriage return character, '\r'.

Output processing by the terminal driver is not as sophisticated as the input processing. For the most part, characters are transmitted unchanged to the screen. One action is that when a program outputs a linefeed character, the terminal driver will normally insert a carriage return character. The translation of tab characters into spaces is an optional service provided by the driver for terminals which do not understand the concept of tab stops. The driver will also optionally create time delays to slow the transmission rate to terminals that have trouble keeping up after certain screen actions. For example, some terminals can accept characters at a very rapid rate as long as the characters appear one after the other on the same line. But when a linefeed character is received by the terminal, it may be temporarily unable to receive new characters until it has finished scrolling the screen image up.

There are actually two different terminal drivers available with Berkeley-based UNIX systems, the old driver and the new driver. The new driver must be used if you use the `csh` command shell, since only the new driver supports the *Control-Z* control character and understands job control. The old driver is perfectly usable, however, if you use the *sh* shell. We will assume that you use `csh` and therefore also need to use the new terminal driver. To force use of the new driver, you should include a line similar to

```
stty new crt
```

in your ".login" file. The `stty` command is the normal method of changing modes or options for the terminal driver. The argument `crt` in our command, above, requests that all options suitable for a CRT terminal should be selected. The command can also be used to see what the current options are set to. You may execute the following command to see a rather complete list.

```
stty everything
```

The terminal driver operates in one of three main modes: *cooked*, *cbreak* or *raw*. The cooked mode (called so because it is the opposite of raw) is the normal mode. In raw mode, no processing is performed at all on input characters. Each character is passed immediately to the executing program without being echoed. The cbreak mode is intermediate between the other two. Characters are immediately passed to the executing program without being buffered, but they are echoed as normal and most special characters still have effect.

Most programs that you write will operate quite happily when they read from or write to a terminal in the normal cooked mode. The only feature of the cooked mode that might get in your way is the fact that the program cannot read any characters from a line until you type the carriage return at the end of the line. Some programs, such as the `vi` editor, use raw mode. The `vi` editor must read each character as you type it so that it can immediately update information on the screen. The cbreak mode is unsuitable for vi because many characters that have special meaning to vi are intercepted by the terminal driver and may cause unwanted effects.

If you write a program, such as a game or a full-screen editor, where you need to read and respond to characters immediately, you should avoid using raw mode. If your program puts the terminal or display window into raw mode and then goes wrong, you will find out that there is no way to stop the program. All the usual methods of stopping a program, such as typing *Control-C*, *Control-\* or hitting the break key, do not work. These characters are simply sent as input to your program. (Hitting the break key in raw mode generates a null byte.) If you do not believe this, just enter the two commands

```
stty raw; yes
```

and then try to stop the output! If you type those commands on a dumb terminal, the only way you can stop the yes program is disconnect the terminal. (When the terminal driver detects the disconnection, it sends a SIGHUP signal to the program and that will finally stop it.) If you type the commands in one window on a workstation, the best approach is to open up another window and enter a kill command in that window to stop the yes process.

If you are writing a program like a full-screen editor, you should set the terminal mode to cbreak and turn off the echoing of characters. If you want to perform actions such as moving the cursor up one line when a letter *k* is typed, you do not want to have the *k* echoed on the screen. It is possible to set the terminal driver to this mode with the stty command. You would just need to execute the following.

```
stty cbreak -echo
```

However, if you do this, the next command that you type will not be echoed – and that can be a little disconcerting. Ideally, of course, you want your program to change the terminal driver modes at the start of its execution and to reset the modes at the end. Hence, you could perform the function call

```
system("stty cbreak -echo");
```

in the program initialization and make the following call just before the program ends.

```
system("stty -cbreak echo");
```

A greater degree of control over the terminal driver modes can be obtained, and rather more efficiently too, with the ioctl function. The code to set the cbreak mode and disable echoing is as follows.

```
#include <sgtty.h>
struct sgttyb oldmode, newmode;
...
ioctl( 0, TIOCGETP, &oldmode );
newmode = oldmode;
newmode.sg_flags |= CBREAK;
newmode.sg_flags &= ~ECHO;
ioctl( 0, TIOCSETP, &newmode );
```

The first argument to `ioctl` is a file descriptor associated with the terminal. If the terminal is associated with the standard input of our program, as it normally would be, we can use zero. The second parameter is a service request code. The names for these codes are included by the <sgtty.h> header file. The `TIOCGETP` code requests that the current terminal modes be copied into the structure specified in the third argument. After this first call to `ioctl`, we create a modified copy of this structure where we have set a bit to turn on `cbreak` mode and unset a bit for echoing (to turn echoing off). Then, we call `ioctl` with the `TIOCSETP` request code to set the new modes from our modified structure. After our program has finished its work, it can reset the terminal driver back to its original state by executing this call.

```
ioctl( 0, TIOCSETP, &oldmode );
```

For changing the current erase character (usually the *backspace* or *delete* key on the keyboard), the current line kill character (usually '@' or *Control-U*), or a wide variety of processing flags, the `sgttyb` structure is used in the `ioctl` call. For changing other options, different request codes are passed as the second argument and different structures passed as the third argument. More complete details can be obtained by looking at the header files for use with `ioctl` and from the on-line manual entry under the heading `tty`. You must type

```
man 4 tty
```

to see this entry because there is a command named `tty` too.

When you are debugging a program that changes terminal driver modes, you are likely to find that it sometimes leaves your terminal or your workstation window in a strange state. If your program has terminated and you have received a prompt for a new command, but nothing you type appears on the screen, the terminal driver is either in *no-echo* mode or in *raw* mode. If your characters echo but backspacing over characters to correct them does not seem to work, the driver is in *cbreak* mode. The sure-fire method to get your terminal or window back into a usable state is to type the following sequence of 7 characters:

*Control-J*   r   e   s   e   t   *Control-J*

You must type these characters whether or not anything is echoed on the screen. If your keyboard has a key labelled *linefeed*, you may use that instead of *Control-J*. The `reset` command resets the terminal driver modes, as its name suggests. The linefeed (or *Control-J*) character should be used to terminate the command rather than a carriage return. The reason is that the terminal driver translates the carriage return character (which is the same as a *Control-M* character) into a linefeed in the cbreak and cooked modes, but not in raw mode. Thus only a linefeed is guaranteed to work.

## 11-2 The Termcap Database

Each manufacturer of terminals seems to have a different idea as to what capabilities a terminal should have. Some CRT terminals recognize special control character sequences that cause a line to be deleted in the middle of the screen (with the bottom half of the screen being scrolled up) and others do not. Some terminals support underlining of characters on the screen, others do not, and so on. Even if two terminals support the same capability, such as character underlining, they may use different control sequences to perform the underlining action. Although there is a standard for terminal control sequences, the ANSI X3.64 standard, only about 50% of terminals conform to the standard. Of those that conform, most do not implement all the control sequences defined in the standard and most have their own special extensions. Windowing environments that run on workstations provide windows that work much like the screens of terminals. Just as with CRT terminals, special command sequences are provided for scrolling the window, deleting a line, and so on.

To enable programs to take advantage of special terminal or window capabilities, the Berkeley UNIX system provides a database that describes most terminals in common use and windows for standard windowing systems. This database is the file "/etc/termcap". System V implementations of UNIX provide an equivalent database known as "/etc/terminfo".

The format of a terminal description in the `termcap` file is described in the on-line manual. You should execute

```
man 5 termcap
```

to see the manual entry. Each terminal description lists various kinds of terminal attributes or capabilities, organized as fields separated by colon characters. There are three kinds of attribute or capability. The simplest kind is a Boolean flag to indicate whether the terminal has the corresponding capability or not. For example, the presence of the `pt` capability indicates that the terminal understands tab characters. A second kind gives a numeric value for some attribute or capability. For example, the field `co#80` indicates that the terminal has 80 columns. (If a terminal can be switched from 80 columns to 132 columns, say, there would be two separate entries for this terminal in the database.) The third kind of entry gives control sequences for performing various actions. For example, a field such as `dl=\e[M` gives the three character control sequence for deleting a line in the middle of the screen. (The notation `\e` is a readable way of specifying the ASCII *escape* character.)

It is not a good idea for ordinary programs to make extensive direct use of the terminal capability database. If the program assumes the existence of certain capabilities, such as `dl`, on the terminal, the program will only be able to work on terminals that have that capability. If the program must work on a wide variety of terminal types, the program must provide alternate methods of performing actions on terminals that lack various capabilities. For example, if the program does need to delete a line in the middle of the screen when there is no `dl` capability, it could erase and rewrite the entire bottom half of the screen or it could take advantage of the scrolling region capability provided on VT100-compatible terminals. These concerns are best left to sophisticated full-screen programs such as the `vi` editor.

Generally speaking, an ordinary program should use the terminal capability database only for simple operations. A program that wants to produce menu-like screen layouts needs only the capability to clear the screen and to move the cursor to arbitrary coordinate positions on the screen or within the workstation window. These are capabilities that almost all CRT terminals have. If your program needs to perform more sophisticated screen updating operations, it should use the family of library functions known as curses. The curses library is described briefly in the next section of this chapter.

There are functions in a special program library for extracting terminal capabilities and working with them. When you compile a program that uses these functions, you should supply the -ltermcap flag on the cc or gcc command that performs the final linking operation. Figure 11-1 shows code needed to fetch the clear screen (cl) and cursor motion (cm) capabilities, and determine the screen size for our terminal. The routine that performs the actual cursor motion requires that a few more capabilities are loaded too.

The principle behind the various function calls is fairly simple. First, the tgetent function is called to read the terminal description into a local array. Like most terminal handling software, it is assumed that the environment variable TERM gives the name of the kind of terminal in use. If the entry cannot be found or the termcap file cannot be read, the function returns error codes 0 and -1 respectively. Success is indicated by a result of 1.

The other functions, tgetstr, tgetnum and the unused tgetflag, search the local array to find values of capabilities. The tgetnum function returns an integer value for a capability/attribute, or -1 if the capability is not present. The tgetstr function returns a pointer to a string containing a command sequence, or NULL if the capability is not present. This string is copied into a buffer supplied by the caller, which explains the second argument to the function. The tgetflag function (not used in our example) is used similarly to tgetnum to obtain a Boolean value for a capability. A result of 1 indicates that the capability is present; 0 indicates that it is absent.

Using these capabilities is not completely straightforward. The control sequences cannot (always) be sent directly to the terminal because some sequences are preceded by integers that indicate a time delay to allow the terminal to complete the screen update. A function named tputs is provided to output control sequences. Another problem is that the control sequence for cursor motion is parameterized. Somewhere in the sequence encoded values of the desired line number and column number must appear. Different manufacturers have chosen to encode the information in different ways. Therefore the tgoto function is provided to insert the line number and column number into the control sequence. The result is a string which can be passed to tputs to actually move the cursor. Note that the line and column numbers that you pass to tgoto are assumed to have a zero origin. For example, if there are 24 lines on the screen, you should specify line numbers in the range 0 to 23.

Figure 11-2 shows a function that could be used to output a menu onto a screen, using the capabilities extracted with the function of Figure 11-1.

## Figure 11-1  Loading Terminal Capabilities

```c
#include <stdio.h>
#include <stdlib.h>
char  PC;          /* padding character */
char *BC;          /* backspace character */
char *UP;          /* cursor up sequence */
char *CM;          /* cursor motion sequence */
char *CL;          /* clear screen sequence */
int   LI;          /* number of lines */
int   CO;          /* number of columns */

void read_termcap(void) {
    char  tc_entry[1024];
    static char tcbuff[256], *tcbuffp = tcbuff;
    char *term, *temp;

    term = getenv("TERM");
    if (term == NULL) {
        fprintf(stderr, "No TERM env. variable\n");
        exit(1);
    }
    if ( tgetent(tc_entry, term) != 1 ) {
        fprintf(stderr, "Cannot get %s capabilities\n",
            term );
        exit(1);
    }
    temp = tgetstr("pc", &tcbuffp);
    PC = (temp != NULL)? *temp : '\0';
    UP = tgetstr("up", &tcbuffp);
    CL = tgetstr("cl", &tcbuffp);
    CM = tgetstr("cm", &tcbuffp);
    LI = tgetnum("li");
    CO = tgetnum("co");
    if (LI < 0) LI = 24;  /* Some reasonable defaults */
    if (CO < 0) CO = 80;  /* for missing values       */
    if (CM == NULL || CL == NULL) {
        fprintf(stderr,"cm & cl capabilities needed\n");
        exit(1);
    }
}
```

---

**Figure 11-2   Use of Terminal Capabilities**

```
typedef struct menu_item {
    int y, x; /* coordinates for the item */
    char *item;
} MENU_ITEM;


/* Table entry == ( Line #, Col #, Text ) */
MENU_ITEM menu1[] = {
    { 0, 25, "MAIN MENU" },
    { 5, 10, "1. Quit" },
    { 7, 10, "2. Edit" },
    { 9, 10, "3. Compile" },
    { 11, 10, "4. Link" },
    { 13, 10, "5. Run" },
    { 0, 0, NULL } /* terminator */ };


void out1(int ch) { putchar(ch); }


void output_menu( MENU_ITEM *menuptr ) {
    MENU_ITEM *mp; char *cstr;

    /* clear the screen */
    tputs(CL, LI, out1);
    /* loop through the menu items */
    for( mp = menuptr; mp->item != NULL; mp++ ) {
        cstr = tgoto(CM, mp->x, mp->y);
        tputs(cstr, 1, out1);
        fputs(mp->item, stdout);
    }
}
...
    /* display the menu */
    output_menu(menu1);
...
```

The tputs function requires three arguments. The first is the string to be output; the second specifies the number of lines on the screen that will be affected by the output (this information is needed to create appropriate time delays when dealing with certain kinds of terminals); and the third argument names a function that will output one character to the terminal. Our use of tputs to clear the screen affects all lines on the screen so we pass the value of LI, the number of lines on the screen.

## 11-3 The curses Screen-Handling Package

As explained above, you would have to put a lot of effort into your program if you wanted it to perform full-screen output for a wide variety of terminals. Rather than expend this effort, you should acquaint yourself with a package of library functions called curses.

The curses package supports an interface to an idealized terminal that has most of the features that you would find on a sophisticated CRT terminal. It also supports multiple windows, although, in practice, most programs treat the terminal screen as being a single window. There are functions in the package for moving the cursor and writing characters at different positions on the screen, for inserting or deleting lines, for scrolling the screen, and so on. These functions will work regardless of whether the actual terminal in use has corresponding capabilities. The curses functions will translate your screen update requests into whatever control sequences are needed to produce the desired effect on the real terminal. In fact, curses makes some attempt to produce the shortest possible control sequences that accomplish the screen update.

Curses also provides functions to help with input from the terminal. It will, on request, disable echoing and enable cbreak mode in the terminal driver. Some books containing more details about the curses package are listed in the *Further Reading* section.

## 11-4 Further Reading

If you need more information about the terminal capability database than is available from the on-line manual, there is a book *Termcap and Terminfo*, third edition, by J. Strang, T. O'Reilly and L. Mui (O'Reilly and Associates 1988). Another title in the same series from that publisher explains the curses library. It is called *Programming with Curses* by J. Strang (O'Reilly and Associates 1986). A more recent book on the same subject is *Unix Curses Explained* by B. Goodheart (Prentice-Hall 1991). The original documentation on curses is quite readable and is provided as supplementary documentation with releases of Berkeley UNIX. It is titled *Screen Updating and Cursor Movement Optimization: A Library Package* and was written by K. Arnold.

# CHAPTER 12   *COMMUNICATING BETWEEN PROCESSES*

---

## *12-1   Inter-Process Communication*

In a multiprocessing operating system, it is normal for processes to exchange data. In some operating systems, two processes may have access to the same region of memory and one process can therefore store a value in a variable for later retrieval by the other process. This is sometimes referred to as a *shared-memory model*. In other operating systems, message passing is provided as a basic system operation and can be used to transmit data.

In the original UNIX system, there were only two ways for processes to share data. One mechanism was for one process to write its data to a output stream that is linked by a pipe to an input stream of a second process. Indeed, the pipe facility is provided by the command shell for connecting the standard output of one program to the standard input of the next program. The second mechanism is for the first process to write the data to a file, where it can be retrieved by other processes.

The pipe facility is still an important part of UNIX and we will look at it in the next section of this chapter. However, it is extremely limited because the two communicating processes must be related (for example, the two processes may share a common parent). If the two processes are unrelated, a different mechanism must be used. Furthermore, computer networks have become standard and it would be desirable for the mechanism to be powerful to permit the two processes to be located on two different computers.

The System V version of UNIX provides a mechanism known as *STREAMS* for interprocess communication. Berkeley UNIX, on the other hand, added a generalization of pipes known as *sockets*. We will cover a simple example using sockets later in the chapter. However, sockets are a relatively low-level concept and it is tedious to get all the programming details right. An alternative to sockets is the *remote procedure call* (RPC). We will look at RPC too in this chapter. RPC is not as powerful as sockets and is not available on all Berkeley-based UNIX systems, but its interface is so much simpler that it should be used whenever appropriate.

## 12-2  Pipes

In the shell command language, output from one command can be piped to the input of another command. This command, for example, prints a formatted listing of a C source file:

```
cb program.c | lpr
```

Since the shell command processor is just another C program, a method of starting up processes and connecting the standard output of one process to the standard input of another process is needed. But before we get to the actual procedure of making these connections, we should take a look at how input-output and multiprocessing coexist.

When a new process is created, it inherits exactly the same set of open files as its parent possessed when it executed `fork`. This means that if both the parent and the child continue execution and both write to their standard outputs, the output will be interleaved. Indeed, if output is being buffered, any output that was in the buffer when `fork` was executed can be output twice. Similarly, if both processes read from their standard inputs, they will both read characters that were in the buffer at the time of the fork. After this, the two processes are in competition for input characters. The input will sometimes go to one process and sometimes to the other, but never to both processes.

To avoid such chaos, it is advisable for the parent process to wait for the child to finish before performing any more input or output. It is also a good idea for the parent process to execute `fflush(stdout)` before calling `fork`. If input is line-buffered, as `stdin` from the keyboard is by default, the parent process need only make sure that it has read a complete line of input before executing the `fork`.

At the low-level input-output interface to the system, it is easy to rearrange file descriptors. If you recall from Chapter 8, open files correspond to slots in an object description table. When the shell invokes a program, it opens files as necessary so that standard input for the program corresponds to slot 0, standard output to slot 1 and standard error output to slot 2. The index position of an open file in this table is called its *file descriptor*, so standard input has the file descriptor 0. When a new file is opened, the system uses the lowest numbered empty slot in the table. Therefore, if you want your program to read from the file "/tmp/junk" when it reads from the standard input, you need only include the following lines of code in your program:

```
close(0);        /* close standard input */
if (open("/tmp/junk", O_RDONLY, 0) != 0)
    fprintf(stderr,"oops!\n");
```

Yes, you are allowed to close the standard input or output files! Closing the standard input frees slot 0 in the object descriptor table, so that the next file we open will be given this slot. This change affects stream input-output too. When stdin is supplied as a parameter to the stream-oriented functions, these functions use file descriptor 0 to read more input. Thus, next time that they read new data into the buffer, they would read from the file.

Since it is possible to replace the open file in a particular slot in the table, is it also possible to exchange two entries? If we close and reopen the two files, we could achieve such an exchange. But closing and reopening a file is undesirable. Not only is it inefficient, it would also lose the current position in the file. To do the job properly, we need the help of either the dup or dup2 system functions. If we make a call like

```
newfd = dup(oldfd);
if (newfd < 0) { perror( "dup" );   exit(1); }
```

where oldfd is a descriptor for an open file, the function creates a duplicate file descriptor and returns this descriptor as the result. (If dup fails for some reason, the result is -1.) Afterwards, output to the file can be performed by calling the write function with either file descriptor. Similarly, input operations on the file could use either descriptor. When dup creates the new entry in the object descriptor table, it uses the slot with the lowest numbered position. The dup2 function is used if we want to force the new descriptor to have a specific number. (The name dup2 appears to be an abbreviations for *duplicate to*.) If we make the call

```
returncode = dup2(oldfd, newfd);
```

then the table slot at position newfd is forced to contain a duplicate of the slot at position oldfd. Any open file already occupying position newfd is automatically closed by dup2. To clarify, here is how we could use dup2 to replace standard input with input from "/tmp/junk" again:

```
char *filename = "/tmp/junk";
fd = open(filename, O_RDONLY, 0);
if (dup2(fd, 0) < 0) { perror(filename);   exit(1); }
if (close(fd) < 0) { perror(filename);   exit(1); }
```

The close of the fd entry still leaves slot 0 open for input from the file. This code, used for replacing the standard input with another input source, should be preferred over the code given previously. The dup2 call explicitly specifies which file descriptor number to use and automatically takes care of any previous uses for that file descriptor.

After all this preamble dealing with file descriptors, we can now get back to the subject of pipelining. We can create a pipe with the system call pipe (what else?). The call creates an internal system buffer and two file descriptors. One file descriptor is used for writing and the other for reading. Writing causes data to be put into the buffer, whereas reading extracts it from the buffer. Unlike a file which has a very large output capacity, the buffer used for a pipe has a modest size – only 4096 bytes. If a process writes a lot of data and fills the buffer, the process will be suspended until the reading process has caught up a little and removed some data from the buffer. Similarly, if the reading process reads fast enough to empty the buffer, it will be suspended when it attempts to read some more.

The only problem with pipe is that we usually want the standard output of one program to write into the buffer and the standard input of another process to read from the buffer. And that is why we first went through all the details of how to rearrange file descriptors. Figure 12-1 gives a simple example of a program creating two child processes connected by a pipe. One process executes the cb program and the other executes the lpr program.[1]

All the calls to dup2 and close will, no doubt, make this example seem rather confusing. On the other hand, if you can follow the logic of this program, you will have an excellent understanding of file descriptors. Now for a quick tour through the program. First, if the executable form of the program has the name cprint, the program can be invoked with a command similar to

```
cprint prog1.c prog2.c
```

This command will send a beautified version of "prog1.c" to the printer, and then it will send a beautified version of "prog2.c" to the printer. One minor difficulty is that some versions of cb do not take a filename argument. Therefore, inside the main processing loop, our program replaces the standard input with input from the next argument file. It does this using dup2 and then closes the superfluous file descriptor. Next, we create the pipe. The pipe function stores two file descriptors in the array fd. The first entry is for reading and the second for writing.

A child process to run cb is now forked off. This process will be reading from the standard input and we have already taken care of that. (Recall that a child process inherits standard input and output from its parent.) We have to redirect standard output, however, to go into the pipe. Therefore, we use dup2 to perform the substitution and then we close the duplicate file descriptor and the (superfluous) file descriptor for the read side of the pipe. Then the child can transfer control to an invocation of cb via the execl call.

Next, a child process to run lpr is forked off. Its standard input has to be replaced with input read from the pipe. The code used to achieve this is similar to that found in the first child. Then control is transferred to the lpr program.

---

1. In the interests of keeping all the code for the example on a single page, the return codes from some of the functions such as close and dup2 are not checked.

## Figure 12-1  The cprint Program

```
/*      Program to print beautified C source code.
        Usage:      cprint file file ...                     */
#include <stdio.h>
#include <stdlib.h>
#include <sys/file.h>
#define PRINTER "-Plwp"  /* passed as argument to lpr */
int cb_pid, lpr_pid, pid, status, fd[2], filefd;

int main(int argc, char *argv[]) {
    register int i;
    for( i=1; i<argc; i++ ) {
        filefd = open(argv[i], O_RDONLY, 0);
        if (filefd < 0) {
            perror(argv[i]);  continue;
        }
        dup2(filefd, 0);
        close(filefd);
        pipe(fd);
        if ((cb_pid = fork()) == 0) {     /* cb process */
            dup2(fd[1], 1);
            close(fd[0]);  close(fd[1]);
            execl("/usr/bin/cb", "cb", (char *)0);
            _exit(1);
        }
        if ((lpr_pid = fork()) == 0) {   /* lpr process */
            dup2(fd[0], 0);
            close(fd[0]);  close(fd[1]);
            execl("/usr/ucb/lpr", "lpr",
                    PRINTER, (char *)0);
            _exit(1);
        }
        close(fd[0]);  close(fd[1]);
        do {
            pid = wait(&status);
            if (pid == cb_pid) cb_pid = 0;
            if (pid == lpr_pid) lpr_pid = 0;
        } while(cb_pid != lpr_pid && pid != -1);
    }
    return 0;
}
```

The main program closes its file descriptors for the pipe, since it will not be using the pipe itself, and then waits for both child processes to complete. Subsequently, the main processing loop can be repeated for the next file provided as an argument in the command line. Note that it is quite important for superfluous file descriptors to be closed in all processes. If, for example, we do not close all the extra descriptors for writing to the pipe, the process that is reading from the pipe will never be given an end-of-file indication. And that causes the lpr process in our example to hang, waiting for more input.

## 12-3   Remote Procedure Call

When a function A calls a function B, there are three main steps. First, the function arguments are passed from A to B, then B executes, and finally the results from B are passed back to A. The concept of a *remote procedure call* is very similar. A process A makes a remote procedure call on a process B by sending the arguments to B and then waiting for the results to come back. When B receives its arguments, it performs a computation, sends the results back to the caller (i.e., A) and then goes to sleep waiting for more arguments. We can diagram the interaction between A and B as shown in Figure 12-2.

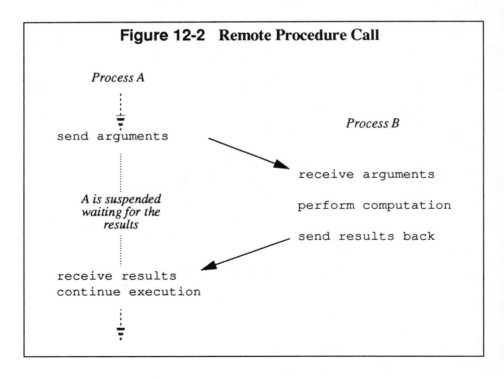

**Figure 12-2   Remote Procedure Call**

*Process A*

send arguments

*Process B*

receive arguments

perform computation

*A is suspended
waiting for the
results*

send results back

receive results
continue execution

The two processes may be located on the same machine or on two different machines. Clearly, in the latter case, the arguments and the results must be transmitted as messages between computers. The original remote procedure mechanism, as described in Nelson's doctoral dissertation,[2] allowed reference parameters to be used and provided a mechanism for the remote procedure to access global data on the same computer as the caller (thus providing a complete simulation of a normal procedure call as in the Pascal language).

The remote procedure call service (RPC) provided with the SunOS UNIX operating system does not support reference parameters or global data. All the information that the remote procedure requires must be passed by value in the call. However, even with (or, perhaps, because of) this restriction, RPC provides a very efficient mechanism for passing data from one process to another. It is so efficient, in fact, that SUN use RPC to implement some important system software such as the Network File Server and the Network Information Service.

Unfortunately, RPC is not standard across UNIX or even Berkeley UNIX systems. SUN have made the source code for their RPC available in the public domain and therefore it is reasonably likely that your non-SUN system has the facilities described below. If RPC facilities are not available, your alternatives would be the streams mechanism of System V UNIX or the socket mechanism of Berkeley UNIX. If RPC is available, and if it meets your needs, you should ignore the alternatives and use RPC. We will now examine the SUN implementation of RPC and go through a simple programming example.

The interaction between the two processes follows the *client-server* model. The process that makes the call is the client and the process that executes the remote procedure and sends the results back is the server. The server process must be started up first and after registering itself as available to execute one or more specific functions, goes to sleep and waits for a client to invoke it. Subsequently, a client on any machine in the network may send a request for a calculation to the server.

The client has to send the argument values to the server, and a mechanism analogous to performing stream input-output is used for sending the values. Whatever the datatypes of the arguments, their must be converted to a sequential series of bytes for transmission. At the receiving end in the server, the series of bytes must be used to reconstruct the original argument values. An added complication is that different machines in the network may represent data values in different ways. For example, the integer hexadecimal value $0x01020304$ is stored on a SUN-3 or SUN-4 computer with the $01$ byte at the lowest address and $04$ at the highest address (so-called *little-endian* order), whereas the order is reversed on a VAX computer with the $01$ byte at the highest address (so-called *big-endian* order).

---

2. Bruce Jay Nelson, Remote Procedure Call. Technical Report CMU-CS-81-119, Dept. of Computer Science, Carnegie-Mellon University, 1981.

To facilitate communication of data values in RPC calls, SUN have defined a standard external data representation (abbreviated as *XDR*) for the various C data types and provide functions for converting between C values and the XDR representations. If both the client and the server processes use the XDR conversion functions, it will not matter if one process is on one kind of computer and the other on a different kind of computer.

That is probably sufficient introduction for the sample program to be understood. While the sample program is not very sophisticated and could be improved to make it more usable and more general, it solves a useful program. If you have accounts on different computers in a network, you will often have duplicates of some of your files on several different machines. If these files require occasional updating, it is easy to lose track of which files have been changed. Therefore, a program to compare files on two different computers and report if they are the same would come in useful. Of course, the easy way to solve this problem is to copy the file on one machine to the other machine and then run either the cmp or the diff program to perform the comparison. But suppose that the files are very large and we would like to avoid unnecessary remote file copying. In that situation, we could compute a hash code for the file and transmit just the hash code across the network. We can then compare two hash codes. If they differ, the files are definitely not the same. If they are the same, there is a small chance that the hash function has yielded a false hit and a difference between the two files will go unnoticed. However, by choosing a good function and using enough bits for the hash value, we can make the chance of a false hit as small as we please.

We intend to use our program in a manner similar to rcp. That is, the user could type a command like

```
rcmp sirius:myfile.o gemini:source/myfile.o
```

to compare the files located on two machines named *sirius* and *gemini*, and the command would reply with one of the two responses:

```
The files are definitely different
```

or

```
The files are probably identical.
```

To achieve the desired effect, we need to have a server process running on every machine where are files are located. Each server process will implement a remote procedure that computes the hash value of an arbitrary file located on its machine. The single argument of the procedure is the pathname of the file. The result will be a structure containing a status code and the hash value. The status code will indicate possible error conditions, such as the file being unreadable, and so warn the client process to ignore the hash value.

The code for the main part of the server is shown in Figure 12-3. Since the server compares hash codes of remote files and operates as a daemon, we call the server program rcmpd (the trailing *d* in a program name conventionally denotes a daemon). As usual, the function main is executed when the server process is initially started. Its very first action is to create a subprocess with fork and exit. This is a trick that leaves the child process

## Figure 12-3   The rcmpd Server Program: File "rcmpd.c"

```c
#include <stdio.h>
#include <stdlib.h>
#include <rpc/rpc.h>
#include <errno.h>
#include "fhash.h"

FHR *fhash(char **pathp) {
    static FHR result;
    FILE *f;
    unsigned int hash = 0;
    register int ch;

    f = fopen(*pathp, "rb");
    if (f == NULL) {   /* pass the error code back */
        result.stat = errno;
        result.hash = 0;
        errno = 0;   /* reset errno for next client */
        return &result;
    }
    for( ; ; ) {
        ch = getc(f);
        if (ch == EOF) break;
        hash = hash*13753 + ch;
    }
    fclose(f);
    result.stat = 0;
    result.hash = hash;
    return &result;
}

int main(void) {
    if (fork() != 0) exit(0);
    svc_unregister(SERVICENUM, VERSION);
    registerrpc(SERVICENUM, VERSION, PROCNUM,
                fhash, xdr_wrapstring, xdr_FHR);
    svc_run();
    fprintf(stderr, "svc_run should never return\n");
    return 1;
}
```

running independently as the daemon, while the original process terminates. Thus, we can execute the shell command

```
% rcmpd
```

and this command will start up the daemon without making you wait for it to finish. The next action is to unregister the RPC service that is being offered (in case an older faulty version of our program previously registered the service and subsequently crashed). Now we register the service using the `registerrpc` function. We have to identify our server program by a number (this is the SERVICENUM parameter) and, because one program may support several different remote procedures, we must also supply a procedure number (the PROCNUM parameter). Provision is also made for the server program being replaced by a newer version. Since we cannot hope to replace every copy of a server program and of every client program simultaneously, we should allow different versions of the server to coexist. Thus another parameter of the call is a version number (the VERSION parameter).

The actual remote procedure that is being registered is the function `fhash`. The parameter `xdr_wrapstring` is the name of the XDR function that will be called to decode the function argument from the external representation and convert it to a C string before passing that string to `fhash`. Similarly, the parameter `xdr_FHR` is the name of a function that will be used to encode the result from `fhash` for transmittal back to the client process. The SUN XDR library contains encode/decode functions for all standard C datatypes – thus `xdr_wrapstring` is one of the functions provided. However, the FHR type is a structure type of our own creation, defined in the header file "fhash.h". This file is reproduced in Figure 12-4. Therefore, we must provide our own function for encoding values of type FHR. Since the FHR type is a structure containing two fields with simple datatypes, we can synthesize `xdr_FHR` from the two standard XDR functions provided by SUN. The coding of the function is shown in Figure 12-5.

Registration of the remote procedure as a server program requires that we identify it with a number. We cannot pick a number that clashes with any other registered programs. What number can we use? SUN have decreed that numbers in the range 0 to $0x1fffffff$ are for use by operating systems programs and those in the range $0x20000000$ to $0x3fffffff$ are available for use by local users, either for local software or for developing new software. Thus we have picked an arbitrary number in that latter range as the value for SERVICENUM. If you want to verify that this arbitrary number is not already in use, you may (on a SUN system) execute the command

```
/usr/etc/rpcinfo
```

and obtain a list of the currently registered services. But, given that there are $2^{29}$ (about 500 million) different service numbers to choose from, it is probably not worth checking in advance.

Our remote file compare daemon program, `rcmpd`, may be compiled with a command like the following.

```
gcc rcmpd.c fhash.c -o rcmpd
```

---

## Figure 12-4   The fhash.h Header File

```
#define SERVICENUM    0x20001234
#define VERSION       1
#define PROCNUM       1
#define MAXSTRLEN     1024

typedef struct {
      int stat;
      unsigned int hash;
   } FHR;

int xdr_FHR(XDR *xdrsp, FHR *fhrp);
```

---

## Figure 12-5   The fhash.c File

```
#include <rpc/xdr.h>
#include "fhash.h"

int xdr_FHR(XDR *xdrsp, FHR *fhrp) {
    if (!xdr_int(xdrsp, &fhrp->stat)) return 0;
    if (!xdr_u_int(xdrsp, &fhrp->hash)) return 0;
    return 1;
}
```

The source of the main part of the client program, rcmp, is listed in Figure 12-6. For each of the two command line arguments, the client program decomposes it into a hostname and a filename. The rcmpd server daemon on the computer whose name is hostname is invoked as a remote procedure by using the callrpc function. The SERVICENUM, PROCNUM and VERSION arguments match those used by the rcmpd daemon to register its service. The next pair of arguments supply the input argument to the remote procedure. The first member of the pair is the name of the function to perform the encoding to the external data representation, and it is followed by a reference to the actual argument to pass to the remote procedure. If the remote procedure actually required more than one parameter, we would have to combine the parameters into a single structure and pass that structure. Note that the XDR function for encoding the string for transmission is the same function that the rcmpd server program uses for decoding the received string. All the XDR functions supplied by SUN are programmed so that they can perform both encoding and decoding. Finally, the last two arguments to callrpc specify the disposition of the result from

## Figure 12-6   The rcmp Client Program: File "rcmp.c"

```c
#include <stdio.h>
#include <stdlib.h>
#include <string.h>
#include <rpc/rpc.h>
#include <errno.h>
#include "fhash.h"

void usage(char *prog) {
    fprintf(stderr,
        "Usage: %s host1:file1 host2:file2\n", prog);
    exit(1);
}

int main(int argc, char *argv[]) {
    FHR result[2];
    int i, stat;
    char *hostname, *filename;

    if (argc != 3) usage(argv[0]);
    for( i = 0; i < 2; i++ ) {
        hostname = argv[i+1];
        filename = strchr(hostname,':');
        if (filename == NULL) usage(argv[0]);
        *filename++ = '\0';
        stat = callrpc(hostname, SERVICENUM, VERSION,
                    PROCNUM, xdr_wrapstring, &filename,
                    xdr_FHR, &result[i]);
        if (stat != 0) { clnt_perrno(stat);  exit(1); }
        if (result[i].stat != 0) {
            fprintf(stderr, "%s:", hostname);
            errno = result[i].stat;  perror(filename);
            exit(1);
        }
    }
    if (result[0].hash == result[1].hash)
        printf("The files are probably identical\n");
    else
        printf("The files are definitely different\n");
    return 0;
}
```

the remote procedure. The first member of the pair is the XDR function for decoding the result value and the second member is a pointer to the variable where the decoded value should be stored. Note again that the XDR function is the same as that used by rcmpd for encoding its result prior to transmission, so that the code in the "fhash.c" file can be shared by the two programs.

The `rcmp` client program may be created with the command:

```
gcc rcmp.c fhash.c -o rcmp
```

That is all there is to the example. If this program is found to be sufficiently useful, the local administrator of your system could be prevailed upon to have the `rcmpd` daemon automatically started as a public service whenever the system is re-booted. (The likely place to put the `rcmpd` command is in the file "/etc/rc.local", which contains local commands to execute at system start-up.) However, you would be advised to make improvements to the `rcmp` program first. The program, as presented, does not allow you to type a command like

```
rcmp thisfile gemini:thatfile
```

to compare a file on your local machine with a file on the remote machine *gemini*. Instead, if your local machine is named *sirius*, you have to type the command as follows.

```
rcmp sirius:thisfile gemini:thatfile
```

A better version of the program would supply the missing hostname automatically. A second, and more serious, deficiency is that the file pathname used by the `rcmpd` daemon is relative to the current working directory that was in effect when `rcmpd` was started. If `rcmpd` is to be a public service for use by many users, the client program should pass the name of the user as an additional argument and `rcmpd` should change its working directory to be the home directory of the user before opening a file with a relative pathname.

The XDR library functions are much more extensive in scope than one might suppose from the preceding descriptions. It is possible, without too much trouble, to convert arbitrary data structures into the sequential coding scheme used by XDR. Further information may be obtained from the on-line manual pages (the command "`man 3 xdr`" gives a list of all the functions available) and from the document cited at the end of this chapter.

The RPC functions described above correspond to the middle level of the RPC interface. A higher-level interface, requiring less C coding, is provided by the program tool `rpcgen`. Functions that provide a lower-level interface are also available. These are useful if you do not find the defaults provided by the middle-level interface to be appropriate. For example, the current implementation of `callrpc` limits the amount of data that can be transmitted in either direction to 8K bytes and there is no time-out if the server daemon fails to respond. Both limitations may be overcome by using the lower-level routines.

The RPC mechanism is implemented using sockets, the next topic in this chapter. The middle-level interface with callrpc uses the UDP/IP communication protocol. The lower-level interface allows TCP/IP to be selected instead.

## 12-4  Sockets

### What Are Sockets?

Two processes cannot communicate via a pipe unless they have inherited file descriptors for that pipe from a common ancestor. This means that the `talk` program, for example, cannot use pipes to communicate between two users. Communication between two unrelated processes could, conceivably, take place through files. Process A could append its message to a file, and process B could check that file at regular intervals and read from it whenever it contains anything new. This approach would be rather inefficient though. The Berkeley UNIX system provides a better solution to the problem in the form of *sockets*.

A socket is like the end point of a UNIX pipe. We can describe a pipe as being comprised of two sockets that are linked by some sort of communications software.[3] A single socket is used in exactly the same way as a file descriptor. When a socket is created, it is allocated a slot in the object descriptor table exactly as for an open file. After the socket has been linked to another socket, the slot number may be used as the file descriptor parameter in calls to the `read` and `write` functions.

Two (or more) sockets must be connected before they can be used to transfer data. There are many kinds of connection to choose from. We can begin, though, by grouping connections into two categories. First, we can have a connection that is implemented just as a pipe is. That is, the system allocates a buffer; writes to a socket cause the data to be stored in the buffer; and reads from a socket at the other end cause that data to be removed from the buffer. Secondly, we can have a connection between processes on two different computers where writes to a socket cause the data to be sent out over a transmission line to the process on the other computer. It is becoming common for several computers running the UNIX system to be linked in a *local area network* (LAN) using coaxial cable or fibre optic cable for high-speed communication. Transmissions over communications lines are usually grouped into message packets constructed and transmitted according to special rules known as a *protocol*. Several different protocols are supported by the Berkeley UNIX system. Most system software which performs socket communication between computers uses either the *Internet Transmission Control Protocol* (TCP) or the *Internet User Datagram Protocol* (UDP).

To make matters more confusing, the different kinds of protocol are grouped into families. The TCP and UDP protocols both belong to the Internet family (INET). The INET family is known as a *communications domain*. Development of the INET communications domain was funded by the Defense Advanced Research Projects Agency (DARPA) of the United States government. There are several other domains which have protocols corresponding to standards set by private manufacturers or standards organizations. A list of do-

---

3. Indeed, a pipe is implemented as a pair of sockets.

main names can be seen in the file "/usr/include/sys/socket.h". These names all begin with the prefix 'AF_', which is short for *address family*. Not all the communications domains listed in this file may actually be implemented on your system. And, within any domain, not all the protocols listed in documentation for that domain may be implemented. The reason is that intercomputer communications is a relatively recent UNIX facility and still subject to ongoing development.

It would be inappropriate to go into details about communications and protocols in this book. This chapter will continue with just a brief glimpse at the two most important domains on Berkeley-based UNIX systems and give only two small program examples.

## Types of Socket

There are three kinds of socket which may be used in one or more of the communications domains. They are named SOCK_STREAM, SOCK_DGRAM and SOCK_RAW. The first kind provides byte-by-byte stream communication in a manner similar to pipes. Sockets of this kind may be used for transmission in either direction.

The second kind, SOCK_DGRAM, is used for datagram transmission, again, in either direction. A datagram is nothing more than a packet of data along with some control information, such as a packet sequence number. However, the normal user would probably not wish to use datagrams directly because the system does not guarantee delivery of datagrams in the order that they are transmitted or any delivery at all! To use datagrams, you would either have to limit communications to a single packet or else you would have to implement your own datagram-handling protocol to put packets into the correct order, to request retransmission of missing packets and to ignore duplicate packets.

The third kind, SOCK_RAW, is provided only for users who want a high degree of control over message transmission. For example, this raw interface might permit the user to specify the exact path to use when sending packets over a complicated network.

This chapter does not give any information about the usage of the SOCK_DGRAM nor SOCK_RAW form of sockets. For more information, you should consult the references given at the end of this chapter.

## The UNIX Domain

When both ends of a socket connection are located in the same computer, we can use a simple communications domain called the UNIX domain. A simple example of the use of sockets in the UNIX domain appears in Figure 12-7 and Figure 12-8. Our example is motivated by the following situation. We imagine that there is a user, user A, who wishes to receive files or data sent by other users on the system. Possibly, user A uses a hardcopy terminal and is providing a line printer service for other people; or, possibly, user A has connected a special hardware device such as a bit-mapped raster display and wishes to have other users send picture images to him. In order to receive the data, user A starts the

## Figure 12-7   The Receive Program

```c
#include <stdio.h>
#include <stdlib.h>
#include <string.h>
#include <sys/types.h>
#include <sys/socket.h>
#define SOCK_PREF        "/tmp/#"
#define oops(msg)        { perror(msg); exit(1); }

struct sockaddr saddr;
int slen, s, rfd, ch;
FILE *rf;
char *username;

int main(int argc, char *argv[]) {
                /* construct the socket name & length */
    saddr.sa_family = AF_UNIX;
    strcpy(saddr.sa_data, SOCK_PREF);
    if ( (username = getenv("USER")) == NULL ) {
        fprintf(stderr,"can't get username\n"); exit(1);}
    strcat(saddr.sa_data, username);
    slen = sizeof(saddr);
    unlink(saddr.sa_data);
    s = socket(AF_UNIX, SOCK_STREAM, 0);
    if (s == -1) oops("socket");
    if (bind(s, &saddr, slen) != 0) oops("bind");
    if (listen(s,1) != 0) oops("listen");
    for( ; ; ) {                 /* wait for a connection */
        rfd = accept(s, NULL, NULL);
        if (rfd == -1) oops("accept");
        rf = fdopen(rfd, "r");
        if (rf == NULL) oops("fdopen");
        ch = '\f'; /* start with a form-feed */
        do {
            putchar( ch ); ch = getc(rf);
        } while( ch != EOF );
        fclose(rf);
        fflush(stdout);
    }
    return 0;
}
```

## Figure 12-8  The Send Program

```c
#include <stdio.h>
#include <stdlib.h>
#include <string.h>
#include <sys/types.h>
#include <sys/socket.h>

#define SOCK_PREF           "/tmp/#"
#define oops(msg)           { perror(msg);  exit(1); }

struct sockaddr saddr;
int slen = sizeof(saddr);
int s, ch;
FILE *sf;

int main(int argc, char *argv[]) {
    if (argc != 2) {
        fprintf(stderr,"Usage: %s recipient\n", argv[0]);
        exit(1);
    }
    saddr.sa_family = AF_UNIX;
    strcpy(saddr.sa_data, SOCK_PREF);
    strcat(saddr.sa_data, argv[1]);
    s = socket(AF_UNIX, SOCK_STREAM, 0);
    if (s == -1) oops("socket");
    if (connect(s, &saddr, slen) != 0) oops("connect");
    sf = fdopen( s, "w" );
    if (sf == NULL) oops("fdopen");
    /* send data to socket */
    fprintf(sf,"Data from %s::\n", getenv("USER"));
    while((ch = getchar()) != EOF)
        putc(ch, sf);
    fclose(sf);
    return 0;
}
```

`Receive` program shown in Figure 12-7, which sets up a socket ready to receive data. The received data is generated as the standard output of this program. User A might invoke the program as

```
Receive > data_in
```

Later, another user, user B say, would execute the `Send` program of Figure 12-8, which connects with A's socket. User B might execute the program as

```
Send A < some_data
```

where *A* represents the user id of A. Any data provided to the standard input of `Send` will be transmitted to A.

Although the two programs start similarly, they soon diverge. Let us begin with the `Receive` program in Figure 12-7. This program acts as a server, passively waiting for client processes (invocations of the `Send` program) to connect with it. `Receive` creates the socket with a call to the `socket` function. The first parameter gives the communications domain (or address family) as UNIX. The second parameter specifies SOCK_STREAM type sockets. The third parameter could be used in other domains for specifying a particular protocol, but it is inapplicable here.

After creating the socket, we must give it a name. If it did not have a name, there would be no way for the `Send` program to say what socket it wanted to connect to. Just as you can choose names for files, you can choose names for sockets in the UNIX domain. In fact, in the current Berkeley implementation of sockets, socket names and file path names share the same name space. That is, the program must choose a socket name that could also be a valid name for a new file. Our program chooses a path name that begins "/tmp/..." because files (and hence sockets) in the "/tmp" directory should be accessible to all users. The name is constructed and copied into a structure, whose name and size are passed to the `bind` function. Our call to this function will cause an entry in the "/tmp" directory to be created and associated with the socket. Next, `Receive` tells the UNIX system that it will be listening for connections on this socket. The second parameter in the call to `listen` tells the system how big a backlog of waiting connections it should be prepared to handle. Then, `Receive` calls `accept` to wait for a connection to be made. The process will be suspended until the connection occurs, or until some interrupting signal arrives.

If a connection is made, the `accept` function returns a file descriptor as its result. This file descriptor may be used for both input and output communication with the client process at the other end of the communications link. In our example, we will only use the file descriptor for reading. Our `Receive` program converts the file descriptor into an ordinary stream pointer, using `fdopen`, and reads from the stream. At the end of input from the stream, it closes the stream. Closing the stream causes the file descriptor to be closed and that breaks the socket connection. But breaking the connection does not delete the entry we created in the "/tmp" directory. This is why the program began by attempting to delete (unlink) this entry – in case there was a socket left from a previous invocation of `Receive`. After closing the connection, the program resumes its wait for another connection.

The sending program, `Send`, in Figure 12-8 is a little less complicated. It creates a socket, just as `Receive` did. This socket, however, needs to be connected to the socket created by `Receive`. Therefore, `Send` constructs the same socket name as that used by `Receive` and passes this name to `connect`. If the connection can be made (i.e., the entry in the "/tmp" directory exists), the call will return a zero result. After a successful connection, the `Send` program can use the socket as though it were a file descriptor. (Both file descriptors and sockets are implemented as indexes into the same object descriptor table.) Our program converts the file descriptor to a stream for convenience, writes data to the socket and closes the stream when finished. Closing the stream causes `Receive` at the other end to receive an end-of-file indication.

## The INET Domain

There are several networking programs provided with the Berkeley UNIX system. They include `rlogin`, `finger` and `talk`. All the networking programs use the Internet communications domain. Within this domain, the commonly used protocols are TCP and UDP. TCP (Transmission Control Protocol) provides reliable byte-stream message transmission and is used to support the `SOCK_STREAM` form of socket. UDP (User Datagram Protocol) is used to support the `SOCK_DGRAM` form of socket. UDP is more efficient, in that there is less software overhead associated with its use, but it is unreliable; the system does not guarantee that packets will arrive at the other end. Our example programs will use `SOCK_STREAM` sockets and therefore the TCP protocol.

A major difference between the UNIX and INET domains is the form of the socket names. In the UNIX domain, file pathnames are used to name sockets. In the INET domain, network addresses must be used. A network address consists of three numbers. The first number specifies the network or address family (INET in our case), the second number identifies the computer and the third identifies a port on that computer.

A program that communicates with a program on another computer needs to know the network address of that other program. But how does it find out what address to use? For the networking programs that form part of the UNIX system, there is a facility akin to the directory assistance service provided by a telephone company. Most networking software fits the client/server model. For example, on each UNIX machine in a network, there is a remote login server (the `rlogin` daemon) waiting for clients on other computers to make a connection. When a user on some machine executes the `rlogin` program, it determines the number for the machine specified as the `rlogin` argument by searching for the machine name in a small database that lists the machines on the network. This database is the file "/etc/hosts". The program then determines the port number for the `rlogin` service by searching another small database. This other database corresponds to the file "/etc/services". The file also says which protocol each service uses for communication. The numbers found in the two databases are combined to create an INET address. Then `rlogin` attempts to make the connection. (There is an assumption that the port numbers for the `rlogin` service are the same on all machines.)

Our small programming example of the use of sockets in the INET domain takes the form of a computerized bulletin board. The idea is that a server program on our machine will send today's bulletin board announcements (copied from a file) to any client located on any machine in the network. Unless we have *super-user* privileges, we cannot add the port number for our bulletin board service to the "/etc/services" database. Therefore, we have just picked an arbitrary port number, 2000, and built it into the program. With luck, no-one else will have already taken this port number. (At the end of this section, we tell you what to do if you do not want to rely on luck.) Now let us begin with the client program. We call the program b_board and it appears in Figure 12-9.

The program requires one command-line argument that provides the name of the machine on which the bulletin board server program is located. This allows us to have different bulletin boards on different computers. The program begins by constructing the network address in the structure named bba. This structure has a different format to that used in the previous example for the UNIX domain. First, our program uses the memset function to clear the structure to hold zeros. (This is actually unnecessary here because static storage is initialized with zeros anyway.) Second, the address format code (the network number) is set to indicate INET. Next, we need to know the number for the machine named on the command line. We use a library routine, gethostbyname, to look up the number in the database and we put the number into the network address. A routine, memcpy, is used to copy the number because this makes our code independent of the number of bytes in the number. Finally, we put the port number into the address. The function htons (host-to-network, short) is used to convert the number into a standard form used in network communications. This function overcomes a potential problem caused by different computer manufacturers having chosen to order the bytes within an integer differently. The host-to-network conversion function puts the bytes in the order that all computers on the network are programmed to expect.[4] (There was no need to convert the machine number because gethostbyname returns the number with the bytes in the proper network order.) If we had desired to connect to a standard service rather than our own unofficial one, we would have used a library function, getservbyname, to look up the proper port number to use.

Having constructed the network address, the b_board program creates a socket and attempts to connect it to the address. In the call to socket, there is again no need to specify a protocol in the third parameter because TCP will be used automatically for a socket of type SOCK_STREAM. If we had wanted, we could have used the getprotobyname function to look up a code number for the TCP protocol and passed that number as the third argument.

After establishing a connection, we can use the socket as though it were a file descriptor. Our program reads from the socket and copies the data to the standard output.

---

4. The same reason motivates the XDR functions used with remote procedure calls.

## Figure 12-9  The b_board Client Program

```c
#include <stdio.h>
#include <stdlib.h>
#include <string.h>
#include <sys/types.h>
#include <sys/socket.h>
#include <netinet/in.h>
#include <netdb.h>
#define PORTNUM 2000
#define oops(msg) { perror(msg);  exit(1); }

struct sockaddr_in bba;
struct hostent *hp;
FILE *rf; int s, rfd, ch;

int main(int argc, char *argv[]) {
    if (argc < 2) {
        fprintf(stderr, "Usage: %s hostname\n", argv[0]);
        exit(1);
    }
    /**** build the network address ****/
    memset(&bba, 0, sizeof(bba));
    bba.sin_family = AF_INET;
    hp = gethostbyname(argv[1]);
    if (hp == NULL) oops("no such computer");
    memcpy(&bba.sin_addr, hp->h_addr, hp->h_length);
    bba.sin_port = htons(PORTNUM);
    /**** make the connection ****/
    s = socket(AF_INET, SOCK_STREAM, 0);
    if (s == -1) oops("socket");
    if (connect(s, &bba, sizeof(bba)) != 0)
        oops("connect");
    /**** read and print data read from the socket ****/
    rf = fdopen(s, "r");
    if (rf == NULL) oops("fdopen");
    while( (ch = getc(rf)) != EOF)
        putchar(ch);
    fclose(rf);
    return 0;
}
```

Now we can turn our attention to the server program which will be left running on one or more computers. The source code for this program is given in Figure 12-10. We call the program b_board_d (again, the *d* suffix indicates that the program is a daemon).

The b_board_d program begins in a similar way to the client program. It first builds a network address, its own address. We use a function, gethostname, to obtain the name of the machine on which the program is running. After building the network address, we create a socket and bind the address to it. Next, we tell the system that we are prepared to listen for connections and wait in the accept call for some client process to make a connection. When a connection is made, we copy the contents of the bulletin board file to the socket, close the connection, and return to the beginning of the loop to wait for a new connection.

You may have questioned the arbitrary assumption made in this example that we could use port number 2000 for the bulletin board service. If you want to eliminate the assumption that a particular port number is free for use, the b_board_d program should be modified to use port number zero. When the program makes the bind call, the UNIX system will automatically substitute the number of an available port. After the bind call, the program can call the getsockname function to determine what port number was assigned. This number can be printed and made available to all potential users of the bulletin board service. That is, code like the following can be inserted in the program just before the call to listen:

```
slen = sizeof(saddr);
if (getsockname(s, &saddr, &slen) != 0)
    oops("getsockname");
printf("Service available on port %d\n",
    ntohs(saddr.sin_port));
```

## 12-5  *Multiplexed Input-Output*

It is not hard to conceive of programs that have two sources of input and must respond, without delay, to input that becomes available from either source. The talk program provides a good example. After talk has established a socket connection with another instance of talk, perhaps on another computer, the program has two sources of input and two destinations for output. The program must wait for input to come from either the socket or from the keyboard. Input received from the socket must be copied onto the lower half of the screen. Input received from the keyboard must be echoed to the upper half of the screen and also written to the socket. Clearly, the talk program must respond instantly, or nearly instantly, to a new character becoming available from either source.

But how do we write a program that accepts input from either source without knowing in advance which source will provide some input first? If the program calls getc (or

## Figure 12-10   The b_board_d Server Program

```c
#include <stdio.h>
#include <stdlib.h>
#include <string.h>
#include <sys/types.h>
#include <sys/socket.h>
#include <netinet/in.h>
#include <netdb.h>
#define PORTNUM            2000
#define BBD_FILE          "/u0/jack/bulletin.brd"
#define oops(msg)         { perror(msg);  exit(1); }

struct sockaddr_in saddr;  struct hostent *hp;
char hostname[256];  int slen, s, sfd, ch;
FILE *sf, *bbf;

int main(int argc, char *argv[]) {
    /**** build our own network address ****/
    memset(&saddr, 0, sizeof(saddr));
    saddr.sin_family = AF_INET;
    gethostname(hostname, sizeof(hostname));
    hp = gethostbyname(hostname);
    memcpy(&saddr.sin_addr, hp->h_addr, hp->h_length);
    saddr.sin_port = htons(PORTNUM);
    /**** create the socket and bind the address ****/
    s = socket(AF_INET, SOCK_STREAM, 0);
    if (s == -1) oops("socket");
    if (bind(s,&saddr,sizeof(saddr)) != 0) oops("bind");
    /**** repeatedly wait for clients to connect ****/
    if (listen(s, 1) != 0) oops("listen");
    for( ; ; ) {
        sfd = accept(s, NULL, NULL);
        if (sfd == -1) oops("accept");
        sf = fdopen(sfd, "w");
        if (sf == NULL) oops("fdopen");
        bbf = fopen(BBD_FILE, "r");
        if (bbf == NULL) fprintf(sf, "No information\n");
        else {
            while((ch = getc(bbf)) != EOF) putc(ch, sf);
            fclose(bbf);
        }
        fclose(sf);
    }
    return 0;
}
```

some similar function) to read from one source, the program will be suspended until input from that source arrives, while ignoring the other source of input. A possible solution to the problem is to use a *non-blocking* read instead of `getc`. You could program your own version of `getc` which returns an input character if one is available or returns a special code, say `'\0'`, if one is not available. (Such a function can be programmed because it is possible to test to see how many input characters could be read before the program would be suspended.[5]) By alternating non-blocking reads on both input sources, we could be sure of seeing an input character as soon as it arrives. But, this approach would be very wasteful of CPU time.

A better solution, and the normal solution used in non-Berkeley versions of the UNIX system, is for the program to fork into two processes. One process reads from one source and the second process reads from the other source. This way, a process would be unblocked and would read as soon as input became available. If we were trying to implement *talk*, we would still have a small problem trying to prevent the two processes from writing to the screen simultaneously. But with a little effort, the problem can be solved using signals to synchronize the actions of the two processes.

However, the Berkeley-based UNIX systems provide a simpler solution to the problem of reading from two or more sources simultaneously. The system function, `select`, can be passed a mask which has one bits in positions corresponding to the file descriptors for these input sources. When control returns, there will be one bits set only for the input sources that you can read without having to wait. Actually, `select` takes three separate masks. One for reading, one for writing (remember that writes to pipes or slow output devices can cause the writing process to be suspended), and a third for watching for exceptional conditions associated with a file descriptor. There is also an optional time-out value that can be passed. This specifies a limit on how much time the process should be blocked waiting for possible input-output or exceptions on the selected file descriptors.

A simple example of the use of `select` is shown in Figure 12-11. The <sys/types.h> header file contains macros for manipulating the bit masks, which are defined with type `fdset`. As shown, FD_ZERO clears all bits in the mask, and FD_SET sets an individual bit in the selected position. In the example, we wait for input from either the standard input (descriptor 0) or from the source associated with descriptor `fd`. The first parameter to `select` is a limit on the range of descriptor values to check. We obtain the maximum number of descriptor values that are possible from the `ulimit` function. (If this function is not available on your system, the older Berkeley UNIX function `getdtablesize` may be called instead.) After the `select` call, the result stored in `nf` is the total number of bits that are set in the three masks on return from the function. The FD_ISSET macro may be used, as shown, to test file descriptors correspond to bits set in the mask.

---

5. Better still, the `fcntl` function or the `ioctl` function can be used to modify the behavior of standard input to become non-blocking.

---

**Figure 12-11** Using select for Multiplexed I/O

```
#include <sys/types.h>
...
int numfds, nf;
fdset rmask[1], wmask[1], xmask[1];
int fd;                    /* a socket or file descriptor */
...
FD_ZERO(rmask);   FD_SET(0, rmask);   FD_SET(fd, rmask);
FD_ZERO(wmask);   FD_ZERO(xmask);
numfds = ulimit(4, 0);
nf = select(numfds, rmask, wmask, xmask, NULL);
if (FD_ISSET(0, rmask)) {
    /* read from standard input */
    ...
}
if (FD_ISSET(fd, rmask)) {
    /* read from descriptor fd */
    ...
}
```

## 12-6  Further Reading

Much of the material in this chapter was prepared using the SUN document called *Network Programming Guide*, Part Number 800-3850-10. If your system includes a SUN computer, your systems administrator should have a copy. Chapters 2 through 7 cover the SUN implementation of remote procedure call and chapters 10 through 12 provide a tutorial introduction to sockets. A book, *The Art of Distributed Applications: Programming Techniques for Remote Procedure Calls* by J. Corbin (Springer-Verlag 1991) gives an extensive coverage of RPC. A more general book on networking, that covers both sockets and RPC, is *UNIX Network Programming* by W. R. Stevens (Prentice-Hall 1990).

Some older material related to sockets is still relevant but, before any code is copied, the on-line manual pages should be checked for changes to the interfaces. These older documents are as follows: *Tutorial Examples of Interprocess Communication in Berkeley UNIX 4.2bsd* by Stuart Sechrest, Report UCB/CSD 84/191, Computer Science Division, University of California, Berkeley; *A 4.2bsd Interprocess Communication Primer* by S. J. Leffler, R. S. Fabry and W. N. Joy, available as supplementary documentation supplied with Berkeley UNIX 4.2bsd system, July 1983; *4.2BSD Networking Implementation Notes* by S. J. Leffler, W. N. Joy and R. S. Fabry, also provided as supplementary documentation with the Berkeley UNIX 4.2bsd system, July 1983.

# SECTION III

# *Managing and Maintaining Software*

# CHAPTER 13

*DEVELOPING LARGE C PROGRAMS*

---

## 13-1 *Multi-File Compilation*

Large C programs should be developed in several pieces. These different parts should be held in different files and may be compiled separately. All it takes is a little care to ensure that the different pieces fit together correctly. The way to make sure that the pieces match up properly requires the use of C *header* files. We will refer to these as '*.h*' files because that is the filename suffix normally used in C programming. However, to be certain that the general principles are understood first, we will forego their use in the following example.

A complete C program consists of a sequence of external declarations for variables and functions. Executable statements may only appear inside function declarations. The declarations can be split into two or more files and compiled separately, provided that some information gets repeated. Let us consider a trivial example. Suppose that we have three functions named main, fn1 and fn2; and we have three global variables x1, x2, x3. We will assume that each function needs to access all of the global variables. A possible way of splitting the program into two files is shown in Figure 13-1.

The storage for the global variables, x1, x2 and x3, is declared and initialized in the first file. These variables may, of course, be referenced from within the two functions, fn1 and fn2. In addition, we have declared a variable localvar in the first file. The keyword static on the declaration causes the variable to be local to this file. It cannot be refer-

---

**Figure 13-1    A Two File Program**

*File 1* (named "prog1.c")

```
int x1 = 5;
char *x2[] = { "message 1", "message 2", "message 3" };
float x3 = 4.500;
static float localvar = 0.0;
static void fn2(char);

float fn1( int a, int b ) {
    /* body of fn1 appears here */
}

static void fn2( char a ) {
    /* body of fn2 appears here */
}
```

*File 2* (named "prog2.c")

```
extern int x1;
extern char *x2[];
extern float x3;
extern float fn1(int,int);
static int localvar, anothervar;

int main( int argc, char *argv[] ) {
    /* body of main program appears here */
}
```

enced from any other source file. Similarly, the function fn2 has been given the static attribute. This means that it can be called only from functions within the first file.

In the second file, we want the main program (the main function) to be able to access the variables, x1, x2 and x3, declared in the first file as well as the function fn1. Clearly, declarations for x1, x2, etc. are needed, even if only to provide type information to the C compiler. However, we do not want storage to be allocated and initialized for these external variables, because the storage allocation and initialization is taken care of in File 1. When the extern attribute is used in front of a declaration, it indicates that we are providing type information only for variables or functions defined in another file. The extern attribute need not be supplied for a function declaration because the compiler assumes this attribute as the default. However, it is probably good practice to include it in order to give a positive indication that this function is used or defined in other files. The second file contains a local variable named `localvar`. This variable is distinct from the variable declared with the same name in the first file.

Our two files may be compiled separately. The first file might be compiled with the command

```
gcc -c prog1.c
```

This command will create a relocatable object file named "prog1.o". Similarly, the second file might be compiled with

```
gcc -c prog2.c
```

to create the file "prog2.o". Finally, the two object files may be merged and loaded into an executable program by executing

```
gcc prog1.o prog2.o -o prog
```

where the executable program has been named "prog". This last step is relatively fast compared to the first two because no compilation is performed. The `gcc` command will invoke only the system loader (`ld`) to merge the object files and any library functions that they may reference into a complete, executable, program.[1]

The advantage of this approach is that the whole program need not be recompiled if, say, we later change the `fn1` function. We could make the changes to the first file, recompile just this file and then repeat the final merge step. Recompilation is particularly easy if the `make` utility is used. As we will see shortly, this versatile UNIX program can be set up to recompile automatically just those files that have been changed since the executable program was last created.

## Effective Use Of '.h' Files

We have just seen one way in which a large program can be split into files for separate compilation. There is, however, an obvious danger in this approach. It is clearly necessary for the pieces of the program to interface correctly. And it would be very easy to make a change in one file but to forget to make a matching change in another file. Perhaps, the resulting mismatch might be quite obvious. For example, we may now be calling a function with three arguments whereas, in the definition for that function, only two parameters are declared. But, regardless of how obvious the mismatch is, the C compiler has no way of telling that the mismatch exists, precisely because the source files are compiled separately. Even if we compile two source files at the same time, as in the command

```
gcc -c prog1.c prog2.c
```

---

1.  If you wish to compile and link both files in a single step, you may execute
```
gcc prog1.c prog2.c -o prog
```

the C compiler will not remember any information from the first file when it comes to compile the second file. With classic C code, the `lint` processor can find most such mismatches. Unfortunately, an ANSI C version of lint is not currently available. Perhaps it does not matter very much because, by using *.h* files properly, the C compiler can find the mismatches too.

Let us consider an example. Suppose that we are developing a large program which makes use of queues of integers that obey a First-in, First-out (FIFO) queuing discipline. We will further suppose that the operations to be performed on these queues include

1. creating a new (empty) queue,
2. appending an integer to the end of a queue,
3. removing the first integer from a queue, and
4. finding the length of a queue.

Modern programming practice would consider the FIFO queue to be an *abstract data type* whose implementation details should be encapsulated in a separate file and kept secret from the remainder of the program. Regardless of whether you believe in the philosophy of abstract data types, it does make good sense to separate the functions that implement the abstract data type from the remainder of the program. You will find programs that follow this scheme to be easier to develop and debug.

For our example, we shall place the declarations for the various FIFO queue functions in a file named "intqueue.c", say. Our problem now is to make sure that the other source files use the FIFO queues correctly and without requiring any knowledge of how the queues are implemented. Thus, we should provide a header file, which we can name "intqueue.h", that defines the FIFO queue data type and its operations. Quite plausibly, the "intqueue.h" file could contain the definitions reproduced in Figure 13-2.

Our structure definitions indicate that the queue is to be implemented as a linked-list and that we will keep pointers to the first and last queue elements in a separate structure. Users of the queue manipulation package will work with pointers to the queue header structure, using the type name `FIFO_Q`. They will work with pointers to the structure rather than with the structure directly because some of the functions need to change the list header structure. In other words, we are using pointers to achieve the effect of call-by-reference (or PASCAL `var`) parameter passing.

Users of the FIFO queue data type should neither directly reference any field names in the two structures nor should they use the structure tag identifiers. We note that, in C, it is difficult to prevent users of the package from using these field names and structure tags and thus writing code that is dependent on the queue implementation. However, we will shortly see a couple of ways to discourage direct access to the queue implementation. (Some of the more modern programming languages, such as ADA, provide better support for abstract data types and can completely deny access to the internal details of the implementation.)

---

### Figure 13-2   The intqueue.h Header File

```
/*  These two structure definitions represent the queue
    implementation. These definitions are used only in
    the functions which implement the FIFO queue
    operations. */
struct q_element {
        int value;
        struct q_element *link;
    };
struct q_header {
        struct q_element *first, *last;
    };

/*  Instances of FIFO queues are declared with the FIFO_Q
    type. All operations on these queues are performed
    via the four access functions listed below. */
typedef struct q_header *FIFO_Q;
extern FIFO_Q make_new_q(void);
extern int remove1(FIFO_Q), q_length(FIFO_Q);
extern void append1(FIFO_Q,int);
```

The "intqueue.c" file which implements the various queue manipulation operations might contain the code reproduced in Figure 13-3. This sample code has been deliberately written in a straightforward manner. The code can be considerably shortened through full use of C language features, but we leave that as an exercise to the reader.

It must be stressed that this file, which implements the queue operations, should be the only file where the structure tags q_element and q_header are used, and where field names first, last, value and link are used in association with FIFO queues.

One may object that including the "intqueue.h" header file in the "intqueue.c" file causes declarations for the various functions, make_new_q and the rest, to be seen twice by the C compiler. That is quite correct. However, the declarations in the .h file provide only data type information. When the compiler later reaches the full declarations, it will check that the data types in the full declarations match the data types provided in the .h file. The data type checking is important to us because it verifies that our function definitions are consistent with invocations of these functions contained in other files.

The other files that comprise the rest of our large program can create and use FIFO queues, as in the code fragment shown in Figure 13-4. This code fragment might conceivably appear as part of a discrete event simulation program.

## Figure 13-3  The intqueue.c File

```c
#include <stdio.h>
#include <stdlib.h>
#include "intqueue.h"

FIFO_Q make_new_q(void) {
    FIFO_Q qh = (FIFO_Q)malloc(sizeof(*qh));
    qh->first = qh->last = NULL;
    return qh;
}

int length_q( FIFO_Q qh ) {
    struct q_element *tp;  int length = 0;
    for( tp=qh->first; tp!=NULL; tp=tp->link ) length++;
    return length;
}

void append1( FIFO_Q qh, int new_element ) {
    struct q_element *tp;
    tp = (struct q_element *)malloc(sizeof(*tp));
    tp->value = new_element;
    tp->link = NULL;
    (qh->last)->link = tp;
    qh->last = tp;
    if (qh->first == NULL) qh->first = tp;
}

int remove1( FIFO_Q qh ) {
    struct q_element *tp;  int result;
    tp = qh->first;
    if (tp == NULL) {
        fprintf(stderr, "remove1: argument is empty");
        abort();
    }
    qh->first = tp->link;
    if (qh->first == NULL) qh->last = NULL;
    result = tp->value;
    free(tp);
    return result ;
}
```

---

**Figure 13-4   Using the intqueue Package**

```
#include "intqueue.h"
#define MAXINT 0x7fffffff      /* largest integer value */
FIFO_Q customer_queue;
int time_now, next_arriv_time, finish_time;

    . . .

    customer_queue = make_new_q();
    finish_time = MAXINT;
    next_arriv_time = arrival_interval();
    do {
        if (finish_time < next_arriv_time) {
            time_now = finish_time;
            if (length_q(customer_queue) == 0)
                finish_time = MAXINT;
            else
                finish_time = remove1(customer_queue);
        } else {
            time_now = next_arriv_time;
            append1(customer_queue, service_time());
            next_arriv_time += arrival_interval();
        }
    } while(time_now < 10000);

    . . .
```

## 13-2   *Encapsulation of Abstract Data Types in C*

It was mentioned in the previous section that there are ways to discourage users of the queue package from directly accessing internal details of the queue implementation. One technique[2] is to make use of the C preprocessor and cause a header file like "intqueue.h" to expand differently depending on whether the file that contains the #include directive is the implementation file ("intqueue.c") or some other file. Following this idea, we can change the "intqueue.h" file as shown in Figure 13-5. If the preprocessor flag INTQUEUE_IMPLEMENTOR is set when the header file is included, the expanded file

---

2. See the book by Darnell and Margolis (listed under *Further Reading* at the end of the chapter) for a larger example that uses this technique.

contains the full implementation of the `FIFO_Q` data type (albeit in a slightly indirect fashion). If the preprocessor flag is not set, however, the expanded file contains only a dummy definition for `FIFO_Q`.

The implementation file "intqueue.c" would have to contain the two lines

```
#define INTQUEUE_IMPLEMENTOR
#include "intqueue.h"
```

to compile correctly. Other files would not have that `#define` directive and they would be unable to access any fields inside `FIFO_Q` objects (other than a meaningless field named `_x`).

The dummy definition of `FIFO_Q` is chosen so that if the user should write code like

```
FIFO_Q q1;
q1 = (FIFO_Q)calloc(sizeof(*q1), 1);
```

then at least the correct amount of storage will be allocated for the object referenced by `q1`. (This would actually be incorrect because only the `make_new_q` function should be used to create a new `FIFO_Q` object – but it is probably preferable to have the user's code crash because the object has not been initialized correctly than to have the code crash because an object has the wrong size.)

---

### Figure 13-5    Revised intqueue.h File Using Encapsulation

```
struct _private_q_header {
        struct _private_q_element *first, *last;
    };
struct _private_q_element {
        int value;
        struct _private_q_element *link;
    };

#ifdef INTQUEUE_IMPLEMENTOR
    typedef struct _private_q_header *FIFO_Q;
#else
    typedef struct {
            char _x[sizeof(struct _private_q_header)];
        } *FIFO_Q;
#endif

extern FIFO_Q make_new_q();
extern int remove1(FIFO_Q), q_length(FIFO_Q);
extern void append1(FIFO_Q, int);
```

---

## 13-3   The make Program

A really large C program might consist of scores of standard source files (files with the *.c* suffix) and dozens of include files (files with either a *.h* or *.i* suffix). If the program is under development or being debugged, there may be frequent changes to the source files. Every time that a *.c* file is changed, we must remember to perform a compilation and recreate the corresponding *.o* file. If an include file has been changed, all the *.c* files that include it usually need to be recompiled. If a *.h* file includes a *.i* (or, as is quite legal, another *.h* file), the situation becomes a little unclear. A change to the *.i* file may require recompilation of all *.c* files that include the original *.h* file.

The fact of the matter is that it is altogether too easy to forget to recompile some source file. Then, when the different object code files are merged, we may end up with a program that does not work, and is hard to debug because it does not correspond to the current source code. A simple, but wasteful, way to avoid this kind of problem is to recompile every source file after a series of changes have been performed.

The `make` program is a software tool that can be used to keep track of which files need recompiling after any changes have been made and to actually issue the sequence of commands that performs all the necessary recompilations. Because `make` is a general tool, it can be used for much more than just keeping C programs properly up-to-date. However, we will not go into the full details here.

### The Basic Concepts of *make*

To know which files need recompiling after a change, we need to know how the files depend on each other. For example, if some file, "prog1a.c" say, contains the declaration

```
extern int zflag;
```

and another file, "prog1b.c" say, contains the declaration

```
int zflag=25;
```

then the two files are interdependent. We must not change the type of the variable from `int` to `short` in one file without making a matching change in the other file. It is actually rather poor practice to have files that are interdependent in this manner. The correct approach is to place the declaration:

```
extern int zflag;
```

in a *.h* file, "prog1ab.h" say. We will treat this particular declaration as being the only place in the program where the data type of `zflag` is determined. All other files will have to agree with this definition and we will force them to agree by having them include "prog1ab.h". The file "prog1a.c" would have to contain the `#include` directive

```
#include "prog1ab.h"
```

and file "prog1b.c" would have to contain the two lines

```
#include "prog1ab.h"
int zflag = 25;
```

This breaks the direct interdependence between the files "prog1a.c" and "prog1b.c". We can say that "prog1a.c" depends on data type information that is defined only in "prog1ab.h". Similarly, "prog1b.c" depends on information defined only in "prog1ab.h" too. Therefore, if the approach that we described earlier as *correct* is followed religiously, all file dependencies must be revealed by #include directives. We will now take the sanctimonious attitude that all dependencies do in fact correspond to uses of #include directives.

To illustrate the use of make, we will hypothesize a relatively small C program, which we will name displayprog. That is, our executable version of the program will be held in a file with this name. The files comprising the program contain #include directives as below. We omit #include directives for <stdio.h> and any other header files contained in the standard library.

*File "main.c":*
```
#include "treepack.h"
#include "listpack.h"
```

*File "treepack.c":*
```
#include "treepack.h"
#include "graphpack.h"
```

*File "listpack.c":*
```
#include "listpack.h"
#include "graphpack.h"
```

*File "graphpack.c":*
```
#include "graphpack.h"
```

*File "graphpack.h":*
```
#include "tables.i"
```

The make utility has to be told the name of the target program, which is "displayprog", how this target program is to be built, how files used in the building process are themselves to be built, and what the dependencies are. All this information is kept in another file, called "Makefile" (or, optionally, "makefile"). If we were unsophisticated users of the make utility, we might set up our "makefile" to look like the one shown in Figure 13-6.

If you have all the source files and the makefile in the current directory, you need do no more than type the command

```
make
```

and then sit back and wait for all the necessary compilations to be performed automatically. If you subsequently change one or two source files and, perhaps, delete an object file, you need only repeat the magic command

```
make
```

to bring everything up-to-date. The make utility will recompile only those files that need to be recompiled and then recombine the object files to create the new version of "displayprog".

Before proceeding to explain how it all works, let us first run through the syntax of a makefile. Comments are introduced by a hash mark symbol (#) and continue up to the end of the line. An identifier that begins in the first column and is followed by a colon is called a *target*. It is usually, but not necessarily, the name of a program or file to be built. The identifiers that follow the target on the same line are called the *prerequisites*. These are usually the names of files which the target depends on. After the line defining a target and prerequisites, command lines may appear. These are commands which will be executed by the *sh* shell program when make needs to create the target or bring it up-to-date. Command lines must begin with a tab character, *space characters do not work.* (**NOTE THIS!!**)

---

### Figure 13-6    A Simple Makefile for 'displayprog'

```
# makefile to create 'displayprog'

displayprog: main.o treepack.o listpack.o
        gcc main.o treepack.o listpack.o -o displayprog

main.o: main.c treepack.h listpack.h
        gcc -c main.c

treepack.o: treepack.c treepack.h graphpack.h
        gcc -c treepack.c

listpack.o: listpack.c listpack.h graphpack.h
        gcc -c listpack.c

graphpack.h: tables.i
        touch graphpack.h
```

---

Now we are ready to look at how it all works. Let us assume that none of the object files currently exists. The make program first discovers that its target is "displayprog". This is determined by the fact that "displayprog" is the first target to appear in the makefile. And make sees that the prerequisites for "displayprog" are the files "main.o", "treepack.o" and "listpack.o". If make had access to up-to-date versions of these files, it would be able to create "displayprog" from them by executing the commands that immediately follow in the makefile. However, make has to defer executing these commands until it is sure that it has up-to-date versions of the named object files. Thus, make now has three sub-targets. It takes each sub-target in turn, starting with "main.o", the first file listed. Make now searches the makefile for a line that gives "main.o" as a target. When make finds it, make discovers that the prerequisites for "main.o" are the files "main.c", "treepack.h" and "listpack.h". On the line following is a command that instructs make on how to construct a new version of "main.o". But before it can execute this command, it must check the three new sub-targets. The first one is "main.c". Because make cannot find a line defining "main.c" as a target and because "main.c" is (or should be) an existing file, make assumes that "main.c" is up-to-date. Next, the process is repeated for "treepack.h" and then for "listpack.h". Having verified that these files all exist, make now returns to execute the command

```
gcc -c main.c
```

which implicitly creates or re-creates the file "main.o". Having attained a sub-goal of providing an up-to-date version of "main.o", make proceeds to its next sub-target, which is "listpack.o". And so on. Eventually, make will achieve all its subtargets and perform the final command that links all the object files to create "displayprog". (We will defer explanation of the touch command, which appears in the makefile, until later.)

Having created the main target and all the object files that are subsidiary targets, let us suppose that we now change some file, say "treepack.h". What happens when we invoke make again? How does make avoid performing unnecessary re-compilations? The short answer is that make simply checks the times at which files were created (or last modified) to determine whether files are obsolete. In our example, "treepack.o" is shown as depending on "treepack.h". If the time of creation of "treepack.o" precedes the time of last modification of "treepack.h" then make knows it has to execute the commands that create an up-to-date version of "treepack.o". It should be noted that make still has to go through the process of checking targets, sub-targets, sub-sub-targets and so on. If make were to immediately compare the time of creation of "displayprog" against the times of creation for "main.o", "treepack.o" and "listpack.o", it would appear that "displayprog" is up-to-date. So, make does indeed follow the chains of dependencies making sure that all the files are up-to-date. Make does not check the creation time of "displayprog" against those of the three object files until after it has guaranteed that they are up-to-date. Thus, if a recompilation of "treepack.c" has been performed, make will now find "displayprog" to be out-of-date and will execute the command to link the object files.

The strange command

```
touch graphpack.h
```

which appears in one of the rules is there to force the files which use "graphpack.h" to become out-of-date. The touch command is a standard UNIX command, though normally used only in makefiles. This command does not alter a file, it just causes the time of last modification for that file to be reset to the current time. Thus if the file "tables.i" has been changed, we will fool make into thinking that "graphpack.h" has been changed too. And this is exactly the behavior we desire, so that programs which include "graphpack.h" (and thus indirectly include "tables.i") will be recompiled.

The sample makefile defined five targets in all – one main target and four sub-targets. If you wish, you may create any subset of these targets by naming them on the command line. For example, we may run the command

```
make treepack.o
```

and just the commands needed to create an up-to-date version of "treepack.o" will be executed. Similarly, the command

```
make treepack.o listpack.o
```

is possible too. Note that the commands

```
make displayprog
```

and

```
make
```

are equivalent only because displayprog is the first target defined in the makefile.

## Macros and Default Rules in *make*

The makefile used in the preceding example is, in fact, unnecessarily detailed. This is because make has many built-in rules for creating object files. Consider one of the sub-target files, say "treepack.o", and suppose that the makefile contains no rules for creating this file. In this situation, make will discover for itself that "treepack.c" exists and will automatically apply the classic C compiler (i.e., the cc command) to this file to create "treepack.o". If "treepack.c" does not exist, but "treepack.p" exists, make would invoke the Pascal compiler, pc. If we do not wish to have the default C compiler or the default Pascal compiler applied to the source file, it is easy to supply different default rules. We will look at some examples shortly.

Make supports a simple macro facility. Macros may be used to parameterize a makefile or just to simplify it. A few special macros change their definitions dynamically and are used when writing default rules.

Taking advantage of these more advanced features of make, we can improve our makefile to that shown in Figure 13-7.

In the example makefile, the identifier OBJS is a macro which is assigned a list of names of the object files. The dollar symbol must be used when accessing the value of the

## Figure 13-7 An Improved Makefile for 'displayprog'

```
# makefile to create 'displayprog'

OBJS= main.o treepack.o listpack.o

## re-define default compiler and compilation flags
CC = gcc
CFLAGS = -ansi -g

displayprog: $(OBJS)
        $(CC) $(CFLAGS) $(OBJS) -o $@

main.o: treepack.h listpack.h

treepack.o: treepack.h graphpack.h

listpack.o: listpack.h graphpack.h

graphpack.h: tables.i
        touch $@
```

macro, as in the two subsequent uses of it. If the macro name has more than one character, the name must be surrounded by either parentheses or braces. The example uses `$(OBJS)` to access the value of `OBJS`, but we could equally well have written `${OBJS}`.

The macro CC is used as the name of the command that `make` uses in an implicit compilation of a *.c* file (i.e., when you have not supplied an explicit rule to use). The macro CFLAGS is used as an extra argument to an implicit C compilation. Your makefile might contain the setting

```
CFLAGS = -ansi -g
```

while a program is being developed and, possibly, the setting

```
CFLAGS = -ansi -O
```

after the program is working and fully debugged. The special macro `$@` yields the name of the current target. It can be used to shorten command lines, as in our example, and to reduce the amount of editing work if we ever decide to rename our files.

The implicit rule used to perform a C compilation is defined in a file that make reads when it starts up. This rule and many others are called *default rules*. The default rule for obtaining a *.o* file from a *.c* file might read as follows:[3]

```
CC = cc
CFLAGS =
.c.o:
        $(CC) $(CFLAGS) -c $<
```

The target .c.o is treated specially by make because it consists of two filename suffixes placed adjacently. The macro $< expands to the name of the subject file (i.e., the file whose suffix is *.c*). If you need to refer to the subject file in the rule but with a different suffix, the macro $* yields the filename with the suffix stripped off.

You are free to define your own default rules in a makefile. These may be entirely new default rules or they may replace some of the default rules that make reads from its start-up file. However, if your default rule uses a new kind of filename suffix, you have to declare it. An example which does this appears in Figure 13-8. The example is based on the LaTeX text formatting program. Given a LaTeX input file called, say, "doc.tex", we would normally have to execute the command

```
latex doc.tex
```

twice in succession to create an intermediate form in a new file named "doc.dvi". (The second pass is required if the document contains forward references to such things as items in the bibliography.) The dvi file is a device-independent representation of the formatted document and requires only a minimal amount of extra processing to convert it into a control file for a laser printer. If the laser printer uses PostScript[4] as its command language, there is a program (typically called dvi2ps) to convert a dvi file to PostScript. Thus, we might wish to execute a command pipeline similar to

```
dvi2ps doc.dvi | lpr -Plaser1
```

for creating the Postscript code and sending it directly to a laser printer named *laser1*.

The default rules in the example makefile provide for two possibilities. If the current directory contains the file "mydocument.tex", we may execute the command:

```
make mydocument.dvi
```

and the .tex.dvi default rule will be executed to create the dvi form (assuming that the dvi file does not already exist and is not more recent than the tex file). The other possibility is that we may execute this command:

```
make mydocument
```

---

3. The default rule provided with the SunOS version of make is a little more complicated.

4. *PostScript* is a trademark of Adobe Systems Inc.

Note that there is no suffix on the target. This forces make to use either the default rule labelled by *.tex* or the rule labelled by *.dvi*. In either case, the result is to print a copy of the document. (If both "mydocument.tex" and "mydocument.dvi" exist, the default rule that uses the dvi form will be used because that default rule is given before the other one.)

## Command-Line Arguments to make

As you may have gathered, make is a useful but complicated tool. It has many command-line options, of which only a few of the more useful possibilities are described below. For a full list of the options, you should consult the on-line manual pages.

Apart from listing the targets which you wish make to create, you may provide values for macros and you may set flags. Using, for example, the makefile of Figure 13-8, we may send a document to a different printer from the one named in the makefile by executing a command like

```
make LW=ccprinter document
```

---

### Figure 13-8   Defining Extra Default Rules in a Makefile

```
## define additional filename suffixes
.SUFFIXES:   .tex .dvi

## define the default printer and print command
LW = laser1
LPR = lpr -P$(LW)

## rule to create a dvi file from a latex file
.tex.dvi:
        latex $<
        latex $<

## rule to print a dvi file
.dvi:
        dvi2ps $< | $(LPR)

## rule to print a latex file
.tex:
        latex $<
        latex $<
        dvi2ps $*.dvi | $(LPR)
        rm -f $*.dvi      ## remove the dvi file again
```

---

The value provided for the LW macro overrides the one given in the makefile. Similarly, using the makefile of Figure 13-7, we can change the flags passed to the C compiler by using a command similar to

```
make CFLAGS=-O
```

(But if you want to be sure that all the C source files are compiled with the −O flag in effect, you must remove all the *.o* files first.)

We will now cover just a few of the possible command-line options.

The −t flag lets you avoid having make perform unnecessary re-compilations. Suppose that you simply change a comment in a *.h* file. This innocuous change could easily result in several wasted compilations the next time you use make. You could prevent the re-compilations by manually typing a touch command for all the object files involved. However, make has an option that will cause it to perform the touching actions. Executing the command

```
make -t
```

will cause make to touch whatever files are necessary to make all of them appear to be up-to-date. No re-compilations whatsoever will be performed. Obviously, this command must be used very carefully.

Other flags are useful when debugging makefiles. If you construct a fairly complicated makefile, you may have some difficulty understanding why make simply prints a message like

```
make: Fatal error: Don't know how to make target `x'
```

or why it re-builds a program that has not changed. The −n flag lets you perform dry runs, trying out make targets without really building them. For example, if the command

```
make -n prog
```

is executed, make will simply report all the actions that it would perform if it were to be invoked normally to create the target prog. That is, make simply prints the shell commands without actually executing them. A second flag, −d, is available for tracing through the interpretation of a makefile. When the command

```
make -d prog
```

is executed, make performs all the actions that bring the program prog up-to-date, but it also explains why it is performing each action. That is, make prints out exactly which rules it is using and prints modification and creation times for all the files involved. The output is lengthy, but reasonably easy to follow.

## Special Targets

With a little imagination, it is possible to use make as an interesting alternative to a shell script file. (Since the commands executed by make are passed to instances of a command shell, perhaps there is not much of a distinction between the two anyway.) Users of make often add fictitious targets to the makefiles that cause useful side-effects to happen. A typical example is the target *clean* (found in most makefiles that come with software source code distributions). This target is normally defined by the rule

```
clean:
        rm -f core a.out *.o
```

and when the user types the command

```
make clean
```

the result is that all superfluous files are removed. The −f flag to rm suppresses a warning from make if one of the arguments (say "a.out") does not exist. The command would normally be executed after the program being built has been successfully installed and now we wish to reduce the amount of disk storage.

Other special targets that are sometimes included in makefiles are *help* (to obtain a list of targets), *compress* (to squash all the source files and reduce disk usage as much as possible), *tarfile* (to create a tar archive file of all the source files) and *tarfile.Z* (to make a compressed tar archive file). Since these targets provide instructive examples of using make, sample rules for making these targets are shown in Figure 13-9. Note in the definition of the macro SRCS that a long line may be split and continued on the next line by typing a backslash character immediately before the newline character. The *help* target in this makefile should need only minimal explanation − echo is the command built into the shell for displaying a one-line text message. The '@' character that prefixes the command is special to make. Normally make prints each command just before it executes it. The @ prefix suppresses this behavior. The *tarfile* target shows a relatively complicated sequence of shell commands. Note that a new instance of a shell is created to execute each command line in the makefile. This implies that a cd (change directory) command in one line will therefore have no effect on the command in the next line. (Each instance of the shell is started with its working directory the same as for the make program.) If you need to change the directory before executing the next command, both commands must be on the same line of the makefile separated by a semicolon (which is a command separator for the shell).

## Figure 13-9   Some Special make Targets

```
## define a list of all source code files
SRCS = graphpack.h treepack.h listpack.h tables.i  \
       main.c treepack.c listpack.c


## all files needed for a software distribution
ALLFILES = README Makefile $(SRCS)


help:
        @ echo "Targets for make are:"
        @ echo "    compress   - compress source files"
        @ echo "    uncompress - restore source files"
        @ echo "    tarfile    - make an archive"


compress:
        compress $(SRCS)


uncompress:
        uncompress *.Z


tarfile: $(ALLFILES)
        mkdir /tmp/TAR
        cp $(ALLFILES) /tmp/TAR
        (cd /tmp/TAR; tar cf - ./*) > tarfile
        rm -r /tmp/TAR


tarfile.Z: tarfile
        compress tarfile
```

# 13-4  Make Reference Guide

To save having to search through the preceding explanations for specific details, some usage instructions for make are collected below. Note that the version of make provided on your system may have many additional features (such as support for library archives and SCCS files) beyond those described here. You should check your on-line system documentation to see what is available.

## Makefile Format

The input file to make normally has the name "makefile" or "Makefile". Either will work. If both files exist, the name "makefile" will take precedence over "Makefile". Alternatively, you may use any other name for the file but then you are required to use the −f command line flag on the make command.

A comment in the makefile is introduced by the '#' character. The comment continues to the end of the line. The makefile contains a sequence of definitions, where each definition takes one of the three forms below.

1. A macro definition of the form:

        NAME = text string

    The text string is terminated by the end of line. A long text string may be continued over several lines if each embedded newline is prefixed with a backslash character. Once defined, a macro may be used anywhere in the makefile. If the macro name is ABC, say, a use of the macro is written as either $(ABC) or ${ABC}. The parentheses may be omitted only if the macro name consists of a single character.

2. A default rule of the form:

        .suffix1.suffix2:
                one or more command lines ...

    or of the form:

        .suffix:
                one or more command lines ...

    The double suffix form defines a rule for obtaining a file with the second suffix from a file that has the first suffix. The single suffix form defines a rule for obtaining a file with no suffix from a file that has the given suffix. Each of the command lines must be indented by a single tab character (not by space characters). Note that the suffixes must have been declared (either in the start-up file read by make) or by defining a rule with the special target ".SUFFIXES".

3. An explicit rule of the form:

        target: prerequisite1 prerequisite2 ...
                zero or more command lines ...

    As before, the command lines must be indented by a single tab character.

Several special macros are built into `make`. These include the following:

| | |
|---|---|
| `$@` | the target of the current rule. |
| `$<` | the subject file (i.e. input file) being used in a default rule. |
| `$*` | the subject file with its suffix stripped off. |
| `$?` | a list of those prerequisite files that are newer than the target. |
| `$(MFLAGS)` | the command line flags passed to `make`. |

Each command line contains text that is passed as input to a new instance of the Bourne shell (the `sh` command). Multiple `sh` commands may be placed on one line if they are separated by semicolon characters. Long command lines may be split into several lines if each embedded newline is prefixed with a backslash character. If the `sh` command returns a non-zero result code, `make` will normally halt. If the command line is prefixed with a hyphen, the return code is ignored. (The special ".IGNORE" target may be defined to cause return codes on all commands to be ignored.) The default behavior is for `make` to echo each command immediately before it is executed. Prefixing the command line with an *at* character, `@`, suppresses echoing of that line.

Special targets include the following.

.SUFFIXES    is used to add extra suffixes to the list known to `make`. For example,
```
.SUFFIXES: .Z .tex .dvi
```
adds three new suffixes to the list. The list is cleared to empty if no prerequisites are given. For example, the two consecutive rules
```
.SUFFIXES:
.SUFFIXES: .Z .tex .dvi
```
cause the list of known suffixes to contain only the three shown.

.IGNORE    causes the return codes from shell commands to be ignored. The makefile simply has to contain this rule.
```
.IGNORE:
```

.SILENT    causes all command lines to be executed without being echoed. The makefile simply has to contain this rule.
```
.SILENT:
```

.PRECIOUS    tells `make` not to remove certain files when it is interrupted. Normally, if you interrupt `make` while it is building, say, a *.o* file, that file will be automatically removed. Listing the file as a prerequisite to a rule with the target .PRECIOUS will suppress that behavior.

The start-up file read by `make` contains default rules for most standard processors on the UNIX system. These rules cause `make` to behave intelligently when dealing with C, Pascal, Fortran77, Ratfor, assembler, object, lex and yacc files, for instance.

The command line that invokes `make` may include the names of one or more targets to be built, macro definitions to override or to use in addition to those given in the makefile, and various options. If no targets are listed, the target of the first explicit rule in the makefile will be built. Macro definitions take the form NAME=TEXT. If the text contains space characters, you will need to enclose the entire macro definition in quote characters. Command-line options include the following possibilities.

| | |
|---|---|
| $-f$ *name* | gives the name of a makefile to use (instead of the default names "makefile" or "Makefile"). |
| $-d$ | causes debugging output to be generated. |
| $-n$ | causes make to list the commands that it would execute to build the target(s), without actually executing the commands. |
| $-t$ | causes make to touch files so that the named targets appear to be up-to-date. |
| $-i$ | causes make to ignore all return codes, as though the .IGNORE target had been used in the makefile. |
| $-s$ | causes make to suppress echoing of all command lines, as though the .SILENT target had been used in the makefile. |

## 13-5   *Further Reading*

The book *C: A Software Engineering Approach* by P. A. Darnell and P. E. Margolis (Springer-Verlag 1990) contains a good explanation of multi-file compilation. It is also the source of the encapsulation technique used for hiding the implementation of the FIFO_Q abstract data type, shown as an example in this chapter. A good initial source of information about make is the on-line manual entry. If your computer is a SUN, the system documentation manual *Programming Utilities and Libraries* (part number 800-3847-10) contains a 50 page tutorial titled "make User's Guide." An appendix describes the enhancements made to the SunOS version of make. Alternatively, there is a book available: *Managing Projects with Make* (2nd Edition) by S. Talbott (O'Reilly 1988). However, it has a System V orientation.

# CHAPTER 14 *PROJECT MANAGEMENT AND VERSION CONTROL*

## 14-1  *A Description of the Problem*

If you develop and then maintain a software product, the source code will normally progress through a series of versions. Each version will differ from its preceding version because of corrections to erroneous or incomplete code, tuning of the code to make it more efficient, addition of new functionality, changes required to keep in step with evolving operating system environments, and so on. If the software is in use by a large community of users and if it performs reasonably sophisticated functions, evolutionary change is to be expected.

A systematic software developer will keep a history of all the changes made to the software. One benefit is that the history will enable him or her to recover from errors more easily. For example, if a user of the software reports that a feature that used to work in version 2.7 no longer works in version 3.2, the developer may want to successively re-create all the versions between 2.7 and 3.2 to discover where the bug was first introduced. Then a particular set of changes may be examined in detail to find the exact cause of the error. A managerial benefit is that the quality of software and the amount of effort spent on maintenance may be estimated from the volume of changes. If changes are documented with explanations of how and why the code was changed, the documented version history may be used to help newly hired programmers understand the functionality of software components.

Complications arise if the software must be created in multiple versions for different operating environments. For example, the software used to format the text of this book (FrameMaker) currently has different versions to run on the Macintosh, on the NeXT and on SUN-3 and SUN-4 computers under the SunView, OpenWindows and X-windows environments. Each of these versions may have to undergo an independent series of revisions.

The evolutionary chart of a software product tends to have a tree structure. Consider a hypothetical program which is initially developed to run in a standard UNIX environment. After some bug fixes, a separate DOS version is produced. Subsequently, it is found convenient to release an X-windows variant of the UNIX product. The tree might then look something like the following.

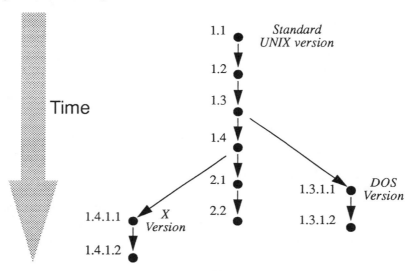

Following conventional practice, the different versions along the main branch of the tree (corresponding to the standard UNIX version) are labelled with two numbers separated by a period. The first component is called the *release number* and the second is called the *level number*. The main branch is sometimes called the *trunk* of the tree.

There is no clear convention for labelling releases that do not lie on the main branch of the tree. The two systems for version management that we will look at shortly, SCCS and RCS, have different rules for numbering branches. The two systems, however, differ only when branches themselves divide into branches. Thus the four digit numbers used in the above example are correct under both systems.

It would be a needless waste of disk storage to maintain full copies of all the different source code versions. Furthermore, unless the software developers maintain a strict discipline, it would be easy to misplace versions of the code or to lose the records that describe how one version has evolved from another. In a large project with several software developers on the payroll, there are additional complications to worry about. Different developers may be simultaneously working on different parts of a source code file. When both developers store their revised files back in the master directory, one set of revisions is likely to be lost.

Version control software is intended to take care of all the concerns listed above. The two programs normally available on UNIX systems are SCCS (Source Code Control System) and RCS (Revision Control System). The facilities they offer are somewhat similar. Both systems reduce the amount of disk storage by saving only one version of a source file in its entirety. One version is obtained from another version by applying simple updates (in the form of an edit script). Since the differences between two successive versions tend to be small compared the size of the file, the approach saves a lot of disk space at the expense of the CPU time required to apply the updates.

There is nothing magic about how SCCS and RCS determine the differences between versions. There is a standard UNIX program, `diff`, which compares two files and reports differences. One of the options to `diff` causes it to output the differences as an edit script (suitable for input to the `ed` editor) which, if applied to the first file, would convert it into the second file. Both SCCS and RCS use `diff`.

The version control programs *own* all the source code files. The files are saved under different names and with write permission disabled. If you want to modify one of the files, you have to ask the version control program to *check out* the file. The program will then make a copy of the file for you to access. When you have finished updating it, you have to *check in* the file again. When checking in the file, you are required to provide a description of the changes you made. (No system can force you to provide a sensible description, but the fact that you are forced to say something is an important part of maintaining good discipline.) Two people are not permitted to have the same files checked out simultaneously. The version control system will deny the check out request of the second person and report who currently has the file(s) checked out. However, if you just wish to browse through a file, you are allowed to check out a read-only copy but you would not normally be allowed to check that file back in again later.

Given a file named, say, "F" that is under version control, both SCCS and RCS save one complete version of "F" plus all the differences between versions and the change history concatenated (with suitable separators) in a single new file. SCCS saves this composite file under the name "s.F" while RCS saves it under the name "F,v".

SCCS and RCS differ in how they store the differences between versions of a file. To adopt the normal terminology of this subject, the difference between two successive versions of a file is known as a *delta*. SCCS uses *forward deltas*, whereas RCS mostly uses *reverse deltas*. To go back to our example, above, of a program that comes in three versions, SCCS would store only release 1.1 in its entirety. It stores the difference between 1.1 and 1.2 as a delta, between 1.2 and 1.3 as a delta, and so on. If you wish to obtain a copy of a file from the latest release of the standard UNIX version of the software, SCCS would conceptually apply five successive deltas (running the editor five times) to obtain the desired file. In contrast, RCS stores the latest release of the software along the main trunk in its entirety (i.e., release 2.2 in the tree diagram). The differences between 2.2 and 2.1, between 2.1 and 1.4, between 1.4 and 1.3, ... are stored as reverse deltas. Thus, if you want to obtain any release along the main trunk, a sequence of reverse deltas must be applied. However, if you want, say, the latest release of the DOS version of the software, RCS would (conceptually) use reverse deltas to go up the tree to the common ancestor, release 1.3, and then use forward deltas to go down the DOS branch of the version tree.

The word *conceptually* is used in the preceding descriptions because both SCCS and RCS use an optimization technique to reduce the number of times that an edit script must be applied. The only safe statement that can be made about the relative efficiency of checking out a particular version is that RCS provides faster access to the latest release of the main version of the software, while SCCS provides faster access to the original version of the file, version 1.1. Common sense would suggest that RCS has optimized the more frequent case. But, unless your files are unusually large, you are unlikely to observe any noticeable delay in extracting a particular version of a file.

## 14-2   The Source Code Control System, SCCS

The Source Code Control System, SCCS, is delivered with the SunOS implementation of UNIX and is used by SUN to maintain their own software. Thus, if your computer is a SUN machine, you will find that there is more support for SCCS (for example, by the `make` tool) than for RCS.

### Starting a Project Under SCCS

Suppose that you have a directory containing several source files. These files may contain source code, lex input, yacc input, documentation – anything you wish. The first step you should take is to identify each file with a comment or string that will be used to record the current SCCS version number for the file. If the file is a *.h* file, you may add a C comment similar to the following at the top of the file:

```
/* %W% %G% */
```

If the file is a *.c* file, you would normally choose to add this declaration at the top:

```
static char sccsid[] = "%W%\t%G%";
```

If the file is documentation in `troff` or `nroff` form, you would add a comment line like:

```
\" %W% %G%
```

and if the file is a shell script or a makefile, the comment line would read as follows.

```
# %W% %G%
```

When a copy of the file is later checked out, SCCS will expand the combination %W% to a string that contains the name of the file and the number of the version that was checked out. SCCS similarly expands %G% to the date that that version was previously checked in. For example, the identification line in a checked out .c file might expand to:

```
static char sccsid[] = "@(#) foo.2  3.4  05/26/91";
```

Note that the form recommended for a .c file causes the identification string to be embedded in the .o file after compilation. (The what command will subsequently be able to find that string by searching for the @(#) prefix and tell you the version number of the .c file that the .o file was created from.)

When you have added identification lines to all the files, you must create a project directory named "SCCS" where SCCS is to keep the files. The most convenient location is as a subdirectory of the directory where you intend to edit the project files and construct versions of the program. (If you wish to use a different place, the PROJECTDIR environment variable should be set to the full pathname of the directory that contains the SCCS subdirectory.) Assuming you choose the easy option, all you need do is execute

```
% mkdir SCCS
```

and you are ready to proceed with transferring all your files over to the control of SCCS. For each file "bigprog.c", say, that you wish to hand over, you should execute the command

```
% sccs enter bigprog.c
```

SCCS will assign the version number 1.1 to the file, move it to the project directory but under a modified name and set the access mode to be read-only.

The sccs command is a front-end that executes the subcommand listed as its first argument. If you wish, you may set your path environment variable to include a reference to the directory where all the SCCS subcommands reside and then use the subcommands directly.

## Checking a File Out

If you wish to inspect a file without making any changes to it, you simply use the get subcommand. For example, a session with the computer might proceed as follows.

```
% ls
Makefile  SCCS
% sccs get bigprog.c
1.1
1037 lines
% ls
Makefile  SCCS  bigprog.c
%
```

The `get` subcommand causes SCCS to place a read-only copy of the latest version of the named file in your working directory. You may do anything you like with the file (it is only a copy) but, because the file was not checked out for update, you are not allowed to change the mode to permit updates, modify it and check it back in. (At least, not without jumping through hoops.) The various identification codes, `%W%` etc., are expanded in the copy of the file retrieved by `get`.

If you wish to edit a file, you must check it out with the `edit` subcommand. For example,

```
% sccs edit bigprog.c
1.1
new delta 1.2
1037 lines
%
```

retrieves a writable copy of the latest version of the file. The information listed by SCCS informs you of the version that was retrieved and the new version number that it will have if and when you check it in again. In the retrieved copy of the file, occurrences of `%W%` and other identification codes are not expanded.

If you wish to check out a version of a file other than the latest, you may specify either a version number or a date. For example,

```
% sccs get -r2.3 foo.i
```

obtains version 2.3 of the named file, while

```
% sccs get -c910527 foo.i
```

obtains whatever version was current at 0:00 on May 27, 1991. By adding more digits to the date string, you can specify the time instant down to the second! The `-r` and `-c` options are equally applicable to the `edit` subcommand.

If you wish to retrieve working copies of all the files that are under SCCS control, the command

```
% sccs get SCCS
```

(where "SCCS" is, of course, used here as the name of the project directory). The same method works for checking out all the files with the `edit` subcommand.

If you are about to make some major functional changes to the program, you would normally choose to increment the release number. To do this, you should use the edit subcommand with the -r option specifying the new release number. Thus,

```
% sccs edit -r2 bigprog.c
```

would give you version 2.1 of the file when it is checked back in. Similarly,

```
% sccs edit -r2 SCCS
```

would cause all the files to be numbered 2.1 when they are checked in again.

## Checking a File In

If you previously checked a file out for update and you have finished editing the file copy that was retrieved, you may check it back in again with the delta subcommand. When you check it in, SCCS prompts you for a one-line description of the changes that were made to the file. You can actually continue your description over as many lines as you wish, as long as you escape each embedded newline character with a back slash. For example, the dialogue with SCCS might proceed as follows.

```
% sccs delta bigprog.c
comments? Global variable read was renamed to \
read_input to avoid a clash with a library \
function of the same name.
1.2
27 inserted
27 deleted
1010 unchanged
%
```

After integrating the changes and the description with the corresponding history file in the SCCS subdirectory, SCCS removes the working copy of the file.

As the SCCS documentation recommends, you should not casually check a modified file back in – it would be a good idea to check that the program works as intended after the changes have been applied. Otherwise, other members of the project who retrieve the latest version of a file may be exposed to buggy code. Therefore, before checking the file back in, you should build the program (presumably using make, see below), test it, and debug as necessary. Only after everything seems to work correctly should you check the modified files in again.

If you need to have a working copy of the file immediately after checking a version in, there are two useful subcommands. The first, delget, is equivalent to performing the delta subcommand immediately followed by the get subcommand. The second, deledit, is equivalent to the combination delta, edit.

## Working with Several Files

A large program or system is normally constructed from many source files. SCCS allows you to update individual files and, therefore, you would naturally expect to reach a situation where one file has version number 2.3 while another file is numbered 2.17, and so on. If the version numbers are not uniform across all the files, it becomes tedious to re-construct a previous release of the program. You will either have to keep track of which versions of the files were used in the program or else you will have to use dates. That is, you can retrieve all the versions that were extant on a particular date and make the program from those.

RCS handles the problem better than SCCS because it permits a symbolic name to be associated with a particular version of a file. Thus RCS would allow you to retrieve all the file versions that comprise the 'UNIX-2.5alpha' release, say, of your program. In the absence of this feature, the easiest approach with SCCS would be to keep all the version numbers in lock step. Whenever one file is updated, all files have their version numbers incremented.

## Creating a New Branch

If you refer back to the tree diagram on page 300, you will see that the tree forked after version 1.3. Perhaps while one group of developers were working on release 1.4 of the main UNIX product, others were working on DOS release 1.3.1.1. (Alternatively, version 1.3.1.1 might have been created much later but the developers decided that 1.3 was a better starting point than a later release on the trunk of the tree.)

Branches in the tree should not be created without a great deal of forethought. Therefore, the default operation mode of SCCS disallows branches. If you decide that a branch in the version tree is needed, the first step is to use the appropriate administrative command and enable branch creation. You may choose to allow only a particular file to have branches if you execute the command as

```
% sccs admin -fb bigprog.c
```

or you may permit branches for all the files with

```
% sccs admin -fb SCCS
```

Then, to create the branch of the "bigprog.c" file corresponding to version 1.3.1.1 in the diagram, you specify the -b option when checking the file out for update, as follows.

```
% sccs edit -r1.3 -b bigprog.c
```

If you are following the advice given above and all your version numbers are being kept in lock step, you would check out all the files with

```
% sccs edit -r1.3 -b SCCS
```

When the edited files are checked back in, they will be assigned a version number of 1.3.1.1. If you later wish to browse files belonging to that release, you must explicitly request retrieval of the files on that branch of the tree by giving the release number. For example,

```
% sccs get -r1.3.1.1 bigprog.c
```

will obtain the named version, or

```
% sccs get -r1.3.1 bigprog.c
```

will obtain the latest version along that branch of the tree.

If version 1.3.1.1 is checked out for update and checked in again, the new version number will be 1.3.1.2. All versions along the new branch of the tree will have numbers that begin with 1.3. If some version along the branch is later selected as the base of yet a new branch, all the versions on that new branch would be numbered 1.3.2.1, 1.3.2.2 and so on.

## SCCS Administration and Utility Commands

At first sight, the SCCS approach to source code management is very simple. But, after some experience with the system, you are likely to encounter complications. A user will at some time or other have an accident and corrupt or delete a checked out file. What do you do? SCCS will not let you check out the file again, it reports that the file is already checked out. What do you do if you start a new version of a file and then change your mind and decide not to? What if you notice that your description of a change was wrong? How do you find out who has files checked out? And so on. After SCCS has been extended to provide the means to answer all the questions and to solve all the little problems, it is no longer such a simple system but it does become a useful aid to programming productivity. We will briefly review a selection of the extra SCCS features.

### Controlling Access in a Group Project

In a group project, the source files must be located in a directory accessible to all the project members. The directory would presumably belong to one of the project members who is responsible for administration of the files. By default, only the owner of the directory is allowed to check out files for update. Other users have this privilege only if permitted by the administrator and by appropriate UNIX access permissions on the project directory. For example,

```
% sccs admin -ajackz SCCS
```

will add the user *jackz* to the list of users permitted to make deltas to all files under SCCS control in the "SCCS" directory. Conversely,

```
% sccs admin -ejackz SCCS
```

would revoke that privilege again. The UNIX file permissions would normally be handled by creating a group to which the project members belong. (Groups and their members are listed in the file "/etc/group", a file that is maintained by the UNIX system administrator.) The directory would have group ownership by the project, and its access permissions would be set to permit read, write and execute access by group members.

Regardless of the access control performed by SCCS, other users are permitted to retrieve read-only working copies of files, subject only to the normal UNIX file access permissions.

## Seeing Who Has Checked-Out Files

On a multi-person project, it is important to see who is working on which file. The command

```
% sccs info
```

will give you that information.

## Reporting Differences

If you have checked out a file and started editing it, you may see a listing of the changes that have been made so far by executing the `diffs` subcommand. For example,

```
% sccs diffs bigprog.c
```

The differences between any two checked-in versions of a file may be seen with a command like the following.

```
% sccs sccsdiff -r1.2 -r2.3 bigprog.c
```

## Seeing the Version History of a File

If you execute the command

```
% sccs print bigprog.c
```

where "bigprog.c" is one of the files under SCCS control, you will be given a list of all the versions of the file that exist, accompanied by the descriptive comments. The output concludes with a listing of the latest version of the file where each line is annotated with the number of the version where that line was first introduced.

## Replacing a Checked-Out File

If you accidentally remove or damage the contents of a checked-out file beyond repair, you can obtain a fresh copy of the checked out file by using the `-k` option on the get subcommand. Suppose, say, that you have corrupted the "myprog.c" file. Executing the two commands

```
% sccs get -k myprog.c -Gtemp
% mv temp myprog.c
```

will first obtain a fresh writable copy under the name "temp", and then replace the corrupted file with the new copy.

## Correcting Changes

If you check in a file but then find that there were errors, there is (provided that no-one else has already checked that file out again) a way to get that file back again to complete the job properly. If you execute a command like

```
% sccs fix -r2.3 bigprog.c
```

you will obtain the specified release of the file again. This is only permitted if the requested release is at a leaf position in the version tree and if no-one has the file checked out. When you check the file in again, it will replace the version that was previously checked in. (I.e., a new version number is not created.)

## Deleting a Version

If you have checked in a new version of a file and then change your mind about wanting that new version, the command

```
% sccs rmdel -r2.3 bigprog.c
```

will destroy all trace of that version. Again, the version must be a leaf of the version tree and no-one can have the file checked out.

## Excluding Deltas

If the new version of a file, say version 2.4, should turn out to be easier to create from version 2.2 than from version 2.3, you would like to exclude the 2.3 differences from the file you check out. The −x option (for *exclude*) on the edit subcommand provides this possibility. For example,

```
% sccs edit -x2.3 bigprog.c
```

will retrieve the latest version of "bigprog.c" but excluding the changes introduced in version 2.3. The concept generalizes so that you may exclude changes introduced in more than one version. For example,

```
% sccs edit -x1.2,2.3 bigprog.c
```

obtains a working copy that excludes the changes of versions 1.2 and 2.3.

It is possible that excluding a particular delta will conflict with other changes introduced in a later version. If there is such a conflict, SCCS will indicate the line numbers where conflicts exist and it is up to the user to verify and, if necessary, correct these lines.

## Combining Deltas

If you have ignored the advice not to check in new versions lightly, you are likely to have obtained a very tall version tree where the differences between successive versions tend to be small. If you would like to reduce the number of versions, it is possible to combine deltas. For example, if you wish to coalesce as many deltas as possible for file "bigprog.c", execute the two commands:

```
% sccs comb bigprog.c > combscript
% sh -v combscript
```

The first command creates a Bourne (sh) shell script. When it is executed in the second command, it applies changes to reduce the number of versions of "bigprog.c" to the minimum possible while retaining the shape of the version tree. (The −v option to sh causes each command in the script file to be echoed before it is executed; the option is useful only if you are curious as to what the script is doing.) Another reason to combine versions is that it tends to reduce the amount of disk space occupied by the SCCS history file (but, as the on-line manual page points out, a reduction is not guaranteed). **NOTE**: once you have executed the shell script, destroy it! If you should execute the script a second time, you are likely to cause irreparable damage to the SCCS history file.

More selective control over which deltas should be combined is obtained by use of either the –p or the –c option. For example,

```
% sccs comb -p2.3 bigprog.c > combscript
```

creates a script to merge all versions up to and including version 2.3 into a single version that will be numbered 1.1. All later versions will still exist as separate versions, and will be numbered 1.2, 1.3, etc.

Alternatively,

```
% sccs comb -c1.2,2.3 bigprog.c > combscript
```

specifies that SCCS should attempt to collapse the version tree so that there are only two versions left – those being the versions currently numbered 1.2 and 2.3. After the script has been executed, the two remaining versions will be numbered 1.1 and 1.2.

The advice of the SCCS documentation is to make sure that back-up copies of the SCCS files exist before running the shell script to merge versions. You may discover that the script may not result in a desirable version tree, and the back-up copies also provide a safeguard against something going wrong with the script.

## Using *make* with SCCS

The make program distributed with the SunOS version of UNIX has been extended to provide automatic support for SCCS. The following discussion will assume that you have this version of make. If not, the description of how to use make with RCS on page 320 can easily be adapted to apply to SCCS instead.

The make extension uses an additional special target, .SCCS_GET. The start-up file read by make contains a default rule for .SCCS_GET that reads as follows.

```
SCCSFLAGS=
SCCSGETFLAGS=-s
.SCCS_GET:
            ?sccs $(SCCSFLAGS) get $(SCCSGETFLAGS) $@ -G$@
```

The extended make program checks for source files in the "SCCS" subdirectory. If it finds a source file with the 's.' prefix on its name and if the file is newer than the target(s) created from it, make executes the .SCCS_GET rule to obtain a copy of the source file. For example, if the requested target requires "s.bigprog.o" and "s.bigprog.c" in the "SCCS" subdirectory is newer than "bigprog.o" in the current directory, make will execute the command

```
sccs get -s bigprog.c -Gbigprog.c
```

to retrieve the latest version of the file and then it will proceed as normal. (The −s flag on the get subcommand causes SCCS to suppress its information messages about which version is being retrieved and how large it is).

The overall effect is that the makefile requires no special additions to be able to build the latest version on the main trunk of the version tree. For example, the following is a perfectly correct, if trivial, makefile set up as illustrated by a dialogue with the computer.

```
% ls −F
Makefile            SCCS/
% ls SCCS
s.foo.h             s.foo.c             s.main.c
% cat Makefile
# Makefile for the foo program

foo:    foo.o main.o
        $(CC) $(CFLAGS) −o foo foo.o main.o

foo.o: foo.h

%
```

If the command make is entered, the dialogue might continue as follows.

```
% make foo
sccs get −s foo.h −Gfoo.h
sccs get −s foo.c −Gfoo.c
cc −c foo.c
sccs get −s main.c −Gmain.c
cc −c main.c
cc −o foo foo.o main.o
% ls −F
Makefile    SCCS/       foo*        foo.c       foo.h
foo.c       foo.o       main.c      main.o
%
```

Note that after make has successfully finished, duplicate copies of all the source files are held in the working directory. They may be removed with the command:

```
% sccs clean
```

SCCS will only remove files that can be re-extracted from the history files. It is much safer to use than the obvious command:

```
% rm *.c *.h
```

If you wish to build a version of the program that is not the latest release, you have to be slightly careful as make does not understand SCCS version numbers. It cannot tell if the "foo.o" file in the current directory is constructed from version 2.5 of "foo.c" when you would like to use version 1.3. Provided that you have been keeping the version numbers of all your files in lock step, the procedure for building an older version of the program, version 1.3 say, would be as follows.

```
% sccs clean
% rm -f *.o
% make SCCSGETFLAGS=-r1.3 foo
```

If you need to be working on two versions of a program at the same time, a better approach is to use different directories for building the program in. Doing so eliminates the possibility of combining inconsistent object files.

## 14-3   The Revision Control System, RCS

The Revision Control System, RCS, is public-domain software, distributed by the Free Software Foundation (the same organization that distributes the Gnu C compiler). It may be obtained by `ftp` from any of a large number of sites. While RCS gives the appearance of being functionally equivalent to SCCS, it is superior in some respects. For example, if a single user wishes to maintain source files with RCS, the strict locking controls that prevent two users from updating a file simultaneously need not be used. The `rcsfreeze` program also allows a set of files with different version numbers to be given a symbol release name. Thus, users do not have to keep version number of all the files in lock step. Finally, the expected time needed to retrieve a file version tends to be slightly less with RCS.

### Starting a Project Under RCS

As with the SCCS explanation, we will start by assuming that you have a directory containing several source files. And, as with SCCS, the first step you should take is to identify each file with a comment or string that will be used to record the current RCS version number of the file. The standard identification marker is $Id$, and this four character combination should be placed in a *.h* file as a C comment:

```
/* $Id$ */
```

In a *.c* file, you would place this declaration at the top:

```
static char rcsid[] = "$Id$";
```

In a `troff` or `nroff` file, you would place a comment line at the top like:

```
\" $Id$
```

Finally, for a shell script or a makefile, the comment line would read as follows.

```
# $Id$
```

When a copy of the file is later checked out, RCS will expand the combination $Id$ to a string that contains the name of the file, the number of the version that was checked out, the author's name and the state of the file. The state of a file is a symbolic string that may be chosen by the user to indicate a status. The default status name chosen by RCS is Exp (short for *Experimental*). Other status names recommended in the RCS documentation are Stab (for *Stable*) and Rel (for *released*). As with the equivalent SCCS construct, the C declaration form recommended for a *.c* file causes the identification string to be embedded in the *.o* file after compilation. The ident command may subsequently be used to identify the version number of the source file used to create a *.o* file.

Assuming the files all contain the appropriate identification strings, you next need to create a directory named "RCS" that RCS will use to hold the project files. The directory should be a subdirectory of the working directory where you will build versions of the program. If that is not convenient for you, you may instead create a symbolic link named "RCS" that references the actual directory where the project files are located. Having "RCS" either as a subdirectory or appear to be a subdirectory simplifies the RCS commands that you type because, unlike SCCS, RCS does not support an environment variable that can be set to the pathname of the RCS directory. After creating the subdirectory, you have to execute the RCS check-in command, ci, for every file that you wish to put under RCS control. RCS will prompt you for a description of each file, and then save it as version 1.1. A dialogue with the computer might proceed as follows.

```
% mkdir RCS
% ci zapper.c
RCS/zapper.c,v  <--  zapper.c
initial revision: 1.1
enter description, terminated with single '.' or
    end of file:
NOTE: This is NOT the log message!
>> Module to zap the execution priority of running
>> processes that consume too much CPU time.
>> .
done
%
... and so on, for checking in the other files
```

The initial line output by the ci command indicates that the "zapper.c" file is to be moved to the "RCS" directory under a modified name. The description of the file's purpose is entered at successive '>>' prompts.

## Checking a File Out

A file is retrieved for browsing with the co (check out) command. For example,

```
% co zapper.c
```

obtains the latest version of the file (on the trunk of the revision tree). If you wish to retrieve the file for updating, the −l option should be specified, as in

```
% co -l zapper.c
```

The −l option causes the file to be locked, so that other users cannot also obtain copies of this file for updating.

If you wish to obtain a copy of an earlier version of the file, the −r option may be used to specify the version number, exactly as with SCCS. If you wish to obtain the version of a file that was current on a particular date, the −d option is used to provide a date. The date is acceptable in almost any imaginable format. Here are a few examples.

```
% co -r2.1 bigprog.c
% co "-d May 27, 1991 19:08 PST" zapper.c
% co '-d 27-May-1991' zapper.c
```

Note that quotes must be used around an argument if it contains spaces (otherwise the command shell will decompose it into several arguments). The time zone defaults to UTC (Coordinated Universal Time, formerly known as Greenwich Mean Time) unless a time zone is specified.

## Checking a File In

The command for checking a file in after a revision is ci (check in), the same command as was used for initial registration of the file with RCS. An example use is as follows.

```
% ci zapper.c
RCS/zapper.c,v <-- zapper.c
new revision: 1.5, previous revision: 1.4
enter log message
(terminate with single '.' or end of file)
>> Changed program so that it will not
>> attempt to zap processes owned by root.
>> .
done
%
```

As the first line of output indicates, the checked-in file is moved to the "RCS" directory and renamed (by appending ',v' to its old name). The log message that you are asked to enter is supposed to describe the changes that have been made to the file.

If you supply a version number on the ci command, you can increment the release number component. The only requirement on the supplied version number is that it must be higher than any version number on the branch to which it belongs, or else it must start a new branch (see below). For example, to check in the file as version 2.1, the command is as follows.

```
% ci -r2.1 zapper.c
```

## Creating a New Branch

It could hardly be simpler to create a new branch in the version tree. One simply checks in the file using the desired multidigit version number. Consider, once again, the version tree shown on page 300. If we are just about to create the DOS branch of the tree, we would first check out version 1.3 of the file(s) and modify them as required for the DOS version. When checking the new file(s) back in again, we would simply use a command similar to the following.

```
% ci -r1.3.1 main.c
```

The command creates a new branch and checks the file in as version 1.3.1.1. Subsequent revisions of this same file, checked in with the same $-r1.3.1$ option, will be numbered 1.3.1.2, 1.3.1.3, and so on.

Unless you intend to create a complicated version tree, you do not need to read any further. However, if you wish to create branches of branches, you have to understand the numbering scheme for versions (it is different to the scheme used by SCCS). Any node of the version tree may be used as the basis for more branches. One branch leading from that node will be a main branch, where the last digit of the version number is successively incremented. If the basis node is numbered N, then the first non-main branch to be created will lead to a node numbered N.1.1, the second non-main branch will be numbered N.2.1, the third one will be N.3.1, and so on. These rules imply that a version number can have an unlimited number of components – for example, we could have 1.3.1.2.2.3.1.4 as a valid version number. A sample version tree numbered according to the RCS scheme is drawn below.

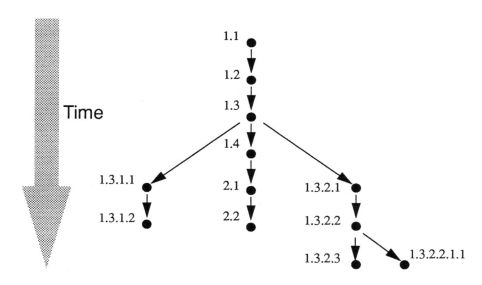

## RCS Administration and Utility Commands

RCS provides similar capabilities to those available with SCCS. Only a selection of all the possible operations on RCS files are described below. For more complete information, the RCS documentation should be consulted.

### Controlling Access in a Group Project

Similarly to SCCS, the file access mode bits on the "RCS" directory should be set so that those project members who will be making updates to files have read, write and execute permission. The UNIX system administrator should establish a group for your project members in the "/etc/group" file, and the group ownership of the directory should be changed to the project group. The owner of the "RCS" directory should be the only person to act as the RCS administrator.

In addition to the normal restrictions imposed by the UNIX file access mechanism, RCS allows the administrator to select which project members may check out files for update. To permit the three users *joan*, *jack* and *jean* to update a particular file, the administrator may execute a command similar to

```
% rcs -ajoan,jack,jean zapper.c
```

or if permission to update all the files under RCS control is to be given, the command would be as follows.

```
% rcs -ajoan,jack,jean RCS/*,v
```

The right may be revoked with the −e option, as in this example command.

```
% rcs -ejack,bill RCS/*,v
```

### Seeing Who Has Checked-Out Files for Update

The `rlog` command provides various information about RCS files. To see who is updating a particular file, "bigprog.c", you would execute

```
% rlog -l -R bigprog.c
```

and to see a list of all the files checked out by user *bill*, you would execute

```
% rlog -lbill -L -R RCS/*,v
```

### Reporting Differences

To see what changes you have made to a file that you have checked out, you may execute a command like the following.

```
% rcsdiff zapper.c
```

If the file you checked out was not the latest release, you have to give the version number on the command. For example, if you were editing version 1.3, you would execute

```
% rcsdiff -r1.3 zapper.c
```

Finally, you may see the differences between any two versions of a file. For example,

```
% rcsdiff -r1.3 -r1.4 zapper.c
```

shows the changes introduced in version 1.4 of the file.

### Seeing the Version History of a File

The default behavior of the `rlog` command (mentioned above) is to give a full history of a file. The various modifiers on this command generally cause parts of the output to be omitted. So, to obtain complete information about the version history of a file, just use the command with no options, as in the following.

```
% rlog zapper.c
```

### Changing the Status of a File

RCS associates a status with each file. The default status for a checked-in file is `Exp` (for *Experimental*). Other recommended statuses are `Stab` (for *Stable*) and `Rel` (for *Released*). You may change the status of a version of a file from `Exp` to whatever you like by supplying the `-s` option on the `rcs` command. For example, to change the status of version 1.3 of "zapper.c" to Stable, one would execute the command:

```
% rcs -sStab:1.3 zapper.c
```

### Strict versus Non-Strict Locking

If you are the only person working on a project, you should not really need to have RCS enforce file locking. It is, presumably, unlikely that you would check out a file twice to work on two incompatible updates at the same time. If you execute the command

```
% rcs -U zapper.c
```

RCS will subsequently not require you to use the `-l` option when you check out the file for updates. Similarly, non-strict locking for all files may be achieved with this command,

```
% rcs -U RCS/*,v
```

You may enable strict locking again by using `-L` instead of `-U` on the `rcs` command.

### Replacing a Checked-Out File

If you check out a file for update, you may possibly change your mind about performing those updates. In that case, you would like to release the lock without checking the file back in again. The command to accomplish such unlocking for file "zapper.c" is

```
% rcs -u zapper.c
```

If you had checked out a version other than the latest on the trunk of the version tree, you need to supply the number of the version being unlocked, as in the command

```
% rcs -u1.3 zapper.c
```

Normally, only the person who checked out the locked file should unlock it. If any other project member performs the action, a mail message is sent automatically to the original locker of the file.

The unlocking capability also provides the capability of throwing away changes and starting to make them afresh, or of replacing a damaged or destroyed working copy. Since, after unlocking the file, all you need do is remove your working copy and then check it out for update again.

## Combining and Deleting Deltas

If your version tree is overly tall and skinny because of too many new versions with minor updates having been checked in, you can simply delete nodes from the tree. For example, the command

```
% rcs -o1.3 zapper.c
```

deletes version 1.3 from the tree, leaving all preceding and all succeeding versions intact. (The letter *o* for the option is supposed to suggest the word *outdate*.) The effect, therefore, is equivalent to having merged the updates of version 1.3 with those of version 1.4 (assuming that that is the number of the next revision in the tree). When you print out the revision history of the file, you will see that version 1.3 is missing – all of the other versions will still be there with the same numbers. Note that you are not permitted to delete a version that is currently checked out or delete a node that is the basis for branch versions.

Other effects of combining or removing deltas can be obtained with the `rcsmerge` command. This command determines the changes required to convert one version of a file into a second version, and then applies those same changes to the working copy of the file. The result will, by default, replace the working copy of the file but you may choose to have the result diverted elsewhere if you wish. We will look at one example of its use.

Suppose that the latest release of a file "fuzzy.c" is numbered 1.7 and further suppose that you now consider the changes introduced in version 1.4 to be a mistake and ought to be undone. What you can do is check out that latest release and then edit it with the changes needed to convert version 1.4 into version 1.3 (thus undoing the 1.4 changes). The commands and responses might proceed as shown in Figure 14-1.

## Using Symbolic Version Names with RCS

A program is normally composed from several source files. The program itself will progress through a series of revisions, corresponding to changes in the component source files. However, it would be an unnatural constraint to require that version 2.3 of the program be composed from version 2.3 of all the component files. (However, this is what you would have to do in SCCS to simplify construction of older versions of a program.) If development of a particular module has been troublesome, you would naturally expect the files for that module to have been through more revisions than some other files.

RCS provides an elegant solution. You may choose symbolic names for releases of the program or system, and associate those names with particular versions of the compo-

---

### Figure 14-1    Undoing an RCS Delta

```
% co -l fuzzy.c
RCS/fuzzy.c,v  -->  fuzzy.c
revision 1.7 (locked)
done
% rcsmerge -r1.4 -r1.3 fuzzy.c
RCS file: RCS/fuzzy.c,v
retrieving revision 1.4
retrieving revision 1.3
Merging differences between 1.4 and 1.3 into fuzzy.c
merge: overlaps or other problems during merge
% vi fuzzy.c
... edit the file to fix up conflicting
... changes, as indicated in the file itself
% ci fuzzy.c
RCS/fuzzy.c,v  <--  fuzzy.c
new revision: 1.8; previous revision: 1.7
enter log message:
(terminate with single '.' or end of file)
>> undid the 1.4 changes that misguidedly replaced
>> a hash table structure with a binary search tree.
>> .
done
%
```

---

nent files. The association may be established when the file is checked in or, later, by use of the `rcs` command. For example,

```
% ci -nV2.3alpha zapper.c
```

checks the "zapper.c" file in as a new version on the main branch of the tree and associates the name *V2.3alpha* with that version. If that symbolic name has been previously associated with an older version of the file and you wish to move the name to the newest version, you would check the file in using this version of the command,

```
% ci -NV2.3alpha zapper.c
```

If you wish to attach a symbolic label later on, you may use the `rcs` command to make the association between the name and an arbitrary version. For example,

```
% rcs -r1.4 -nV2.3alpha zapper.c
```

makes the association between version 1.4 and the supplied name. If you later wish to transfer that symbolic name to a different version, you may execute a command similar to:

```
% rcs -r2.1 -NV2.3alpha zapper.c
```

Finally, a shell script is available as a command for associating a symbolic name with the latest versions of the entire collection of files under RCS control. If you have just checked in the revised files that form a compatible configuration of the program, you may execute a command similar to

```
% rcsfreeze V2.4beta
```

and that name will be attached to the latest version of every file. You should be sure to run `rcsclean` first, however, because `rcsfreeze` will not complain if you have not checked all the files undergoing revision back in.

## Using *make* with RCS

The Gnu version of `make` (distributed by the Free Software Foundation and, like RCS, available by `ftp`) has been extended to provide automatic check-out of RCS files as required. We will assume, however, that you do not have this version of `make` installed on your system. If you use a standard (but fairly recent) version of `make`, it has a special .DEFAULT target that may be defined in a way that achieves automatic check-out. If a file that `make` needs (for the purposes of checking whether a target is up-to-date or for building a target) is missing, the rule associated with the target .DEFAULT is executed. An example makefile, equivalent to the SCCS example given earlier, is shown in Figure 14-2.

There is one complication that should be noted. If the target "foo.o" is defined as depending only on "foo.h", with no associated command for building "foo.o", the makefile will not work properly. A makefile that does not have a .DEFAULT rule would work because the default rule labelled by ".c.o" will be applied – and that default rule implies the dependency on "foo.c" and provides the required C compilation command. But consider the case when the .DEFAULT target is defined and when neither "foo.c" nor "foo.h" is present in the working directory. In this situation, `make` will first see the dependency of "foo.o" on "foo.h". Next, it will discover that "foo.h" is not present and will look for a rule that builds it. Not finding it, it applies the .DEFAULT rule with the built-in macro $< defined as "foo.h". After executing that rule, make considers that it has finished. The absence of a "foo.c" file implies that the default ".c.o" rule never gets triggered. The solution is to associate an explicit compilation command with every *.o* file target, and to show an explicit dependence on the corresponding *.c* file, exactly as in the sample makefile.

The `clean` target shown for `make` removes all the checked-out (but unlocked) source files under RCS control by invoking the `rcsclean` command, as well as removing the usual *.o* files.

If you wish to build a version of the program that uses older versions of the source files, it is easy if you have associated symbolic names with the file versions that need to be combined. (Symbolic version naming is a facility that makes RCS superior to SCCS.) All you need do is remove all current working copies of RCS files and then invoke `make` with

---

**Figure 14-2   A Makefile for use with RCS**

```
# Makefile for the foo program

## Set CFLAGS to -O for the production version and
## to -g for debugging versions
CFLAGS = -g

CC = gcc

.DEFAULT:
        co $(RCSFLAGS) $<

foo:    foo.o main.o
        $(CC) $(CFLAGS) -o foo foo.o main.o

clean:
        rcsclean
        rm -f a.out core *.o

foo.o: foo.h foo.c
        $(CC) $(CFLAGS) -c foo.c

main.o: main.c
        $(CC) $(CFLAGS) -c main.c
```

---

the appropriate setting for the RCSFLAGS parameter. For example, to make a version with the symbolic name *V2.4alpha*, you would execute:

```
% make clean
% make RCSFLAGS=-sV2.4alpha
```

## 14-4   *Further Reading*

A good tutorial introduction to SCCS is provided by chapter 4 in the SUN system documentation manual *Programming Utilities and Libraries* (part number 800-3847-10). The original description of SCCS appeared as *The Source Code Control System* by M. J. Rochkind, IEEE Transactions on Software Engineering, vol. SE-1, no. 4 (Dec. 1975), pages 364-370. If you intend to be a serious user, you should print out copies of the on-line manual pages for all the SCCS commands. You can access them under the names sccs,

`sccs-admin`, `sccs-cdc`, `sccs-comb`, `sccs-delta`, `sccs-get`, `sccs-help`, `sccs-prs`, `sccs-rmdel`, `sccs-sact`, `sccs-sccsdiff`, `sccs-unget`, `sccs-val`, and `sccsfile`.

The philosophy of RCS was explained in *RCS – A System for Version Control* by W. F. Tichy, Software – Practice & Experience, vol. 15, no. 7 (July 1985), pages 637-654. An updated version of this publication is provided in `troff` source form with the source code for RCS. If you wish to print a complete set of the on-line manual pages, the command names to locate are: `rcsintro`, `ci`, `co`, `ident`, `rcs`, `rcsclean`, `rcsdiff`, `rcsfreeze`, `rcsmerge`, `rlog`, and `rcsfile`.

# CHAPTER 15

# *DEBUGGING &*
# *PROFILING C CODE*

## *15-1   Insertion of Debugging Code*

Unless you are unusually careful when constructing programs and you use verification techniques on the code, it is unlikely that your programs execute correctly on the first attempt. Even after the typographical errors and other errors detected at compilation time have been removed, it is (unfortunately) very likely that your programs will contain logic errors. A wise programmer plans ahead for execution errors and includes extra statements that would help locate problems. These extra statements would normally perform tests on the validity of data, check whether assertions hold, or simply output the values of variables at critical points in the program's execution.

You can use the C preprocessor to good advantage. It can expand macros into debugging statements that would otherwise be too repetitive to keep typing into the program. It can also conditionally include debugging statements depending on the state of a preprocessor flag. The `assert` macro defined in the ANSI C header file <assert.h> is particularly useful for checking assertions about the code. Its expansion into executable code is controlled by the `NDEBUG` flag. Additional macros that may be useful are given in Figure 15-1.

The `assert` macro in <assert.h> tests assertions. If, for example, at some point in the program, you believe that the pointer variable `ptr` should have the value `NULL`, you can insert the line

```
assert( ptr==NULL );
```

---

## Figure 15-1   Additional Debugging Macros

```
#ifndef NPDEBUG
extern void *sbrk(int);
extern int end;
static void *_p_t_r;

/* check that ptr is a credible non-NULL pointer */
#define PCHK(ptr)      \
    if((_p_t_r=(ptr))<(void*)&end || _p_t_r>=sbrk(0)){  \
    fprintf(stderr,"Bad pointer: line %d in `%s'\n",    \
        __LINE__, __FILE__ ); abort();      \
    } else (void)0
#else
#define PCHK(ptr)        ((void)0)
#endif

#ifndef NXDEBUG
static int _i_x;

/* check that ix is in the range 0 <= ix < size */
#define XCHK(ix,size)    \
    ( _i_x = (ix), assert(_i_x < size), _i_x )
#else
#define XCHK(ix,size)    (ix)
#endif
```

into the program at this point. If you compile the program without defining the preprocessor macro NDEBUG (which disables assert), the expression provided as the argument to assert will be tested each time control reaches that point in the program. If your belief turns out to be wrong, a message similar to the following will be generated on the standard error stream.

```
Failed assertion `p!=NULL' at line 22 of `buggy.c'.
Abort (core dumped)
```

The second line is a result of a call to the abort function, which deliberately terminates the program in an ungraceful way to generate a *core* file. The file "core" allows you to use a debugger to obtain more information about the state of the program when it was halted. Use of the dbx debugger for this purpose is explained later in the chapter.

The PCHK macro, shown in Figure 15-1, is intended to test whether a pointer variable is not NULL and refers to storage that was dynamically allocated (via malloc or calloc). If you want to check the validity of a pointer cp in the program before you dereference it in a statement, you can modify the statement by preceding it with a use of the PCHK macro, as in the following example

```
PCHK(cp); cp->code = '*';
```

Compiling the program with the NPDEBUG preprocessor flag set disables the checks.

The tests performed by the PCHK macro assume that dynamically allocated storage begins at a data address with the label end (this label is defined by the system loader, the ld program, which is invoked as the last stage of a C compilation). The address of the end of dynamically allocated storage increases as the program executes (as a result of calls to malloc or calloc). The function call sbrk(0) returns the address of the next byte of memory after the area that has been dynamically allocated. Before you use PCHK in your program, you should note that an assignment like

```
cp = &xyz;
```

assigns a perfectly valid pointer value to cp, but this pointer value fails the check implemented by PCHK. The function checks *only* if the pointer value refers to an address in the region of memory managed by malloc and calloc.

If you have already run some C programs, you will probably have discovered that C does *not* check array indexes to see that they are in range. If you want such a check, you have to do it yourself and the XCHK function is designed to make this check easy. If, say, an array buff is declared in the program as

```
char buff[80];
```

then a use of the array, as in

```
buff[i] = '*';
```

can be replaced by

```
buff[ XCHK(i,80) ] = '*';
```

The subscript expression in this use of the array will now be checked to see if it is in range. Checking is disabled by compiling with the NXDEBUG preprocessor flag set.

Some explanation of the rather complicated macro definitions is probably called for. One complication is that macros should not evaluate an argument more than once. Otherwise, the user is liable to be surprised by an argument that has side-effects when evaluated. For example,

```
buff[ XCHK(i++,80) ] = '*';
```

is a usage of the XCHK macro that requires us to be careful. If the first argument of XCHK is used twice in the macro expansion, the effect will be to increment i twice. Both macro definitions solve that problem by making a temporary copy of the argument's value. The XCHK macro has been defined so that its use may be embedded inside the actual array reference. It is not always possible to insert a statement without rewriting some of the surrounding code. It would have been nice to have designed PCHK to be embeddable also, so that a usage like

```
PCHK(cp)->code = '*';
```

would be accepted. Unfortunately , it does not appear possible to write this as an ANSI C macro whose argument has an arbitrary pointer type without evaluating the argument more than once.[1]

A final point that might be puzzling – why is there an "else (void) 0" clause on the **if** statement that implements the PCHK macro? The **else** clause is semantically re-dundant (it has no effect if executed, yielding a value that is simply discarded). But it en-ables the macro to be used in all contexts where a statement is syntactically acceptable. If the else clause is omitted, the following use of PCHK would give surprising results.

```
if (cp != NULL)
    PCHK(cp);
else
    break;
```

(The else would pair with the if keyword used inside the macro, rather than with the out-er if.) And why the cast to the void type in front of the constant 0? The cast is an explicit indication to the compiler that the value will not be used, averting a possible warning from the compiler will not be generated.

As stated earlier, all uses of the debugging macros and functions may be left in the program source code. If you ever think the tests are no longer needed, simply re-compile the program with the PDEBUG and XDEBUG preprocessor flags set. For example,

```
% gcc -DPDEBUG -DXDEBUG -DNDEBUG buggy.c
```

compiles the "buggy.c" file with all checking disabled. This is preferable to deleting the de-bugging statements from the source code file. You never know when you may need them again.

Some source code debugging systems (the *Saber C* debugger is an example) automat-ically check array subscripts and pointers while a program is executed under their control. If you have access to such a product on your computer, you should take full advantage of it for testing and debugging your C code.

Some errors that are particularly difficult to track down are caused by incorrect usage of the storage allocation and de-allocation functions. A typical error is continuing to use a pointer after the object it references has been de-allocated by the free function. An error that may cause the storage allocation functions to fail sometime later is to de-allocate stor-age that was never obtained via malloc or calloc. To help detect these, and similar, er-

---

1. The Gnu C compiler supports a C extension (the typeof operator) that makes such a macro pos-sible.

rors, debugging versions of the storage allocation functions are available on Berkeley UNIX-based systems. They may be used instead of the standard, non-checking, implementations of the functions by including the appropriate binary file in the final compilation step when linking is performed. For example, if our program is composed of two files named "buggy.c" and "main.c", the final step could, on the SunOS system, be modified to:

```
% gcc -o buggy main.o buggy.o /usr/lib/debug/malloc.o
```

The debugging package includes two extra functions. One, debug_level, varies the thoroughness with which integrity checks on the storage allocator's data structures are performed. The maximum degree of checking is obtained by executing the call

```
debug_level(2);
```

The other function, malloc_verify requests an immediate check of these data structures and is useful to check for evidence of corruption of the heap storage area.

## 15-2 The dbx Debugger

When a C program goes wrong at execution time, the sole error message is likely to be something similar to

```
Segmentation fault (core dumped)
```

The first part of the message describes the error from the machine's point of view – a segmentation fault indicates that there was a reference to a memory location somewhere outside the program (usually caused by dereferencing a pointer that contains an erroneous value or by using a wildly wrong array index). The last, parenthesized, part of the message means that the UNIX system has created a file named "core". It contains a memory image of the data area of the program at the moment of error. (The name of the file dates back to the time when the main memory of the computer was built from ferrite cores.) The "core" file can be analyzed with the dbx debugger to see where the program went wrong and, in many cases, why it went wrong. If a post-mortem analysis of the crashed program does not readily reveal the cause of the error, dbx may be used to trace program execution and to give detailed information about the values of variables and which statements are being executed. We will look at the dbx debugger in some detail.

Older releases of Berkeley UNIX systems had a debugger called sdb (symbolic debugger). It has been supplanted by dbx. Another debugger that is still available, and is also available on most System V UNIX systems, is adb (assembler debugger). It can analyze "core" files and trace execution too, but at the machine instruction level. Since dbx can also perform tracing at the instruction level, there is no great need to learn how to use adb.

dbx is a source code, statement-level, debugger. It allows you to discover the values of variables by using their names in the source program, and it allows you to trace the execution of a program one statement at a time. But to obtain the full benefit of dbx it is necessary to compile your C files with the −g flag in effect. It causes the C compiler to include extra symbol table information in the binary files. The information includes the names and locations of all variables in the program, the names of all functions and their arguments, the datatypes of all objects declared in the program, and the path names of the source code files used to compile the program. The −g flag is incompatible with optimization. If you supply both the −g and −O flags to the standard C compiler, cc, the −O flag will be ignored. The Gnu compiler, gcc, accepts both flags but you risk confusing yourself when debugging the program. In particular, optimization may cause some assignments to variables to be suppressed or deferred and it becomes much harder to deduce what is wrong with a program.

If your computer is a SUN workstation, you will have access to a program named dbxtool. It provides a window-oriented interface to the same dbx program as is described below. The main differences are that the source code of the program being debugged may be viewed in a window and that mouse selection may be used instead of equivalent dbx commands. An understanding of dbx concepts is a prerequisite to being able to use dbxtool effectively. The dbx program also has similarities to other debuggers, such as the Gnu debugger, gdb, and the *Saber C* debugger.

By the way, if you find a core file and you have forgotten or do not know which program generated that file, try executing the command

```
% file core
```

You will usually be given the name of the program.

## 15-3  *Analyzing a Core File with dbx*

Suppose that you have just executed a program that halted with a core dump, as follows

```
% myprog datafile > results
Arithmetic exception (core dumped)
```

If you have no idea why the myprog program might have crashed, an almost automatic next step is to type the dbx command, and the dialogue would continue similarly to this.

```
% dbx prog
Reading symbolic information...
Read 394 symbols
program terminated by signal FPE (integer divide by
            zero)
(dbx)
```

The last line, (dbx), is a prompt from dbx for you to enter a subcommand. The dbx command that you will almost always want to use is where. It tells you the position in the source code where the program was halted – furthermore, it shows you the chain of function calls that led to the stopping place. Our dialogue with the dbx might proceed as follows:

```
(dbx) where
.div() at 0x3174
rotate(arr=0xf7ff8210, flag=1), line 67 in "rf.c"
doit(A=0xf7ff8210), line 132 in "rf.c"
main(argc=2, argv=0xf7fffa0c), line 17 in "main.c"
(dbx)
```

The list of active functions is printed in reverse order. Thus, this program crashed in a function named '.div', an internal subroutine used to perform integer division on SUN-4 computers. Since '.div' is a library routine not compiled with the −g flag, dbx cannot give us the argument values or tell us a source line location (the hexadecimal number 0x3174 is the address in memory where the entry point of the '.div' subroutine is located). The second line is more interesting however. It tells us that we were inside a function named rotate. We are told the argument values (as they were when the program halted – recall that C allows assignments that may change the argument variables). Finally, we are given the exact line number where the program stopped. The final line shows that rotate was called from the main function, and gives the source line location of the function call.

If your output from the where command should come out looking something like

```
(dbx) where
.div() at 0x3174
rotate(0xf7ff8210, 0x1) at 0x20e4
doit(0xf7ff8210) at 0x2788
main(0x2, 0xf7fffa0c) at 0x2450
```

or, worse, not even showing hexadecimal argument values, the program was not compiled with the −g flag in effect. (Observe that no source file line numbers and no argument names are supplied for the functions.) In this case, you will not be able to obtain much more information than you already have from the where output.[2] Another possibility is that when dbx is started up, you get the message

```
warning: no symbols
```

This indicates that the executable file has been *stripped* to remove the entire symbol table. If you try the where command, you will not see any function names listed (just hexadecimal numbers). The strip command is often used to remove the symbol table from a production program because it saves disk space, but it makes the program practically impossible to debug with dbx. In either case (a missing −g flag or a stripped symbol table), you should re-compile the program with the −g option enabled before you continue debugging.

2. Unless you can understand disassembled machine code.

After you have obtained intelligible output from where, you would probably like to continue by listing the source code in the neighborhood of the error and by checking the values of same variables. Our sample dialogue with dbx might proceed in this manner ...

```
(dbx) list 65,68
65          k = arr[len/2];
66          for( j = 0; j < len/2; j++ ) {
67              if ( arr[j]/k > arr[len-j] )
68                  break;
(dbx) print k
k = 0
(dbx) print arr[len/2], len
arr[0] = 37
len = 1
(dbx) quit
```

This dialogue illustrates that you can list lines of source code without leaving dbx and that you can print the values of C expressions.

Some of the dbx commands that should be useful for analyzing core files are listed below in Table 15-1. The print command is possibly the most useful command of all. It automatically prints variables or expressions in formats that suit their datatypes. For example, if a variable is declared in the program to have the type (char *), then the storage that the variable references is printed as an ASCII character string up to the terminating null byte. If there are several variables with the same name, print will print the instance of the variable that belongs to the current function. To print the value of a different instance, it is either necessary to qualify the name or to change the current function and/or the current file. A full qualification for a variable name includes both the name of a source code file and a function name. For example:

```
print prog3'foo'x
```

will print the variable x inside function foo which is defined in the C source file "prog3.c". The filename prefix is required only if the program contains more than one function named foo (as is possible if foo has the static attribute). The which command is useful for finding out what dbx expects as the full qualification for a variable. The whereis command prints the fully qualified names of all the variables with a given name in the program.

To save you having to prefix variables with filenames and function names, you may change dbx's notion of the current file and/or current function. The up and down commands will transfer attention from the current function to the adjacent function in the call chain, towards and away from the main function respectively. When you use up or down, the current file automatically changes to match the current function. You may also explicitly change the focus of attention to a particular function with the func command. For example,

```
func foo
```

## Table 15-1   Some dbx Commands for Analyzing a Core File

| | |
|---|---|
| `where` | prints a list of the active procedures and functions. |
| `dump` | prints out the values of all active variables. |
| `print` *expr-list* | prints the values of particular values or expressions. |
| `up` | changes the current function to the caller of the current one. |
| `down` | changes the current function to the one called by the current function. |
| `list` *funcname* | lists the first 10 lines of the source code for the named function in the current file. If no argument is provided, the next 10 lines are printed. |
| `func` *funcname* | changes the current function to the named function. |
| `file` *filename* | changes the current file to the one specified. (If no argument is provided, the name of the current file is printed.) |
| `which` *vrbl* | prints the fully qualified names of the named variable. |
| `whereis` *vrbl* | prints the fully qualified names of all occurrences of the named variable in the program. |
| `help` | gives a summary of available `dbx` commands. |
| `quit` | exits from `dbx`. |

changes the current function to be `foo`. However, `foo` must be active (i.e., be present in the call path from `main` to the place where the program stopped) for you to be able to inspect local variables belonging to `foo`.

While inspecting the values of variables in a program, it is nice to see a listing of the program source code. The command

```
list 35,54
```

lists the lines numbered 35 through 54 in the current file that `dbx` is looking at. More conveniently, perhaps, you can type a command like

```
list foo
```

which lists the first few lines at the beginning of the function named `foo`. It does not matter which file `foo` is located in unless the program contains more than one `foo` function. In that case, you will either need to prefix the function name with the desired file name or to change the current file, as explained below.

If you type the `list` command with no arguments, the next ten lines in the source file are listed. This command is handy for continuing the printout of a function definition.

If the source code for your program is contained in several files, you may have to tell `dbx` when to change files. As mentioned above, `dbx` has a notion of a current file. You can find out which is the current file by executing

```
file
```

The `list` command will print functions only from the current file. When you need to print from another file, you can execute the `func`, `up` or `down` commands to reach a function in the other file, or you may use a command similar to

```
file prog2.c
```

which changes the current file to "prog2.c".

If you use `dbx` a lot, you will probably grow tired of typing out the full command names. The solution is to define some suitable abbreviations. You should create, in your home directory, a file named ".dbxinit". Into this file, you should place lines similar to

```
alias p print
alias l list
alias f func
alias fi file
     etc.
```

When you next use `dbx`, you may then use `p` as a synonym for `print`, and so on.

## 15-4 Tracing Program Execution with dbx

Perhaps every programmer has encountered bugs that elude detection for a long time. After re-reading the source code many times and after puzzling over the values of variables at the point of failure, the only recourse might be to monitor the program while it executes. The programmer can easily insert debugging output statements into the program in the way suggested at the start of this chapter. This practice is recommended for any large program. It is quite possible, however, that the debugging output will not reveal the source of the error (perhaps the wrong variables are being printed or the wrong conditions are being tested). It is even possible that the error symptoms will go away when the debugging statements are included and re-appear when the statements are removed![3]

The ultimate resort is to use `dbx` to trace the program's execution. Many `dbx` commands that are useful for tracing execution are summarized in Table 15-2. We will now explain how they are used.

---

3. If this happens, you should suspect that the program is using an uninitialized variable or that the program is accessing a location just beyond the end of an array.

## Table 15-2  Dbx Commands for Statement-Level Tracing

| | |
|---|---|
| trace *func* | causes a line showing the function name and argument values to be printed whenever the function is entered. |
| trace *vrbl* | prints information about every assignment to the named variable. |
| stop in *func* | causes dbx to halt execution when control enters the named function. |
| stop *vrbl* | causes dbx to halt execution when the named variable is about to be changed. |
| stop at *line* | causes dbx to halt execution when control reaches the specified line number. (If the line is not in the current file, the line number should be prefixed by the full file-name in double quotes and a colon.) |
| run *args* | causes execution of the program to begin, passing in the command line arguments (if any). If the program reads from standard input, the input can be taken from a file by adding <*filename* to the command. If the program writes to standard output, that output can be sent to a file by adding >*file*name to the command. |
| cont | causes execution to resume after it has halted as a result of the stop command or as a result of an interrupt. |
| step | resume execution just for a single statement. |
| next | resume execution for a single statement or for one function call. |

Before starting up dbx, any "core" file should be removed from the current directory. Next, you may invoke dbx with the same kind of command as before, namely

```
% dbx prog
```

where prog is the name of the troublesome program. If you wish, you may invoke dbx with no arguments and supply the name of the program with the debug subcommand, as follows.

```
% dbx
(dbx) debug prog
```

Using your knowledge of the problem symptoms exhibited by the program, you probably have some idea of which functions are performing incorrect actions or which variables are being assigned the wrong values. You should type `trace` or `stop` commands for such functions and variables. You would use a `trace` command if knowledge about the function argument values or about the value being assigned to a variable (and where the call or assignment is taking place) is sufficient for your purposes. You would use a `stop` command if you want to retain the freedom to inspect any variable in the program just before or just after the call or assignment has taken place. Here are a few examples,

```
trace cnt
trace foo'ptr
trace rotate_function
stop in print_function
stop at "buggy.c":137
```

Now you can start execution of the program using the `run` command. If the program normally has no arguments, the command

```
run
```

will suffice. If you would normally invoke the program with arguments, as in

```
prog -x bananas
```

you would type

```
run -x bananas
```

If your program normally reads from its standard input, the running program will, by default, read from the keyboard. If you have input data in some file, "indata" say, you can type the `run` command as

```
run -x bananas < indata
```

Similarly, if your program writes to its standard output, that output will, by default, appear on the screen. If there is much output, or if it contains non-ASCII characters, this output will interfere with the information displayed by `dbx`. In this case, you would want to redirect the output into a file. An example of a redirection is

```
run -x bananas > output
```

After the `run` command has been entered, the program is executing. If you had previously entered any `trace` commands, `dbx` will automatically display tracing information on the screen. If you had entered any `stop` commands, execution will halt when control reaches the specified point in the program or when an assignment to a specified variable occurs. When execution halts like this, `dbx` informs you of where and why execution was halted and then gives you a prompt for a new command.

While the program is halted, you may enter any `dbx` commands. You may print the values of variables, specify new functions to be traced, do almost anything. If you subsequently wish to resume execution from the point where the program was halted, the `cont` command should be used. Alternatively, you may single step through the program executing one statement at a time. The `step` and `next` commands are used for this purpose –

both execute one statement and halt again. They differ in that `next` treats a call to a function as a single statement and will only halt again when control returns from the function.

If your program does not stop, appearing to be stuck in an infinite loop, the *break* key or *Control-C* character combination will generate an interrupt that causes execution to halt. Then `dbx` will report the current program location and prompt for a command.

If your program needs to run a long time before exhibiting the error symptoms that you are interested in, you should take advantage of conditional `stop` commands. Any of the various forms of `stop` command listed in Table 15-2 may be modified by appending an `if` condition. A plausible use of an `if` condition is

```
stop at "buggy.c":326 if (p == NULL || i < 0)
```

Any C expression involving variables that are currently visible (which is not to say that they are necessarily visible at the specified line to stop at) may be used in the condition.

If you discover that a variable has the wrong value, you may assign it any desired value and resume execution to verify that the program will now work correctly. To change a value, you should use the set command. For example,

```
set i = j*2
```

changes i to have the current value of `j*2`.

If you discover that you have omitted a statement from the program logic, you do not need to re-compile the program to test if inserting the missing statement will fix the error. For example, if there is an assignment statement missing between lines 23 and 24 in the current file, you may execute a dbx command similar to this.

```
when at 24 set i = 0
```

(Of course, `dbx` commands other than `set` are acceptable after the `when` prefix.)

If your program contains a function for printing the contents of a complicated data structure, you may invoke it. For example, if `print_list` is one of your functions, you could enter a dbx command like

```
call print_list( foo'p )
```

where `foo'p` is a reference to variable p belonging to function `foo`. Of course, there should be no errors in `print_list` for this call to be useful.

The `dbx` debugger has more commands and more modes of operation than those described above. For further information, you should refer to the on-line manual pages or to the system documentation.

## 15-5  *Improving Execution Efficiency*

If a program is likely to be executed a great number of times or if the program executes for a very long time, it is worthwhile improving the program to make it efficient. A certain amount of speed-up, perhaps 10%-20%, can be achieved by compiling the program with the optimize flag, −o, in effect. However, much larger speed improvements can usually be obtained by tuning the program.

Some relatively easy ways of making a C program execute more efficiently are listed below. As we will argue in the next section of this chapter, it is not worth the effort of following these suggestions throughout the entire program. They need only be adopted in those regions of the program where the most execution time is spent.

- Use the **register** attribute. Variables which are used as loop indexes and other variables which receive heavy use inside loops should be given the **register** attribute. Any simple variable which is declared locally inside a function and which has the **int** or **float** type may be given the **register** attribute. The number of registers that are available depends on the computer and on the C compiler being used. The variables that will give the largest speed-up if kept in a register should be declared first, because the C compiler processes the declarations in order. Note that the Gnu C compiler, gcc, attempts to keep important variables, such as loop indexes, in registers anyway – thus lessening the importance of a register declaration.

- Use macros instead of functions. Simple functions that contain only one or two statements can usually be replaced by equivalent macros. This reduces the number of instructions executed because function arguments do not have to be pushed onto the stack and accessed from stack locations. However, the use of macros can make it harder to debug the program. It is a good idea to defer replacement of functions with macros until the program is working and, even then, replace only functions that are called a large number of times.

- Move code out of loops. You should attempt to minimize the number of statements and the complexity of those statements inside loops.

- Avoid repeating calculations. You should not repeat calculations that are much more complicated than a simple addition or subtraction. Instead, save the result of the calculation in a temporary variable and use that variable rather than recalculate the value. Temporaries can be implemented as local automatic variables, as in

```
{   float temp = f(a);
    printf( "%.2f, %.2f\n", temp, a*temp );
}
```

- Avoid floating-point calculations. If you can, you should calculate quantities using only integers. Integer arithmetic is normally much faster than floating-point arithmetic. If you need to manipulate values that are not integers, you can probably scale the values by a convenient power of 2 or a power of 10.

- Use pointers instead of array indexing. When you are making a pass through an array, perhaps searching for a particular element, the normal coding approach is to use an index variable that ranges from zero up to the greatest index. However, a C program will normally execute faster if you use a pointer to the first array element and increment that pointer on each loop iteration. For best results, the pointer variable should have the **register** attribute.

The execution speed improvements achieved by using the preceding suggestions are not the end of the story by any means. The greatest speed improvements will normally come from careful algorithm design and making appropriate choices of data structures. The importance of algorithm design is often illustrated in computer science books with the problem of sorting an array. To be slightly different, let us look at the problem of maintaining a list of English words. (Actually our program will work with arbitrary character strings, so there is nothing that intrinsically restricts it to English words.) We will provide just one operation on the list. This operation, Check_Word, will search the list to see if its argument is a member of the list. If it is a member, the function returns a result of *true* (one). If it is not a member, the word is inserted into the list and the function returns a result of *false* (zero). If we are bold enough to place a limit on the number of words in the list, we might quickly rattle off C code similar to that shown in Figure 15-2.

Our first version of the code searches through the list relatively slowly. If the word we are seeking is actually in the list, we would have to search half way through the list on average. And if the word is not present in the list, we have to search the entire list. We could speed the search loop up a little by using a pointer to the array elements rather than an index into the array, as suggested above. But the improvement in speed would be minimal compared to what can be achieved by changing the search algorithm. If we realize that the searches are going to be too slow, we might consult a book on algorithms and discover the binary search technique. (The book cited at the end of the chapter might be consulted.) At the cost of making insertions of new words much more expensive, we can reduce the number of loop iterations involved in searching to about the logarithm (to base 2) of the number of words in the list. Our new version of the functions would look similar to that given in Figure 15-3.

Binary search requires that the list of words be maintained in sorted, lexicographic order. This is why the word insertion code has become much more complicated. The words already in the list have to be moved down to make a space for the new word to be inserted at its correct position. However, we might find that a word search function is still too slow. For one thing, comparisons between words require the strcmp function to be called and that is relatively expensive. Our third and final version of the program appears in Figure 15-4.

The third version uses a data structure called a *hash table*. To be technical, it is called an *open hash table*. More information about open hashing and alternative hashing methods can be found in the book cited at the end of the chapter. Our words are held in linked lists, known as *buckets*. The hash function, named hash in the code, selects which of the 64 buckets our word will be kept in. When we want to find out if the word is in our table, we

## Figure 15-2  Version #1 of Check_Word

```
#include <stdio.h>
#include <stdlib.h>
#include <string.h>
#define MAXWORDS 4096
char *wordlist[MAXWORDS];
int wordcnt = 0;

int Check_Word( register char *word ) {
    register int i;
    char *newstring;
    for( i=0; i<wordcnt; i++ ) {
        if (strcmp(word,wordlist[i]) == 0)
            return 1;
    }
    if (wordcnt>=MAXWORDS) {
        fprintf(stderr, "check_word: table overflow!\n");
        exit(1);
    }
    newstring = (char *)malloc(strlen(word)+1);
    strcpy(newstring, word);
    wordlist[wordcnt++] = newstring;
    return 0;
}
```

first determine which bucket to search. Then we perform a linear search through all the words in the bucket. If the word is not found, we insert it at the front of the bucket.

To help you visualize the hash table and the linked lists, Figure 15-5 shows a small-scale version of a hash table. In this diagram, the table is scaled down to have only eight buckets and it is shown containing the words from the fragment of English text "It was nice to have had." To make the diagram more interesting, we have assumed that the hash function returned the same value, one, for the words 'had' and 'was'. Similarly, the hash function returned four for each of the three words in the second linked list and six for the word in the third list. In practice, we would expect to find the words distributed more evenly between the different hash buckets than this.

Now a linear search through a linked list is, in itself, no more efficient than the linear search through an array that was performed in the first version of the program. The advantage of the hash table method is that the number of words in one of our buckets is, on average, one sixty-fourth of the number of words that would have been in the array. Therefore

## Figure 15-3   Version #2 of Check_Word

```c
#include <stdio.h>
#include <stdlib.h>
#include <string.h>

#define MAXWORDS 4096
char *wordlist[MAXWORDS];
int wordcnt = 0;

int Check_Word( register char *word ) {
    register int first, last, middle, t;
    register char *newstring;

    first = 0; last = wordcnt;
    while( first < last ) {
        middle = (first + last) >> 1;
        t = strcmp(word,wordlist[middle]);
        if (t == 0)
            return(1);
        if (t < 0)
            last = middle;
        else
            first = middle+1;
    }
    if (wordcnt++ >= MAXWORDS) {
        fprintf(stderr, "check_word: table overflow!\n");
        exit(1);
    }
    newstring = (char *)malloc(strlen(word)+1);
    strcpy(newstring, word);
    if (t < 0)
        first = middle;
    /* 'first' indicates where new word must go */
    for( last=wordcnt; last >= first; last-- ) {
        wordlist[last+1] = wordlist[last];
    }
    wordlist[first] = newstring;
    return 0;
}
```

---

## Figure 15-4 Version #3 of Check_Word

```c
#include <stdio.h>
#include <stdlib.h>
#include <string.h>

typedef struct listitem {
        char *word;
        struct listitem *next_item;
    } item, *itemptr;

#define NBUCKETS  (1 << 6)    /* must be a power of two */
itemptr bucket[NBUCKETS];


int hash( register char *word ) {
    register int len = strlen(word);
    return (word[0]*379 + word[len-1]*73 + len)
           & (NBUCKETS-1) ;
}

int Check_Word( register char *word ) {
    register itemptr bp;
    register int ix;
    char *newstring;

    ix = hash(word);
    for( bp=bucket[ix]; bp!=NULL; bp=bp->next_item ) {
        if (strcmp(bp->word,word) == 0) return 1;
    }
    newstring = (char *)malloc(strlen(word)+1);
    strcpy(newstring, word);
    bp = (itemptr)malloc(sizeof(item));
    bp->word = newstring;
    bp->next_item = bucket[ix];
    bucket[ix] = bp;

    return 0;
}
```

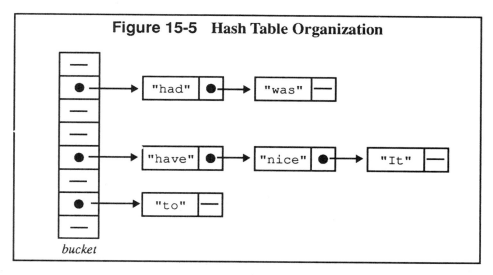

**Figure 15-5** Hash Table Organization

bucket

the search should proceed about 64 times faster. And if the speed-up factor of 64 is insufficient, we simply have to change the constant 64 (written as 1<<6) in the program. It could be increased to any suitable power of 2. As an added bonus, our code does not place any prior limit on the number of words that can be entered into the table. It is limited only by the amount of memory available for dynamic allocation by the `malloc` function (several megabytes, at least).

## 15-6 Execution Profiling with prof and gprof

The previous section attempted to stress the importance of choosing an efficient algorithm and of choosing suitable data structures. Should we write a large program using the most efficient algorithms and the most suitable data structures throughout? The answer is almost certainly no. The fastest algorithms are usually longer, more complicated and more difficult to debug than equivalent simple-minded algorithms. Furthermore, data structures that promote execution speed are likely to require more memory than simpler data structures.

The best approach is to use the fastest algorithms, with their corresponding data structures, where it matters the most. That is, we should be extra careful only in those parts of the program where the most execution time is spent. An often quoted observation is that 90% of the execution time of a program is spent in only 10% of the code. If you know which statements comprise the important 10% of the program, you will know where to concentrate your effort.

There are two tools to help you identify those regions of a program where the most time is spent. One tool, available on most versions of the UNIX system, is called `prof` (short for *Program Profiler*). The other tool, special to the Berkeley UNIX-based systems, is called gprof (a contraction of *Graph Profiler*).

## The *prof Profiler*

To illustrate the use of prof, we will run through its use on an actual program. Suppose that we want a program to count the number of distinct words that appear in a document. By an amazing coincidence, this program will need the Check_Word function that we designed in the previous section of this chapter. The main program to count distinct words that calls Check_Word is listed in Figure 15-6. We started by combining the code of Figure 15-6 with the implementation of Check_Word given in Figure 15-2 to create a file named "count1.c". Next, we compiled the program with the command

```
gcc -p count1.c -o count1
```

### Figure 15-6   A Program to Count Words

```c
#include <stdio.h>
#include <stdlib.h>
#include <ctype.h>

int main(void) {
    char wordbuff[128], *wp;
    int ch;
    int word_cnt = 0;
    while((ch = getchar()) != EOF) {
        if (isspace(ch) || ispunct(ch)) continue;
        wp = wordbuff;
        do {
            *wp++ = ch;
            ch = getchar();
        } while( !isspace(ch) && !ispunct(ch) );
        *wp = '\0';
        if (Check_Word(wordbuff) == 0)
            word_cnt++;
    }
    printf("There are %d distinct words\n", word_cnt);
    return 0;
}
```

The −p flag tells the C compiler to insert extra instructions in the program to count and to time all function calls. Then we performed a sample execution of the program, using the command

```
count1 < /usr/man/cat1/csh.1
```

This command uses the formatted version of the on-line documentation for the csh command as the sample input file.

After whirring away for a surprising long time, the program prints a message that the file contains 1619 distinct words and then halts. This is exactly the behavior that we would expect. However, the −p flag has had an important side effect. While the program was executing, all function calls were being timed. And when the program finished, it created a file named "mon.out" which contains the results of the timing measurements. This file does not contain ASCII characters. A readable printout of the file is created by the prof program. If we now execute the command,

```
prof count1
```

we obtain output like that shown in Figure 15-7.

In this tabular output, there is one line for each function in the program. Several functions are not immediately recognizable as belonging to the program. Many of these functions are automatically included in the program from the C library to perform input-output handling (included because of our use of the getchar macro and the printf function). Several more are included because they are used by the extra profiling code that times the function calls and creates the "mon.out" file.

The first column of the table shows how much each function contributes to the total running time. We see that 39.9% of all execution time is spent performing more than 3 million calls to the strcmp function. The second column keeps track of the cumulative total of the execution time consumed by the functions listed so far. Thus the first three lines in the table account for 14.07 seconds out of the 14.55 seconds used by the program as a whole. The second line in the table is for mcount. This is a function added by the −p option that keeps track of the time spent in each of the other functions. It has to be ignored as the unavoidable overhead of collecting profile information.

The prof output tells us that if we want to make the program faster, the biggest gain in speed would come from making strcmp faster or by reducing the number of calls to strcmp. (Since strcmp is a carefully tuned library function, it is unlikely that we would be able to replace it with a faster equivalent.) The second biggest source of improvement would come from optimizing or changing the algorithm used in the Check_Word function.

The binary search strategy of Figure 15-3 should both make Check_Word itself much faster and reduce the number of calls to strcmp. Repeating the execution profile experiment using the implementation given in Figure 15-3, gives us the output shown in Figure 15-8. Only the first several lines of the table are reproduced here. Although

---

## Figure 15-7  Output of prof for count1

| %time | cumsecs | #call | ms/call | name |
|-------|---------|-------|---------|------|
| 39.9 | 5.80 | 3312331 | 0.00 | _strcmp |
| 33.1 | 10.61 | | | mcount |
| 23.8 | 14.07 | 10315 | 0.34 | _Check_Word |
| 2.7 | 14.47 | 1 | 400.00 | _main |
| 0.3 | 14.51 | 3 | 13.33 | _cfree |
| 0.1 | 14.53 | 1622 | 0.01 | _malloc |
| 0.1 | 14.54 | 11 | 0.91 | _read |
| 0.1 | 14.55 | 1619 | 0.01 | _strlen |
| 0.0 | 14.55 | 7 | 0.00 | .udiv |
| 0.0 | 14.55 | 3 | 0.00 | .umul |
| 0.0 | 14.55 | 4 | 0.00 | .urem |
| 0.0 | 14.55 | 1 | 0.00 | __doprnt |
| 0.0 | 14.55 | 11 | 0.00 | __filbuf |
| 0.0 | 14.55 | 2 | 0.00 | __findbuf |
| 0.0 | 14.55 | 1 | 0.00 | __wrtchk |
| 0.0 | 14.55 | 1 | 0.00 | __xflsbuf |
| 0.0 | 14.55 | 1 | 0.00 | _exit |
| 0.0 | 14.55 | 3 | 0.00 | _free |
| 0.0 | 14.55 | 1 | 0.00 | _fstat |
| 0.0 | 14.55 | 2 | 0.00 | _ioctl |

*... remaining output omitted*

---

## Figure 15-8  Output of prof for count2

| %time | cumsecs | #call | ms/call | name |
|-------|---------|-------|---------|------|
| 38.5 | 0.45 | 10315 | 0.04 | _Check_Word |
| 23.9 | 0.73 | 1 | 280.00 | _main |
| 18.8 | 0.95 | 92417 | 0.00 | _strcmp |
| 12.8 | 1.10 | | | mcount |
| 2.6 | 1.13 | 11 | 2.73 | _read |
| 1.7 | 1.15 | 1622 | 0.01 | _malloc |
| 0.9 | 1.16 | 3 | 3.33 | _cfree |

*... etc.*

Check_Word and strcmp still account for 57.3% of all execution time, the total time spent in these two functions has been considerably reduced. Together, they now consume only 0.67 seconds of execution time (as opposed to 9.26 seconds previously).

If we were striving for a very efficient program, we would see from Figure 15-8 that the best place to concentrate our efforts is still the Check_Word function. This should encourage us to completely change our strategy and, for example, use a hash table implementation. Substituting the code of Figure 15-4 to create program "count3", and repeating the program profile leads to the results shown in Figure 15-9. The new timings reduce the importance of Check_Word to the point where we would have to turn our attention to the input loop in the main function for significant improvements. Some experimentation to tune the hash function, without increasing the amount of computation that it performs, would achieve a minor improvement. However, a simple increase in the number of buckets would be easier and more effective.

---

### Figure 15-9    Output of prof for count3

| %time | cumsecs | #call | ms/call | name |
|-------|---------|-------|---------|------|
| 30.3 | 0.30 | | | mcount |
| 28.3 | 0.58 | 1 | 280.00 | _main |
| 16.2 | 0.74 | 10315 | 0.02 | _Check_Word |
| 15.2 | 0.89 | 138937 | 0.00 | _strcmp |
| 3.0 | 0.92 | 11 | 2.73 | _read |
| 3.0 | 0.95 | 11934 | 0.00 | _strlen |
| 1.0 | 0.96 | 11 | 0.91 | __filbuf |
| *... etc.* | | | | |

---

## The Call-Graph Profiler, *gprof*

Our sample program was a little too simple to illustrate any deficiencies in prof, but it is easy to find a situation where we would like to have more information than is provided by prof. In, say, the count3 program, the strcmp, strcpy and malloc functions were called only by the Check_Word function and these were the only functions that Check_Word called. Therefore, if we wanted to know how much time is spent executing Check_Word, including all functions called by Check_Word, we just have to add the times for the four functions together. If some other function in the program had also contained a call to strcmp, say, we would no longer be able to compute total execution times at all accurately. The gprof profiler is designed to overcome the deficiency.

As well as producing a table of function times similar to that produced by prof, it also shows figures for functions depending on the caller.

To use `gprof`, it is necessary to supply the `-pg` compilation flag to `cc` or `gcc`. For example, the command might be

```
gcc -pg -ansi count3.c main.c -o count3
```

When we execute the program, it creates a file named "gmon.out", which contains the timing information. Finally, executing the command

```
gprof count3
```

outputs a voluminous amount of timing information – approximately 10 pages, of which, the first two pages provide an explanation of how to interpret the subsequent tables. An extract of the `gprof` output for the `count3` program is shown in Figure 15-10. (The lines have been slightly compressed to make them fit on a page in this book.)

---

## Figure 15-10  Extract from *gprof* Output for count3

```
                                called/total      parents
index %time     self descendents  called+self  name        index
                                called/total      children

                                                  <spontaneous>
[1]    66.2    0.00      0.50                   start [1]
               0.20      0.30       1/1           _main [2]
               0.00      0.00       1/1           _on_exit [21]
               0.00      0.00       1/1           _exit [143]

-------------------------------------------------

               0.20      0.30       1/1           start [1]
[2]    66.2    0.20      0.30       1           _main [2]
               0.12      0.14   10315/10315      _Check_Word [3]
               0.00      0.04      11/11          __filbuf [7]
               0.00      0.00       1/1           _printf [22]

-------------------------------------------------

               0.12      0.14   10315/10315      _main [2]
[3]    34.4    0.12      0.14   10315          _Check_Word [3]
               0.10      0.00  138937/138937     _strcmp [4]
               0.00      0.03    3238/3241        _malloc [10]
               0.01      0.00   10315/10315      gcc_compiled.
               0.00      0.00    1619/11934      _strlen [131]
               0.00      0.00    1619/1619       _strcpy [132]
... etc.
```

---

Let us take a look at the section of the Figure 15-10 output that is tagged by the '[3]' index marker. This section of the gprof table is concerned with how much execution time is consumed by the Check_Word function. The line on which the index marker appears tells us that 34.4% of the entire program execution is spent inside Check_Word or inside functions invoked by Check_Word. The next two numbers on the same line tell us that, in fact, 0.12 seconds were spent inside Check_Word itself and 0.14 seconds inside the functions called by Check_Word. There were five functions called by Check_Word and they are listed on the five succeeding lines, namely strcmp, malloc, an internally generated gcc function, strlen and strcpy. Taking the second one of these as an example, the line says that Check_Word made 3238 calls to malloc out of a total of 3241 times that malloc was invoked. The 3238 calls to malloc used 0 seconds of execution time within the function itself (actually, we should say that less than 0.01 seconds were used) plus 0.03 seconds within the functions called by malloc. The lines that precede the Check_Word line list the functions that call Check_Word. There is only one, main, and it called Check_Word 10315 times out of a total of 10315 times that Check_Word was invoked. Furthermore, the calls from main accounted for 0.12 seconds of execution time within Check_Word plus 0.14 seconds in functions called from Check_Word (i.e., calls from main accounted for 100% of the work performed by Check_Word).

There are a few more aspects to the output produced by gprof. If any functions in the program call themselves, either directly or indirectly, gprof will generate a section of the output listing for each cycle in the call graph. And since there may be a fairly large number of sections to the output, gprof outputs an index table so that you can quickly locate where a particular function is listed. Finally, gprof also prints a table similar to that created by prof.

## 15-7 Further Reading

A good tutorial introduction to the dbx debugger is contained in the SUN document *Debugging Tools Manual* (Part Number 800-3849-10). The binary search and hash table techniques used as the subjects of the experiments on profiling are explained in most text books on algorithms. One such book is *Data Structures and Algorithms* by A. V. Aho, J. E. Hopcroft and J. D. Ullman (Addison-Wesley 1983). The book *Writing Efficient Programs* by J. L. Bentley (Prentice-Hall 1982) surveys a wide variety of techniques for improving the execution efficiency of code.

# APPENDIX A  *THE EMACS EDITOR*

---

## A-1  *Preliminaries*

Many versions of emacs exist. This appendix describes *Gnu emacs*, which is available at no charge from the Free Software Foundation. It is likely to be the version installed on a UNIX system. Furthermore, this appendix assumes that your local installation has not customized emacs by providing a local file of key bindings.

The emacs and vi editors are competitors on UNIX systems. Users seem to learn one of the two editors and faithfully stick with it for the remainder of their UNIX careers. Both editors are visual in nature, displaying a screenful (or a window-full on a workstation) of lines from the file being edited. Both provide commands for moving the cursor through the file and modifying the contents of the file using brief keyboard commands. The emacs editor is, however, the more powerful of the two. It allows the screen to be split and display different sections of the same file in multiple subscreens, or even display several different files at the same time. The emacs editor also allows customization in that the user can define new commands, using a variant of the lisp language, and bind them to the desired combinations of key strokes.

Unlike vi, emacs does not have separate command and insert modes. You can think of emacs as always being in insert mode. Whenever an ordinary character is typed, it is inserted into the file at the current cursor position. This simplification implies, however, that various combinations of control characters must be typed in order to perform actions such as deleting a line or moving the cursor around.

Emacs uses two kinds of control character. One kind is formed with the control key. For example, the emacs documentation indicates that C-g is the command to abort a search for a regular expression. This means that you should use the *control-G* combination formed by depressing the *control* and *g* keys simultaneously. The other kind of control character requires a modifier key that works in a similar manner to the shift or control keys on the keyboard. The emacs documentation calls this the *meta* key. For example, one of the commands is M-v which scrolls backwards through the file by one screenful. However, you are unlikely to find a key actually labelled *meta* on your keyboard. If you use a SUN workstation, you will find that both of the keys labelled *left* and *right* operate as the *meta* key in emacs. On other keyboards, it may be labelled *alt* (for *alternate*) or ◇. If your keyboard does not provide a suitable *meta* key, you may use the *escape* key instead. But you must type it as a separate keystroke. Thus, you can type the M-v command as the two consecutive keystrokes *escape*, *m*. A few emacs commands require use of both the control and meta keys together. One such command is C-M-v. To enter this command if you do not have a meta key, you would first type *escape* and then C-v.

The UNIX system allows you to choose an erase character that, when typed, causes the character under the cursor to be erased and the cursor to back up by one position. The usual choice is one of the characters produced by the *backspace* key or the *delete* key (possibly labelled *rubout* on some terminals). Emacs ignores your *erase* character setting and forces you to use the *delete* key for deleting characters. The *backspace* key generates the *control-h* character (C-h in emacs notation) and that is the emacs command to obtain help information.

## A-2  Starting the Editor

To start emacs, you need only type the command

    emacs

Alternatively, if emacs has been customized at your computer installation with a local key-bindings file, you may suppress loading of that file (and hence revert to the default Gnu emacs bindings described in this appendix) by starting up emacs with the command

    emacs -q

On an ordinary terminal, the whole screen will be taken over by the emacs program and a few information lines will be displayed at the top and bottom. On a workstation running X-windows, a separate window may be created.[1] This window is used in the same manner as the screen of an ordinary terminal.

---

1. The emacs program must have been created with X-windows support enabled and the environment variable DISPLAY must be set.

Just as with vi, the correct operation of emacs depends on it knowing the correct terminal (or window) type. That is, the TERM and/or TERMCAP environment variables must be set correctly. If you should find that the information displayed on the screen is consistently garbled or displayed with a strange layout, you should suspect that these environment variables are improperly set.

To read in a file for editing or browsing, type C-x C-f. The full pathname of the current directory will be displayed on the bottom line of the screen and the cursor will be positioned at the end of the line. Emacs calls this last line the *echo area*. The echo area normally contains information messages, but it is sometimes used as a *minibuffer*, where text strings such as file names or search patterns are composed. For example, after typing the command C-x C-f to load a file, the minibuffer contents may be shown as:

```
Find file: ~/project-X/src/█
```

where █ represents the cursor and where "project-X/src" was the working directory when emacs was invoked. You may type additional characters and erase displayed characters (using the *delete* key) to construct the pathname of the desired file. There is a filename completion facility that may be used to reduce the number of keystrokes required. If, for example, you wish to edit the file named "globals.c" and there are no other files with names starting with the letters 'gl', you may type the 'gl' and then type a *tab*. The tab character causes completion of as much of the name as possible. When the name is correct, hit the *return* key and a copy of the file will be displayed in the window. The emacs documentation considers the file copy to be held in a *buffer*. When you make changes, the changes affect only the contents of the buffer. The actual file on disk is not altered unless you explicitly write the buffer back to the disk file.

As an alternative to using C-x C-f to read in a file, you may provide the names of one or more files to be edited on the command line. For example,

```
emacs src/mangler.c
```

will start emacs with the named file already loaded and ready for editing.

After you have made changes to the copy of the file in the buffer (as explained below), you may store the buffer back to disk by typing the command C-x C-s. If you have created a new file or you want to store an edited file back under a different name, use the command C-x C-w and you will be prompted for the file name on the last line.

Exit emacs with the C-x C-c command. Alternatively, as the emacs documentation recommends, you may simply suspend emacs by typing *control-Z* and return to it later by bringing it to the foreground. A csh job control command such as fg or %emacs will make the editor active again.

## A-3   Moving Around in the File

### Cursor Motion

Commands are provided for advancing the cursor forwards or backwards over units of text. The possible units include single characters, words, sentences, lines, and paragraphs. A sample command is

        C-n

which moves the cursor down to the next line. The backwards version of the command is C-p which moves the cursor up to the previous line. A more complete list of cursor motion commands is provided in the Tables at the end of this Appendix.

### Scrolling

The screen may be scrolled up and down. The commands C-v and M-v are used to scroll down to the next screen and up to the previous screen, respectively.

Long lines that are too wide to fit in the display window are normally wrapped onto succeeding lines (a backslash character in the rightmost column is an indication that the line has been wrapped). However, if you prefer, the line wrapping may be disabled and you may use left-right scrolling for viewing long lines. Also, if you split the screen into two side-by-side windows, line wrapping is normally disabled for these narrow windows. The commands C-x < and C-x > are used for left-right scrolling. A dollar symbol in the rightmost column is an indication that the line has been truncated and that more of it may be seen by scrolling the screen left.

### Searching

Searching for a pattern provides a different way of moving the cursor. You may search for simple strings or regular expressions in either the forwards or backwards directions. Suppose that you wish to search forward for the misspelled word *Misteak* in our file. First, you type the command for searching forwards, C-s. Then, you type the letter m and the cursor will jump forward to just past the next occurrence of *M* or *m* in the file. (The default search process is not case-sensitive.) Next, you type i and the cursor jumps forward to just past the next occurrence of the letter combination *Mi*. In other words, as you make the pattern longer, emacs immediately advances to where that combination occurs. (This is called *incremental search* in the emacs documentation.) The cursor will probably be at the word *Misteak* before you have finished typing the entire string.

If you wish to immediately search forward to another occurrence of *Misteak*, you need only type C-s again. If you wish to back up to the previous occurrence by searching backwards, type C-r. You may extend the search pattern by typing the additional characters before executing the C-s or C-r command.

If, instead of searching for new occurrences of *Misteak*, you wish to edit the text and correct the misspelling, type the *escape* character. This character terminates the incremental search, leaving the cursor at the position where the pattern was detected most recently. The C-g command also terminates a search, but it causes the cursor to jump back to its original position before the search commenced. C-g may also be used to abort a search in progress (although it would take an extremely large file to give you enough time to type that command before the search is completed).

An easier way to change multiple occurrences of one string into another string is to use the *query-replace* command. The emacs command for query-replace is M-%. When you type this, the cursor jumps to the last line and you see

```
Query replace: ■
```

Next, you type the string to be found followed by a *return* character. If the search string is *Misteak*, the last line will change to

```
Query replace Misteak with: ■
```

and you should type the replacement text, followed by a return character. If you type the correction to *Misteak*, the cursor will jump to the next occurrence of *Misteak* in the text while the last line (the minibuffer) displays the message

```
Query replacing Misteak with Mistake:
```

You may now hit the space character to perform the replacement followed by an immediate search forwards to the next occurrence of the search string. Typing the *delete* character performs a search forward without performing the substitution on the text matched at the current position. If you type an exclamation mark character, !, all occurrences from the current position to the end of file are replaced. You may terminate the query-replace mode by typing an *escape* character.

Commands are provided for using regular expressions in conjunction with incremental search and query-replace. An incremental search with a regular expression pattern is requested by the command C-M-s. The regular expression notation is similar to that used in other UNIX software (vi, lex, awk, etc.) but with some additions. All the extra constructs are introduced with the backslash character, so you can almost always type an expression that would be valid for lex, say, and have it work correctly. The emacs regular expression notation is summarized in Table A-7.

To use the query-replace command with regular expression matching, you have to type this rather long command:

```
M-x query-replace-regexp
```

## Marking a Position and Creating a Region

The C-@ or C-*space* command sets a mark at the current cursor position. You may subsequently move the cursor back to this marked position by typing C-x C-x, which has the effect of exchanging the mark with the current cursor position.

The text between the current cursor position and the mark forms the current *region*. Several commands are available for deleting, checking or modifying the text in a region. The current paragraph or the entire file may made into the current region by using one of the commands listed in Table A-6.

## A-4 *Editing Text*

### Insertion

Inserting ordinary text is easy. Just move the cursor to the desired place in the file and type the new text. The text is inserted immediately in front of the cursor position. If you should need to insert a control character, such as the ASCII alert character (*control-G*), into the file, it must be prefixed by C-q (the *quote* command). Thus, C-q C-g would insert the alert character. You may also use a three-digit octal code to define a character, so, for example, C-q 0 0 7 would be another way of inserting the alert character.

### Deletion

For deletion of text, there are several commands to choose among. The first choice to be made concerns the kind of textual unit to delete. The possible units include characters, words, lines, and sentences. Furthermore, you have an additional choice as to whether you wish to delete forwards, removing the textual unit immediately after the cursor position, or to delete backwards, removing the textual unit from just before the cursor position. With the exception of a deleted character, the deleted text may be subsequently *yanked* back into the buffer. Yanking therefore provides a way of moving text from one place to another. A list of useful deletion commands appears in Table A-5.

The C-k command is slightly anomalous. If used on a non-empty line, it deletes up to the end of line. If used on an empty line, it deletes the line. Thus, to delete a non-empty line, you would move the cursor to the beginning of the line and then use the C-k command twice in succession.

If you wish to delete a multiple of a standard unit, you may prefix the delete command with a count modifier (called a *universal argument* in the emacs documentation). For example, suppose that you wish to delete 10 lines in the forwards direction from the cursor.

The basic delete command is C-k; the universal argument modifier is C-u 10. That is, you must type the four characters,

```
C-u 1 0 C-k
```

Almost all commands, not just deletion commands, accept an argument in this way. If the count modifier is a number in the range 1 to 9, you may save a keystroke by using M-1, M-2 ... M-9 instead of C-u 1, etc.

To delete text that cannot easily be described as a small number of characters, words or lines, you should use the operation described as *cut* in the following paragraphs.

## Cut-Copy-Paste Operations

By making use of regions, you may obtain the same effects as the cutting, copying and pasting operations provided by mouse-based editors. A region is formed between the current cursor position and the place where a mark was previously set. Either of the commands C-@ or C-*space* set the mark at the current cursor position. (Two commands are provided because some terminals do not generate the expected ASCII code for one of the control character forms.) Additionally, the M-h command creates a region around the current paragraph and C-x h forms a region around the entire file.

One you have formed a region, you may *cut* it (i.e., delete it) from the file using the C-w command. The deleted text is still available for re-insertion in the yank buffer. Alternatively, you may *copy* the current region into the yank buffer using the M-w command. You can now move the cursor elsewhere in the file and *paste* the contents of the yank buffer back into the file using the C-y command.

## A-5   Handling Files

Emacs allows you to work on several files simultaneously. Furthermore, you may swap between different files in the same window or you may split your window into two or more smaller windows and see the files in different windows. For the moment, we will assume that you wish to do all your work in a single window.

The C-x C-f (find-file) command for loading a file into the window for editing or browsing has already been introduced. What was not mentioned is that you may enter this command at any time. If you are in the middle of updating one file and find that you need to consult another file, just type C-x C-f. This will cause emacs to prompt you for the name of the new file and then display it in the window. The previous file that you were working on is *not* stored back to disk (recall that you always work on a copy of the file, known as a buffer), but neither are your updates lost. After consulting or editing the second file, you may return to the first file by using the C-x C-f command again and giving the name of the file. Emacs will switch back to the buffer that you were previously working on.

If you wish to save an altered file back to disk, use the C-x C-s (save-buffer command). This saves the current file in the window, provided that the file has been altered. If you have been working on several files, you may interactively select some or all of these files to be written back to disk with the C-x s (save-some-buffers) command.

When you have completely finished working with a file and you wish to edit another file instead, you should use the C-x C-v (find-alternate-file) command. This will cause emacs to close the file currently being edited and read a new file for editing. If the current file has been modified, emacs asks if it should be saved.

To create a new file, you may simply enter the desired name for the new file after the C-x C-f or C-x C-v commands. The window will show no lines in the buffer and the echo area will show the file status as *New File*. If you have been editing an existing file and you wish to save the changed file under a different name, the command C-x C-w (write-file) should be used. This will write the file and remember the new name as corresponding to the current buffer.

## A-6    Multiple Windows

It is frequently useful to have two (or more) kinds of information displayed on the screen simultaneously. Some commands, such as the help facility, create an extra window automatically so that you can see the help information without leaving the window holding the file being edited. Another situation where multiple windows are useful occurs when you are editing program source code. You may wish to keep referring to global declarations near the beginning of the file while you are editing executable statements located somewhere else. To achieve this effect, emacs allows you to split the window into two sub-windows. The sub-windows may then be scrolled independently so that they let you look at and edit two different parts of the file. Some commands, such as the help facility, create an extra window automatically.

A window may be split either vertically or horizontally. With vertical splitting, you get two sub-windows, one above the other. Each window shows only a few lines, but they will be full length. With horizontal splitting, you obtain two sub-windows placed side-by-side. Here, you have more lines but they have only half the width. To split the screen vertically, the command is C-x 2; to split horizontally, the command is C-x 5. With the side-by-side windows, emacs will, by default, not fold long lines. Instead, long lines are truncated and you may need to use horizontal scrolling to view the truncated parts of lines. A dollar in the rightmost column is an indication that the displayed line has been truncated and that horizontal scrolling will reveal more of the line.

Once you have two or more windows, you will want to be able to switch between them, resize them and delete them again. The basic command for switching windows is C-x o (other-window). It causes another window to become the focus of attention. The windows are maintained in a cyclic order so that if you execute C-x o a few times, you will return to the original window. If all you want to do is to scroll the other window and then return to the original window, there is a short-cut. The command C-M-v scrolls the next window without changing the current focus of attention. If the division of space between the different windows on the screen does not suit you, the command C-x ^ may be used to make the current window one line larger and the command C-x } makes it one column wider (subject in both cases to there being space in other windows that can be transferred). Both resizing commands may be prefixed with a numeric argument. For example, M-3 C-x ^ adds three lines to the current window. When you no longer need a sub-window, there are commands to delete them. The command C-x 0 (delete-window) deletes the current window, while C-x 1 (delete-other-windows) deletes all windows except the current one.

When you split a window, you create two sub-windows that both show the same file. It is a simple manner to have, instead, different files displayed in different sub-windows. One method is to use the command C-x 4 f (find-file-other-window) which causes you to be prompted for a filename in the minibuffer and then that file to be loaded into the other window. If you only had one window originally, a second window is created for you. If you have previously been editing a file, you may recall that file to the other window with C-x 4 b (select-buffer-other-window). Another method is simply to execute C-x f (find-file) in one of the windows.

## A-7   Running a Compiler

Unless you are a very careful typist, the first version of a new program is likely to contain many minor syntax and semantic errors. It is common to alternate between editing a file and running the compiler several times before all the little errors have been fixed. The emacs editor makes this process easy.

Suppose that you have just been editing a file named "program.c" and that you now wish to compile the file and correct any mistakes that are detected by the compiler. The first step is to save the file with the C-x C-s command. Now, if you enter the emacs command

```
M-x compile
```

you will be prompted for a shell command in the minibuffer. If this is a simple compilation, you might enter the command

```
gcc -g program.c
```

The editor now spawns a child process to execute that command. If the expected happens and the compiler reports errors, the messages are collected in an emacs buffer named "*compilation*". You are, of course, free to scroll through that buffer using the appropriate scrolling commands. But, much more conveniently, you can simply use the C-x ` command. This command causes emacs to read the next compiler message and move the cursor to the location of the error in the source file. By repeating C-x ` as necessary, you can step through all the errors, correcting them one-by-one.

If you are editing a more complicated program composed of several files, the shell command that you enter may compile all the files. For example, you might enter the command

```
gcc -g *.c -o prog
```

If there are error messages, the C-x ` command will take you to the error location in whichever file it belongs to. A better way to compile a multi-file program is through the make facility. Thus, the command that you enter would normally be make.

If you need to re-execute the same shell command as the previous time, you need only enter a blank line. That is, just hit the *return* key. (If there was no previous shell command, emacs will execute make -k.)

Instead of running make or a compiler, you may execute the grep program instead. The command M-x grep causes you to be prompted for the arguments to the grep program in the minibuffer. Then the grep program is run as a child process, with emacs collecting the output in the "*compilation*" buffer. The effect of C-x ` is to advance the cursor successively through each position that matches the pattern supplied to grep.

## A-8   *Obtaining On-line Help*

There is an elaborate help facility built into emacs. It is triggered by the C-h command. (C-h is the character generated by the *backspace* key.) The next character is an option letter that selects among several kinds of help information. The C-h C-h command shows a list of valid option letters, C-h C-h C-h displays both the list and their meanings. A few of the more useful help options are as follows.

C-h a     (command-apropos) is used to display a list of commands whose names include a particular string.

C-h c *key*   (describe-key-briefly) gives the name of the command that is run when key *key* is pressed; *key* represents any command or meta combination.

C-h k *key*   (describe-key) gives both the name and a description of the command that is run when key *key* is pressed.

C-h i     (info) runs the info program, which allows you to browse through the on-line emacs documentation. The info program provides instructions for its use.

C-h t     (help-with-tutorial) displays the emacs tutorial document. The tutorial is recommended reading for a first-time emacs user.

## A-9   Further Reading

For space reasons, many interesting `emacs` features have not been covered in this appendix. (These features include the directory editor, macro definitions, customizing `emacs` with your own commands, and much more.) A full description of `emacs` is provided in the *Gnu Emacs Manual* by Richard Stallman. The manual is distributed as a `tex` file along with the source code of `emacs`. Your system administrator should be able to help you locate the `tex` file and print it. (Be warned, however, that the manual is about 300 pages long.) Alternatively, copies may be purchased from the Free Software Foundation. The address of FSF may be found in the on-line help information for `emacs` or any other Gnu program.

## A-10   Emacs Reference Tables

**Notation**: In the following tables, C-x means hold down the *control* key and then depress the *x* key. The notation M-x means hold down the *meta* key (possibly labelled *alt*, ✧, *left* or *right* on your keyboard) and then depress *x*. If the keyboard does not provide a suitable *meta* key, you may instead type *escape* followed by *x* as two separate keystrokes. A notation like C-M-x means hold down both the *control* and *meta* keys while pressing *x*. If the keyboard has no *meta* key, type *escape* and then enter C-x.

**Argument Prefixes**: Many commands may be prefixed with an argument. For example, a command that deletes one word may be prefixed with a modifier to make it delete 7 words, say. If the prefix is an integer in the range 0 to 9, the argument prefix is M-0, .. M-9. If the prefix is a negative integer, say -27, you may use M-- (i.e., meta-minus) followed by the digits 2 7. An alternate prefix notation that works with non-numeric arguments or with arbitrary integers (both positive or negative) is introduced by C-u. To prefix a command with an argument of 99, say, enter the three characters C-u 9 9.

## Table A-1   Emacs: Exiting & Error Recovery

| | |
|---|---|
| Terminate `emacs` | `C-x C-c` |
| Restore buffer to its original contents | `M-x revert-buffer` |
| Recover a file lost by a system crash | `M-x recover-file` |
| Undo one batch of changes | `C-x u` or `C-_` |
| Redraw a garbled screen | `C-l` |
| Abort the current command | `C-g` |

## Table A-2   Emacs: Basic Help Commands

| | |
|---|---|
| List the commands whose names contain a given string | `C-h a` *string* |
| Give brief help about using help | `C-h C-h` |
| Give detailed help about using help | `C-h C-h C-h` |
| Give the full name of the command tied to character *k* | `C-h c` *k* |
| Describe the command tied to character *k* | `C-h k` *k* |
| Run the `emacs` tutorial | `C-h t` |
| Run the `info` browser program | `C-h i` |

## Table A-3   Emacs: File Handling

| | |
|---|---|
| Read a file into `emacs` | `C-x C-f` |
| Save file back to disk | `C-x C-s` |
| Insert another file at current cursor position | `C-x i` |
| Write buffer to a different file | `C-x C-w` |
| Read another file instead of current file | `C-x C-v` |

## Table A-4  Emacs: Screen & Cursor Motion Commands

| Action | Backwards | Forwards |
|---|---|---|
| Move over one character | C-b | C-f |
| Move over one word | M-b | M-f |
| Move over one line | C-p | C-n |
| Go to line beginning / end | C-a | C-e |
| Move over one sentence | M-a | M-e |
| Move over one paragraph | M-[ | M-] |
| Move over one page | C-x [ | C-x ] |
| | | |
| Go to first / last line | M-< | M-> |
| Go to a particular line number | M-x goto-line | |
| | | |
| Scroll up, scroll down | M-v | C-v |
| Scroll left, scroll right | C-x < | C-x > |
| | | |
| Incremental search[†] | C-r | C-s |
| Regular expression search[†] | | C-M-s |

[†] After a search has begun, use

| | |
|---|---|
| C-s | to repeat the search forwards, |
| C-r | to repeat the search backwards, |
| *escape* | to exit the search, |
| *delete* | to delete the last character of the pattern and back-up to the previous match without that character, and |
| C-g | to abort the search. |

## Table A-5  Emacs: Deleting, Replacing, & Moving Text

| Action | Backwards | Forwards |
|---|---|---|
| Delete one character | *delete* | C-d |
| Delete[†] one word | M-*delete* | M-d |
| Delete[†] to start / end of line | M-0 C-k | C-k |
| Delete[†] sentence | C-x *delete* | M-k |
| Delete[†] to next occurrence of $c$ | | M-z c |
| Delete[†] the active region | | C-w |
| | | |
| Yank back deleted or copied text | | C-y |
| Exchange yanked text with previously deleted text | | M-y |
| | | |
| Join current line with previous line | | M-^ |
| | | |
| Interactively replace a string | | M-% |
| Interactively replace a regular expression[‡] | M-x query-replace-regexp | |

[†] The deleted text is available to be reinserted in the buffer with the yank-back command, C-y.

[‡] In query-replace mode, use:

| | |
|---|---|
| *space* | to replace the current match and find the next match, |
| , | to replace the current match and do not move, |
| *delete* | to skip to the next match without replacing, |
| ! | to replace all remaining matches, |
| ^ | to back-up to the previous match, |
| *escape* | to exit query-replace, and |
| C-r | to recursively edit the pattern |

## Table A-6   Emacs: Marking and Region Operations

| | |
|---|---|
| Set the *mark* at the current position | `C-space` or `C-@` |
| Set mark after end of next word | `M-@` |
| Interchange the mark and the current position | `C-x C-x` |
| Form a region around current paragraph | `M-h` |
| Form a region around the entire buffer | `C-x h` |
| Cut the region | `C-w` |
| Copy region into the yank buffer | `M-y` |
| Paste yank buffer back into buffer | `C-y` |
| Extend selection (enlarge region) | `C-M-w` |
| Change text in region to lower-case | `C-x C-l` |
| Change text in region to upper-case | `C-x C-u` |

## Table A-7   Emacs: Regular Expression Notation

| | |
|---|---|
| Match any single character | `.` |
| Repeat preceding construct zero or more times | `*` |
| Repeat preceding construct one or more times | `+` |
| Repeat preceding construct zero or one times | `?` |
| Match any character in the set | `[ ... ]` |
| Match any character not in the set | `[^ ... ]` |
| Match beginning of the line | `^` |
| Match end of the line | `$` |
| Match special character *x* | `\x` |
| Separator of two alternatives | `\|` |
| Group a sub-expression together | `\( ... \)` |
| Match same text as *n*-th bracketed group | `\n` |
| Match the beginning of the buffer | `` \` `` |
| Match the end of the buffer | `\'` |
| Match the beginning of a word | `\<` |
| Match the end of a word | `\>` |
| Not the beginning or end of a word | `\B` |

## Table A-8   Emacs: Multiple Window Control

| | |
|---|---|
| Delete current window | C-x 0 |
| Delete all other windows | C-x 1 |
| | |
| Split window vertically | C-x 2 |
| Split window horizontally | C-x 5 |
| | |
| Switch cursor to other window | C-x o |
| Scroll other window | C-M-v |
| | |
| Enlarge current window vertically | C-x ^ |
| Enlarge current window horizontally | C-x } |
| Shrink current window vertically | M-x shrink-window |
| Shrink current window horizontally | C-x { |
| | |
| Visit file in other window | C-x 4 f |
| Select buffer in other window | C-x 4 b |

## Table A-9   Emacs: Running Make, Compilers, Grep & Spell

| | |
|---|---|
| Run a compiler or make as a separate task | M-x compile |
| Run grep as a separate task | M-x grep |
| Kill the compiler or make task | M-x kill-compiler |
| Kill the grep task | M-x kill-grep |
| | |
| Move the cursor to the location of the next compilation error or grep match | C-x ` |
| Return to first compilation error or grep match | C-u C-x ` |
| | |
| Run the spelling checker on the buffer | M-x spell-buffer |
| Run spelling checker on current region | M-x spell-region |

# *CONVERTING ANSI C TO K&R C*

All the programming examples have been coded in ANSI C rather than one of the older dialects of C. This choice was deliberate. A major reason is that ANSI C is less error-prone because the compiler checks function calls against function prototypes. A second reason is that ANSI C will gradually supplant classic C as compilers become more widely available.

In the unfortunate circumstance that your computer system does not have an ANSI C compiler available or that there are other compelling reasons to stay with classic C, you will need to convert the code supplied throughout this book. For the most part, the conversion is easy. (Only a subset of ANSI C has been used, so few constructs need changing.) For convenience, the conversion process has been structured into four stages involving – lexical and preprocessor constructs, syntactic constructs, semantic rules of the language, and calls to ANSI C library functions.

For completeness, all the new or changed ANSI C features are listed below. Those which have been used somewhere in this book are flagged with a warning ☞ symbol.

## B-1  Lexical and Preprocessor Constructs

| | |
|---|---|
| `'\a'` | (Alert character code.) New in ANSI C. It can be replaced with `'\007'`. |
| `'\v'` | (Vertical tab character code.) New in ANSI C. It can be replaced with `'\014'`. |
| trigraphs | New in ANSI C. |
| `123L` | The 'L', 'l', 'U', 'u', 'UL' and 'ul' suffixes on integer constants to indicate long and/or unsigned values are new in ANSI C. |
| `0.3e2F` | The 'F', 'f', 'L' and 'l' suffixes on floating-point constants to indicate `float` or `long double` values are new in ANSI C. |
| catenation | Concatenation of two adjacent string constants to form a single string is new in ANSI C. A string constant may be continued on an additional line in classic C by preceding the linefeed character with a backslash. |
| macros | Recursive instances of macros are not expanded. |
| unary `+` | New in ANSI C. |
| `'\x3a'` | Hexadecimal character constants are new in ANSI C. They may be replaced with equivalent octal constants. |
| `#` | (The stringize preprocessor operator.) No equivalent in classic C. |
| `##` | (The token catenation preprocessor operator.) No official equivalent in classic C although tricks to obtain similar effects exist. |
| `#elif` | Not available in all implementations of classic C. May need expansion to its `#else #if` equivalent. |
| `#error` | New in ANSI C. |
| `#pragma` | New in ANSI C. |
| defined | (The preprocessor test on a macro name.) Not available in all implementations of classic C. May need to be replaced by equivalent uses of the `#ifdef` and `#ifndef` directives. |
| `__DATE__` | (And, similarly `__TIME__`.). Probably not defined in classic C implementations. |
| ☞ `__FILE__` | Not available in all implementations of classic C. |
| ☞ `__LINE__` | Not available in all implementations of classic C. |
| ☞ `__STDC__` | Should definitely not be defined in a classic C compiler. |

## B-2   *Syntactic Conversion*

☞ Functions

ANSI C provides an extended syntax for function prototypes and function declarations. If, for example, a function declaration reads as

```
int *get_pointer(int *ap, float delta){
    ... }
```

it should be transformed to the following.

```
int *get_pointer( a, delta )
int *ap;  float delta;
{ ... }
```

If you wish to modify the code so that it is acceptable to both ANSI and classic C compilers, expand the function declaration to this ...

```
#ifdef __STDC__
int *get_pointer(int *ap, float delta)
#else
int *get_pointer( a, delta )
int *ap;  float delta;
#endif
{ ... }
```

☞ prototypes

Function prototype declarations in all files (both '.c' and '.h' files) should be stripped of their argument declarations. For example,

```
extern int *get_pointer(int *, float);
static void exec_error(int severity);
```

should be transformed to:

```
extern int *get_pointer(/*int*, float*/);
static void exec_error(/*int severity*/);
```

(The original argument declarations as comments provide useful documentation to anyone who subsequently reads the program.)

`const`

New in ANSI C. Simply removing the keyword should be sufficient.

`enum`

Not available in some classic C implementations.

`signed char`

Not available in some classic C implementations.

`unsigned char`

Not available in some classic C implementations.

☞ `volatile`

New in ANSI C. Removing the keyword from code should usually work (but it depends on the compiler being cooperative).

initialization

Permitted for statically or automatically allocated structures, unions and arrays in ANSI C.

## *B-3   Semantic Conversion*

☞   `void *`   Used in ANSI C to represent a generic pointer. To convert to classic C, use the `char*` type instead.

☞   Also, `void*` values are automatically coercible to any other pointer type in ANSI C. To convert the code to classic C, explicit casts should be inserted in the code.

arguments   In ANSI C, an argument being passed to a function is automatically coerced to the type declared for that argument in the function prototype or function heading (provided that the ANSI C syntax is used for the function arguments). Explicit casts of arguments may need to be inserted into the code.

conversions   The ANSI C rules for converting values between the `signed` and unsigned varieties of the `char`, `short`, `int` and `long` types are different.

## *B-4   Library Function and Header File Replacement*

The ANSI C standard introduced many new library functions and re-organized the standard header files. Therefore, the following lists of changes are fairly long. Many of the functions listed in the ANSI C standard were adopted from System V UNIX. These functions may have been installed in your Berkeley UNIX system to simplify porting of software. A sensible approach that eliminates unnecessary work would be to attempt to compile your program and let the preprocessor tell you which header files are unavailable and let the loader tell you which library functions are missing.

Here are the functions and macros that are different or may be missing if your C compiler pre-dates ANSI C. In some cases, Berkeley UNIX equivalents are suggested. In other cases, some re-programming may be necessary to remove a call to the missing function.

☞   `assert`   May not be available in all classic C implementations.

`atexit`   New in ANSI C.

`bsearch`   New in ANSI C.

`fprintf`   (and `printf`, `sprintf`, `fscanf`, `scanf` and `sscanf`). Some format codes work differently under the ANSI C standard. You would be wise to check the on-line documentation.

| | | |
|---|---|---|
| | `fgetpos`<br>`fsetpos` | New in ANSI C. Uses of these functions can normally be replaced by calls to the `ftell` and `fseek` functions. |
| | `isalnum` | A function in ANSI C but a macro in classic C. Similarly for all the character testing functions (`isalpha`, `isdigit`, etc.). This difference is unlikely to affect your code. |
| | `isgraph` | New in ANSI C. |
| | `ldiv` | New in ANSI C. |
| ☞ | `malloc`<br>`calloc` | They return results of type `void*` in ANSI C. The results have type `char*` in classic C. |
| | `mblen` | (and the other multibyte functions `mbtowc`, `wctomb`, `mbstowcs` and `wcstombs`). New in ANSI C. |
| | `memchr` | May not be available in all classic C implementations. |
| | `memcmp` | May not be available in all classic C implementations. A Berkeley UNIX equivalent is the `bcmp` function. |
| ☞ | `memcpy`<br>`memmove` | May not be available in all classic C implementations. A close Berkeley UNIX equivalent is the `bcopy` function. |
| ☞ | `memset` | May not be available in all classic C implementations. When the value being stored in memory is zero, `memset` may be replaced by the Berkeley UNIX function `bzero`. |
| | `remove` | New in ANSI C. The Berkeley UNIX equivalent is `unlink`. |
| | `setlocale` | (and `localeconv`). New in ANSI C. |
| ☞ | `strchr` | (and `strcspn`, `strpbrk`, `strrchr`, `strspn`, `strstr` and `strtok`). May not be available in classic C implementations. A Berkeley UNIX equivalent to `strstr` is the `index` function. |
| | `strcoll` | New in ANSI C. |
| | `strerror` | New in ANSI C. |
| | `strtod` | (and `strtol` and `strtoul`). New in ANSI C. |
| | `strxfrm` | New in ANSI C. |
| | `tmpfile` | New in ANSI C. |
| | `tmpnam` | New in ANSI C. Close equivalents in Berkeley UNIX are `mktemp` and `mkstemp`. |
| ☞ | `va_start` | (and the other variable argument handling functions). Defined differently in classic C. |

The re-organization of header files is also likely to cause some trouble. Here is a commented list of the ANSI C header files.

☞    &lt;assert.h&gt;        Not available in all classic C implementations.

☞    &lt;ctype.h&gt;        Pre-ANSI versions of this file define `isalnum`, etc., as macros, not as functions.

     &lt;errno.h&gt;

     &lt;float.h&gt;        New in ANSI C.

     &lt;limits.h&gt;      New in ANSI C.

     &lt;locale.h&gt;     New in ANSI C.

     &lt;math.h&gt;

     &lt;setjmp.h&gt;

     &lt;signal.h&gt;

☞    &lt;stdarg.h&gt;     The equivalent, pre-ANSI, Berkeley UNIX header file is named &lt;varargs.h&gt;. However, the usage of the variable arguments handling macros, `va_start` and the rest, is not identical. Check the on-line manual before revising the code.

     &lt;stddef.h&gt;     New in ANSI C.

     &lt;stdio.h&gt;

☞    &lt;stdlib.h&gt;     New in ANSI C.

☞    &lt;string.h&gt;     The pre-ANSI equivalent in Berkeley UNIX is called &lt;strings.h&gt;. If the header file &lt;memory.h&gt; exists, it contains prototypes for `memchr` and a few related functions.

     &lt;time.h&gt;

# INDEX

# FUNCTION INDEX